Exchange Rates and International Financial Economics

Exchange Rates and International Financial Economics

History, Theories, and Practices

by

John N. Kallianiotis

palgrave
macmillan

EXCHANGE RATES AND INTERNATIONAL FINANCIAL ECONOMICS

Softcover reprint of the hardcover 1st edition 2013 978-1-137-28322-1

First published in 2013 by
PALGRAVE MACMILLAN®
in the United States—a division of St. Martins Press LLC,
175 Fifth Avenue, New York, NY 10010.

Where this book is distributed in the UK, Europe and the rest of the world, his is by Palgrave Macmillan, a division of Macmillan Publishers Limited, registered in England, company number 785998, of Houndmills, Basingstoke, Hampshire RG21 6XS.

Palgrave Macmillan is the global academic imprint of the above companies and has companies and representatives throughout the world.

Palgrave® and Macmillan® are registered trademarks in the United States, the United Kingdom, Europe and other countries.

ISBN 978-1-349-44896-8 ISBN 978-1-137-31888-6 (eBook)
DOI 10.1057/9781137318886
Library of Congress Cataloging-in-Publication Data

Kallianiotis, John N., 1951–
Exchange rates and international financial economics : history, theories, and practices / by John N. Kallianiotis.
pages cm
Includes bibliographical references and index.

1. Foreign exchange rates. 2. International finance. I. Title.

HG3851.K25 2013
332.4'5—dc23 2013013236

A catalogue record of the book is available from the British Library.

Design by Newgen Knowledge Works (P) Ltd., Chennai, India.

First edition: October 2013

10 9 8 7 6 5 4 3 2 1

To *Katerina* (*Κατερίνα*) and *Nicholas* (*Νικόλαος*)

Contents

Illustrations

Exhibits

Figures

Graphs

Tables

Permissions

Chapter 1:

Table A1.1: Consolidated Statement of Condition of All Federal Reserve Banks.

Federal Reserve Bulletin, Board of Governors of the Federal Reserve System, Volume 98, November 8, 2012. www.federalreserve.gov. Reprinted with permission.

Chapter 5:

Exhibit 5.2: Euro Futures, U.S. $/€ (CME), € 125,000. Currency futures, *The Wall Street Journal*, October 4, 2012, p. C11. Reprinted by permission from *The Wall Street Journal* (2012).

Exhibit 5.6: Euro Currency Options Detail. *NASDAQ*, http://www.nasdaq.com/aspxcontent/optionsWC.aspx?symbol=^XDE&qm_page=25122&qm_symbol=^XDE. Reprinted by permission from The NASDAQ OMX Group (John Jacobs).

Exhibit 5.7: Currency Futures Options. *The Wall Street Journal*, http://online.wsj.com/mdc/public/page/2_3024-futopt_currency.html_ Reprinted by permission from *The Wall Street Journal* (2012).

Table A5.1: Cumulative Probabilities of the Standard Normal Distribution Function. *Engineering Statistics Handbook*, http://www.itl.nist.gov/div898/handbook/eda/section3/eda3671.htm. Reprinted with permission.

Preface

The abandonment of the gold exchange standard regime, the introduction of the flexible (market determined) exchange rate, the role of the US dollar as international reserve, the European integration, the imposition of the new common currency (the euro) on the Economic and Monetary Union (EMU) member nations, and the latest global financial crisis (systemic risk) have changed the entire international monetary and broader economic system. The internationalization of business, the interdependence among nations, the enormous capital mobility, the foreign exchange market that provides the payments and instruments for all these international transactions, the risk that is involved among markets, economies, and businesses require studies, instruments, and empirical work on international financial economics.

All these phenomena prove that we are living in increasingly integrated and uncertain world markets and economies. Current business students and professionals must be absolutely cognizant of the international dimensions of this open world that we live in and how it affects businesses and the well-being of individuals. This book, *Exchange Rates and International Financial Economics: History, Theories, and Practices*, aims to provide, mostly, students and researchers with knowledge about and tools of analysis of these markets and the exchange rates involved in their transactions.

The book is intended for undergraduate seniors specializing in international finance, international business, international economics, and other related areas. Also, it is designed for MBA students, especially those who are specializing in international studies, as mentioned above. It has theories and empirical work that can be useful for practitioners, traders, and for anyone involved in international finance. It can also be used in itself as a complete text on international finance or employed to supplement a reference book devoted to international finance or multinational business or international financial economics. In addition, it includes many policy issues, such as monetary and fiscal, trade policies, and others of open economies.

The book deals with six topics on exchange rates, which are part of international financial economics. Much of the book contains lectures given by the author in the last twenty-five years, and it was inspired by and based on the economic events of the last ten years since the introduction of the common currency in the European Union (EU) and the current dramatic years since 2007, with the global financial crisis and its consequences on the Euro-zone, such as the debt crisis, which requires a renewed thinking and outlook. The topics covered include the foreign exchange market, exchange rate theories, exchange rate determination and forecasting, exchange rate risk and its hedging, and others. Also, a central issue discussed here is the role of exchange rate volatility and its use as an instrument of trade policy, which is necessary for a country to pursue its public policy objectives.

Chapter 1 gives a brief history of the exchange rate from ancient times to the medieval period to the nineteenth-century classical gold standard to the present-day international financial system. It deals with the fixed exchange rate (currencies were pegged to gold) of the early twentieth century and the gold exchange standard after World War II with the creation of different international institutions (IMF, World Bank, etc.). Then, the creation of the Eurocurrencies in Europe took place and the fixed exchange rate was abandoned in 1973. The emerging markets crisis in the 1990s and later in the 2000s is presented as a historic lesson. The European Monetary System and the introduction of the new common currency, the euro, in the European Union changed the entire international monetary system, and the euro became the major competitor of the US dollar. Finally, there is some discussion regarding what lies ahead in our intergraded world, and what history can teach us to avoid similar mistakes.

Chapter 2 introduces us to the environment of the foreign exchange market, its institutions, its participants, its functions, its different transactions, its quotations of the different exchange rates, and the foreign currency trade. The role of central banks, as policy makers, and commercial banks, as market participants, in the foreign currency market is covered extensively. Also, the role of the foreign exchange market in multinational corporations is emphasized in this chapter. It also covers bonds and stocks denominated in foreign currency and loans offered by foreign banks.

Chapter 3 deals with the exchange rate determination. The different theories in determining exchange rates are covered here: from the monetary approach to the asset market approach to the exchange rate overshooting, and other models based on assumptions, mathematical models, and empirical results using econometrics. The output from the empirical analysis is presented in an appendix at the end of the chapter that contains a lot of econometric work and more detailed explanations.

Chapter 4 elaborates on the previous one by forecasting the exchange rate. Different econometric models are presented, such as the time series, fundamentals, purchasing power parity, asset market approach, maker-based forecast (using forward rates), currency betas (using exchange rate indexes), technical forecasting, and mixed forecasting. Also, efficiency in the foreign currency markets is analyzed and tested econometrically. The statistics, econometrics, and empirical results are placed in details in an appendix at the end of the chapter, which helps students apply this work to their own projects, and researchers to reproduce or investigate exchange rates in the future.

Chapter 5 discusses the foreign currency derivatives. The operations of the foreign exchange forward and futures markets are covered in detail and the pricing and applications of these contracts are described. A more rigorous treatment of the pricing and modeling of the foreign currency options market is presented. Also, currency swaps and interest rate swaps are described too. These derivatives are used in the next chapter to hedge exchange rate risk.

Chapter 6 deals with foreign exchange risk (exposure) and its management. The unanticipated movements of exchange rates increaserisk to market participants (mainly MNCs). The objective is to measure these exposures (accounting, tax, operating, and mostly transaction exposure) and to manage them using instruments to hedge the exchange rate risk. Businesses need certainty, and for this reason we see, lately, a growing new field on financial risk management. The differences between hedging of receivables and payables are covered extensively. The techniques that are used are mostly related to transaction exposure; they are (1) forward market hedge, (2) futures market hedge, (3) money market hedge, and (4) options market hedge. The operating exposure is managed by using (1) parallel loans, (2) currency swaps, (3) leads and lags, (4) diversification of operations, and (5) other techniques.

Acknowledgments

I would like to acknowledge the assistance provided by Nicholas J. Kallianiotis, Katerina I. Kallianiotis, Vinaykumar H. Jani, and Asad I. Akram. I am indebted to these scholars listed below for the insights they provided on reading the chapters of this book. Also, I would like to thank the editor for his enormous work on my manuscript. The usual disclaimer applies. Then, all remaining errors are mine.

1. Dr. Aram Balagyozyan, University of Scranton, aram.balagyan@scranton.edu
2. Dr. Theologos H. Bonitsis, NJIT, bonitsis@adm.njit.edu
3. Dr. Paul Kutasovic, NYIT, pkutasov@nyit.edu
4. Dr. Mary L. Lo Re, Wagner College, mlore@wagner.edu
5. Dr. Christos Pargianas, University of Scranton, christos.pargianas@scranton.edu
6. Dr. Jordan Petsas, University of Scranton, iordanis.petsas@scranton.edu
7. Dr. Louis Rivera, Dowling College, riveral@dowling.edu
8. Dr. Richard Torz, St. Joseph's College, rtorz@sjcny.edy
9. Dr. Cathyann Tully, Wagner College, cathyann.tully@wagner.edu

With great respect and many thanks for their valuable work,

John N. Kallianiotis
University of Scranton
Scranton, PA, March 1, 2013

About the Author

Dr. Ioannis (John) N. Kallianiotis is a professor of Finance at the Economics/Finance Department, The Arthur J. Kania School of Management, University of Scranton, Scranton, PA, USA. He has a BA in Business Economics from the Aristotelian University of Thessaloniki, Greece (1978), an MA in Business Economics from Queens College, CUNY, New York (1982), an MPhil in Financial Economics from Graduate Center, CUNY, New York (1984), and a PhD in Finance (International Finance and Monetary Theory and Financial Institutions) from Graduate Center and Baruch College, CUNY, New York (1985).

He has taught at nine different colleges and universities over the last twenty-eight years and has worked at a few other jobs (as accountant, banker, and researcher) in the private sector for six years. He was an officer in the Greek Army, where he served at a NATO base for three years. He is married for 39 years and has one son. He is a president or a member on the board of directors or on the council of many editorial boards, in academic, professional, community, charitable, and spiritual societies and associations across America, Europe, and in the international arena.

His research is focused on international finance, the financial markets, the European Union, and business in general, where he has published over 200 articles in different journals, including *Quarterly Economic Review, Greek Economic Review, Economicos Tachydromos, International Journal of Commerce and Management, American Business Review, Pennsylvania Economic Review, Journal of Business and Society, North Central Business Journal, Economic Modelling, Journal of Business and Economic Studies, Global Business and Economic Review, Spoudai, Indian Journal of Economics and Business, The Journal of American Academy of Business, The Business Review, The Journal of European Research Studies, The International Research Journal of Finance and Economics, The International Journal of Applied Business and Economic Research, The American Journal of Economics and Business Administration, Journal of Business and Economics, International Journal of Business and Commerce*, and others. Many of his articles appeared in books such as *International Research in the Business*

Disciplines, Emerging Markets in Asia, Quantity and Quality in Economics Research, Business and Economics for the 21st Century, International Public Policy and Regionalism at the Turn of the Century, Applied Economic Research, Contemporary Issues of Economic and Financial Integration: A Collection of Empirical Work, Financial Crises, Impact and Response: The View from the Emerging World, Social Welfare, etc. He was coeditor of a book titled *Balance of Payments Adjustment* (Greenwood Press, 2000) and has also reviewed many books. He has many articles and interviews published in magazines and newspapers (Politico.com, *The Washington Times, US News & World Report, Times Leader, Scranton Times, Northeast Business Journal,* etc.). His work has also been published in numerous conference proceedings.

In addition, he has published extensively in other areas, including History, Philosophy, Culture, Education, Greek Language, and others. His other work has been published in Orthodoxos Typos, Salpigx Orthodoxias, Ekklisiastiki Paradosis, Dimosiographiki, Agios Kyprianos, Orthodox Tradition, Ellinochristianiki Agogi, Agios Agathagelos, Voanerges, Hellas on the Web, Antibaro, Christian Vivliografia, Serbia Martira, Macedonia Hellenic Land, Hellenes Online, and elsewhere.He has also published different pamphlets, books, chapters, etc. on similar topics. There are numerous unpublished manuscripts too, written by him and based on business and social issues.

E-mail: ioannis.kallianiotis@scranton.edu
Web: http://academic.scranton.edu/faculty/jnk353/
http://matrix.scranton.edu/academics/ksom/eco-fin/faculty/John-Kallianiotis.shtml

1

History of Exchange Rate

In finance, an exchange rate or a foreign exchange rate or a forex rate or an FX rate (i.e., $e_t(\$/€)$) between two currencies is the rate at which one currency will be exchanged for another. Exchange rate is the price (value) of one country's currency in terms of another country's currency. The history of money goes back thousands of years. Numismatics is the scientific study of moneys and their history in all their varied forms and functions. Many items have been used as commodity money, such as animals, barley, wine, oil, cowrie shells, beads, and naturally occuring rare precious metals and stones, as well as many other things that be considered as valuable to the average person. Most ancient moneys started to become tokens a long time ago. The word "*nomisma*"[1] (derived from *nomos* = anything assigned, a usage, a custom, a law, an ordinance), meaning coin, was and still is used by Greeks for "currency" and "money." Historically, the island of Aegina (Greece) participated in the early days of coinage (silver coins since 670 B.C.), the first money in Europe. Then, coins were minted in Athens, Corinth, Euboea, Syracuse, and in other Greek city-states and their colonies. Hence, objects of gold or silver or copper present many of money's essential properties. Modern money appeared in paper currency form (banknotes) as early as the Ptolemaic Egypt (first century BC), and in Europe during the fourteenth century AD, and as coins much earlier. The industrial revolution, the independence of European nations, the economic boom, and the increase in trade of the late nineteenth and early twentieth centuries led us to a need for a more formalized system of payments and settling international trade balances.

Lately, world reserve currencies or anchor currencies are currencies that are held in significant quantities by many governments, central banks, and institutions as part of their foreign exchange reserves (foreign assets). They also tend to be the international pricing currencies for products traded on a global market, and commodities such as oil, gold, coffee, etcetera. These currencies are, today, the US dollar (62.1 percent) and lately, its weak competitor the over-sweating euro (25 percent). The advantage for the issuing countries is that they can purchase the commodities at a marginally lower rate than the other nations, which must exchange their domestic currencies for the reserve currency with each purchase and pay a transaction cost too. For major currencies, this transaction cost is negligible with respect to the price of these commodities. These reserve currencies also permit the governments issuing the currencies to borrow money at a better rate, as there will always be a larger market for these currencies than the others. But, these world reserve currencies must be national currencies and not common currencies of diverse and unequal sovereign nations because their risk is higher, as the current euro experience proved to us.

Of course, reserve currencies come and go, as the size and power of different countries change over time. International currencies in the past have included, first, the Greek drachma and others with the passing of time. The word "nomisma," meaning coin, as mentioned earlier, was used by Greeks; also, specialization, futures contracts, and many other terms used in economics, today, have Greek origin. According to Herodotus, money,[2] in the sense of coinage (drachmas), began to circulate in the Aegean in the early seventh century B.C. Xenophon (430–354 B.C.), a disciple of Socrates, is the "Father of Economics" (*Oeconomicos*).[3] The other international currencies were the Chinese Liang, the silver punch-marked coins of fourth century B.C. in India, the Roman denari, the Byzantine solidus and the Islamic dinar of the Middle Ages, the Venetian ducato of the Renaissance, the Dutch guilder of the seventeenth century AD, and of course, more recently, the British sterling, the US dollar, and the novel euro.

Before 1944, the world reserve currency was the British pound sterling. After World War II, with the decline of the United Kingdom and the growth of the United States as a global power, the international financial system was governed for about three decades by a formal agreement, the Bretton Woods System. Under this system, the US dollar was placed deliberately as the anchor of the system, with the US government guaranteeing other central banks that they could sell their US dollar reserves at a fixed rate ($35/oz) for gold.[4] During that period, European countries and Japan deliberately devalued their currencies against the dollar in order to boost exports and development ("beggar-thy-neighbor" policy). In the late 1960s and early 1970s, the system suffered setbacks due to problems pointed out by the Triffin dilemma,[5] a general problem with any fiat currency[6] under a fixed exchange rate regime, as the dollar was in the Bretton Woods system.

The US dollar is the most widely held currency in the allocated reserves, today. Throughout the last six decades, an average of two-thirds of the total allocated foreign exchange reserves of countries has been in US dollars. For this reason, the US dollar is said to have "reserve-currency status," making it somewhat easier for the United States to run higher trade deficits with greatly postponed economic impact or even postponing a currency crisis. Central bank reserves held in dollar-denominated debt, however, are small compared to private holdings of such debt. If non-US holders of dollar-denominated assets (China, Japan, OPEC nations, etc.) decide to shift holdings to assets denominated in other currencies, there could be serious consequences for the US economy. Changes of this kind are rare, and typically take place gradually over time; the markets involved adjust accordingly, too. However, the dollar remained until recently the favorite reserve currency because it has relative stability along with assets such as US Treasury securities that have scale, liquidity, and hopefully, no risk. This dominant position of the US dollar in global reserves is very much challenged currently, because of the growing share of unallocated reserves, and because of the doubts regarding dollar stability in the long term, due to the enormous debts incurred by the United States.[7]

Currently, the euro is the second most commonly held reserve currency, comprising a quarter of the allocated holdings. After World War II and the rebuilding of the German economy, the German Deutsche Mark gained the status of the second most important reserve currency (15.8% in 1995) after the US dollar. When the euro was launched, in electronic form on January 1, 1999, and in bank notes on January 1, 2002, replacing the Mark, French Frank, and seventeen other European currencies so far, it inherited the status of a major reserve currency from the Mark. Since then, its contribution to official reserves has risen continually (from 17.9 percent to 25.0 percent) as banks seek to diversify their reserves, as some nations have started mistrusting the US foreign policy, and as trade in the Euro-zone continues to expand. The euro could compete and might replace the US dollar as the world's primary reserve currency. But the latest US-initiated worldwide credit crunch, its related recessions, and the Euro-zone sovereign debt crisis have had an adverse impact on the euro and will slow its adoption for many years, provided there are no bankruptcies in any Euro-zone nation.

Historically, for many centuries, the currencies of the world were backed by gold ("gold standard" and "gold exchange standard"). That is, a piece of paper currency issued by any world government represented a real amount of gold held in a vault by that government. In the 1930s, the United States set the value of the dollar at a single, unchanging level, which was 1 ounce of gold was worth $35. After World War II, with the Bretton Woods Agreement, other countries based the value of their currencies on the US dollar. Since everyone knew how much gold a US dollar was worth, the value of any other currency against the dollar could be based on its value in gold.

A currency worth twice as much gold as a US dollar was, therefore, also worth two US dollars (i.e., $e_t = 2\$/FF$). Unfortunately, the imbalances of the real world of economics outpaced this system. The US dollar suffered from inflation (its value relative to the goods it could purchase decreased), while other currencies became more valuable and more stable. Eventually, the United States could no longer pretend that the dollar was worth as much as it had been, and its value was officially reduced so that 1 ounce of gold was worth in the market for \$70. Thus, the dollar's value was cut in half. Finally, in 1971, the United States took away the gold exchange standard altogether. This meant that the dollar no longer represented an actual amount of a precious substance; market forces alone determined its value. Today, the US dollar still dominates many financial markets. In fact, exchange rates are often expressed in terms of US dollars. Currently, the US dollar (62.1 percent) and the euro (25 percent) account for approximately 87 percent of all currency exchange transactions in the world. Adding to the list, the British pound (3.9 percent), the Japanese yen (3.7 percent), the Swiss franc, the Canadian dollar, and the Australian dollar account for over 95 percent of currency exchanges altogether.

1.1 History of Currencies

A large proportion of the world aggregate demand (AD), about one-fifth, represents exports (X) and imports (M) among countries. The same amount represents also capital flows among nations because the current accounts (CA) are approximately equal to the capital accounts (KA), assuming official settlements (OS) zero [$B\ of\ P = CA + KA + OS = 0$]. In all these enormous transactions, there is a need for exchanging one currency for the other, so the relative price between two currencies plays a major role in this international economic and financial environment. International trade is as old as the political history of the nations on earth. In these early societies, the city-states exported and imported products among themselves and each one of them had its own currency. The currency exchanger had his bench (*trapeza, banco, banca, banque* = moneychanger's table) in the middle of the marketplace (*agora*) and exchanged the different currencies with the local one for merchants to buy products they needed, like wine, oil, spices, food, and others. Thus, there was an exchange rate between these currencies that the "banker" (*trapezitis*) knew and used in these transactions.

Technological and technical advances followed the philosophical and social tenets practiced by these ancient nations (Hellenes, Egyptians, Assyrians, Sumerians, Babylonians, and others of those days). We see all these, today, from the archeological findings, their existing structures, and their literature. They were really advanced societies and, for this reason, we can say that their economic innovations were advanced too. The Greek philosopher Socrates had introduced many new ("*kaina daimonia*") sociopolitical "innovations and beliefs," and his student Xenophon introduced, as it was mentioned, a new science that he called "*Oeconomicos*," the management of household (*oecos* = household and *nemo* = manage). These unique advances occurred 2,500 ago, but they led to lasting benefits for the entire world, and for us, they are the foundations of our profession and form the core of our current international socioeconomic system.

Without a monetary unit (1 Dr., £1, $1, €1, etc.) to provide a common basis, in which to express values, to provide a unit of account (*numeraire*), to become a medium of exchange, and to represent the currency of the country, the international economy could not be carried very far because transactions between the residents of different countries have to be carried out continuously. Thus, an exchange rate regime was necessary to determine the relative value of these currencies (the exchange rates). Also, reserve currencies (foreign assets) were needed to be transferred in settlement of deficits. Lastly, an adjustment mechanism had to be found to avoid financing the imbalances and adjusting them with changes in the exchange rate, instead of losing gold reserves.

The abandonment of barter in favor of a monetary economy brought efficiency, but also macroeconomic instability (unemployment and inflation); it brought exchange rates, but also current account imbalances; it brought monetary policy, but also bias toward the market; it brought trade policy, but also devaluation of currencies to improve the domestic economy by acting against the rest of the world ("beggar-thy-neighbor" policy). "No good is pure of bad" (*ouden kalon amiges kakou*).

1.2 Fixed Exchange Rate

In eighteenth-century Europe, we had the classical "gold standard" (fixed exchange rate), which contained an automatic adjustment mechanism, the "price-specie-flow" mechanism (Hume's [1752] essay in Cooper's [1969]). The gold standard, as an international monetary system, achieved acceptance in Europe at the end of nineteenth century (1870) and in the United States officially in the year 1879. The countries, under the gold standard, fix the values of their currencies in terms of gold[8] (mint parity theory) and the ratio between two mint parities was the exchange rate of the currencies of these countries. Before World War I, the mint parity of the US dollar was $20.67/oz of gold and the British pound sterling £4.2474/oz of gold.

Thus, their exchange rate was: $e = 4.8665$ \$/£. The balance of payment surpluses and deficits between countries was settled by transferring gold without sterilizing the effects of these gold flows on money supply. Gold was shipped from the country with deficit to the other country to settle payments. The countries thus exchanged their currencies at this fixed exchange rate to settle their payments, and if there was not enough currency for the payments, the deficit country paid by sending gold to settle the payment deficit. Thus, maintaining adequate reserves of gold to back its currency's value was very important for a country, but very difficult at the same time because gold is not in abundance and thus, the money supply was limited.

1.2.1 *Payments of Current Account Deficits*

A payment deficit caused a loss of reserves (gold), which reduced the money supply and brought down the price level. Then, the home country products got cheaper, more competitive, therefore exports increased and import fell, and the balance of payments improved. This process continued until the deficit was eliminated:

$$CA < 0 \Rightarrow OF_{Gold} \Rightarrow M^s \downarrow \Rightarrow P \downarrow$$
$$\Rightarrow TOT \uparrow = \frac{\bar{e}P^*}{P\downarrow} = \frac{P_M}{P_X} \uparrow (P_M > P_X) \Rightarrow Competitiveness \uparrow$$
$$\Rightarrow X \uparrow \& M \downarrow \Rightarrow CA \uparrow$$

where, CA = current account, OF_{Gold} = outflow of gold, M^s = money supply, TOT = terms of trade or real exchange rate, $\bar{e}$ = fixed exchange rate, P = domestic price, P^* = foreign price, P_M = price of imports, P_X = price of exports, X = exports, and M = imports.

With the fixed exchange rate, an incipient payment deficit leads to a loss of reserves (outflow of gold).[9] This reserve loss will lead to a fall in the domestic money supply (if the central bank follows a nonsterilization policy, it does not increase domestic credit to offset the decline in reserves). During the period of the gold exchange standard, countries did not follow a sterilized policy. Then, a loss of reserves led to multiple reduction of the money supply, due to the money multiplier (see Appendix [A1.1] for correlation and causality between M^s and P):

$$GC + FA \downarrow + DC = C + R \downarrow = MB \downarrow \Rightarrow MB \downarrow m_M = M^s \downarrow \Rightarrow P \downarrow$$

where, GC = gold certificate, FA = foreign assets, DC = domestic credit, C = currency, R = reserves, MB = monetary base, m_M = money multiplier, M^s = money supply, and P = price level.

The fall in the money supply led to a price decline in this classical economic view (monetarist view). The equation of exchange (quantity theory of money) says:

$$M\overline{V} = P\overline{Q} \tag{1.1}$$

where, M = money supply, V = velocity of money, P = price, and Q = quantity of output (production). The economy was at full employment (Q^F), thus $\overline{V}$ and $\overline{Q}$ were constants.

A fall in domestic prices increases international competitiveness (domestic products become less expensive). The balance of trade (TA) will improve, as is discussed in Chapter 3, depending on the price elasticity of demand for imports (ε_M) and the price elasticity of supply of exports or the foreign demand for imports (ε_{M^*}). The improvement in competitiveness depends on the size of these two elasticities (elastic demands) and in this case, the Marshall-Lerner condition must be satisfied:

$$|\varepsilon_M| + |\varepsilon_{M^*}| > 1 \tag{1.2}$$

where, $\varepsilon_M = -\frac{\Delta M}{\Delta TOT}\frac{TOT}{M}$ = price elasticity of demand for imports and $\varepsilon_{M^*} = \frac{\Delta M^*}{\Delta TOT}\frac{TOT}{M^*}$ = price elasticity of supply of our exports (foreign imports).

Also, a loss of reserves (reduction of money) leads a central bank to raise the interest rate to attract a capital inflow. This high interest rate leads to a decline in aggregate demand (AD), a fall in production (AS), and consequently, to a fall in imports (M), which improves the current account (CA), according to the Keynesian view:

$$M^s \downarrow \Rightarrow i \uparrow \Rightarrow CIF \Rightarrow AD \downarrow (= C \downarrow + I \downarrow)$$
$$\Rightarrow AS \downarrow \Rightarrow Y \downarrow \Rightarrow M \downarrow \Rightarrow CA \uparrow$$

where, i = interest rate, CIF = capital inflow, AD = aggregate demand, AS = aggregate supply, C = consumption, I = investment, and Y = income.

1.2.2 Gold Standard before World War II

The gold standard worked before World War I, but during the war, it was abandoned when fixed exchange rates fluctuated because trade flows and free movement of gold were interrupted, and nations suspended the operation of the gold standard. International speculators were selling the weak currencies short,[10] causing them to fall further in value than that warranted by economic factors. An attempt was made to restore the gold standard after the war, but the newly established Federal Reserve System (1913) sterilized the gold inflows, and the Great Depression forced countries to leave the gold standard. After the collapse of the Austro-Hungarian Empire (1918), the objective of the Allies was again the stabilization of Europe.

During World War I, convertibility of the currencies into gold was suspended by all the belligerent nations, except the United States. Paper currencies were exchanged on the basis of floating exchange rates, and many countries devalued their currencies. After the war, countries started going back to the previous regime, except Germany and other East European countries, which experienced hyperinflations.[11] In 1925, a system of "gold exchange standard" came into being, when Britain reestablished the gold convertibility of the pound sterling at its prewar par and many other nations followed. At that time, many nations were holding a part of their reserves in currencies, like British sterlings and US dollars. This regime was again a fixed exchange rate system. Now, gold and leading currencies are held as international reserves.

The Wall Street crash of 1929[12] led to a cessation of US capital outflows, which had been a major source of money used by Germany to pay reparations. Then, Germany stopped making reparation payments. In 1931 came the crash of the Austrian banking system, and a wave of bank runs spread all over Europe. On September 21, 1931, Britain "went off gold." A monetary anarchy was generated, and countries created currency blocs (a sterling bloc, a dollar bloc, and a gold bloc). Some currencies floated, with intervention by their central banks. Others remained pegged to gold, and some were depreciated in a bid to improve trade and their domestic economies. Trade fell drastically, and the international capital market ceased to function. The United States adopted a modified gold standard in 1934 when the US dollar was devalued by 69.33 percent to $35/oz of gold from $20.67/oz that was before. The United States started trading gold only with foreign central banks and not with private citizens. From 1934 until the end of World War II, exchange rates were determined by each currency's value in terms of gold. During World War II and the hyperinflation in some European nations, many trading currencies lost their convertibility, except the US dollar.

1.2.3 After the Bretton Woods

After World War II, the West was clearly intent on creating a new international economic order. The British thinker and negotiator between Britain and the United States, John Maynard Keynes, and others aimed to create a liberal multilateral order that would be the opposite of the restrictions and bilateralism of the 1930s. Three international economic institutions were created to supervise this new liberal order, the International Trade Organization (ITO),[13] the World Bank,[14] and the International Monetary Fund (IMF). Britain and the United States invited the other wartime allies to a conference in July 1944 in Bretton Woods in New Hampshire to make official their objectives. This order (agreement) and the principal controversies surrounding its design, with regard to a new exchange rate regime, can be called as the *gold exchange standard* or reserve regime or adjustment obligations. This Bretton Woods Agreement established a US dollar–based international monetary system.

The Bretton Woods agreement was signed by 44 nations, but the agreement was negotiated by only two nations, the United States and the United Kingdom. The two principal individuals involved in the negotiations, and who "persuaded" all the other representatives, were Harry Dexter White,[15] representing the United States, and John Maynard Keynes,[16] representing Great Britain. Each fund member established a par value for its currency and maintained the exchange rate for its currency within $\pm 1\%$ of par value. A fund member could change its par value only with fund approval and only if the country's balance of payments was in "fundamental disequilibrium." The IMF received gold and currencies from its members through "subscription." Countries would have to make a payment (subscription) of gold and currency in order to become members of the IMF. Subscription quotas were assigned according to a member's size and resources. Payment of the quota was 25 percent in gold and 75 percent in the member's own currency. The voting rights were distributed according to the size of the members.

The Bretton Woods agreement committed member countries to peg exchange rates to the US dollar and allowed them to fluctuate with a $\pm 1\%$ margin around a declared par value. The central bank had a fixed price for its currency (i.e., $e_1 = 4\ DM/\$$ or $e_2 = 33.33$ Drs/$). and if someone wanted to trade a currency for dollars, he had to deal with the central bank. The price of the currency was fixed by altering either the supply of or the demand for these assets. The Fed fixed the price of gold at $35/oz by supplying unlimited amounts of gold to the market to drive the price back down, whenever the price of gold exceeded the $35/oz. In order to peg the price of gold, the United States needed a large stock of gold to supply to the market whenever there was pressure on the market price of gold to go up. When a foreign bank wanted to peg the exchange rate, it had to have a stock of its own currency and a stock of dollars. The domestic currency could be created at itswill, but dollars were a problem to the foreign central banks. Dollars were the foreign central banks' reserves.

When a country was running a balance of payments deficit, its central bank was losing reserves; there was an excess demand for foreign currency (an excess supply of domestic currency), at the rate at which the central bank was pegging. When the country was running a balance of payments surplus, it was gaining reserves; it was an excess supply of foreign currency (an excess demand for domestic currency) at the pegged exchange rate.

The United States was committed to trade gold with foreign officials at a fixed price of $35/oz. This commitment meant that the United States needed a very large stock of gold to sell and keep its price at $35/oz. By the end of World War II, the United States had about 60 percent of the total world stock of gold. At the end of 2010, the world stock of gold was 165,000 metric tons, of which central banks and IMF held 30,807.6 tons (18.67 percent) and private hands held 134,192.4 tons (81.33 percent). The United States had 26.4 percent, Germany 11.02 percent, and IMF 9.13 percent of the total gold in the central banks and IMF.[17] For exchange intervention, foreign central banks needed a supply of dollars. The Cold War assured European nations enough dollars to play the intervention game and to "stop the spread of communism internationally." This policy was satisfied by the European Recovery Program (Marshall Plan). Its objective was to supply capital to Western European economies, to enable them to rebuild their nations after the war, and to become capable military allies (through NATO membership) of the United States against the socioeconomic system of the Soviet Union. The Organization for European Economic Cooperation, which was renamed as the Organization for Economic Cooperation and Development (OECD), was set up to administer the Marshall Plan aid to Europe.

This plan reduced the "dollar shortage" in Europe and made it possible for European nations to build up foreign exchange reserves. The Marshall Plan aid constituted 4 percent of the European GNP, but it was 40 percent of European receipts of hard currency. Also, European countries were encouraged by the United States. to liberalize their trade. Then, the idea of the European integration was created, and the goal of this common market was the free trade and the free mobility of factors of production among member nations. The European Economic Community (EEC) was established, and the Treaty of Rome was signed by six European nations (Belgium, France, Italy, Luxembourg, the Netherlands, and West Germany) on March 25, 1957.

Of course, the IMF was the key institution in the new international monetary system since 1944, but it lost its public acceptance, especially during the major financial crises, due to its oppressive policies toward nations that ask for its assistance. Criticism against the IMF is enormous, and reforms are necessary to improve its functions and policies.[18] The IMF has provided loans to Russia and many other former Soviet republics, also to Brazil, Argentina, Mexico, Poland, Ghana, Turkey, Indonesia, South Korea, Hungary, Greece, Portugal, Spain, Ireland, and many others during its history.[19]

During that period, as was mentioned, the dollar exchange rate was also fixed ($1 was valued as 1/35 ounces of gold). This was the par value of the dollar in terms of gold, and all the other currencies had a fixed exchange rate with the US dollar. The par value of any currency could be adjusted, if the country was requesting it and of the IMF agreed that a change was necessary to correct a "fundamental disequilibrium" in that country. A special position was that the United States. will defend the dollar by buying and selling gold, while other countries will defend their currencies by buying and selling dollars. Participating countries agreed to try to maintain the value of their currencies within $\pm 1\%$ of par by buying or selling foreign currency (dollars) or gold as needed. Also, devaluation was not allowed to be used as a competitive trade policy; but if it was difficult for a country to defend its currency, due to current account deficit and lack of reserves, a devaluation of up to -10% was permitted without formal approval from the IMF.

The IMF was formally created after 1944, but it accomplished very little in 1940s because of its limited resources (endowments), which were insufficient to make any impact on the postwar reconstruction and on the chronic European payment deficits. Actually, the Bretton Woods system moved into its golden age at the end of 1950s. Exchange rate policy was ruled out by the Bretton Woods agreement (fixed exchange rate), by which devaluation was the ultimate weapon, whose use was a national disgrace. Countries had to finance their deficits instead of devaluating their currencies. But, it was obvious that there was a problem of long-run viability of the system by converting dollars into gold. In addition, the Bretton Woods agreement had established the British pound sterling as an international reserve currency along with the US dollar. In 1950s, the exchange rate between these two reserve currencies was $e = 2.80$ \$/£.

Actually, the exchange rates between the US dollar and the other European currencies were roughly their equilibrium market values. The only problem was with the deutschemark; its exchange rate had been set too high ($e = 10\ DM/\$$),[20] which means that the DM was undervalued and the dollar overvalued. This had generated a balance of payments (*CA*) surplus in Germany and it was accumulated in US dollars. By 1960, total foreign dollar claims on the United States were greater than the total value of the US gold stock at $35 per ounce. If the foreign central banks turned in their dollars for gold, the US gold was not enough to meet this demand, unless the United States would have increased the dollar price of gold, which means devaluation of the dollar.

The United States started having a balance of payment deficits; but everyone expected the dollar to be a riskless asset (as we believe, today too, that the US Treasury securities are riskless assets). The excess demand for dollar reserves caused a deficit to the United States, and supplying all these reserves caused an enormous capital outflow. Presidents John Kennedy and Lyndon Johnson put a series of credit restrictions and capital controls to avoid the deficits. The objective of the US authorities was to keep dollars out of foreign hands and thus, they could not insist on other countries to buy gold from them and reduce their gold reserves. These restrictions, together with the competition between the two superpowers, contributed to the growth of the Euro-dollar market. During the early years of the Cold War, the Soviet Union began to fear expropriation of its dollar deposits in New York, and for this reason, it switched ownership of these deposits to Soviet-controlled banks in Europe, like the Moscow Narodny Bank in London and the Banque Commercial pour l' Europe du Nord in Paris.

The practice of fixing (coordinated intervention, which maintained the gold price within a narrow range around $35/oz) the gold price began in 1919. It continued until 1939, when the London gold market (the Bank of England, which intervened in the private market via the daily gold price fixing at N. M. Rothschild) was closed as a result of World War II. The market was reopened after the war, in 1954. When the central bank gold pool began officially in 1961, the Bank of England (as agents for the gold pool were Mocatta & Goldsmid, a trading arm of Standard Chartered Bank; Sharps, Pixley, a broker owned by the merchant bank Kleinwort Benson; N. M. Rothschild & Sons, whose representative acts as the auctioneer; Johnson Matthey, a metallurgical firm; and Samuel Montagu, a merchant banking subsidiary of Midland Bank) maintained an open phone line with N. M. Rothschild during the fixing. If the fixing price was above $35.20 or below $34.80, the Bank of England was selling or buying gold to bring the price within the prescribed bands.

In 1962, France began to convert its dollar reserves into gold, which signified the end of the Bretton Woods Agreement. Officials in France were frustrated by the seigniorage[21] gains accruing to the United States as a result of the dollar's role under this agreement. As the provider of foreign exchange reserves, the United States could ensure that foreign central banks held dollars. In turn, most reserves were kept in the form of US Treasury securities. French officials believed that such securities were not yielding a competitive rate of interest and for this reason, seigniorage gains accrued to the United States. After France, other nations started selling their dollar reserves thinking that the dollar was overvalued. Any time the

Exhibit 1.1 Central Bank (Fed) Balance Sheet

Assets	*Liabilities*
GC	C
FA	R
DC	
V_{Assets}	$V_{Liabilities}$

Note: GC = gold certificate, FA = foreign assets, DC = domestic credit, C = currency, and R = reserves.

central bank intervenes in a market to buy or sell a foreign currency, it changes the side of its assets and consequently, its liabilities and through the money multiplier, a multiple change in money supply takes place, as is shown at the central bank's balance sheet, in Exhibit 1.1, and is presented with eqs. (3) and (4).

$$C + R = MB \tag{1.3}$$

$$MB\, m_M = M^s \tag{1.4}$$

where, C = currency in the hands of the public, R = reserves of financial institutions in the central bank, MB = monetary base, m_M = money multiplier, and M^s = money supply.

Also, a consolidated statement of condition (balance sheet) of all Federal Reserve banks is presented in table A1.1.

1.2.4 Special Drawing Rights

Thus, negotiations on international monetary reform started in earnest among the Group of Ten (G10) in 1965. Despite French (de Gaulle's) opposition on the gold standard, negotiations to create a new reserve asset were brought to the IMF's annual meetings in Rio de Janeiro in September 1967. The new reserve asset was called "Special Drawing Right (SDR)," which was defined as having a value of 1/35 of an ounce of gold (1 SDR = 0.888671 grams of fine gold or 0.028571428 oz of gold). It carried an interest rate of 1.5 percent per annum, and it was to be used the same way as gold (countries in deficit were offering SDRs to cover it). It was approved in July 1969. The first SDRs were allocated on January 1, 1970, when there was a belief that a liquidity shortage exists in the international financial system, and therefore there was a need for a new reserve (the SDR). SDRs could be sold by a country in deficit to a strong-currency country in exchange for currencies that could be used for intervention in the exchange markets. SDRs were allocated to members in proportion to their quotas in the fund and they supplemented the existing foreign exchange reserves. Despitethis new international reserve, the US monetary policy was easing, and this enormous outpouring of dollars devalued the dollar in the following years.[22] Individual countries hold SDRs in the form of deposits in the IMF, which are part of their international monetary reserves, along with official holdings of gold, foreign currencies, and their reserve position at the IMF to settle their international transactions.

From the end of World War II up to 1965, US monetary and fiscal policies were conducted in such a way that they were not inflationary. However, as world trade began expanding, the relative importance of Germany and Japan grew, and the international financial system needed a consensus among the three economic powers (the United States, West Germany, and Japan). After 1965, the US economic policy began to be in conflict with that desired by West Germany and Japan. The United States began a strong expansion, then, a moderate inflation started as a result of the Vietnam War and the Great Society program. The DM and the yen were undervalued with respect the US dollar, and the United States urged these two nations to revalue their currencies upward. Germany and Japan argued that the United States should revise its economic policy (to curb money supply growth, tighten credit, and cut government spending) to be consistent with those in Germany and Japan. In April 1971, the Bundesbank started intervening in the foreign exchange market by buying dollars and selling its own currency.

In November 1967, the British pound sterling was devalued from 2.80 \$/£ to 2.40 \$/£. Then, central banks that were holding sterling reserves took a 14.29 percent capital loss in dollar terms. This raised the question on the exchange rate risk of the other reserve currencies, too. Thus, if the US dollar was devalued with respect to gold, a capital gain in dollar terms could be made by holding gold. Since that time, demand for gold rose and gold pool sales in the private market tried to hold down the price of gold.[23] In March 1968, the effort to control the private market price of gold was abandoned and a two-tier system started. During that month, British authorities closed the London gold market. Since that time, central banks were trading gold among themselves at \$35/oz and the private market was trading gold at the market price. Its price immediately jumped to \$43/oz and by November 1973 had reached \$100/oz.

In 1974, the value of the SDR was redefined and made it equal to the value of a basket of the 16 major currencies of the world.[24] The weights are updated every five years by the IMF because the economies of the countries are altered. Defining the SDR as equal to a basket of the major currencies enabled it to serve as a unit of international account equal to an average of the currencies of the countries with the largest trade. Also, the IMF interest rate on the SDR loans was raised about halfway toward a market rate, which is determined weekly. Further, another decision was the promulgation of a set of guidelines for floating exchange rates. Lastly, they decided on the creation of a high-level committee to meet about twice a year to supervise the IMF. Of course, the major holders of gold were dissatisfied with the extent to which gold had been immobilized. The market price of gold had risen far above the official price, but central banks were forbidden to sell gold above the official price. They were using it only as collateral for borrowing. An agreement was arrived at in a meeting of the Interim Committee of the IMF in Jamaica in January 1976 regarding the gold deposits at the fund by its members.[25] The allocation of SDRs were SDR 21.4 billion in 1981, and in 2009 it increased to SDR 204 billion, to help mitigate the effects of the latest global financial crisis.

1.2.5 The Abandonment of the Gold Exchange Standard

The "gold exchange standard" (fixed exchange rate system) was required to prevent nations from changing exchange rates and generating competitive advantages. Also, currency reserves were required to maintain exchange rates within narrow boundaries. This system required the United States to maintain a reserve of gold and the other nations to maintain a reserve of dollars. In order for the stock of currency (dollar) reserves to finance growing world trade, the United States was running a balance of payment (current account) deficits and this way, the other nations were accumulating dollar reserves, which was reducing the US ability to convert dollars into gold at the official price of $35 per ounce (Triffin paradox).[26]

In early 1968, a run from the dollar into gold started. From 1968 to 1971 many speculative crises took place in different European currencies. By August 1971, there were signs of uneasiness on the part of official holders of dollars. This "dollar standard" had not been serving US national interests because the dollar was seriously overvalued. On August 15, 1971, President Richard Nixon closed the gold window, and many economists mark the death of Bretton Woods and the fact that the United States went bankrupt on that date because of the suspension of gold convertibility. The United States had a record $30 billion trade deficit at that time and a 10 percent surcharge was placed on all its imports and a program of wage and price controls was instituted too. It was obvious that currency values had to be realigned in order to restore a more balanced flow of payments between countries. In December 1971, a conference among representatives of various nations concluded with the Smithsonian Agreement, which called for a devaluation of the dollar by about 8 percent against the other currencies (to $38/oz of gold). Also, boundaries for the currency values were expended to $\pm 2.25\%$ of the rates initially set by the agreement. The major countries finally accepted the fact that they have to move to a system of generalized floating exchange rate.[27]

The US suspension of gold convertibility left the other major countries with little alternative but to float their currencies, which did it with great reluctance. Almost everyone agreed that negotiations to construct a new international monetary system to succeed the defunct Bretton Woods system was an urgent necessity. The first step in this reconstruction was agreed to be the reestablishment of a new structure of pegged exchange rates system. This was accomplished at the conference held in the Smithsonian Institute in Washington. This agreement started to unravel in middle of 1972, when a run on the pound led the British authorities to let sterling floating again. In February 1973, came more speculative runs, which led to a new wave of currency realignments and speculative pressures. The adjustable peg had become unworkable, and the major countries accepted the fact that we are moving to a new system of generalized floating.

1.2.6 The "Golden Age" of the Twentieth Century

In brief, from 1876 to 1913, exchange rates were dictated by the "gold standard" system. Each country's currency was convertible into gold at a specified rate (its mint parity). Thus, the exchange rate between two currencies was determined by their relative convertibility rates per ounce of gold. Each country was using gold to back its currency. When World War I began in 1914, the gold standard was suspended. Some countries reverted to the gold standard in the 1920s, but abandoned it as a result of a banking panic in the United States during the Great Depression and in Europe a little later. In the 1930s, some countries attempted to peg their currencies to the US dollar or the British pound sterling, but there were frequent revisions, due to trade deficits. As a result of these instabilities in the foreign exchange market and the severe restrictions on international transactions, during that period, the volume of international trade had declined. In 1944, a new international agreement (the Bretton Woods Agreement) called for fixed exchange rates between currencies ("the gold exchange standard"). Exchange rates were established between currencies, and the governments or central banks intervened to prevent exchange rates from moving more than ±1% above or below their initially established levels. This agreement lasted until 1971. With the Smithsonian Agreement, the US dollar was devalued relative to the other currencies ($38/oz of gold) and the exchange rates were allowed to fluctuate by ±2.25%.

The above exchange rate regime, which was negotiated at Bretton Woods and monitored by the IMF worked relatively well during the post–World War II period of reconstruction and rapid growth in world trade and in domestic economies. Of course, differences existing in national monetary, fiscal, and trade policies, as well as in inflation and unemployment rates among countries, and many external shocks (wars, oil prices, etc.) led the system to its demise. Actually, it was a rigid monetary system, which caused serious problems mostly to small economies. The US dollar was the main reserve currency held by central banks, but it had many problems because the United States ran persistent and growing deficits in its trade accounts. An enormous capital outflow of dollars to finance the deficits and the demand for dollars resulted in a lack of confidence by foreigners toward the ability of the United States to meet its commitment, which was to offer gold and keep the exchange rate fixed. The United States lost a tremendous amount of gold until the suspension of the official sales of gold in 1971. The dollar was devalued until March 1973, when the major foreign exchange markets closed for a few weeks, and when they reopened, currencies were allowed to float depending on the market conditions.

A country on the "gold standard" and on the "gold exchange standard" allowed its residents and its businesses to ship gold abroad to finance their payment deficits. The central banks also were buying or selling gold by accepting their own currencies. Gold was serving as the principal reserve asset up to 1971, when President Nixon abandoned the sale of gold from the Federal Reserve System. In the late years of the gold standard system, some countries began holding reserves in the form of currencies (mainly pound sterlings; later dollars; and now dollars, euros, and other hard currencies). The gold standard was imposing adjustment obligations and was also providing an adjustment mechanism (through the price-specie-flow mechanism, interest rate effects on capital flows, income effects, and terms of trade effects). Loss of gold signified the obligation to accept monetary contraction and a gain of gold implied an obligation to expand money supply. Gold was provided as the world's monetary base during that period, "the golden age" period. There was a period of thriving international capital market intermediating funds mainly from United Kingdom and France to investors in the lands of recent settlement and elsewhere (in regions that nations were financing their wars of independence). But, the inflexibility of these systems caused serious balance-of-payments problems and consequently, employment and welfare reductions.

1.3 Floating Exchange Rate

After the fall of the Bretton Woods System, the unsuccessful compromises with the Smithsonian Agreement, the oil crises on the early 1970s, and the continued devaluation of the dollar, the system of floating exchange rates that appeared in 1971 was adopted by many leading industrialized nations, but the official ratification took place in April 1978. Even with the wider bands, due to the Smithsonian Agreement, governments still had many difficulties maintaining exchange rates within the ±2.25% boundaries. By March 1973, these official boundaries were eliminated. The widely traded currencies were allowed to fluctuate in accordance with market forces. Floating exchange rates were deemed acceptable by the IMF and gold was officially demonetized and sold off.[28] This new "non-system" (because it made no attempt to subject countries to obligations or to impose any order, as the gold exchange standard) was legalized by the Interim Committee at the Jamaica meeting in January 1976. Under a freely floating exchange rate system, exchange rates would be determined (through demand and supply of currencies) by market forces and without government or central bank interventions, as graph 1.1 shows.

The exchange rates that exist today lie between fixed and freely floating.[29] Exchange rates are allowed to fluctuate on a continual basis without official boundaries, but from time to time central banks intervene and alter their currency's market value. This type of system is known as a

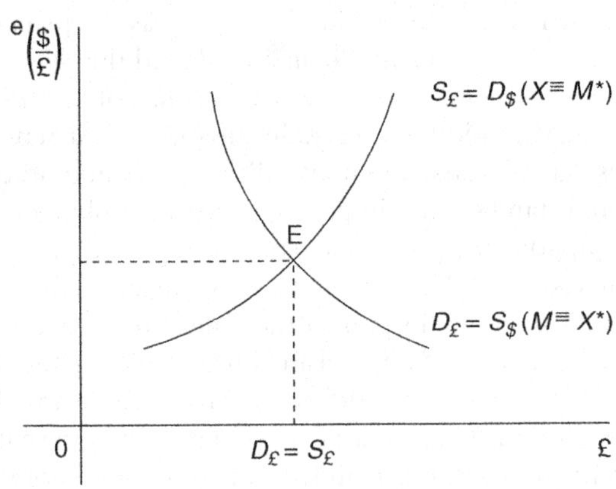

Graph 1.1 Determination of flexible exchange rate.

Note: e = spot exchange rate($/€), e_0 = equilibrium spot exchange rate, E = equilibrium point, D = demond, S = supply, M = domestic imports, X = exports, M* = foreign imports, and X* = foreign exports "managed" float or "dirty" float system. The degree to which a home currency is managed varies across nations. Some central banks smooth the exchange rate movement, some establish implicit exchange rate boundaries, and others react to disturbances or use it as tool for their domestic trade policy. For example, when the Fed wants to force a depreciation of the dollar, it uses (sells) dollars to purchase foreign currency reserves. To force a dollar appreciation, the Fed purchases dollars by selling foreign reserves (assets). Studies have found that the effectiveness of central banks' interventions in the foreign exchange market does not have a permanent effect on the exchange rates. A central bank may consider depreciating its currency through selling it in the foreign exchange market in order to alleviate a domestic trade deficit. The devaluation of the currency may improve the deficit in the long run, but in the short run the deficit may worsen because precontracted imports will cost more in domestic terms, due to depreciation of the domestic currency (the *J*-curve effect).

As price theory shows how price flexibility can clear competitive markets, variations in the price of foreign exchange could ensure that the foreign exchange market clears (see graph 1.1). The rate will adjust to the point where the demand for foreign currency to buy imports and make other current payments will equal the supply of exports and other current receipts denominated in foreign currency. In terms of graph 1.1, the exchange rate would be determined at the value of e_0, where demand for pound sterlings equals the supply. The main point of our work is to study how the exchange rate is determined, when it is induced by market forces.

With the failure of the Bretton Woods system and the "Nixon shock" in 1971, the Smithsonian Agreement set bands of $\pm 2.25\%$ for currencies to move relative to their central rate against the US dollar. This provided a "tunnel" in which European currencies were allowed to trade. However, it implied much larger bands in which they could move against each other. For example, if currency A started at the bottom of its band, it could appreciate by 4.5 percent against the US dollar, while if currency B started at the top of its band, it could depreciate by 4.5 percent against the dollar (if both happened simultaneously, then currency A would appreciate by 9 percent against currency B). This was seen as excessive, and the Basle Agreement in 1972 between the six existing European Economic Community (EEC) members (France, West Germany, Italy, Belgium, Netherlands, and Luxembourg) and the three (Denmark, Ireland, and the United Kingdom) about to join, established a "snake in the tunnel" with bilateral margins between their currencies limited to $\pm 2.25\%$, implying a maximum change between any two currencies of 4.5 percent, and with all the currencies tending to move together against the dollar. The "snake in the tunnel" was the first attempt at European monetary cooperation in the 1970s, aiming at limiting fluctuations between the different EEC currencies. It was an attempt at creating a single currency band for the EEC, essentially pegging all the EEC currencies to one another. The "tunnel" collapsed in 1973, when the US dollar floated freely. The "snake" proved unsustainable, with several currencies leaving and in some cases rejoining. Also, in August 1971, a special arrangement was made between the National Bank of Belgium and the Netherlands Bank to limit fluctuations among the Benelux currencies to ±1.5% (the "worm"), which was maintained until March 1976. Since March 1973, the exchange rates have become floating, but not a freely floating exchange rate system because there are interventions by central banks and governments to prevent their currencies from moving too far in a certain direction. Thus, our system, is today, a "managed" or "dirty" floating system.

1.4 Eurodollars and Eurocurrencies

Euro-dollars are US dollars time deposits in banks outside the United States. They cannot be found in demand deposits and they cannot be created as the bank's liabilities by offering loans. These Euro-dollars deposits are transferred by wire or by cable or by depositing cash or checks from a bank located within the United States and are kept abroad in the form of dollars. In general, Euro-currencies are time deposits in banks outside of the countries that have issued these currencies. Any convertible currency can exist in "Euro-" form, which has nothing in common with the new currency of the Economic and Monetary Union (EMU), the "euro". Thus, we have Euro-pound sterling, Euro-yen, and of course, Euro-euros (euros on time deposits outside the EMU). The exact size of the Euro-currency market is difficult to measure, but it is a growing wholesale market since 1950s, and it is continuing not only abroad, but also in the United States since December 1981, with the creation of international banking facilities (IBFs) inside the country.

Euro-currency deposits are efficient and convenient ways for banks to hold excess corporate liquidity and to offer short-term loans to finance international transactions (trade and capital flows). Banks accepting Euro-currencies as deposits are called Euro-banks. Thus, a Euro-bank is an intermediary that accepts time deposits and offers loans in a currency other than that of the country in which the bank is located, as Exhibit 1.2 shows. A Euro-bank can be a department of a large commercial bank in any country accepting Euro-currencies.

Exhibit 1.2 Euro-bank Balance Sheet

Assets	*Liabilities*
Loans to Banks	Time Deposits
Loans to Companies	CDs
and Governments	Floating Rate Notes
Fixed Assets	Loans from
V_{Assets}	$V_{Liabilities}$

Note: A = assets and L = liabilities.

1.4.1 History of Euro-Currency Market

The history of Euro-dollars and Euro-banks is as follows. In 1950s, during the period when the Cold War was intense, Soviet Union countries and their banks that were holding dollars were afraid to deposit them in the United States. This was because they feared that in case of a conflict between the two philosophical systems (communism and capitalism), the United States might freeze these deposits.Therefore, Eastern Europeans deposited their dollars in two Soviet banks in Western Europe. The first was the Moscow Narodny Bank in London and the second one, the Banque Commerciale pour l' Europe du Nord in Paris. These banks redeposited those dollars to other European banks and offered loans in dollars because they were paying interest on their dollars time deposits and at the same time, there was a huge demand for dollar loans by all the multinational corporations and central banks. Other central banks and commercial banks started depositing their funds denominated in dollars at these Euro-banks because of their higher deposit rates. Also, in 1957, British monetary authorities, after a devaluation of the pound sterling, imposed restrictions on UK banks from lending sterlings to non-UK residents. Then, the British banks turned to dollar lending, and for these loans, they needed dollar deposits from the Euro-dollar market. London, due to its expertise and its proximity to major international customers, became the center for international transactions. Also, the European-based dollar market grew in the 1960s as a separate market from the United States because the US domestic capital market was facing many difficulties due to the growing trade account deficits in the country. The Euro-currency market continued to thrive because it is an enormous, efficient, and low-cost market, without reserve requirements, without FDIC insurance, and without regulations or interferences from the authorities, which keeps their operating cost relatively low.

In the Euro-currency market, its reference interest rate is the London Interbank Offered Rate (LIBOR). It is officially defined by the British Bankers Association (BBA), and it is the most accepted interest rate in loans, financial derivatives, and standardized quotations, globally. The BBA calculates the US dollar LIBOR, the Japanese yen LIBOR, the euro LIBOR, and other rates as the mean of 16 non-US banks.[30] Of course, the interbank offered rates are not confined to London; there are also PIBOR (Paris Interbank Offered Rate), MIBOR (Madrid Interbank Offered Rate), SIBOR (Singapore Interbank Offered Rate), FIBOR (Frankfurt Interbank Offered Rate), EURIBOR (Euro Interbank Offered Rate), SHIBOR (Shanghai Interbank Offered Rate), and many other rates. The Euro-currency market is a very efficient one: it is a wholesale market (transactions more than $500,000), it is unsecured, but participants have an excellent credit standing, it has no reserve requirements, it is not subject to many regulations, as the traditional banks (before 1980), and it has a very low overhead cost. For these reasons the market has a very narrow interest rate spread between loan rates and deposit rates (about 1 percent). The competition is higher in these Euro-currency markets, and that is why their deposit rates are higher and loan rates lower when compared with domestic banks.

1.4.2 From the European Monetary System to the Economic and Monetary Union

In March 1979, the EMS was created by the EEC, which established a cooperative exchange rate system and was hoping to prevent large fluctuations among the participating member nations. After the demise of the gold exchange standard in 1971, most of the EEC countries agreed in 1972 to maintain stable exchange rates among themselves by preventing exchange rate fluctuations of more than $\pm 2.25\%$ (the European "currency snake"). This system was replaced by the EMS, and the European Currency Unit (ECU), which was defined as a basket of currencies preventing movements above 2.25 percent (6 percent for Italy). Also, the exchange rate mechanism (ERM) was introduced by the EEC in March 1979 to achieve monetary stability in Europe, and an extension of European credit facilities was arranged, in preparation for the EMU and the introduction of a single currency, the euro, which took place on January 1, 1999. After the adoption of the euro, the policy changed to linking currencies of countries outside the Euro-zone to the euro (having the common currency as a central point).

In October 1972, the European Monetary Cooperation Fund (EMCF) was established, and it allocated ECUs to members' central banks in exchange for gold and US dollar reserves; it was succeeded by the European Monetary Institute (EMI) in 1994, which is now part of the European Central Bank (ECB). In the early 1990s, the EMS was strained by the differing economic policies and conditions of its members, especially, the newly reunified Germany that caused serious problems to the other EU currencies. Britain (which had initially declined to join the EMS and only did so in 1990) permanently withdrew from the system in September 1992. Speculative attacks on the French Franc during the following year led to the so-called Brussels Compromise in August 1993, which established a new fluctuation band of ±15%.

On February 7, 1992, the Maastricht Treaty or Treaty on European Union (TEU) was signed by the members of EEC in Maastricht, Netherlands. On December 9–10, 1991, the same city hosted the European Council, which drafted the treaty. Upon its entry into force on November 1, 1993, during the Delors Commission, it created the European Union (EU) and led to the creation of the single European currency, the euro (€). The Maastricht Treaty has been amended by the treaties of Amsterdam (October 2, 1997),[31] Nice (February 26, 2001),[32] and Lisbon (December 13, 2007).[33] In September 1992, the EMS crisis started, due to increases in German interest rates, which induced massive capital flows into deutsche mark-denominated assets, causing the withdrawal of the Italian lira and the British pound from the EMS's common float. On September 13, 1992, Italy decided to devalue the Italian Lira by 7 percent. On September 16, 1992, the United Kingdom withdrew from the ERM, and on September 17, 1992, Italy did the same.

For the member nations of the EU to be able to join the EMU, five "convergence criteria" or Maastricht criteria were expected to be met by the candidates. They were: (1) The currency of each member nation must have remained within the normal fluctuation margins of the ERM (±2.25%) of the EMS for at least two years prior to the examination. (2) The average inflation rate should be no more than 1.5 percent above the average for the three members of the EU with the lowest inflation during the previous year. (3) The long-term interest rates (on government bonds or comparable securities) of any member nation during the year prior to the examination by the European Commission must have been no more than 2 percentage points above the average long-term interest rate of the three countries with the lowest inflation rates during this same period. (4) The government budget deficit (including central, regional, and local government) of any member nation may not exceed 3 percent of that country's GDP at the time of the examination, unless it is temporary and exceptional. (5) The government debt of any member country may not exceed 60 percent of the country's GDP at the time of the examination. But, this criterion is also satisfied if it is approaching the reference value at a satisfactory speed. In addition, the national central banks must be granted full independence.

In 1994, the EMI, the predecessor to the ECB, was founded in Frankfurt, Germany. The EMS was no longer a functional arrangement in May 1998, as the member countries fixed their mutual exchange rates when participating in the euro. Its successor however, the ERM-II (Stage II), was launched on January 1, 1999, at an exchange rate of 1.19 $/€. In ERM-II, the ECU basket was discarded and the new single currency euro (€) became the anchor for the other currencies participating in ERM-II. Participation in ERM-II is voluntary and the fluctuation bands remain the same as in the original ERM, that is, ±15 percent, once again with the possibility of individually setting a narrower band with respect to the euro.

In 1995, the Madrid Summit of heads of state and government decided on the details of entry into Stage III. They were as follows. As early as possible in 1998, "the European Council will decide which countries can participate in EMU, according to compliance with the convergence criteria achieved in 1997." On January 1, 1999, "the monetary union will begin with the irrevocable fixing of the conversion rates of the countries that qualified for EMU. The European Central Bank will initiate a single monetary policy and a foreign exchange rate policy will be conducted in euro. New tradable public debt will be issued in euro. The ECU will cease to exist." On January 1, 2002, "the new euro notes and coins will be introduced." And on July 1, 2002, "national currencies will be completely replaced and cease to be legal tenders."[34] The 1997 target for EMU was not abandoned even though only two countries (Luxembourg and France) met the five criteria of economic convergence.[35]

In 2000, 11 EU member nations elected to participate in the system. Greece joined in 2001, and Denmark chose to stay out. The ERM-II is sometimes described as the "waiting room" for joining the EMU of the EU. On January 1, 2002, the EMU (Stage III) was launched, where the actual currencies in the participating member nations were replaced by euro banknotes and coins; thus, 12 members entered the Euro-zone. On May 1, 2004, ten more countries joined the EU, expanding the union to 25 (EU-25) members, and lastly, in January 2007, two nations (Bulgaria and Romania) joined the EU making it the EU-27. The euro initially declined and became 0.8525 $/€(2000:10), after that, it started to appreciate and peaked at 1.6001 $/€ (2008:04). Lately, due to the global financial crisis and the European debt crisis, the euro has lost some of its value; on May 17, 2012, the exchange rate was 1.2691 $/€; but, it continues to appreciate with respect the US dollar (1.3193 $/€ on December 31, 2012) because of the "fiscal cliff" in the United States and due to the disagreement between the two political parties, the Democrats and the Republicans.

The ECB is the institution of the EU that administers the monetary policy of the 17 member nations of the Euro-zone. The ECB was established by the Treaty of Amsterdam in 1998, and is headquartered in Frankfurt, Germany.[36] It follows the basic structures of the US Federal Reserve System (Fed) and the German Bundesbank. The primary objective of the ECB is to maintain price stability in the medium term within the Euro-zone, which is the same as keeping inflation low.[37] The governing council defined price stability as inflation (harmonized index of consumer prices) of around 2 percent. Unlike, the US Fed, which has two mandates (maximum employment and stable prices, and also, moderate long-term interest rates), the ECB has only one primary objective, with other objectives subordinate to it. The key tasks of the ECB are to define and implement the monetary policy for the Euro-zone, to conduct foreign exchange operations, to take care of the foreign reserves of the European System of Central Banks, and promote smooth operation of the financial market infrastructure under the Target Payment System and the technical platform (currently being developed) for settlement of securities in Europe (TARGET 2 Securities, T2S). Furthermore, it has the exclusive right to authorize the issuance of currency (euro banknotes). Member states could issue euro coins, but the amount had to be authorized by the ECB beforehand (upon the introduction of the euro, the ECB also had exclusive rights to issue coins; but then, the member nations lost their monetary policy because they could not use domestic money supply as a policy instrument).[38]

1.4.3 The Latest Debt Crisis

In August 2007, a financial crisis started developing from the United States (by investment banks), spread almost globally, and became a financial contagion (systemic risk). The most severe effect of this crisis was on Europe, referred to as the European sovereign debt crisis, which is an ongoing financial crisis that has made it impossible for some countries in the Euro-zone to refinance their government debt (bonds) without the assistance of third parties, like the "Troika" (EU, ECB, and IMF). Since late 2009, fears of a sovereign debt crisis developed among investors, as a result of the rising government debt levels in EU member nations, together with a wave of downgrading of government debt in some EU members. Concerns intensified in early 2010, leading Europe's finance ministers on May 9, 2010, to approve a rescue package worth €750 billion aimed at ensuring financial stability across Europe by creating the European Financial Stability Facility (EFSF). The countries with the worst crisis were Portugal, Ireland, Italy, Greece, Spain (PIIGS), and some others, too.

The EFSF's mandate is to safeguard financial stability in Europe by providing financial assistance to Euro-zone member states. The EFSF must also cooperate within the EU and internationally with third bodies and entities. Finally, it contributes to maintaining a stable financial system and monitoring the banking sector. The latter can be seen, for example, in the bank's intervention during the 2007 credit crisis and the erupted debt crisis in 2009, when it loaned billions of euros to banks to stabilize the financial system. Throughout 2009–2013 various member states of the European Union showed themselves to be increasingly unable to meet financial commitments. The current debt crisis (2009–2013) is the worst in ECB's history and has difficulties confronting it, due to lack of experience and conflict about a common monetary policy among the different members (the wealthy north nations and the poor ones of the south).[39] The crisis of the ECU in 1992 was similar to almost any other financial crisis, but relatively smaller. The latest crisis is, so far, unique in our international economic history.

In October 2011 and February 2012, the Euro-zone leaders agreed on more measures designed to prevent the collapse of member economies. This included an agreement whereby banks would accept a 53.5 percent write-off of some of the Greek debt owed to private creditors, increasing the EFSF's capital to about €1 trillion, and requiring European banks to achieve 9 percent capitalization. To restore confidence in Europe, the EU leaders also agreed to create a European Fiscal Compact including the commitment of each participating country to introduce a balanced budget amendment. This Euro-zone debt crisis has become a big problem for the entire EMU and its currency, the euro. After the French and Greek elections in May 2012, the euro has started losing its value significantly with respect to the US dollar; in 2012 the euro depreciated by 13 percent, but after June 2012 until the end of the year, it appreciated by 7.45 percent with respect to the US dollar. It would appear that the "market knows better" than us.

1.5 Modern Currency Regimes

The current international monetary system is composed of less national currencies compared to the past, and the reason for this is the introduction of the euro (€) on January 1, 1999, in electronic form and on January 1, 2002, in banknotes and coins. Today, 17 countries, without knowing its consequences, have abandoned their domestic currencies and have adopted the euro. These countries are, with their adopted year in parenthesis: Austria (1999), Belgium (1999), Finland (1999), France

(1999), Germany (1999), Ireland (1999), Italy (1999), Luxembourg (1999), Netherlands (1999), Portugal (1999), Spain (1999), Greece (2001), Slovenia (2007), Cyprus (2008), Malta (2008), Slovakia (2009), and Estonia (2011). Also, there is an artificial currency (interest-bearing international reserve asset) introduced by the IMF in 1969, the Special Drawing Right (SDR). The rest of the world currencies are the national currencies of all the sovereign nations. The next section deals with the exchange rate regime.[40]

1.5.1 Exchange Rate Regimes

According to the IMF, exchange rate regimes can be classified as the following:

1. Exchange Arrangements with No Separate Legal Tender
The currency of another country circulates as the sole legal tender (formal dollarization), or the member belongs to a monetary or currency union in which the same legal tender (i.e., euro) is shared by the members of the union. Adopting such regimes implies the complete surrender of the monetary authorities' independent control over domestic monetary policy, which will have negative effects in the long run on these economies and on their society.

2. Currency Board Arrangements
A monetary regime based on an explicit legislative commitment to exchange domestic currency for a specified foreign currency at a fixed exchange rate, combined with restrictions on the issuing authority to ensure the fulfillment of its legal obligation. This implies that domestic currency will be issued only against foreign exchange, and that it remains fully backed by foreign assets, eliminating traditional central bank functions, such as monetary control and lender-of-last-resort, and leaving little scope for discretionary monetary policy. Some flexibility may still be afforded, depending on how strict the banking rules of the currency board arrangement are for the country.

3. Other Conventional Fixed Peg Arrangements
The country (formally or de facto) pegs its currency at a fixed rate to another currency or a basket of currencies, where the basket is formed from the currencies of major trading or financial partners, and weights reflect the geographical distribution of trade, services, or capital flows. The currency composites can also be standardized, as in the case of the SDR. There is no commitment to keep the parity irrevocably. The exchange rate may

fluctuate within narrow margins of less than ±1 percent around a central rate (or the maximum and minimum value of the exchange rate may remain within a narrow margin of ±2 percent) for at least three months. The monetary authority stands ready to maintain the fixed parity through direct intervention (i.e., via sale/purchase of foreign exchange in the market) or indirect intervention (i.e., via aggressive use of interest rate policy, imposition of foreign exchange regulations, exercise of moral suasion that constrains foreign exchange activity, or through intervention by other public institutions). Flexibility of monetary policy, though limited, is greater than in the case of exchange arrangements with no separate legal tender and currency boards because traditional central banking functions are still possible, and the monetary authority can adjust the level of the exchange rate, although relatively infrequently.

4. Pegged Exchange Rates within Horizontal Bands

The value of the currency is maintained within certain margins of fluctuation of at least ±1 percent around a fixed central rate, or the margin between the maximum and minimum value of the exchange rate exceeds 2 percent. It also includes arrangements of countries in the exchange rate mechanism (ERM) of the European Monetary System (EMS) that was replaced with the ERM Stage II on January 1, 1999. There is a limited degree of monetary policy discretion, depending on the band width.

5. Crawling Pegs

The currency is adjusted periodically in small amounts at a fixed rate or in response to changes in selective quantitative indicators, such as past inflation differentials vis-à-vis major trading partners, differentials between the inflation target and the expected inflation in major trading partners, and so forth. The rate of crawl can be set to generate inflation-adjusted changes in the exchange rate (backward looking) or set at a preannounced fixed rate and/or below the projected inflation differentials (forward looking). Maintaining a crawling peg imposes constraints on monetary policy in a manner similar to a fixed peg system.

6. Exchange Rates within Crawling Bands

The currency is maintained within certain fluctuation margins of at least ±1 percent around a central rate (or the margin between the maximum and minimum value of the exchange rate exceeds 2 percent) and the central rate or margins are adjusted periodically at a fixed rate or in response to changes in selective quantitative indicators. The degree of exchange rate flexibility is a function of the band width. Bands are either symmetric around a crawling central parity or widen gradually with an asymmetric choice of the crawl of the upper and lower bands (in the latter case, there may be no preannounced central rate). The commitment to maintain the exchange rate within the band imposes constraints on monetary policy, with the degree of policy independence being a function of the band width.

7. Managed Floating with No Predetermined Path for the Exchange Rate
The monetary authority attempts to influence the exchange rate without having a specific exchange rate path or target. Indicators for managing the rate are broadly judgmental (i.e., balance of payments position, international reserves, parallel market developments) and adjustments may not be automatic. Intervention may be direct or indirect.

8. Independently Floating
The exchange rate is market determined, with any official foreign exchange market intervention aimed at moderating the rate of change and preventing undue fluctuations in the exchange rate, rather than at establishing a level for it.

Today, the most rigidly fixed exchange rate system is the Euro-zone's, which has imposed the common currency (euro) on its member nations. They have no independent national currencies and face even more negative effects compared with the fixed exchange rate regimes of the past. The Euro-zone members have lost their monetary, fiscal, and trade policies, due to the common currency. They have lost their competitiveness, which has tremendous negative effects on exports, trade, investments, employment, production, income, and wealth for the nations. Even the fixed exchange rate regimes require countries to follow restrictive monetary and fiscal policies. These restrictions cause serious economic problems to the countries, like unemployment, low growth and income, and reductions in social welfare. Central banks have to keep large quantities of international reserves (hard currencies and gold), which create a significant burden on the nations. Fixed exchange rates and common currencies are mostly at levels inconsistent (in disequilibria) with the economic fundamentals of the country, which increases inefficiency for the nation.

The ideal currency must have three attributes ("the impossible trinity"):

1. *Exchange Rate Stability:* The value of the currency must be stable (based on the economic fundamentals of a stable economically and

politically country), so participants in investment and trade will have high confidence and very low risk with this currency.

2. *Convertibility and Mobility:* Complete freedom of monetary flows denominated in this currency among countries that investors and traders can maximize their return and minimize their risk.
3. *Independent Monetary Policy:* The domestic monetary policy (money supply and interest rates) must be determined by the central bank of the country, which has the obligation to maximize the social welfare of the nation and not only the market value of the financial assets. The objective of the central bank must be first, zero unemployment ($u \cong 0\%$), then, low inflation ($\pi \cong 0\%$), stable growth ($g_Q \cong 3\%$), moderate long term interest rate ($i_{L-T} \cong 4\%$), current account balance ($CA \cong 0$), and above all, an independent national policy from any external influence.[41]

1.5.2 *Thoughts for a New Financial System*

On September 26, 2008, then French president Nicolas Sarkozy, then also the president of the EU, said, "We must rethink the financial system from scratch, as at Bretton Woods." On October 13, 2008, British prime minister Gordon Brown said, world leaders must meet to agree to a new economic system by emphasizing the continuation of globalization and free trade: "We must have a new Bretton Woods, building a new international architecture for the years ahead." There were tensions between Brown and Sarkozy, who argued that the "Anglo-Saxon" model of unrestrained (deregulated) markets had failed, as the latest crisis has proven. However European leaders were united in calling for a "Bretton Woods II" summit to redesign the world's financial architecture. President George W. Bush was agreeable to the calls, and the resulting meeting was the 2008 G-20 summit in Washington. International agreement was achieved for the common adoption of Keynesian fiscal stimulus, an area where the United States and China were to emerge as the world's leading actors. Yet there was no substantial progress toward reforming the international financial system, and nor was there at the 2009 meeting of the World Economic Forum at Davos. Despite this lack of results, leaders continued to campaign for Bretton Woods II. The Italian economics minister Giulio Tremonti said that Italy would use its 2009 G-7 chairmanship to push for a "New Bretton Woods." He had been critical of the US' response to the global financial crisis of 2008, and had suggested that the dollar may be superseded as the base currency of the Bretton Woods system.

In March 2009, Gordon Brown continued to advocate for reform and the granting of extended powers to international financial institutions like the IMF, at the April G-20 summit in London, and was said to have President Obama's support. Also, during March 2009, Zhou Xiaochuan, the governor of the People's Bank of China, came out in favor of Keynes's idea of a centrally managed global reserve currency. Dr. Zhou argued that it was unfortunate that part of the reason for the Bretton Woods system breaking down was the failure to adopt Keynes's "bancor."[42] Dr. Zhou said that national currencies were unsuitable for use as global reserve currencies, as a result of the Triffin dilemma (the difficulty faced by reserve currency issuers in trying to simultaneously achieve their domestic monetary policy goals and meet other countries' demand for reserve currency). Dr. Zhou proposed a gradual move toward increased use of IMF SDRs, as a centrally managed global reserve currency. His proposal attracted much international attention. Leaders meeting in April at the 2009 G-20 London summit agreed to allow $250 billion of SDRs to be created by the IMF, to be distributed to all IMF members according to each country's voting rights. In the aftermath of the summit, Gordon Brown declared that "the Washington Consensus is over." On January 27, 2010, in his opening address to the 2010 World Economic Forum in Davos, President Sarkozy repeated his call for a new Bretton Woods, and was met with wild applause by a sizeable proportion of the audience. In December 2011, the Bank of England published a paper arguing for reform, saying that the current International Monetary System has performed poorly compared to the Bretton Woods System. The G-8 leaders met at a weekend summit at Camp David on May 19, 2012, and urged Greece to stay within the euro area as momentum gathered for the idea of issuing euro bonds to ease Europe's debt crisis, to reduce the austerity measures from the Euro-zone nations, and to improve growth.[43] The economies of the EU are being gripped by political confusion, as policy makers failed to develop solutions to address the financial crises faced by Greece and other peripheral nations. The euro has lost 5.23 percent against the US dollar in May 2012 (4/27/2012: 1.3229 $/€ and 5/29/2012: 1.2537 $/€) and $4 trillion have been wiped away from equity markets, due to fear that this turmoil in Greece might spread to other members of the Euro-zone. By the beginning of 2013, the Euro-zone turmoil had affected Spain, Portugal, Ireland, Italy, Cyprus, Slovenia, and it is moving to France and almost to every Euro-zone nation.

1.6 Summary

The international monetary system has experienced tremendous changes over the last 2,500 years. Currencies have been defined in terms of commodities, livestock, gold, silver, copper, and other items of value. The international monetary system has been subject to a variety of international agreements, but lately, has shown many deficiencies, due to lack of control (deregulation), complexity, "innovations," debts, excess liquidity, bubbles, and, in general, an artificial pricing of all the global assets and a lack of a code of ethics. The foreign exchange regimes have also changed over the last 100 years. The first (1876–1913) was the "gold standard," the second (1914–1944) was a "modified gold standard," and the third (1944–1971) the "gold exchange standard" (all of them were fixed exchange rate regimes). Then, the flexible rate regime started in March 1973 and continues up to now. For a fixed exchange rate, the government is unwilling to let the country's currency float freely because there are specific rules enforced by an international agreement. The government takes whatever measures are necessary to maintain the rate and prevent it from fluctuating.

Under the fixed exchange rate system, a decrease in the exchange rate (currency gaining value) is called revaluation of the currency, while an increase in the exchange rate (currency losing value) is called devaluation. Devaluation in a fixed exchange rate will cause the current account balance to rise, making a country's exports less expensive for foreigners, and it also discourages imports by making imported products more expensive for domestic consumers. This will lead to an increase in trade surplus or a decrease in trade deficit. The opposite happens in a revaluation. The rigidity of the fixed exchange rate causes serious problems to the countries. Of course, there is certainty in fixed exchange rate. With it, international trade and investment becomes less risky, and there is little or no speculation on a fixed exchange rate.

However, a fixed exchange rate contradicts slightly the "objective" of having free markets, and it is not able to adjust to shocks swiftly like the floating exchange rate. With a fixed exchange rate, countries lose their trade policy; they cannot devaluate their currencies to improve their trade account (reduce imports and stimulate exports), and face low foreign demand for their product and high unemployment domestically.

On the contrary, the floating exchange rate regime consists of the "independent" floating system and the "managed" floating system. The former is where exchange rate is strictly determined by the free movement of demand for and supply of currencies. For "managed" floating systems too, exchange rate is determined by free movement of demand and supply, but the monetary authorities intervene at certain times to "manage" the exchange rate to prevent high volatilities and improve their domestic trade (it is used as trade policy instrument). The floating exchange rate has various merits. First, there is automatic correction in the floating exchange rate, as the country simply lets it to move freely from one to the other equilibrium. Second, there is insulation from external economic events, as the country's currency is not tied to a possibly high world inflation rate, as it is under a fixed exchange rate. The free movement of demand and supply helps to insulate the domestic economy from world economic fluctuations. Third, governments are free to choose their domestic policy, as a floating exchange rate would allow for automatic correction of any balance of payment disequilibrium that might arise from the implementation of domestic policy. Nonetheless, there are also some minor concerns about the exchange rate being unstable and uncertain under the floating exchange rate regime. Graph A1.1 shows the volatility of the US dollar with respect to a trade weighted exchange rate index and graph A1.2 reveals the depreciation of the US dollar with respect to gold. Also, speculation tends to be higher in the floating exchange rate regime, hence, leading to more uncertainty, especially for traders and investors, but at the same time there are hedging techniques that can be used to reduce the exchange rate risk. A review of these systems provides a useful perspective against the mistakes of the past, and historical knowledge can help decision makers avoid the same mistakes in the future.

Of course, changes in our international monetary system were not only in the exchange rate systems, but also in the enormous progress in information technology and telecommunications that had come during the war (how to defeat the enemy) and later, had a profound impact on international financial economics (how to compete with the rival nations and firms). Bretton Woods was an attempt to avoid a repetition of the same mistakes that the Allies made after World War I, when the second war with Germany was over. But, as it is proven, today, with the global financial crisis, the debt crisis in Europe, and the imposition of the anti-growth measures on Europeans, the Allies (actually, the IMF members) have difficulties in learning from their past mistakes.

What lies ahead in our international monetary system is very difficult to predic. But, any sociopolitical-economic system must have as its objective the human beings of our world, and any nation must have as its goal, through public policies (fiscal, monetary, trade, etc.), the maximum social welfare of its citizens. An exchange rate regime must deal with the trade-off between rules (governments have strict intervention requirements, like the gold standard and the gold exchange standard) and discretion (the country's central bank chooses when, whether, and to what degree to intervene in the foreign exchange market), as well as between cooperation (countries participate in a specific system with others, like the EMS) and independence (acting on their own for the benefit of their citizens). The current trend is that there are no rules for the large economies, but they can have a degree of cooperation, as they talk during the G-7 or G-20 meetings. It seems that the best system can be the one that combines some cooperation among all nations, but with more emphasis on individual discretion for the countries to pursue their domestic, financial, trade, economic, and social objectives as sovereign nations.

Appendix I

A1.1 Correlation and Causality

Correlation is a measure of dependence between two variables, for example, M^s and P; it can be measured with the correlation coefficient ($\rho_{M^s,P}$), which shows the degree of their relationship and its value ranges between, $-1 \leq \rho \leq +1$. It can be calculated using the following formula:

$$\rho_{M^s,P} = \frac{Cov(M^s, P)}{\sigma_{M^s}\sigma_P} \tag{A1.1}$$

where, $\rho_{M^s,P}$ = correlation coefficient between money supply and prices, $Cov(M^s, P)$ = covariance between the two variables, σ_{M^s} = standard deviation of money supply, and σ_P = standard deviation of prices.

The correlation does not necessarily imply causation. A Granger causality test can help in the prediction of P by using lagged values of M^s:

$$m_t = \alpha_0 + \alpha_1 m_{t-1} + \cdots + \alpha_l m_{t-l} + \beta_1 p_{t-1} + \cdots + \beta_l p_{t-l} + \varepsilon_{1t}$$

$$p_t = \alpha_0 + \alpha_1 p_{t-1} + \cdots + \alpha_l p_{t-l} + \beta_1 m_{t-1} + \cdots + \beta_l m_{t-l} + \varepsilon_{2t} \tag{A1.2}$$

where, m_t = natural logarithm of money supply (base $e = 2.71828$), p_t = natural logarithm of prices, and ε_t = the error term.

A1.1.1 Correlation Coefficient between ln M^s *and* ln P *in the United States*

The empirical results show an almost perfect positive correlation between m^s and p in the US economy:

	$\ln M^s$	$\ln P$
$\ln M^s$	1.000	0.994
$\ln P$	0.994	1.000

Thus, $\rho_{m^s,p} = +0.994$.

Table A1.1 Consolidated statement of the condition of all federal reserve banks

Millions of dollars

Assets, liabilities, and capital	*Eliminations from consolidation*	*Wednesday Nov 7, 2012*	*Change since*	
			Wednesday Oct 31, 2012	*Wednesday Nov 9, 2011*
Assets				
Gold certificate account		11,037	0	0
Special drawing rights certificate account		5,200	0	0
Coin		2,153	−1	−143
Securities, repurchase agreements, and loans		2,586,419	+5,883	−49,226
Securities held outright[1]		2,585,253	+5,979	−39,787
US Treasury securities		1,651,289	+5,955	−16,822
Bills[2]		0	0	−18,423
Notes and bonds, nominal[2]		1,568,888	+5,869	−1,557
Notes and bonds, inflation-indexed[2]		71,944	0	+2,692
Inflation compensation[3]		10,457	+86	+465
Federal agency debt securities[2]		81,902	0	−25,766
Mortgage-backed securities[4]		852,063	+24	+2,802
Repurchase agreements[5]		0	0	0
Loans		1,166	−96	−9,439
Net portfolio holdings of Maiden Lane LLC[6]		1,572	0	−11,407
Net portfolio holdings of Maiden Lane II LLC[7]		61	0	−9,276
Net portfolio holdings of Maiden Lane III LLC[8]		23	0	−18,131
Net portfolio holdings of TALF LLC[9]		855	0	+61
Items in process of collection	(0)	129	+1	−178
Bank premises		2,343	−10	+164
Central bank liquidity swaps[10]		12,465	−438	+10,505
Other assets[11]		210,153	+2,222	+67,624
Total assets	(0)	2,832,408	+7,658	−10,009
Liabilities				
Federal Reserve notes, net of F.R. Bank holdings		1,104,765	+5,190	+89,573
Reverse repurchase agreements[12]		92,980	−6,768	+5,332
Deposits	(0)	1,567,205	+9,188	−102,175
Term deposits held by depository institutions		0	0	0
Other deposits held by depository institutions		1,511,296	+76,896	−82,341

continued

Table A1.1 continued

Assets, liabilities, and capital	*Eliminations from consolidation*	*Wednesday Nov 7, 2012*	*Change since*	
			Wednesday Oct 31, 2012	*Wednesday Nov 9, 2011*
US Treasury, General Account		23,970	−75,996	−223
US Treasury, Supplementary Financing Account		0	0	0
Foreign official		5,931	−60	+5,806
Other	(0)	26,008	+8,348	−25,417
Deferred availability cash items	(0)	1,040	−18	−441
Other liabilities and accrued dividends[13]		11,611	+18	−4,998
Total liabilities	(0)	2,777,602	+7,611	−12,708
Capital accounts				
Capital paid in		27,403	+23	+1,350
Surplus		27,403	+23	+1,350
Other capital accounts		0	0	0
Total capital		54,806	+46	+2,699

Note: Components may not sum to totals because of rounding. (Table numbers in the footnotes refer to tables in the *Federal Reserve Bulletin.*)

[1] Includes securities lent to dealers under the overnight securities lending facility; refer to table 1A.

[2] Face value of the securities.

[3] Compensation that adjusts for the effect of inflation on the original face value of inflation-indexed securities.

[4] Guaranteed by Fannie Mae, Freddie Mac, and Ginnie Mae. Current face value of the securities, which is the remaining principal balance of the underlying mortgages.

[5] Cash value of agreements, which are collateralized by US Treasury and federal agency securities.

[6] Refer to table 4 and the note on consolidation accompanying table 9.

[7] Refer to table 5 and the note on consolidation accompanying table 9.

[8] Refer to table 6 and the note on consolidation accompanying table 9.

[9] Refer to table 7 and the note on consolidation accompanying table 9.

[10] Dollar value of foreign currency held under these agreements valued at the exchange rate to be used when the foreign currency is returned to the foreign central bank. This exchange rate equals the market exchange rate used when the foreign currency was acquired from the foreign central bank.

[11] Includes other assets denominated in foreign currencies, which are revalued daily at market exchange rates and the fair value adjustment to credit extended by the Federal Reserve Bank of New York (FRBNY) to eligible borrowers through the term asset-backed securities loan facility.

[12] Cash value of agreements, which are collateralized by US Treasury securities, federal agency debt securities, and mortgage-backed securities.

[13] Includes the liabilities of Maiden Lane LLC, Maiden Lane II LLC, Maiden Lane III LLC, and TALF LLC to entities other than the Federal Reserve Bank of New York, including liabilities that have recourse only to the portfolio holdings of these LLCs. Refer to table 4 through table 7 and the note on consolidation accompanying table 9. Also includes the liability for interest on Federal Reserve notes due to US Treasury.

Source: Federal Reserve Bulletin, Board of Governors of the Federal Reserve System, Vol. 98, November 8, 2012. www.federalreserve.gov

Table A1.2 Pairwise Granger causality tests

Date: 05/02/12 Time: 13:31
Sample: 1950M01 2012M12
Lags: 2

Null Hypothesis	*Obs*	*F-Statistic*	*Prob.*
LUSCPI does not Granger cause LUSM2	618	1.92193	0.1472
LUSM2 does not Granger cause LUSCPI		4.63982	0.0100

Note: LUSM2 = natural logarithm of money supply (M2) and LUSCPI = natural logarithm of prices (CPI).

A1.1.2 Pairwise Granger Causality Tests

The output from the computer by performing a causality test between m^s and p is presented in table A1.2.

We cannot reject the null hypothesis that $\ln P$ (LUSCPI) does not Granger cause $\ln M^s$(LUSM2), but we do reject the null hypothesis that $\ln M^s$ does not Granger cause $\ln P$ (because the F-statistic is statistically significant and the probability less than 0.10). Therefore, it appears that Granger causality runs one way from money supply to prices and not the other way.

Thus, $\rho_{m^s,p} = +0.994$ and $m^s \Rightarrow p$ (money supply causes inflation).

A1.2 Linear Trend

The linear trend is a linear regression equation of the exchange rate (dependent variable) with respect to time as the independent variable. A trend analysis consists of the study of past exchange rates to predict the future exchange rate:

$$e_t = \alpha + \beta t + \varepsilon_t \tag{A1.3}$$

where, $E(\varepsilon_t) = 0, E(\varepsilon_t^2) = \sigma^2, E(\varepsilon_t, \varepsilon_{t-1}) = 0$, and $E(X_j, \varepsilon_t) = 0$ (assumptions); e_t = the spot exchange rate, t = time $(1, 2, 3, \ldots, N)$, α = constant term (intercept), β = coefficient (slope of the line), and ε_t = the error term.

The output and graph of the linear trend of the exchange rate appears in table A1.3.

Table A1.3 Linear trend estimation and its graph

Dependent Variable: EUS
Method: Least Squares
Date: 05/15/12 Time: 11:48
Sample (adjusted): 1999M01 2012M02
Included observations: 158 after adjustments

Variable	*Coefficient*	*Std. Error*	*t-Statistic*	*Prob.*
C	0.922543	0.017251	53.47678	0.0000
TIME	0.003562	0.000188	18.92678	0.0000
R-squared	0.696630	Mean dependent var		1.205756
Adjusted R-squared	0.694685	S.D. dependent var		0.195290
S.E. of regression	0.107908	Akaike info criterion		−1.602491
Sum squared resid	1.816497	Schwarz criterion		−1.563724
Log likelihood	128.5968	Hannan-Quinn criter.		−1.586748
F-statistic	358.2232	Durbin-Watson stat		0.102465
Prob (F-statistic)	0.000000			

Note: EUS = spot exchange rate (\$/€) and TIME = time (1, 2, 3, ...).

A1.3 Log Linear Trend

By taking the natural logarithm of $e_t(\ln e_t)$, we can have a better measurement of the coefficient (elasticities):

$$\ln e_t = \alpha' + \beta' t + \varepsilon'_t \tag{A1.4}$$

where, $\ln e_t$ = the natural logarithm of the spot exchange rate, α' = constant, and β' = slope of the line (semielasticity).

The empirical results and graph of the log linear trend of the exchange rate appears in table A1.4.

The above equations, as we see from the empirical results, have a low D-W statistic, which means that two consecutive errors are serially correlated. To correct this serial correlation $[E(\varepsilon_t, \varepsilon_{t-1}) \neq 0]$, an autoregressive $[AR(1)]$ and a moving average $[MA(1)]$ process are used, here.

A1.4 Correction of Serial Correlation

The serial correlation of the error terms gives biased coefficients. To improve the results, we need autoregressive $[AR(p)]$ or/and moving average $[MA(q)]$ processes. Here, to correct the serial correlation of the error term, the linear trend is used, with two extra terms, an $AR(1)$ and a $MA(1)$

Table A1.4 Log linear trend estimation

Dependent Variable: LEUS
Method: Least Squares
Date: 05/15/12 Time: 11:50
Sample (adjusted): 1999M01 2012M02
Included observations: 158 after adjustments

Variable	*Coefficient*	*Std. Error*	*t-Statistic*	*Prob.*
C	−0.070136	0.015115	−4.640220	0.0000
TIME	0.003063	0.000165	18.57151	0.0000
R-squared	0.688561	Mean dependent var		0.173345
Adjusted R-squared	0.686565	S. D. dependent var		0.168875
S. E. of regression	0.094545	Akaike info criterion		−1.866904
Sum squared resid	1.394447	Schwarz criterion		−1.828137
Log likelihood	149.4854	Hannan-Quinn criter.		−1.851160
F-statistic	344.9009	Durbin-Watson stat		0.086738
Prob (*F*-statistic)	0.000000			

Note: LEUS = natural logarithm of the spot exchange rate ($/€) and TIME = time (1, 2, 3, ...).

Table A1.5 Log linear trend estimation with correction of the serial correlation

Dependent Variable: LEUS
Method: Least Squares
Date: 05/15/12 Time: 11:52
Sample (adjusted): 1999M02 2012M02
Included observations: 157 after adjustments
Convergence achieved after 8 iterations
MA Backcast: 1999M01

Variable	*Coefficient*	*Std. Error*	*t-Statistic*	*Prob.*
C	−0.132021	0.087556	−1.507841	0.1337
TIME	0.003398	0.000815	4.170600	0.0001
AR(1)	0.929721	0.028297	32.85639	0.0000
MA(1)	0.193687	0.082832	2.338312	0.0207
R-squared	0.975109	Mean dependent var		0.173509
Adjusted R-squared	0.974621	S.D. dependent var		0.169403
S.E. of regression	0.026987	Akaike info criterion		−4.361769
Sum squared resid	0.111430	Schwarz criterion		−4.283903
Log likelihood	346.3989	Hannan-Quinn criter.		−4.330145
F-statistic	1997.951	Durbin-Watson stat		1.960303
Prob(*F*-statistic)	0.000000			
Inverted AR Roots	.93			
Inverted MA Roots	−.19			

Note: LEUS = natural logarithm of the spot exchange rate ($/€), TIME = time (1, 2, 3, ...), AR(1) = autoregressive process, and MA(1) = moving average process.

Graph A1.1 US trade weighted exchange rate index for major currencies (FC/$).

Note: USXR I = US exchange rate index
Source: *economagic.com*

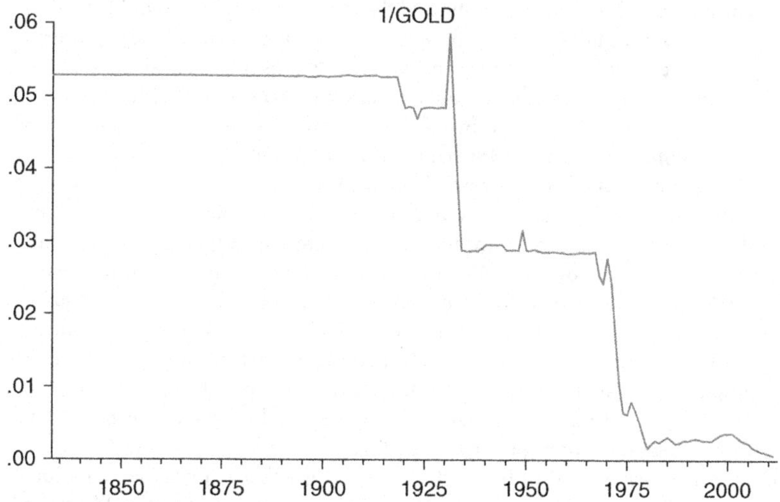

Graph A1.2 The depreciation of the US dollar with respect to gold.

Note: 1/GOLD = the value of US dollar with respect to the price of gold (troy ounces of gold/$).
Source: *Historical Gold Prices-1833 to Present.*
http://www.nma.org/pdf/gold/his_gold_prices.pdf.

process:

$$\ln e_t = \alpha'' + \beta'' t + \gamma'' e_{t-1} + \varepsilon_t + \delta'' \varepsilon_{t-1} \tag{A1.5}$$

where, $e_{t-1} = AR(1)$ process and $\varepsilon_{t-1} = MA(1)$ process.

The output from the computer appears in table A1.5.

The D-W statistic is now 1.960303, which means $E(\varepsilon_t, \varepsilon_{t-1}) = 0$; thus, no first-order serial correlation of the error term exists. For higher order of serial correlation to be tested, a Q-statistic and a Breusch-Godfrey Lagrange multiplier test are needed to see if the coefficients are unbiased.

Notes

1. "But money has become by convention a sort of representative of demand; and this is why it has the name 'money' (*nomisma*) because it exists not by nature, but by law (*nomos*) and it is in our power to change it and make it useless." Aristotle, *Nicomachean Ethics* [1133b 1].
2. The word "money" is derived from the French *monnaie* and the Latin *moneta*, meaning the mint, where coins are struck. See, Davies (1998, p. 101) and Kallianiotis (2011a).
3. The meaning of this new discipline is "the management of household" ([noun] *oecos* = hoursehold and [verb] *nemo* = manage or distribute). Unfortunately, the West ignores history and mistakenly calls Adam Smith, who copied Xenophon, 21 centuries later, as the "father of Economics" (which is also a misspell of the correct word by cutting the two "Os" from the original word "*Oeconomicos*"). See also, Marchant and Todd (1997).
4. The definition of money has varied. For centuries, physical commodities, most commonly silver or gold, served as money. Later, when paper money and checkable deposits were introduced, they were convertible into commodity money. The abandonment of convertibility of money into a commodity since August 15, 1971, when President Nixon discontinued converting US dollars into gold at $35 per ounce, has made the United States and other countries' monies into fiat money—money that national monetary authorities have the power to issue without legal constraints. Many economists have said that this discontinuity of the United States to exchange gold for dollar means that the country defaulted in its payments in 1971.
5. The Triffin Dilemma (or the Triffin Paradox) is a theory that when a national currency also serves as an international reserve currency, there could be conflicts of interest between short-term domestic and long-term international economic objectives. This dilemma was first identified by economist Robert Triffin in the 1960s, who pointed out that the country whose currency foreign nations wish to hold (the global reserve currency) must be willing to supply the world with an extra supply of its currency to fulfill world demand for this "reserve" currency (foreign exchange reserves) and thus, causes a trade deficit.

The use of a national currency (i.e., the US dollar) as global reserve currency leads to a tension between national monetary policy and global monetary policy. This is reflected in fundamental imbalances in the balance of payments, specifically the current account: some goals require an overall flow of dollars out of the United States, while others require an overall flow of dollars into the United States. Currency inflows and outflows of equal magnitudes cannot both happen at once. The Triffin Dilemma is usually used to articulate the problems with the US dollar's role as the reserve currency under the Bretton Woods system, or more generally of using any national currency as an international reserve currency.

6. Fiat money is the money that derives its value from government regulation or law. The term is derived from the Latin *fiat,* meaning "let it be done" or "it shall be [money]," as such money is established by government decree. Where fiat money is used as currency, the term fiat currency is used. The "Nixon Shock" of 1971 ended the direct convertibility of the US dollar to gold. Since then all reserve currencies have been fiat currencies, including the US dollar and the euro.
7. Unfortunately, there is a dollar crisis (underpriced) and a euro one (overpriced) in the world, due to the enormous level of the US deficits and debt: (federal debt = $16.353 trillion, social security liability = $20.5 trillion, Medicare and Medicaid contingent liabilities = $94 trillion, state and local governments = $5.1 trillion, business sector debt = $11.00 trillion, financial sector debt = $15.7 trillion, total personal debt = $16.031 trillion, financial sector bailout = $2.5 trillion, and other debts = $6.1 trillion]. Total Debt (public and private)= $183.1 trillion. The GDP (2012:Q3) in 2012 was $13.653 trillion. This puts the total US debt at 1,341.1 percent of the GDP.
8. See, *Historical Gold Prices-1833 to Present.* http://www.nma.org/pdf/gold/his_gold_prices.pdf
9. On the contrary, with a flexible exchange rate, the country depreciates the domestic currency instead of losing gold reserves, and the competitiveness is restored. Euro-zone member nations cannot depreciate their common currency (the euro) and are forced to "depreciate" their domestic economy, to reduce prices through reductions of cost of production (reduction of salaries and wages), "internal devaluation," which is based on many political and think tanks myths; but, there is no success, as the recent results proved in European indebted nations.
10. Selling short is a speculation technique in which a speculator sells an asset (currency, stock, bond, etc.) without owning it to another party for delivery at a future date. The speculator expects the price of the asset to fall by the date, when the asset must be bought in the market by the speculator for delivery. In September 2008, short selling, exacerbated by naked short selling, was seen as a contributing factor to undesirable market volatility, and was subsequently prohibited by the US Securities and Exchange Commission (SEC) for 799 financial companies for three weeks in an effort to stabilize those companies. In June 2010, due to the financial crisis, Germany permanently banned naked short

selling. In August 2011, France, Italy, Spain, Belgium, and South Korea banned all short selling in their financial stocks. But, unfortunately, this cannot happen in the United States.

11. The effect of World War I and its instability on the German economy was astounding. From January 1919 to January 1922, the German Mark fell from 8.9 DM/$ to DM 191.8 to the US dollar. By June of 1922, the DM had fallen to DM 350 per US dollar and by October of that year, it was DM 4,500 per US dollar. Between January and November of 1923, the value dropped from DM 18,000 per US dollar to DM 4.2 trillion per US dollar. Obviously, this hyperinflation devastated the German economy. See http://voices.yahoo.com/hyperinflation-post-world-war-one-germany-748079.html. During the same period, hyperinflation devastated the economies of Austria, Hungary, Poland, and Russia. After World War II, hyperinflation hit Hungary and Greece. In March 1942, the Nazis "forcibly borrowed" 10,530,120 gold sovereigns from the Central Bank of Greece, as an interest-free loan. The value of that loan today, with 3 percent interest rate amounts to a hefty $17 billion. See http://www.itulip.com/Select/hyperinflation.pdf and http://www.demokritos.org/TRIUMPH.htm.
12. The peak on the Wall Street was on September 3, 1929 (DJIA was 381.17), and its trough was on July 8, 1932 (DJIA was 41.22). This was a decline of the index by 339.95 points or –89.2 percent and with calendar days to bottom 1,038. See Kallianiotis (2012).
13. The International Trade Organization (ITO) was never accepted by the US Congress and was allowed to lapse in 1950. But, it survived an agreement to restrain imposition of trade restrictions; this was the General Agreement on Tariffs and Trade (GATT).
14. The World Bank, with its official name, the International Bank for Reconstruction and Development, was created at the Bretton Woods conference (1944), with the objective of providing a flow of long-term finance to substitute for the then-vanished private capital market. The bank raises money by issuing bonds on commercial terms and lends these funds to developing countries. See IMF History. http://www.imf.org/external/about/history.htm.
15. See, http://en.wikipedia.org/wiki/Harry_Dexter_White.
16. See, http://en.wikipedia.org/wiki/John_Maynard_Keynes.
17. See Grabbe (1986). At a price of $1,900/oz, the metric ton cost $61.1 million and the total value of the world gold stock was $10.1 trillion at the end of 2010. The price of gold fluctuates drastically. See also http://www.321gold.com/editorials/price/price053007.html and http://en.wikipedia.org/wiki/Gold_reserve.
18. Criticisms: (1) The IMF faces the obstacle of being unfamiliar with local economic conditions, cultures, and environments in the countries requiring policy reform. (2) The fund knows very little about what public spending on programs like public health and education actually means, especially in African countries, and lately, in Euro-zone countries due to the debt crises; they have no feel of the impact that their proposed national budget will have on people. (3) The economic advice the IMF gives does not take into consideration

the difference between what spending means on paper and how it was felt by humiliated citizens. (For example, Jeffrey Sach's work shows that "the Fund's usual prescription is 'budgetary belt tightening to countries that are much too poor to own belts"'). (4) The IMF's role, as a generalist institution specializing in macroeconomic issues, needs reforms to become more humane. (5) Conditionality has also been criticized because a country can pledge a collateral of "acceptable assets" in order to obtain waivers on certain conditions. However, this assumes that all countries have the capability and choice to provide acceptable collateral. (6) Another view is that conditionality undermines domestic political institutions. The recipient governments are sacrificing policy autonomy in exchange for funds, which can lead to public resentment of the local leadership for accepting and enforcing IMF conditions. (7) Political instability can result from more leadership turnover as political leaders are replaced in electoral backlashes (as it happened in Greece during the election on May 6, 2012). (8) IMF conditions are often criticized for their bias against economic growth and for reduction of the size of governments and of their public services, which increase unemployment. (9) Another criticism is that IMF programs are only designed to address poor governance, excessive government spending, excessive government intervention in markets, and too much state ownership. IMF assumes that this narrow range of issues represents the only possible problems; everything can be standardized and the differing indigenous contexts of the nations are ignored. (10) A country may also be compelled to accept conditions it would not normally accept, had it not been in a financial crisis and in need of assistance. (11) It is claimed that conditionalities retard social stability and hence inhibit the stated goals of the IMF, while structural adjustment programs lead to an increase in poverty in recipient countries (in Europe, not only poverty, but suicides have also increased drastically). (12) The IMF advocates tough "austerity programs," cutting public spending, laying off public employees, and increasing taxes, even when the economy is weak, in order to bring budgets closer to a balance, thus increasing budget deficits because firms are going bankrupt and individuals are unemployed and tax revenues are declining, which is exactly the opposite of what countries need. (13) Countries are often advised to lower their corporate tax rate, but corporations actually do not pay taxes. This deteriorates the economic conditions of the countries in recession. See also, Stiglitz (2002).

19. See *IMF Lending*. http://www.imf.org/external/np/exr/facts/howlend.htm.
20. See http://www.history.ucsb.edu/faculty/marcuse/projects/currency.htm.
21. Seigniorage can have the following two meanings: (1) Seigniorage derived from specie (metal coins), is a tax, added to the total price of a coin (metal content and production costs), that a customer of the mint had to pay to the mint, and that was sent to the sovereign of the political region. (2) Seigniorage derived from notes is more indirect, being the difference between interest earned on securities acquired in exchange for bank notes and the costs of producing and distributing those notes. Thus, seigniorage is a convenient source of revenue for some governments.

22. US dollar reserves rose by 61 percent in the period between 1970 and 1971, compared with the 22 percent increase in the whole decade of the 1960s. The European-Japanese bloc in the IMF was against this enormous creation of reserves by the United States, and this was their basic objective in reforming the existing system. See Williamson (1983, p. 349).
23. In November 1967, the US Air Force made an emergency airlift of gold from Fort Knox to London, and the floor of the weighing room at the Bank of England collapsed due to the accumulated tonnage of gold bars (bullions). Fort Knox is the US Bullion Depository, which is a fortified vault building located adjacent to Fort Knox, Kentucky, used to store a large portion of US official gold reserves, and occasionally other precious items belonging or entrusted to the federal government. The United States Bullion Depository holds 4,577 metric tons (5,046 tons) of gold bullion (147.2 million troy ounces). This is roughly 2.5 percent of all the gold ever refined throughout human history. Even so, the depository is second to the Federal Reserve Bank of New York's underground vault in Manhattan, which holds 7,000 metric tons (7,716 tons) of gold bullion (225.1 million troy oz.), some of it in trust for foreign nations, central banks, and official international organizations that were shipped into the United States before the war (1 troy ounce=31.1 grams).
24. The weights of the SDR were: 33 percent of the US dollar, 12.5 percent of the Deutschemark, 9 percent of the pound sterling, 7.5 percent of French franc, 7.5 percent of Japanese yen, 6 percent of Canadian dollar, 6 percent of Italian lira, 4.5 percent of Netherlands guilder, 3.5 percent of Belgian franc, 2.5 percent of Swedish krona, 1.5 percent of Australian dollar, 1.5 percent of Danish krone, 1.5 percent of Norwegian krone, 1.5 percent of Spanish peseta, 1 percent of Austrian schilling, and 1 percent of South African rand. The basket of currencies in the SDR was simplified on January 1, 1981, from 16 to 5: 42 percent for the US dollar, 19 percent for the Deutschemark, 13 percent for the French franc, 13 percent for the Japanese yen, and 13 percent for pound sterling. After the introduction of euro (January 1, 2002), the currencies in this basket are four, and the current weights of the SDR are: euro 37.4 percent, Japanese yen 9.4 percent, pound sterling 11.3 percent, and US dollar 41.9 percent. See http://www.imf.org/external/np/exr/facts/sdr.htm and http://fx.sauder.ubc.ca/SDR.html.
25. At this IMF meeting in Jamaica (January 1976), an agreement was reached to sell a portion of the gold that member nations had deposited with the fund as backing for IMF loans. Part of this gold would be sold to member nations at the "official price" of $35/oz, at which they first contributed gold, allowing them to reap the benefits of reselling the gold at the much higher market price. The IMF would sell the remaining part of the gold at the market price and use the proceeds to establish a trust fund for those fund members that had developing-country status.
26. See Triffin (1960).
27. See Williamson (1983, pp. 333–356).

28. According to official doctrine, gold was demonetized in 1971 by the "Group of Seven" governments of the most important trading countries of the world. Demonetization was meted out as a punishment for "bad behavior." In the words of Paul A. Volcker, gold has been tolerated as long as it was content to act as a constitutional monarch. No sooner had gold asserted itself as an absolute monarch, it was dethroned. Indeed, by a stroke of the pen the 5,000-year-old monetary reign of gold was unceremoniously terminated over the entire globe, never again to return.
29. Historical exchange rates are available on a daily basis. See http://www.oanda.com/currency/historical-rates/.
30. See http://www.wsjprimerate.us/libor/index.html. and for LIBOR Rates History, http://www.wsjprimerate.us/libor/libor_rates_history.htm
31. The Amsterdam Treaty, officially the Treaty of Amsterdam amending the Treaty of the European Union, the treaties establishing the European Communities and certain related acts, was signed on October 2, 1997, and came into force on May 1, 1999; it made substantial changes to the Maastricht Treaty, which had been signed in 1992. The Amsterdam Treaty meant a greater emphasis on citizenship and the rights of individuals, an attempt to achieve more democracy in the shape of increased powers for the European Parliament, a new title on employment, a community area of freedom, security, and justice, the beginnings of a common foreign and security policy (CFSP) and the reform of the institutions in the run-up to enlargement.
32. The Treaty of Nice was signed by European leaders on February 26, 2001, and came into force on February 1, 2003. It amended the Maastricht Treaty (or the Treaty on European Union) and the Treaty of Rome (or the Treaty Establishing the European Community, TEC). The Treaty of Nice reformed the institutional structure of the European Union to withstand eastward expansion, a task which was originally intended to have been done by the Amsterdam Treaty, but failed to be addressed at the time. The enforcement of this treaty was doubtful for a while, after its initial rejection by Irish voters in a referendum in June 2001. This referendum result was reversed in a subsequent referendum held a little over a year later.
33. The Treaty of Lisbon or the Lisbon Treaty (initially known as the Reform Treaty) is an international agreement that amends the two treaties, which form the constitutional basis of the EU. The Lisbon Treaty was signed by the EU member nations on December 13, 2007, and came into force on December 1, 2009. It amends the Maastricht Treaty (also known as the Treaty on European Union) and the Treaty establishing the European Communityalso known as the Treaty of Rome. In this process, the Treaty of Rome was renamed as the Treaty on the Functioning of the European Union (TFEU). Some changes included the move from unanimity to qualified majority voting in several policy areas in the council of ministers, a change in calculating such a majority to a new double majority, a more powerful European Parliament forming a bicameral legislature alongside the council of ministers under the ordinary legislative procedure, a consolidated legal personality for the EU and the creation

of a long-term president of the European Council and a high representative of the Union for Foreign Affairs and Security Policy. The Treaty also made the Union's bill of rights, the Charter of Fundamental Rights, legally binding. The stated aim of the treaty was "to complete the process started by the Treaty of Amsterdam (1997) and by the Treaty of Nice (2001) with a view to enhancing the efficiency and democratic legitimacy of the Union and to improving the coherence of its action." Opponents of the Treaty of Lisbon, such as former Danish member of the European Parliament (MEP) Jens-Peter Bonde, argued that it would centralize the EU, and weaken democracy by "moving power away" from national electorates. Negotiations to modify EU institutions began in 2001, resulting first in the treaty establishing a Constitution for Europe, which would have repealed the preexisting European treaties and replaced them with a "constitution." Although ratified by a majority of member states, this was abandoned after being rejected by French and Dutch voters in 2005. After a "period of reflection," member states agreed instead to amend the preexisting treaties, salvaging a number of the reforms that had been envisaged in the constitution. An amending "reform" treaty was drawn up and signed in Lisbon in 2007. It was originally intended to have been ratified by all member states by the end of 2008. This timetable failed, primarily due to the initial rejection of the treaty in 2008 by the Irish electorate, a decision that was reversed in a second referendum in 2009 after Ireland secured a number of concessions related to the treaty. After all these politics, there is no surprise why the EU has so many problems, lately, with the debt crises and the common currency, which abolished domestic public policies of the member nations.

34. See, Kallianiotis (2004, pp. 182–186).
35. See, Pollard (1995).
36. The current president of the ECB is Mario Draghi, who succeeded Jean-Claude Trichet, as president of the ECB on November 1, 2011. He was previously the governor of the Bank of Italy from January 2006 until October 2011. From 1984 to 1990 he was the Italian executive director at the World Bank. In 1991, he became director general of the Italian Treasury, and held this office until 2001. During his time at the Treasury, he chaired the committee that revised Italian corporate and financial legislation and drafted the law that governs Italian financial markets. Draghi was also vice chairman and managing director of Goldman Sachs International and a member of the firm-wide management committee (2002–2005). He is a trustee at the Institute for Advanced Study in Princeton, NJ, and also at the Brookings Institution, in Washington, D.C. In his capacity as governor of the Bank of Italy, he was a member of the governing and general councils of the ECB and a member of the board of directors of the BIS. In April 2006 he was elected chairman of the Financial Stability Forum, which became the Financial Stability Board in spring 2009.
37. The ECB's views are that (1) "inflation is ultimately a monetary phenomenon," and (2) "price stability enhances the potential for economic growth." See, Hall, Swamy, and Tavlas (2012).

38. Although the ECB is governed by European law directly and not by corporate law applying to private companies, its setup resembles that of a corporation, in the sense that the ECB has shareholders and equity (stock) capital. Its capital is €5 billion, which is held by the national central banks of the member states as its shareholders. The initial capital allocation key was determined in 1998 on the basis of the states' population and the GDP, but the key is adjustable. Shares in the ECB are not transferable and cannot be used as collateral.
39. The target rate of the ECB does not fill all the Euro-zone members. The Taylor rule suggests lower target rates for the peripheral countries that have been caught in the sovereign debt crisis. The current monetary rule is in line with the Taylor rule recommendation in the core group (mostly in Germany). See, Nechio (2011) and Chapter 9 of this book. Also, the Austrian ex-minister of Finance Hannes Androsch said that the reunification of Germany cost too much for all Europeans because the exchange rate between the West German mark (DM) and East German ostmark (DDM) was determined arbitrarily at "one to one" (1 DM/ DDM), which increased interest rates in the entire continent of Europe. If Europeans had acted against the reunification of Germany, as Germans are doing now, with the euro crisis, there would have never been their reunification. He also referred to the loans that Greece is receiving; the largest amount never reaches Greece, it is withheld and returned to German and French banks. See *Dailynews24.gr*, June 11, 2012.
40. See, *IMF*, Classification of Exchange Rate Arrangements and Monetary Policy Frameworks. http://www.imf.org/external/np/mfd/er/2004/eng/1204.htm.
41. See, Kallianiotis (2011b).
42. The "bancor" was a supranational currency that John Maynard Keynes and E. F. Schumacher conceptualized in the years 1940–1942 and that the United Kingdom proposed to introduce after World War II. This newly created supranational currency would then be used in international trade as a unit of account within a multilateral barter clearing system—the International Clearing Union—which would also have to be founded.
43. See *The Wall Street Journal*, May 21, 2012, pp. A1, A7, and A9.

Bibliography

Allen, Franklin and Douglas Gale (2009), *Understanding Financial Crises*, Clarendon Lectures in Finance, New York, NY: Oxford University Press.

Cooper, R. N. (ed.) (1969), "Hume's 1752 Essay of the Balance of Trade," in *International Finance*, London: Penguin.

Davies, Norman (1998), *Europe: A History*, New York, NY: Harper Perennial.

Eiteman, David K., Arthur I. Stonehill, and Michael H. Moffett (2010), *Multinational Business Finance*, Boston, MA: Prentice Hall, pp. 106–136.

Grabbe, J. Orlin (1986), *International Financial Markets*, New York, NY: Elsevier.

Granger, C. W. J. (1969), "Investigating Causal Relations by Econometric Models and Cross-Spectral Methods," *Econometrica*, Vol. 37, pp. 424–438.

Hall, Stephen G., P. A. V. B. Swamy, and George S. Tavlas (2012), "Milton Friedman, the Demand for Money, and the ECB's Monetary Policy Strategy," *Review*, Federal Reserve Bank of St. Louis, Vol. 94, No. 3, May/June, pp. 153–185.

Kallianiotis, I. N. (2012), "The Three Indigenous Socio-Economic Troubles of the Free-Market: Uncertainty, Unemployment, Untrustworthiness," in *Financial Crises, Impact and Response: The View from the Emerging World*, edited by Peter Koveos, Athens, Greece: Athens Institute for Education and Research.

———. (2011a), "Europe: A Swift Economic and Financial Historical Journey from the Ancient Times to the Current European Union" unpublished manuscript, *University of Scranton*, June, pages 312.

———. (2011b), "Is the Imposed Global 'Laissez-Faire' Socio-economic System Responsible for the Latest Financial Crisis?" *Journal of Business and Economics*, Vol. 2, No. 5, May, pp. 325–353.

———. (2004), *The European Economic and Monetary Union: Interdependence between the United States of America and the European Union*, Unpublished manuscript, University of Scranton, pages 393.

Keynes, John Maynard (1964), *The General Theory of Employment, Interest, and Money*, A Harvest/HBJ Book, New York: Harcourt Brace Jovanovich.

Marchant, E. C. and O. J. Todd (1997), *Xenophon: Memorabilia, Oeconomicus, Symposium, Apology*, Loeb Classical Library, Cambridge, MA: Harvard University Press.

Nechio, Fernanda (2011), "Monetary Policy When One Size Does Not Fit All," *FRBSF Economic Letter*, Federal Reserve Bank of San Francisco, 6/14/2011, pp. 1–5.

Pollard, Patricia S. (1995), "EMU: Will It Fly?" *Review*, Federal Reserve Bank of St. Louis, Vol. 77, No. 4, July/August, pp. 3–16.

Stiglitz, Joseph E. (2002), *Globalization and Its Discontents*, New York, NY: W. W. Norton & Company.

Triffin, R. (1960), *Gold and the Dollar Crises*, New Haven, CT: Yale University Press.

Williamson, John (1983), *The Open Economy and the World Economy*, New York, NY: Basic Books, Inc., Publishers.

2

The Foreign Exchange Market

The foreign exchange market is a form of international market for the trading of all national currencies. Financial centers all over the world function as anchors of trading among a wide range of different types of buyers and sellers around the clock, with the exception of weekends. This foreign exchange market determines the relative values (exchange rates) of different currencies. It also assists international trade and investment by enabling currency conversion, offering lines of credit in different currencies, and providing instruments of hedging exchange rate risk. Further, it supports direct speculation on the value of currencies and arbitrage profits between different markets, based on different exchange rates and interest rate differentials among countries.

2.1 Functions, Geographical Range, and Size of the Foreign Exchange Market

The foreign exchange market is a unique competitive and efficient market compared with the other financial markets:

(1) It is a market with a huge trading volume, representing the largest asset class in the world leading to high liquidity.
(2) It is geographically dispersed, from one side of the world to the other.
(3) It is a market operating 24 hours a day, except on weekends. Its trading starts from 20:15 GMT on Sunday until 22:00 GMT Friday night.[1]
(4) It is a market with a very large number of factors, information, and expectations that affect exchange rates (domestic, foreign, and global).
(5) It is a market with low margins of relative profit compared with other markets of fixed income.
(6) It is a market that uses leverage to enhance profit.

The foreign exchange market transfers purchasing power among participants in different countries, supplies credit and instruments for international trade and investment transactions, and provides instruments of hedging (redistributing) foreign exchange exposure (risk). The value of the exchange rate (price of one currency with respect to another) is determined in the market, but from time to time there are currency interventions by the central banks. According to the 2010 Triennial Central Bank Survey, coordinated by the BIS, the average daily turnover was $3.98 trillion in April 2010 (vs. $1.7 trillion in 1998).[2] Of this $3.98 trillion, $1.5 trillion was spot transactions and $2.5 trillion was traded in outright forwards, swaps, and other derivatives; a growth of approximately 20 percent over the $3.21 trillion daily volume as of April 2007. Some firms specializing on the foreign exchange market had put the average daily turnover as in excess of $4 trillion.

The trade starts each morning from New Zealand and Australia (Wellington and Sydney), continues to East Asia (Tokyo, Seoul, Manila), moves to Hong Kong and Bangkok, passes to the Middle East (Bahrain and other centers); then, shifts to Europe (Frankfurt, Zurich, Paris, and other centers) and reaches London; then, it proceeds to North America (New York, Chicago, and later Los Angeles and San Francisco). The foreign exchange market is the most liquid financial market in the world. Traders include large banks,[3] central banks, governments, institutional investors, currency speculators, corporations, other financial institutions, and retail investors. The average daily turnover in the global foreign exchange and related markets is continuously growing.

Trading in the United Kingdom accounted for 36.7 percent of the total, making it by far the most important center for foreign exchange trading. Trading in the United States accounted for 17.9 percent, and in Japan accounted for 6.2 percent. Turnover of exchange-traded foreign exchange futures and options have grown rapidly in recent years, reaching $166 billion in April 2010 (double the turnover recorded in April 2007). Exchange-traded currency derivatives represent 4% of OTC foreign exchange turnover. Foreign exchange futures contracts were introduced in 1972 at the Chicago Mercantile Exchange and are actively traded relative to most other futures contracts. In contrast, foreign currency options were introduced in 1982 by the Philadelphia Stock Exchange and followed by the Chicago Mercantile Exchange and other exchanges around the world.

Most developed countries permit the trading of derivative products (like futures and options on futures) on their exchanges. All these developed countries already have fully convertible capital accounts. Some governments of emerging economies do not allow foreign exchange derivative products on their exchanges because they have capital controls. The use of derivatives is growing in many emerging economies. Countries such as Korea, South Africa, and India have established currency futures exchanges, despite having some capital controls.

Foreign exchange trading increased by 20 percent between April 2007 and April 2010 and has more than doubled since 2004. The increase in turnover is due to a number of factors: the growing importance of foreign exchange as an asset class, the increased trading activity of high-frequency traders, and the emergence of retail investors, as an important market segment. The growth of electronic execution and the diverse selection of execution venues have lowered transaction costs, increased market liquidity, and attracted greater participation from many customer types. In particular, electronic trading via online portals has made it easier for retail traders to trade in the foreign exchange market. By 2010, retail trading accounted for up to 10 percent of the spot turnover, or $150 billion per day.[4]

Foreign exchange is an over-the-counter (OTC) market, where brokers/dealers negotiate directly with one another, so there is no central exchange or clearing house. As mentioned previously, the biggest geographic trading center is the United Kingdom, primarily London, which according to TheCityUK[5] estimates has increased its share of global turnover in traditional transactions from 34.6 percent in April 2007 to 36.7 percent in April 2010. Due to London's dominance in the market, a particular currency's quoted price is usually the London market price. For instance, when the IMF calculates the value of its SDRs every day, they use the London market prices at noon that day.

2.2 Market Participants

Unlike a stock market, the foreign exchange market is divided into levels of access. At the top is the interbank market, which is made up of the largest commercial banks and securities dealers. Within the interbank market, spreads, which are the difference between the bid (buying foreign currency) and ask or offer (selling) prices, are razor sharp and not known to players outside the inner circle. The difference between the bid and ask prices widens (e.g., from 0–1 pip[6] to 1–2 pips for a currency such as the euro [EUR]), as you go down the levels of access. This is due to volume. If a trader can guarantee large numbers of transactions for large amounts, he/she can demand a smaller difference between the bid and ask price, which is referred to as a "better spread." The levels of access that make up the foreign exchange market are determined by the size of the "line" (the amount of money with which they are trading). The top-tier interbank market accounts for 53 percent of all transactions. From there, you have smaller banks, followed by large multinational corporations (which need to hedge risk and pay employees in different countries), large hedge funds, and even some of the retail market makers. Central banks also participate in the foreign exchange market to align currencies to their economic needs.

2.2.1 Commercial Companies

An important part of this market comes from the financial activities of companies seeking foreign exchange to pay for goods or services. Commercial companies often trade fairly small amounts compared to those of banks or speculators, and their trades often have little short-term impact on market rates. Nevertheless, trade flows are an important factor in the long-term direction of a currency's exchange rate. Some multinational companies can have an unpredictable impact when very large positions are covered due to exposures that are not widely known by other market participants. Such transactions do not occur in the interbank market (due to their relatively small sizes); instead, they take place in the retail market.

2.2.2 Central Banks and Treasuries

National central banks (or treasuries) play an important role in the foreign exchange markets. They try to control the money supply, interest rates, inflation, growth, employment, et cetera, and often have official or unofficial target rates for their currencies. They settle the remaining payments in balance by using foreign currencies or assets. They can use their often substantial foreign exchange reserves to stabilize the market. Nevertheless, the effectiveness of central bank "stabilizing speculation" is doubtful, because central banks do not go bankrupt if they make large losses, like other traders would, and there is no convincing evidence that they do make a profit trading.

2.2.3 Foreign Exchange Fixing

Foreign exchange fixing is the daily monetary exchange rate fixed by the national bank of each country. The idea is that central banks use the fixing time and exchange rate to evaluate behavior of their currency. Fixing exchange rates reflect the real value of equilibrium in the market. Banks, dealers, and traders use fixing rates as a trend indicator. The mere expectation or rumor of a central bank foreign exchange intervention might be enough to stabilize a currency, but aggressive intervention might be used several times each year in countries with a "dirty" float currency regime. It should be noted that central banks do not always achieve their objectives. The combined resources of the market can easily overwhelm any central bank.

2.2.4 Hedge Funds, Speculators, Arbitragers, and Others

About 70–90 percent of the foreign exchange transactions are speculative. Speculators and arbitragers seek to profit from trading in foreign currencies, operating in their own interest, without serving other clients, as brokers do. Dealers buy for their own account. In other words, the person or institution that bought or sold the currency has no plan to actually take delivery of the currency in the end; rather, they were solely speculating on the movement of that particular currency. Hedge funds have gained a reputation for aggressive currency speculation since 1996. They control billions of dollars of equity and may borrow billions more, and thus may overwhelm intervention by central banks to support almost any currency, if the economic fundamentals are in the hedge funds' favor. Dealers in foreign currencies seek profit from the spread between bid and ask prices. Speculators seek their profit from exchange rate changes, and arbitragers from simultaneous exchange rate differences among different markets. Large banks act as exchange rate dealers, brokers, speculators, and arbitragers as well.

2.2.5 Investment Management Firms

Investment management firms (who typically manage large accounts on behalf of customers such as pension funds and endowments) use the foreign exchange market to facilitate transactions in foreign securities. For example, an investment manager bearing an international equity portfolio needs to purchase and sell several pairs of foreign currencies to pay for foreign securities purchases. Some investment management firms also have more speculative specialist currency overlay[7] operations, which manage clients' currency exposures with the aim of generating profits as well as limiting risk. While the number of such specialist firms is quite small, many of them have a large value of assets under management, and hence can generate large trades.

2.2.6 Retail Foreign Exchange Traders

Individual retail speculative traders constitute a growing segment of this market with the advent of retail foreign exchange platforms, both in size and importance. Currently, they participate indirectly through brokers or banks. Retail brokers, while largely controlled and regulated in the United States by the Commodity Futures Trading Commission (CFTC) and National Futures Association (NFA), have in the past been subjected to periodic foreign exchange fraud. To deal with the issue, in 2010, the NFA required its members that deal in the Forex markets to register as such (i.e., Forex CTA instead of a CTA). Those NFA members that would traditionally be subject to minimum net capital requirements, Futures Commission Merchants (FCMs) and Introducing Brokers (IBs), are subject to greater minimum net capital requirements if they deal in Forex. A number of foreign exchange brokers operate from the United Kingdom under Financial Services Authority (FSA) regulations, where foreign exchange trading using margin is part of the wider OTC derivatives trading industry that includes Contract For Differences (CFD)[8] and Financial Spread Betting (FSB).[9] There are two main types of retail FX brokers offering the opportunity for speculative currency trading: *brokers* and *dealers* or *market makers*. *Brokers* serve as agents of the customer in the broader FX market, by seeking the best price in the market for a retail order and dealing on behalf of the retail customer. They charge a commission or markup in addition to the price obtained in the market. *Dealers* or *market makers*, by contrast, typically act as principals in the transaction versus the retail customer, and quote a price they are willing to deal at.

2.2.7 Non-Bank Foreign Exchange Companies

Non-bank foreign exchange companies offer currency exchange and international payments to private individuals and companies. These are also known as foreign exchange brokers, but are distinct in that they do not offer speculative trading, but rather exchange currency with payments (i.e., there is usually a physical delivery of currency to a bank account). It is estimated that in the United Kingdom, 14 percent of currency transfers/payments are made via foreign exchange companies. These companies' selling point is usually that they will offer better exchange rates or cheaper payments than the customer's bank. These companies differ from money transfer/remittance companies in that they generally offer higher-value services.

2.2.8 Money Transfer/Remittance Companies and Bureaux de Change

High-volume, low-value transfers, generally by economic migrants back to their home country, are done by money transfer/remittance companies.In

2007, the Aite Group estimated that there were $369 billion of remittances (an increase of 8 percent from the previous year). The four largest markets (India, China, Mexico, and the Philippines) receive $95 billion. The largest and best-known provider is the Western Union with 345,000 agents globally, followed by the UAE Exchange. Bureaux de change or currency transfer companies provide low-value foreign exchange services for travelers. These are typically located at airports and stations or at tourist locations and allow physical notes to be exchanged from one currency to another. They access the foreign exchange markets via banks or non-bank foreign exchange companies.

2.3 Trading Characteristics

Lately, technological advancements in telecommunications have changed the interbank market, but there are still transactions executed by phone and face to face (use of trading floors). There is no unified or centrally cleared market for the majority of trades, and there is very little cross-border regulation. In September 2002, the Continuous Linked Settlement (CLS) system was introduced to eliminate losses in settlements and help counteract fraud in the foreign exchange markets.[10] Due to the over-the-counter (OTC) nature of currency markets, there are rather a number of interconnected marketplaces, where different currency instruments are traded. This implies that there is not a *single* exchange rate, but rather a number of different rates (prices), depending on which bank or market maker is trading, and where it is located. In practice, the rates are often very close, otherwise they could be exploited by arbitrageurs instantaneously. Due to London's dominance in the market, a particular currency's quoted price is usually the London market price. Major trading exchanges include the Electronic Broking Services (EBS) and Reuters, while major banks also offer trading systems. A joint venture of the Chicago Mercantile Exchange and Reuters, called FXMarketSpace (FXMS) opened in 2007 and aspired, but failed, to the role of a central market clearing mechanism.

Further, the Society for Worldwide Interbank Financial Telecommunication (SWIFT) system provides the network that enables financial institutions worldwide to send and receive information about financial transactions in a secure, standardized, and reliable environment. SWIFT is a cooperative society under Belgian law, and it is owned by its member financial institutions. SWIFT has offices around the world, but its headquarters are located in La Hulpe, Belgium, near Brussels. SWIFT also markets software and services to financial institutions, much of it for use on the SWIFTNet Network, and ISO 9362 Bank Identifier Codes (BICs) are popularly known as "SWIFT codes." The majority of the international interbank messages use the SWIFT network. As of September 2010, SWIFT linked more than 9,000 financial institutions in 209 countries and territories, exchanging an average of over 15 million messages per day (compared to an average of 2.4 million daily messages in 1995). SWIFT transports financial messages via a highly secure path, but does not hold accounts for its members and does not perform any form of clearing or settlement. SWIFT does not facilitate fund transfer, rather, it sends payment orders, which must be settled via correspondent accounts that the institutions have with each other. Each financial institution, to exchange banking transactions, must have a banking relationship by either being a bank or affiliating itself with one (or more) so as to enjoy these particular business features.

The main trading center is New York, but London, Tokyo, Hong Kong, and Singapore are all important centers as well. Banks throughout the world participate. Currency trading happens continuously throughout the day; as the Asian trading session ends, the European session begins, followed by the North American session, and then back to the Asian session, excluding weekends. The most traded currencies by value (in April 2010) were the US dollar, which was involved in 84.9 percent of the transactions, followed by the euro (39.1 percent), the yen (19.0 percent), and pound sterling (12.9 percent). Volume percentages for all individual currencies should add up to 200 percent, as each transaction involves two currencies.[11]

Fluctuations in exchange rates are usually caused by actual monetary flows (money supply) as well as by expectations of changes in monetary flows caused by changes in gross domestic product (GDP) growth, inflation (purchasing power parity theory), interest rates (interest rate parity, domestic Fisher effect, and international Fisher effect), budget and trade deficits or surpluses, large cross-border mergers and acquisitions (M&A), and other macroeconomic conditions (fundamentals). Major news is released publicly, often on scheduled dates, so many people have access to the same news at the same time. However, the large banks have an important advantage; they can see their customers' order flow. (See, Chapters 4, 5, and 6).

Currencies are traded against one another. Each currency pair, thus, constitutes an individual trading product and is traditionally denoted as *XXXYYY* or *XXX/YYY*, where *XXX* and *YYY* are the ISO 4217 international three-letter code of the currencies involved.[12] The first currency (*XXX*) is the base currency that is quoted relative to the second currency (*YYY*), called the countercurrency (or quote currency). For instance, the quotation *EURUSD (EUR/USD)* 1.2585 is the price of the euro expressed in US dollars, meaning 1 euro = 1.2585 dollars (1.2585 $/€) "Direct or in American terms." The market convention is to quote most exchange rates against the *USD* with the US dollar as the base currency (e.g., *USDJPY, USDCAD, USDCHF*). For example, 79.5330 ¥/$ "Indirect or in Japanese terms." The exceptions are the British pound (*GBP*), Australian dollar (*AUD*), the New Zealand dollar (*NZD*), and the euro (*EUR*), where *USD* is the countercurrency (e.g., *GBPUSD, AUDUSD, NZDUSD, EURUSD*) or quoted in American terms.

Trading in the euro has grown considerably since the currency's creation in January 1999,[13] and how long the foreign exchange market will remain dollar-centered is open to debate, but the current European debt crisis has negatively affected the demand for euros. Until recently, trading the euro versus a non-European currency *ZZZ* would have usually involved two trades: *EURUSD* and *USDZZZ*. The exception to this is *EURJPY*, which is an established traded currency pair in the interbank spot market. As the dollar's value has eroded during 2008, interest in using the euro as reference currency for prices in commodities (such as oil), as well as a larger component of foreign reserves by banks, has increased dramatically. Transactions in the currencies of commodity-producing countries, such as *AUD, NZD, CAD*, have also increased.

2.4 Transactions in the Foreign Exchange Market

The transactions in the foreign exchange market are spot, forward, and swap. Also included are foreign currency futures and option (call and put) contracts.

2.4.1 Spot Transactions

A spot transaction is a two-day delivery transaction (except in the case of trades between the US dollar, Canadian dollar, Turkish lira, euro, and Russian ruble, which settle the next business day). Thus, the standard settlement time frame for foreign exchange spot transactions is $t+2$ days, which means, two business days from the trade date. The exception is when they settle at $t+1$. This trade represents a "direct exchange" between two currencies; it has the shortest time frame, it involves cash rather than a contract, and interest is not included in the agreed-upon transaction. The date of settlement is referred to as the *value date.*

A foreign exchange spot transaction, also known as FX spot, is an agreement between two parties to buy one currency against selling another currency at an agreed price for settlement on the spot date. The exchange rate at which the transaction is done is called the spot exchange rate (S_t). As of 2010, the average daily turnover of global FX spot transactions reached nearly \$1.5 trillion, counting 37.4 percent of all foreign exchange transactions. A spot transaction in the interbank market can be as follows: An American bank signed a contract on Monday for a transfer of €1,000,000 to a French bank in Paris. The spot rate was 1.2563 \$/€. On Wednesday the US bank would transfer €1,000,000 to Paris and the French bank would transfer \$1,256,300 to the US bank in New York at the same time. On the value date, most dollar transactions are settled through the computerized Clearing House Interbank Payments System (CHIPS) in New York, which provides for the calculation of net balances owed by any financial institution to another and for payment by 6:00 p.m. that same day in Federal Reserve Bank of New York funds.

Common methods of executing a spot foreign exchange transaction include the following: (1) *Direct.* Executed between two parties directly and not intermediated by a third party. For example, a transaction executed via direct telephone communication or direct electronic dealing systems such as Reuters Conversational Dealing. (2) *Electronic broking systems.* Executed via automated order matching system for foreign exchange dealers. Examples of such systems are Electronic Broking Services (EBS) (a wholesale electronic trading platform used to trade foreign exchange with market-making banks) and Reuters Matching 2000/2 (D2000–2 or Reuters Dealing 2000–2 was a software system designed by Reuters for foreign exchange trading; this automated electronic trading system allowed a dealer to enter buy and/or sell prices directly into the system, thereby avoiding the need for a human broker. The system recorded the touch price, which is the highest bid and lowest ask price). (3) *Electronic trading systems.* Executed via a single-bank proprietary platform or a multibank dealing system. These systems are generally geared toward customers. Examples of multi-bank systems include FXall, Currenex, FXConnect, Globalink, and eSpeed. (4) *Voice broker.* Executed via telephone communication with a foreign exchange voice broker.

2.4.2 *Forward Transactions*

One way to deal with the foreign exchange risk is to engage in forward transactions. In this transaction (outright forward or forward), money does not actually change hands until some agreed-upon future date. A buyer and seller agree on an exchange rate, the forward exchange rate (F_t) for any date in the future, and the transaction occurs on that date, regardless of what the market rates are then. The duration of the trade can be one day, a few days, months, or years. Usually the date is decided by both parties. Forward exchange rates are normally quoted for value dates of one, two, three, six, and twelve months. Then, the forward contract is negotiated and agreed upon by both parties. Payment is on the second business day after the even-month anniversary of the trade. Thus, a three-month forward transaction entered into on May 24 will be for a value date of August 26 or the next business day, if August 26 falls on a weekend or holiday.

A forward contract or simply a forward is a nonstandardized (custom-made) contract between two parties to buy or sell a currency at a specified future time at a price (forward exchange rate) agreed upon today. The party agreeing to buy the underlying currency in the future assumes a long position, and the party agreeing to sell the currency in the future assumes a short position. The price agreed upon is called the delivery price, which is equal to the forward exchange rate at the time the contract is entered into. Forwards, like other derivative securities, can be used to hedge risk (typically, currency or exchange rate risk), as a means of speculation, or to allow a party to take advantage of the quality of the underlying instrument, which is time sensitive. A contract to deliver (selling forward) pounds for dollars (buying forward) in three months, is one buying dollars forward for pounds and selling pounds forward for dollars. A typical forward transaction is when a US bank sells three-month forward £10,000,000 to a British bank for US dollars at the forward exchange rate quoted today as, $F_3 = 1.5826\$/£$, and it will receive \$15,826,000 three months later. Closely related to the forward contract is a futures contract; they differ in certain respects. Forward contracts are very similar to futures contracts, except they are not exchange traded, or defined on standardized assets. Forwards also typically have no interim partial settlements or "true-ups" in margin requirements, like futures. However, being traded OTC, forward contracts specification can be customized and may include mark-to-market and daily margining. Hence, a forward contract arrangement might call for the loss party to pledge collateral or additional collateral to better secure the party at gain.

2.4.3 Swap Transactions

The most common type of forward transaction is the swap. In a swap, two parties exchange currencies for a certain length of time and agree to reverse the transaction at a later date. These are not standardized contracts and are not traded through an exchange. A deposit is often required in order to hold the position open until the transaction is completed. A foreign exchange swap, forex swap, or FX swap is a simultaneous purchase and sale of identical amounts of one currency for another with two different value dates (normally *spot against forward*). Thus, a foreign exchange swap consists of two legs: a spot foreign exchange transaction and a forward foreign exchange transaction. The dealer buys a currency in the spot market and simultaneously sells the same amount back to the same bank in the forward market. These two legs are executed simultaneously for the same quantity, and therefore offset each other and the dealer incurs no unexpected foreign exchange risk.

There are also some more sophisticated swap transactions, such as the *forward-forward swap*, where both transactions are for (different) forward dates. A dealer sells £10,000,000 forward for dollars for delivery in three months at $F_3 = 1.5826$\$/£ and simultaneously buys £10,000,000 forward for delivery in six months at $F_6 = 1.5817$\$/£. The difference between the buying price and the selling price is equivalent to the interest rate differential $(i_t - i_t^*)$ between the two currencies. A swap can be viewed as a technique for borrowing another currency on a fully collateralized basis. By far the most common use of foreign exchange swaps is for institutions to fund their foreign exchange balances.

Once a foreign exchange transaction settles, the holder is left with a positive (or *long*) position in one currency, and a negative (or *short*) position in another. In order to collect or pay any overnight interest due on these foreign balances, at the end of each day institutions will close out any foreign balances and reinstitute them for the following day. To do this they typically use *tom-next* swaps, buying (or selling) a foreign amount settling tomorrow, and then doing the opposite, selling (or buying) it back settling the day after. The interest collected or paid every night is referred to as the "cost of carry." As currency traders know roughly how much holding a currency position will make or cost on a daily basis, specific trades are put or based on this; these are referred to as "carry trades."[14]

Also, another derivative created in the early 1990s is the *non-deliverable forward (NDF)* that is an outright forward or futures contract, in which counterparties settle the difference between the contracted NDF price or rate and the prevailing spot price or rate on an agreed notional amount (the nominal or face amount on a financial instrument that is used to calculate payments made on that instrument). It is used in various markets such as foreign exchange and commodities. NDFs are prevalent in some countries where forward FX trading has been banned by the government (usually as a means to prevent exchange rate volatility).[15]

The NDF market is an OTC market. NDF markets developed for emerging markets with capital controls, where the currencies could not be delivered offshore. Most NDFs are cash-settled in US dollars. The more active banks quote NDFs from between one month to one year, although some would quote up to two years upon request. The most commonly traded NDF tenors are IMM dates (the four quarterly dates of each year which most futures contracts and option contracts use as their scheduled maturity date or termination date; the dates are the third Wednesday of March, June, September, and December [i.e., between the 15 and 21, whichever day is a Wednesday]), but banks also offer odd-dated NDFs. NDFs are typically quoted with the US dollar as the reference currency, and the settlement amount is also in US dollars.[16]

Originally NDFs were envisioned to be used for currency hedging, but more than 70 percent of them are used in trading for speculative purposes. Pricing of NDFs reflects basic interest differentials, as with regular forward contracts, plus some additional premium charged by the bank for dollar settlement. NDFs are traded and settled outside the country of the subject currency, and therefore are beyond the control of the country's government. In the past, these contracts have created many difficult situations because the NDF market serves as a gray market in the trading of that currency. NDFs have proven to be an imperfect replacement for traditional forward contracts. Today, NDF contracts are very active in the Chinese renminbi (yuan). It is estimated that between 60 and 80 percent of NDF trading is speculative. The main difference between the outright forward deals and the NDFs is that the settlement is made in dollars since the dealer or counterparty cannot settle in the alternative currency of the deal.

2.4.4 Currency Futures

Currency futures are standardized forward contracts and are usually traded on an exchange created for this purpose. The average contract length is roughly three months. Futures contracts are usually inclusive of any interest amounts. (They will be discussed in Chapter 5.)

2.4.5 Foreign Currency Options

A foreign currency option (commonly shortened to just FX option) is a derivative, where the owner has the right, but not the obligation to exchange money (to buy, call option; or to sell, put option) denominated in one currency into another currency at a prev iouslyagreed-upon exchange rate (strike price) on a specified date by paying an option price (premium). The currency options market is the deepest, largest, and most liquid market for options of any kind in the world.

2.5 Speculation

Controversy about currency speculators and their effect on currency devaluations and national economies recurs regularly. Nevertheless, economists including Milton Friedman have argued that speculators ultimately are a stabilizing influence on the market and perform the important function of providing a market for hedgers and transferring risk from those people who do not wish to bear it, to those who do like to gamble (risk takers). Other economists, such as Joseph Stiglitz, consider this argument to be based more on politics and on an extreme free market philosophy than on true economics. Actually, these hedging techniques are "zero sum games" that entail redistribution of risk between the two parties. A zero-sum game is a mathematical representation of a situation, in which a participant's gain (or loss) of utility is exactly balanced by the losses (or gains) of the utility of the other participant. If the total gains of the participants are added up, and the total losses are subtracted, they will sum to zero. Thus, they are not Pareto optimal[17] "innovations."

Currency speculation is considered a highly suspect activity in many countries. While investment in traditional financial instruments, like bonds or stocks, often is considered to contribute positively to economic growth by providing capital (unfortunately, with high risk); currency speculation does not provide anything to society. According to this view, it is simply a form of gambling that often interferes with economic policy. For example, in 1992, currency speculation forced the Central Bank of Sweden to raise interest rates for a few days to 500 percent per annum, and later to devalue the krona.[18] Risk aversion is a kind of trading behavior exhibited by the foreign exchange market, when a potentially adverse event happens, which may affect market conditions. This behavior is caused, when risk averse traders liquidate their positions in risky assets and shift the funds to less risky assets, due to uncertainty.

In the context of the foreign exchange market, traders liquidate their positions in various currencies to take up positions in safe-haven currencies, such as the US dollar. Sometimes, the choice of a safe-haven currency is more of a choice based on prevailing sentiments rather than one of economic fundamentals. An example would be the financial crisis of 2007–2012. The value of equities across the world fell while the US dollar strengthened. This happened despite the strong focus of the crisis in the United States, but also because of the enormous debt crisis in the Eurozone. Another speculative technique is the *currency carry trade*, which refers to the act of borrowing one currency that has a low interest rate in order to purchase another with a higher interest rate. A large difference in rates can be highly profitable for the trader, especially if high leverage is used. However, with all levered investments this is a double-edged sword, and large exchange rate fluctuations can suddenly swing trades into huge losses. The global problem, today, is the enormous leverage (debt), public, private, business, and individual. This wrong economic theory, which is supported by the tax system and the financial institutions, can be disastrous for the entire international financial system. There is hope on some regulations for this completely deregulated financial market, which will improve social welfare.

2.6 Foreign Exchange Rate Quotations

The foreign exchange rate is the relative price of one currency with respect to another. A foreign exchange quotation (quote) is a statement of willingness to buy or sell one currency (which is in the denominator) by offering a number of units of the currency, which is in the numerator. Understanding the quotation and pricing structure of currencies is essential for anyone wanting to trade currencies in the foreign exchange market. If you were looking at the USD/CAD ($/C$) currency pair, the Canadian dollar would be the quote currency, and the US dollar would be the base currency. In the retail market, quotes are given as the home currency price of a foreign currency (i.e., 0.9782 $/C$ and 1.2503 $/€). The professional interbank market has standardized its quotation system.

2.6.1 Direct and Indirect Quotes

A direct quote (in American terms) is the home currency price of a unit of foreign currency (dollars/unit of euro).

$S_1 = 1.2503$ $/€, which says that we need 1.2503 dollars per 1 unit of euro

An indirect quote (in European terms) is the foreign currency price of a unit of home currency (euros/unit of dollar).

$S_2 = 0.7998$ €/$, which says that we need 0.7998 euros per 1 unit of dollar

A quotation that is direct for us (United States) is indirect for the Eurozone and vice versa. The reciprocal of a direct quote is the indirect one ($S_2 = \frac{1}{S_1} = \frac{1}{1.2503} = 0.7998$).

Interbank quotations are stated in European terms (indirect for the United States): 0.7998 €/$. The euro (€), the British pound sterling (£), Australian dollar (A$), and New Zealand dollar (NZ$) are quoted in American terms. American terms are used in quoting exchange rates for most futures and options, too. Foreign exchange traders use nicknames for the major currencies. *Cable* is the exchange rate ($/£), *loonie* is the nickname for Canadian dollar (C$), *kiwi* is used for the New Zealand dollar, *Aussie* is the Australian dollar, *Swissie* is the Swiss franc, and *Sing dollar* means the Singapore dollar.

2.6.2 *Bid and Ask Outright Quotations*

The interbank quotations are given as a bid (the bank is willing to buy the currency in the denominator) and as an ask (or offer) quotation (the bank is willing to sell the currency in the denominator). Banks bid (buy) at a lower price and ask (sell) at a higher price; this spread is their profit. The display below shows the full (spot and forward) *Outright Quotation* between US dollars ($) and British pound sterling (£) in direct or American terms and between Swiss francs (*SF*) and US dollars ($) in indirect or European terms.

Outright Quotations

		Bid($/£)	Ask (Offer)	Bid(SF/$)	Ask (Offer)
Spot	(S)	1.5640	1.5644	0.9601	0.9608
1 month forward	(F_1)	1.5635	1.5640	0.9607	0.9616
3 month forward	(F_3)	1.5630	1.5636	0.9612	0.9621
6 month forward	(F_6)	1.5621	1.5629	0.9633	0.9652

Assume a bank makes the quotations shown in the above display for the British pound (£) and the US dollar ($). The first example of outright quotations ($/£) shows the spot quotations on the first line, which indicates that the bank's foreign exchange trader will buy pounds (£) (i.e., sell dollars [$]) at the bid price of $1.5640/£. The trader will sell pounds (£) (i.e., buy dollars [$]) at the ask (offer) price of $1.5644/£. The forward quotations appear on the second, third, and four lines. We see that the forward rates are falling compared to the spot rate. This is an indication that the market expects the dollar to appreciate because we need fewer dollars to buy the same British pound (the pound is expected to depreciate). In this case, we say that the US dollar is at a forward premium ($fp_{\$}$) and the British pound at a forward discount ($fd£$). There is a *rule of thumb* that says, the currency of the country with higher interest rates will be at a discount from the currency with lower interest rates. (See Appendix [A2.1] for the correlation and causality between these variables):

$$i_t < i_t^* \Rightarrow fp\$ \quad \text{and} \quad fd£$$

or

$$fp\$ \quad \text{and} \quad fd£ \Rightarrow i_t < i_t^*$$

where, i_t = the US (domestic) short-term interest rate and i_t^* = the British (foreign) short-term interest rate.

The second example of outright quotations (SF/$) shows the spot quotations, which indicates that the bank's foreign exchange trader will buy dollars ($) (i.e., sell Swiss francs [SF]) at the bid price of SF0.9601/$. The trader will sell dollars ($) (i.e., buy Swiss francs [SF]) at the ask (offer) price of SF0.9608/$. The forward rates are increasing compared to the spot rate, an indication that the market expects the Swiss franc to depreciate because we need more Swiss francs to buy the same dollar (the dollar is expected to appreciate). Then, the Swiss franc is at a forward discount (fd_{SF}) and the US dollar at a forward premium ($fp\$$), and consequently, $i_t < i_t^*$. An exchange rate that is at a premium in one country, becomes at a discount, when viewed from the other country.

2.6.3 Bid and Ask Points Quotations (Swap Rates)

A bank trader gives the following quotations by phone for the British pound ($/£) exchange rate, which was quoted outright above:

1.5640/4 5/4 10/8 19/15

The first number (1.5640) is the spot bid price, the second (4) represents the digit of the ask that is different from the bid. Thus, the ask price is 1.5644. The forward rates are quoted in terms of points (swap rates). They have been determined by subtracting from the outright quotation the forward rates from the spot rate ($15635 - 15640 = -5$). When the exchange rate is quoted in terms of points, we can determine the outright quotes. The spot bid is given (1.5640), the spot ask is the same as the bid, with the last digit becoming 4 from 0, so we have (1.5644). The points are $5 > 4$, $10 > 8$, and $19 > 15$. If the bid points exceeds the ask points, we subtract (–) the points from the outright spots to determine the outright forward rates.

The second outright quotations of the (SF/$) can be quoted in terms of points as well:

0.9601/8 6/8 11/13 32/44

Then, the outright quotes of the Swiss franc with respect to the US dollar can be determined by taking the given spot bid (0.9601) and changing its last digit to determine the spot ask (0.9608). The outright forward rates are going to be constructed by looking at the swap rates: $6 < 8$, $11 < 13$, and $32 < 44$. The rule here is, if the bid points are less than the ask points, we add (+) the points to the outright spot rates ($9601 + 6 = 9607$ or 0.9607).

In addition, let us take the case where a trader gives his quotations for the Australian dollar (A$) in terms of points and we want to determine the outright quotes for this exchange rate ($/A$):

0.9730/5 25/27 74/71 130/135

The first rate is the spot bid (0.9730 $/A$), the second is the last digit of the spot ask that has changed (0.9735 $/A$). Now, the forward rates in terms of points (swap rates) are given as follows. F_1: 25 <27, then we add (+) these point to the spot rates. F_3: 74 >71, then we subtract (–) these points from the spot rates. Finally, F_6: 130 <135, we add (+) the points to the spot rates.

The Outright Quotations are:

		Bid ($/A$)	Ask (Offer)
Spot	(S)	0.9730	0.9735
1 month forward	(F_1)	0.9755	0.9762
3 month forward	(F_3)	0.9656	0.9664
6 month forward	(F_6)	0.9860	0.9870

With these outright quotes, it is easy to see what prices the bank is willing to use and what are the market expectations regarding these two currencies.

2.6.4 *Forward Quotations in Percentage Terms*

Forward quotations can be expressed as a percent-per-annum deviation from the spot rate. This percent-per-annum forward premium (*fp*) or forward discount (*fd*) facilitates comparing premiums and discounts in the forward market with interest rate differentials between the two countries (see, Chapter 6, Interest Rate Parity).

(1) Direct Quotations:

When quotations are on a direct basis (i.e., $/£), an approximate formula for the percent-per-annum (% p.a.) premium or discount is as follows:

$$fd \quad or \quad fp = \frac{F - S}{S}\frac{12}{n}100 \tag{2.1}$$

where, fd = forward discount, fp = forward premium, F = the forward exchange rate, S = the spot exchange rate, and n = the number of months of the forward contract.

Substituting from the previous example the \$/£ (offer) spot and the three-month forward rate to the above formula, we have:

$$fd_{GBP} \quad or \quad fp_{\$} = \frac{F_3 - S}{S}\frac{12}{3}100 = \frac{1.5636 - 1.5644}{1.5644}\frac{12}{3}100$$
$$= -0.205\%\ p.a.$$

The sign is negative, indicating that the forward dollar is selling at a 0.205 percent per annum premium because its exchange rate is declining (the dollar is appreciated). The British pound is at a 0.205 percent per annum discount (the pound sterling is depreciated).

(2) Indirect Quotations:
Now, when quotations are on an indirect basis (i.e., SF/\$), an approximate formula for the percent-per-annum (% p.a.) premium or discount is as follows:

$$fd \quad or \quad fp = \frac{S - F}{F}\frac{12}{n}100 \tag{2.2}$$

Substituting from the above example, the SF/\$ ask (offer) spot and the six-month forward rate to the above formula, we have:

$$fd_{SF} \quad or \quad fp_{\$} = \frac{S - F_6}{F_6}\frac{12}{6}100 = \frac{0.9608 - 0.9652}{0.9652}\frac{12}{6}100$$
$$= -0.912\%\ p.a.$$

The sign is negative, indicating that the forward Swiss franc is selling at a 0.912 percent per annum discount because its exchange rate is increasing (the Swiss franc is depreciated). The dollar is at a 0.912 percent per annum premium (the dollar is appreciated). The best way to tell if a currency is at a forward discount or premium is to look at the outright quotations. When the currency that is in the numerator is expected to increase in price (you need more units from this currency to buy the currency in the denominator), it means that the currency is losing value (is depreciated); then, this currency is at a forward discount, as is the Swiss franc with respect to the US dollar in the above example.

2.6.5 *Sources of Foreign Exchange Market Information*

Market participants are interested in having access to foreign exchange market information, and there are many sources available today. For currency investing and currency conversion, we can find information in

Yahoo.Finance (http://finance.yahoo.com/currency). Also, *Moneyline Telerate, Reuters* (http://www.reuters.com/), *Bloomberg* (http://www.bloomberg.com/), *X-Rates* (http://www.x-rates.com/), *Rates FX* (http://www.ratesfx.com/rates/), and many others provide information for the public. Foreign exchange rates are quoted in all major newspapers around the world. For the United States quotations are provided by *The Wall Street Journal* (http://online.wsj.com/public/page/news-currency-currencies-trading.html). In Europe, together with many local financial papers, a very popular economic newspaper is *The Financial Times* (http://www.ft.com/intl/markets/currencies).

2.6.6 *Cross Rates*

The foreign currencies in any country are quoted with respect to the domestic currency (direct or indirect quotes). In the United States, all the sources are quoted as foreign currencies with respect to the US dollar. But, on occasion a person dealing in foreign exchange will want to obtain an exchange rate between two currencies (e_3) from their common relationship (e_1 and e_2) with a third currency. For example, the exchange rate between US dollar and Canadian dollar is given as $e_1 = 0.9605$\$/C\$ and the exchange rate between US dollar and euro is $e_2 = 1.2435$\$/€. We need the exchange rate between Canadian dollar and euro, the cross rate (e_3).

Thus, the cross rate is: $e_3 = \frac{e_1}{e_2} = \frac{0.9605}{1.2435}$ \$/CS:\$/€=0.7724 €/C\$.

Suppose *The Wall Street Journal* quotes the following two spot rates: $S_1 = 1.0351$\$/SF and $S_2 = 177.99$¥/\$. We are interested in finding the cross rate between the Japanese yen and the Swiss franc (S_3). This new cross rate will be:

$$S_3 = S_1 S_2(\$/\text{SF} \times \yen/\$) = (1.0351\$/\text{SF} \times 77.99\yen/\$) = 80.727\yen/\text{SF}.$$

(By using the units of the two currencies in our calculations of the cross rates, we do not make mistakes because sometimes we divide the rates and in other cases we multiply the rates to find the cross rate).

2.7 Foreign Exchange Rate Arbitrage

An arbitrage is the practice of taking advantage of a price difference between two or more markets: striking a combination of matching deals that capitalize upon the imbalance, the profit being the difference between the market prices (exchange rates). When used by academics, an arbitrage is a transaction that involves no negative cash flow at any probabilistic or temporal state and a positive cash flow in at least one state; in simple terms, it is the possibility of a risk-free profit at zero cost. In principle, an arbitrage is risk free; but, in common use, as in statistical arbitrage, it may refer to expected profit, though losses may occur, and in practice, there are always risks in arbitrage, some minor (such as fluctuation of prices decreasing profit margins), some major (such as devaluation of a currency or derivative). Simply put, an arbitrage involves taking advantage of differences in price of a single asset (currency).

Thus, arbitrage is possible when the same currency does not trade at the same price on all markets. Arbitrage is not simply the act of buying a currency (£) in one market (Zurich) and selling it in another (New York) for a higher price at some later time. The transactions must occur simultaneously to avoid exposure to market risk or the risk that prices may change on one market before both transactions are complete. In practical terms, this is possible with currencies because they can be traded electronically, and even then, when each leg of the trade is executed the prices in the market may have moved. Missing one of the legs of the trade (and subsequently having to trade it soon after at a lower price) is called "execution risk" or more specifically "leg risk."

2.7.1 Simple Intermarket Arbitrage

Suppose the exchange rate (after taking out the fees for making the exchange) in Zurich is 1.5360 $/£, and the exchange rate in New York is 1.5365 $/£. Converting $1,000,000 to £ in Zurich (buying £) and converting that ($1,000,000: 1.5360 $/£=£651,041.667) into $ (selling £) in New York (£651,041.667 × 1.5365 $/£=$1,000,325.521), for a profit of $325.521 is the arbitrage profit.

2.7.2 Intermarket Triangular Arbitrage

We can look at three different markets by using the cross rates and check on opportunities for intermarket arbitrage in the following three markets: New York, London, and Zurich.

Citibank (New York) is quoting spot $/£ as: 1.5370 $/£.
Barclays Bank (London) is quoting spot £/SF as: 0.6725 £/SF.
And Credit Swiss (Zurich) is quoting spot $/SF as: 1.0365 $/SF.

A trader with $1,000,000 sells that amount spot to Citibank and receives $1,000,000/1.5370 $/£=£650,618.087. Simultaneously, these £650,618.087 are sold to Barclays Bank at the cross rate of 0.6725 £/SF, receiving £650,618.087/0.6725 £/SF=SF967,461.840. Then, immediately he sells

Exhibit 2.1 Intermarket triangular arbitrage

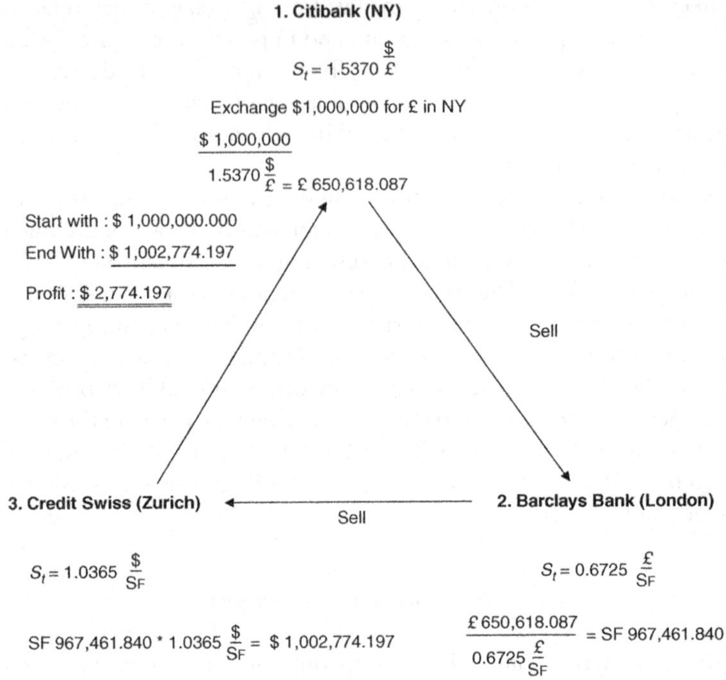

SF967,461.840 to Credit Swiss at the exchange rate of 1.0365 \$/SF and receives SF967,461.840 $\times$ 1.0365 \$/SF=\$1,002,774.197. He started with \$1,000,000 and ended with \$1,002,774.197; then, his triangular arbitrage profit is \$2,774.197, which is a risk-free profit because he is using only the spot market. This triangular arbitrage can continue until exchange rate equilibrium is reestablished, until the calculated cross rate becomes equal to the actual quotations, less any transaction costs. Exhibit 2.1 shows the three steps of the triangular arbitrage.

2.8 Summary

The foreign exchange market is a 24-hour global market, with prices (exchange rates) moving as currencies are traded among the different participants, interbank market (bank and non-bank foreign exchange dealers, brokers, speculators, and arbitragers, central banks, and treasuries) and client markets (firms and individuals). The functions of the foreign exchange market are: (1) transferring of purchasing power, (2) providing credits in foreign currencies, and (3) offering instruments of risk minimization (redistribution). The relative price of two currencies is expressed using the exchange rate of these currencies, which is quoted in two different terms, direct (American terms) and indirect (European terms). The bank quotations are given in outright and points (swap) quotations. From the outright quotes, the forward discount or the forward premium of a currency can be determined as a percentage per annum. The cross rate is the exchange rate of two currencies (€/£) calculated from two other exchange rates ($/€ and $/£). When the cross rates differ from the direct rates between two currencies, interbank arbitrage can take place, and an arbitrage profit equalizes the rates among the different markets.

Appendix 2

A2.1 Correlation and Causality between Interest Rates and Spot Rates

A Correlation and a Pairwise Granger Causality test between the exchange rate (S_t) and the interest rate (i_t) can determine the correlation coefficients and the direction of causality between these variables (tables A2.1 and A2.2).

Thus, the direction of causality that the results show is as follows:

$S \Rightarrow i_{BAA}, S \Rightarrow i^*_{10YGB}$, and $i_{AAA} \Rightarrow S$

A2.2 Example of Points Quotations (Swap Rates)

A foreign exchange trader in New York gives the following quotes for the Russian ruble (RUB or p.) spot, one month forward, three month forward, and six month forward to a US multinational corporation treasurer (\$/RUB):

0.03029/31 5/7 10/9 15/13

(1) Calculate the outright quotes for one month (F_1), three month (F_3), and six month (F_6) forward. (2) If the treasurer of the firm wished to buy

Table A2.1 Correlation Coefficients between exchange rate and interest rates

	LEUS	*STT3M*	*AAA1*	*BAA*	*EU10YGB*
LEUS	1.000000	−0.442187	−0.733932	−0.808572	−0.754290
STT3M	−0.442187	1.000000	0.846844	0.750660	0.621422
AAA1	−0.733932	0.846844	1.000000	0.956234	0.886973
BAA	−0.808572	0.750660	0.956234	1.000000	0.874456
EU10YGB	−0.754290	0.621422	0.886973	0.874456	1.000000

Note: LEUS = natural logarithm of the spot exchange rate (\$/€), STT3M = three-month T-bill rate in the United States, AAA1 = AAA corporate bond rate in the United States, BAA = BAA corporate bond rate in the United States, and EU10YGB = ten-year government bond rate in the EU.

Table A2.2 Pairwise Granger causality tests

Date: 06/05/12 Time: 16:40
Sample: 1964M01 2012M12
Lags: 2

Null Hypothesis:	*Obs*	*F-Statistic*	*Prob.*
STT3M does not Granger cause LEUS	154	0.80048	0.4510
LEUS does not Granger cause STT3M		0.02900	0.9714
AAA1 does not Granger cause LEUS	142	3.23551	0.0424
LEUS does not Granger cause AAA1		0.54958	0.5785
BAA does not Granger cause LEUS	105	1.34084	0.2663
LEUS does not Granger cause BAA		3.25298	0.0428
EU10YGB does not Granger cause LEUS	63	1.13678	0.3279
LEUS does not Granger cause EU10YGB		3.31017	0.0435
AAA1 does not Granger cause STT3M	564	13.8385	1.E-06
STT3M does not Granger cause AAA1		114.509	2.E-42
BAA does not Granger cause STT3M	527	0.74296	0.4762
STT3M does not Granger cause BAA		8.33496	0.0003
EU10YGB does not Granger cause STT3M	123	5.14150	0.0072
STT3M does not Granger cause EU10YGB		0.69612	0.5005
BAA does not Granger cause AAA1	527	493.840	4E-121
AAA1 does not Granger cause BAA		7.18311	0.0008
EU10YGB does not Granger cause AAA1	123	7.31303	0.0010
AAA1 does not Granger cause EU10YGB		2.13100	0.1233
EU10YGB does not Granger cause BAA	123	1.78398	0.1725
BAA does not Granger cause EU10YGB		0.44722	0.6405

Note: See table A2.1

Russian rubles six months forward, how much would he pay in US dollars? (3) If he wished to purchase US dollars three months forward, how much would he have to pay in Russian rubles? (4) If the treasurer wished to sell Russian rubles one month forward, how much would he receive in dollars? (5) Assuming that Russian rubles are being bought by the treasurer, what is the premium or discount, for the one-, three-, and six-month forward rates in annual percentage terms? (6) What do the above quotations imply in respect of the term structure of interest rates in the United States and in Russia?

Solution:

$/RUB 0.03029/31	5/7	10/9	15/13
	$<(+)$	$>(-)$	$>(-)$

(1) Outright Quotes:

	Bid	Ask (Offer)
S	0.03029	0.03031
F_1	0.03034	0.03038
F_3	0.03019	0.03022
F_6	0.03014	0.03018

(2) To buy Russian rubles six months forward, he would pay $0.03018.
(3) To purchase US dollars three months forward, he would he have to pay 0.03019 $/RUB, which are: $\frac{1}{0.03019} = RUB\,33.1236$.
(4) To sell Russian rubles one month forward, he would receive $0.03034.
(5) We use the "ask" price: (we have direct quotes, here);

$$\text{thus, } fp \quad or \quad fd = \frac{F-S}{S}\frac{12}{n}100\ (\%p.a.)$$

$$fp^1_{RUB} \quad or \quad fd^1_{\$} = \frac{0.03038 - 0.03031}{0.03031}\frac{12}{1}100 = 2.772\% \quad p.a.$$

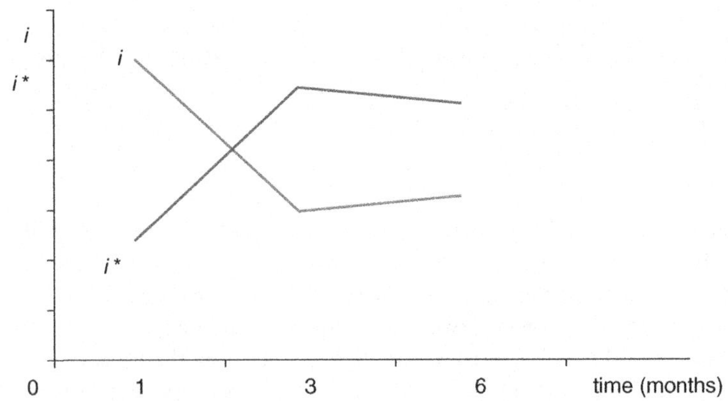

Graph A2.1 The term structure of interest rates.

Note: i_t = the US interest rate and i_t^* = the Russian interest rate.

$$fp_{\$}^{3} \quad or \quad fd_{RUB}^{3} = \frac{0.03022 - 0.03031}{0.03031}\frac{12}{3}100 = -1.188\% \quad p.a.$$

$$fp_{\$}^{6} \quad or \quad fd_{RUB}^{6} = \frac{0.03018 - 0.03031}{0.03031}\frac{12}{6}100 = -0.858\% \quad p.a.$$

(6) The term structure of interest rates in the United States (i_t) and in Russia (i_t^*) is presented graphically in graph A2.1. The interest rate in the United States will be above the Russian one by 2.772 percent (for the one month); then, the US interest rate will be below the Russian by 1.188 percent (the dollar at a forward premium for the three month); and finally the interest rate in the United States will be below the Russian interest rate by 0.858 percent (for the six month).

Notes

1. See The Time Around the World. http://24timezones.com/
2. The $3.98 trillion breakdown is as follows: $1.490 trillion in spot transactions, $475 billion in outright forwards, $1.765 trillion in foreign exchange swaps (a simultaneous purchase and sale of identical amounts of one currency for another with two different value dates [normally spot to forward]), $43 billion currency swaps (a foreign-exchange agreement between two parties to exchange aspects [namely the principal and/or investor payments] of a loan in one currency for equivalent aspects of an equal in net present value loan in another currency; currency swaps are motivated by comparative advantage; a currency swap should be distinguished from a central bank liquidity swap), and $207 billion in options and other products. See, *BIS*, http://www.bis.org/publ/rpfxf10t.htm.
3. The ten larger currency traders (% of overall volume, May 2011): (1) Deutsche Bank: 15.64 percent, (2) Barclays Capital: 10.75 percent, (3) UBS AG: 10.59 percent, (4) Citi: 8.88 percent, (5) JP Morgan: 6.43 percent, (6) HSBC: 6.26 percent, (7) Royal Bank of Scotland: 6.20 percent, (8) Credit Swisse: 4.80 percent, (9) Goldman Sachs: 4.13 percent, and (10) Morgan Stanley: 3.64 percent. Source: *Euromoney* FX survey http://www.euromoney.com/poll/3301/PollsAndAwards/Foreign-Exchange.html.
4. Retail foreign exchange trading is a small segment of the large foreign exchange market. In 2007 it had been speculated that volume from retail foreign exchange trading represents 5 percent of the whole foreign exchange market, which amounts to $50–$100 billion in daily trading turnover. The retail foreign exchange market has been growing. In general, retail customers are able to trade spot currencies. Due to the increasing tendency in the past years of the gradual shift from traditional intrabank "paper" trading to the more advanced and accurate electronic trading, there has been spurring in software development in this field. This change provided different types of trading platforms and tools intended for use by banks, portfolio managers, retail brokers, and

retail traders. One of the most important tools required to perform a foreign exchange transaction is the trading platform providing retail traders and brokers with accurate currency quotes. See, Burrell (2007).

5. TheCityUK is the new, independent membership body for promoting the UK-based financial and professional services industry. It continues the work of International Financial Services London (IFSL) and UKTI's Financial Services Sector Advisory Board (FSSAB). Both were incorporated into TheCityUK.
6. A percentage in point (pip) is the smallest commonly quoted change of an exchange rate of a currency pair. The major currencies, except the Japanese yen, are priced to four decimal places. For these currencies, a pip is one unit of the fourth decimal point, or 1/100th of 1 percent. For the Japanese yen, a pip refers to one unit in the second decimal point, because the yen is much closer in value to 1/100th of other major currencies. This would be different for the other currencies. If the currency pair of the euro versus the US dollar (EUR/USD) is trading at an exchange rate of 1.3000 (1 EUR = 1.3 USD) and the rate changes to 1.3010, the price ratio increases by 10 pips. In this example, if a trader buys 5 standard lots (i.e., 5 × 100,000 = 500,000) of EUR/USD, paying USD 650,000 and closes the position after the 10 pips appreciation, the trader will receive USD 650,500 and achieved a profit of 500 US dollars (i.e., 500,000 (5 standard lots) × 0.0010 = USD 500). Most retail trading by speculators is conducted in margin accounts, requiring only a small percentage (typically 1%) of the purchase price as equity for this transaction.
7. Currency overlay is a financial trading strategy or method conducted by specialist firms who manage the currency exposures of large clients, typically institutions such as pension funds, endowments, and corporate entities. Typically the institution will have a preexisting exposure to foreign currencies, and will be seeking to limit the risk from adverse movements in exchange rates, that is, hedge, and will attempt to profit from tactical foreign exchange views, that is, speculate. The currency overlay manager will conduct foreign exchange hedging on their behalf, selectively placing and removing hedges to achieve the objectives of the client. Many types of currency overlay accounts are more focused on the speculative aspect, that is, profiting from currency movements. These so-called pure alpha mandates are set up to allow the manager as much scope as possible to take speculative positions. As such, they are similar in nature to foreign exchange hedge funds in terms of objective and trading style.
8. A Contract For Difference (CFD) is a contract between two parties, typically described as "buyer" and "seller," stipulating that the seller will pay to the buyer the difference between the current value of an asset and its value at contract time. If the difference is negative, then the buyer pays instead to the seller. In effect CFDs are financial derivatives that allow traders to take advantage of prices moving up (long positions) or prices moving down (short positions) on underlying financial instruments and are often used to speculate on those markets. For example, when applied to equities, such a contract is an equity derivative that allows traders to speculate on share price movements, without

the need for ownership of the underlying shares. CFDs are currently available in the United Kingdom, Hong Kong, the Netherlands, Poland, Portugal, Germany, Switzerland, Italy, Singapore, South Africa, Australia, Canada, New Zealand, Sweden, Norway, France, Ireland, Japan, and Spain. They are not permitted in the United States due to restrictions by the US SEC on OTC financial instruments.

9. Financial Spread Betting (FSB) is by far the largest part of the official market concerning financial instruments in the United Kingdom; the leading spread betting companies make most of their revenues from financial markets, their sports operations being much less significant. FSB in the United Kingdom closely resembles the futures and options markets, the major differences being: (1) in spread betting, the "charge" occurs through a wider bid-offer spread; (2) spread betting has a different tax regime compared with securities and future exchanges; (3) spread betting is more flexible since it is not limited to exchange hours or definitions, can create new instruments relatively easily (e.g., individual stock futures), and may have guaranteed stop losses; and (4) in spread betting, the trading is off-exchange, with the contract existing directly between the market-making company and the client, rather than exchange-cleared, and is thus subject to a lower level of regulation although the spread betting companies themselves are some of the most regulated entities in the city of London. FSB is a way of speculating on financial markets in the same way as trading a number of derivatives, particularly, the financial derivative CFD, which in many ways mirrors the spread bet. In fact a number of financial derivative trading companies offer both FSBs and CFDs in parallel using the same trading platform.
10. Continuous Linked Settlement (CLS) is a process by which a number of the world's largest banks manage settlement of foreign exchange among themselves (and their customers and other third parties). The process is managed by CLS Group Holdings AG and its subsidiary companies and includes CLS Bank, a settlement bank regulated by the Federal Reserve Bank of New York. The group was formed in 1997 and the settlement system has been operational since 2002. As of February 2009, there were 73 shareholders and 62 settlement members as well as 4,576 third party participants (411 banks, corporates, and non-bank financial institutions, and 4,165 investment funds) that participated in the system. CLS Bank settles transactions on a *payment versus payment* (PVP) basis. When a foreign exchange trade is settled, each of the two parties to the trade pays funds in one currency and receives funds in a different currency. PVP ensures that these payments and receipts happen simultaneously. CLS Bank acts as the common counterparty between all participating banks; each party is required to have the funds it is to pay out deposited with CLS Bank in the hours before settlement occurs. Settlement generally takes place during a five-hour window when all the relevant Real-Time Gross Settlement (RTGS) systems are open and able to make and receive payments. Without PVP there is a (potentially devastating) chance that one party could pay its leg of the transaction to the other, but never receive the reciprocal payment (which could happen if the

other institution defaults in the hours between receipt of one leg and payment of the other). This is known as settlement risk (Herstatt risk). On average, CLS netting efficiency is in the region of 95 percent; each trillion dollars of gross value settled might require aggregate pay-ins of only $50 billion. Since it began operations, CLS has rapidly become the market standard for foreign exchange settlement between major banks. On September 21, 2011, it settled a record 1,960,492 instructions a day in 17 currencies (which represent some 95 percent of global foreign exchange trading). These instructions contained a gross value of approximately $8.9 trillion. This new record exceeded the previous record for number of instructions settled of 1,936,790 on November 26, 2010. The single-day record for gross-value settlement, set on March 19, 2008, stands at $10.3 trillion, for 1,113,464 payment instructions.

11. Most traded currencies (April 2010): (1) US dollar (USD): 84.9 percent, (2) Euro (EUR): 39.1 percent, Japanese yen (JPY): 19.0 percent, (4) Pound sterling (GBP): 12.9 percent, (5) Australian dollar (AUD): 7.6 percent, (6) Swiss franc (CHF): 6.4 percent, (7) Canadian dollar (CAD): 5.3 percent, (8) Hong Kong dollar (HKD): 2.4 percent, (9) Swedish krona (SEK): 2.2 percent, (10) New Zealand dollar (NZD): 1.6 percent, (11) South Korean won (KRW): 1.5 percent, (12) Singapore dollar (SGD): 1.4 percent, (13) Norwegian krone (NOK): 1.3 percent, (14) Mexican peso (MXN): 1.3 percent, Indian rupee (INR): 0.9 percent, and other: 12.2 percent. Source: *Bank for International Settlements.* 2010 Triennial Central Bank Survey.
12. ISO 4217 is a standard published by the International Standards Organization, which delineates currency designators, currency codes (alpha and numeric), and references to minor units in three tables: (1) current currency and funds code list, (2) current funds codes, and (3) list of codes for historic denominations of currencies and funds. The tables, history, and ongoing discussion are maintained by SIX Interbank Clearing. The ISO 4217 code list is used in banking and business globally. In many countries the ISO codes for the more common currencies are so well known publicly that exchange rates published in newspapers or posted in banks use only these to delineate the different currencies, instead of translated currency names or ambiguous currency symbols. ISO 4217 codes are used on airline tickets and international train tickets to remove any ambiguity about the price.
13. On the spot market, according to the 2010 Triennial Survey, the most heavily traded bilateral currency pairs were: EURUSD: 28 percent, USDJPY: 14 percent, and GBPUSD (also called "cable"): 9 percent.
14. The currency carry trade is an uncovered interest arbitrage (UIA). The term "carry trade," without further modification, refers to currency carry trade: investors borrow low-yielding currencies and lend (invest in) high-yielding currencies. It is thought to correlate with global financial and exchange rate stability and retracts in use during global liquidity shortages, but the carry trade is often blamed for rapid currency value collapse and appreciation. A risk in carry trading is that foreign exchange rates may change to the effect that the investor would have to pay back more expensive currency with less valuable

currency. In theory, according to uncovered interest rate parity (UIRP), carry trades should not yield a predictable profit because the difference in interest rates between two countries should equal the rate at which investors expect the low-interest-rate currency to rise against the high-interest-rate one. However, carry trades weaken the currency that is borrowed, because investors sell the borrowed money by converting it to other currencies. By early year 2007, it was estimated that some $1 trillion may have been staked on the yen carry trade. Since the mid-90s, the Bank of Japan has set Japanese interest rates at very low levels making it profitable to borrow Japanese yen to fund activities in other currencies. These activities include subprime lending in the United States, and funding of emerging markets, especially resource-rich countries and the BRIC countries. (This is a grouping acronym that refers to the countries of Brazil, Russia, India, and China, which are all deemed to be at a similar stage of newly advanced economic development. It is typically rendered as "the BRICs" or "the BRIC countries" or "the BRIC economies" or alternatively as the "Big Four.") The trade largely collapsed in 2008, particularly in regard to the yen. The 2008–2012 Icelandic financial crisis has among its origins the undisciplined use of the carry trade. Particular attention has been focused on the use of euro (€) denominated loans to purchase homes and other assets within Iceland. Most of these loans defaulted, when the relative value of the Icelandic currency depreciated dramatically, causing loan payment to become unaffordable. The US dollar ($) and the yen (¥) have been the currencies most heavily used in carry trade transactions since the 1990s. There is some substantial mathematical evidence in macroeconomics that larger economies have more immunity to the disruptive aspects of the carry trade, mainly due to the sheer quantity of their existing currency compared to the limited amount used for FOREX carry trades, but the collapse of the carry trade in 2008 is often blamed within Japan for a rapid appreciation of the yen. As a currency appreciates, there is pressure to cover any debts in that currency by converting foreign assets into that currency, so this can be an accelerating effect in currency valuation changes. When a large swing occurs, this can cause a carry reversal. The timing of the carry reversal in 2008 contributed substantially to the credit crunch, which caused the 2008 global financial crisis, though the relative size of impact of the carry trade with other factors is debatable. A similar rapid appreciation of the US dollar occurred at the same time, and the carry trade is rarely discussed as a factor for this appreciation.

15. *List of currencies with NDF market:* Below is a (nonexhaustive) list of currencies, where nondeliverable forwards are traded. Note that not all nonconvertible currencies have an NDF market; on the other hand, a nonconvertible currency to some market participants may be convertible to other market participants: (1) Asia Pacific: CNY Chinese Renminbi (yuan), IDR Indonesian Rupiah, INR Indian Rupee, KRW South Korean Won, MYR Malaysian Ringgit, PHP Philippine Peso, TWD Taiwan Dollar, VND Vietnamese đồng; (2) Europe, Middle East, and Africa: ILS Israeli Shekel, RUB Russian Ruble; (3) Latin America: ARS Argentine Peso, BRL Brazilian Real, CLP Chilean Peso,

COP Colombian Peso, GTQ Guatemalan quetzal, PEN Peruvian nuevo sol, and VEB Venezuela Bolivar. See, http://www.xe.com/symbols.php.

16. See, Lipscomb (2005). http://www.bis.org/publ/cgfs22fedny5.pdf.
17. A Pareto optimal situation is one where it is impossible to make one person better off except by making someone else worse off. See, Layard and Walters (1978). In other words, according to Pareto optimal criterion any change in our socioeconomic system that makes at least one individual better off and no one worse off is an improvement in the social welfare. See Kallianiotis (2012).
18. Former Malaysian prime minister Mahathir Mohamad is one well-known proponent of this view. He blamed the devaluation of the Malaysian ringgit in 1997 on George Soros and other speculators and it cost him the premiership. See also, Tom Redburn, "But Don't Rush Out to Buy Kronor: Sweden's 500% Gamble," *The New York Times*, September 17, 1992. http://www.nytimes.com/1992/09/17/news/17iht-perc.html.

Bibliography

Burrell, Jamaine (2007), *The Complete Guide to Currency Trading and Investing*, Ocala, FL: Atlantic Publishing Group, Inc.

Eiteman, David K., Arthur I. Stonehill, and Michael H. Moffett (2010), *Multinational Business Finance*, 12th Edition, Boston, MA: Prentice Hall.

Kallianiotis, Ioannis N. (2012), "Privatization and Financial Markets in European Union: A Social Welfare Perspective," in *Social Welfare*, edited by Rosario Laratta, Rijeka, Croatia: InTech Publishing, pp. 25–60.

Layard, P. R. G. and A. A. Walters (1978), *Microeconomic Theory*, New York: McGraw-Hill Book Company.

Lipscomb, Laura (2005), "An Overview of Non-Deliverable Foreign Forward Exchange Markets," Federal Reserve Bank of New York, May.

3

Foreign Exchange Rate Determination

Exchange rate determination is very important for financial economists, financial institutions, foreign currency traders, and all professionals in the foreign currency market. This chapter is based on discussions of exchange rate determination on a school of thought, using the asset market approach to solve complex problems. We will explore the different determinants of exchange rates and the theories that deal with its determination. These theories are (a) the monetary approach, divided into the monetarist model (flexible prices) and the overshooting model (sticky prices) and (b) the portfolio balance approach. Other related issues with the exchange rate theories will be discussed, such as efficiency in the foreign exchange market, exchange rate expectations and the "News," money market and exchange rate, exchange rate and freezing funds risk premium (FFRP), public policies and exchange rate, and lastly, oil prices and Euro-zone debt crisis and exchange rates.

3.1 Exchange Rate Theories

The theoretical literature on the asset market view of exchange rate determination has been expanding voluminously since the mid-1970s. The popularity of this view continues for more than 30 years, and generations of economists and practioners are learning and applying them to their theoretical research and their trade practices. The assumption that these models share is the absence of substantial transaction cost, capital control, and other impediments to the flow of capital between nations. Thus, we assume that there is perfect capital mobility among countries. In this case, the exchange rate will adjust instantly to equilibrate the international demand for stocks of national assets. The more traditional view was that the exchange rate adjusts to equilibrate the international demand for flows of national goods. The empirical implication is that floating exchange rates exhibit high variability, which goes beyond the variability of their underlying determinants. Econometric analysis gives specific empirical implications of the various theories. We start with the monetary approach and then, the portfolio balance approach is presented, together with other theoretical and empirical models.

3.1.1 *The Balance of Payments Approach*

The demand for and supply of foreign currency indicates that there is demand for imports and supply of exports. Whenever trade takes place, the demand and supply schedules shift up or down, as shown in figure 3.1.

By using a balance of payments equation, we can determine the factors that affect these two schedules:

$$B\ of\ P_t = CA\left(\frac{S_t P_t^*}{P_t}, Y_t, Y_t^*, \Pi_t, \Pi_t^*\right) + KA(i_t - i_t^*) \quad (3.1)$$

where, CA = current account, S_t = spot exchange rate, P_t = domestic price level, P_t^* = foreign price level, Y_t = real income, Π_t = shift factor (tariffs, subsidies, interventions, etc.), KA = capital account, $i_t - i_t^*$ = interest rate differential, and an asterisk ($*$) denotes the foreign variables.

Under floating exchange rate, balance of payments equilibrium is maintained by a continuing adjustment of the exchange rate. Thus, from

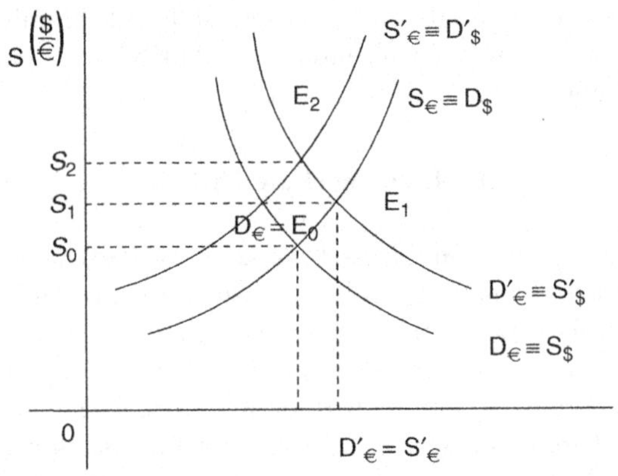

Figure 3.1 Exchange rate determination.

Note: An increase in the demand for euros (€) shifts the demand schedule from D_e to D'_e and the original equilibrium exchange rate s_0 (at the intersection of the demand and supply schedules) increases to s_1.The euro is appreciated and the US dollar is depreciated. A reduction in supply of euros is—a shift of the supply schedule to the left from S_e to S'_e (from E_1 to E_2).

eq. (3.3.1), solving for the exchange rate (S_t) and expressing all the variables in natural logarithms (s_t), except interest rates (variables that are measured as percentages per annum are not transformed to logarithms), we have:

$$s_t = \alpha_0 + \alpha_1(p_t - p_t^*) + \alpha_2(y_t - y_t^*) + \alpha_3(i_t - i_t^*) + \alpha_4(\Pi_t - \Pi_t^*) + \varepsilon_t \quad (3.2)$$

(1) $\alpha_1 > 0$ because an increase in p_t reduces x_t and the CA_t deteriorates (the country loses its competitive position); this will depreciate domestic currency (spot rate will increase, $s_t \uparrow$).
(2) $\alpha_2 > 0$ because a rapid growth in domestic real output tends to increase imports (m_t) and the CA_tdeteriorates; then, domestic currency depreciates ($s_t \uparrow$).
(3) $\alpha_3 < 0$ because an increase in the domestic interest rate, holding the foreign interest rate constant, will cause capital inflows in the country, which will increase the demand for domestic currency, and the domestic currency will appreciate ($s_t \downarrow$).
(4) $\alpha_4 < 0$ because any kind of intervention (domestic trade policy) will have as its objective improvement of the CA_t, which will affect positively the value of the currency ($s_t \downarrow$).

Equation (3.2) can be expanded by using other pairs of variables (i.e., national debt differential: $nd_t - nd_t^*$, investment differential: $\ln I_t - \ln I_t^*$, saving differential: $\ln S_t - \ln S_t^*$, wage differential: $w_t - w_t^*$, etc.).

3.2 Exchange Rate Determination: The Asset Market Models

These theories are part of the *asset market* model of floating exchange rate determination that started developing in the 1970s. The theoretical assumptions that all asset-market models share are: the absence of substantial transaction cost, no capital controls, and no other impediments to the flow of capital between countries (assumption of "perfect capital mobility").

Thus, the exchange rate adjusts instantly to equilibrate the international demand for stocks of national assets. Domestic and foreign bonds are assumed to be perfect substitutes in the asset holders' portfolios. Perfect capital mobility between countries means that actual portfolio composition adjusts instantaneously to the desired portfolio composition. Assuming no risk of default or future capital controls, perfect capital mobility implies covered interest parity,

$$i_t - i_t^* = fd_t \text{ or } fp_t = f_t - s_t \tag{3.3}$$

where, fd_t = forward discount, fp_t = forward premium, f_t = the natural logarithm (ln) of the forward rate, and s_t = the ln of spot exchange rate.

Perfect substitutability between domestic and foreign bonds is a much stronger assumption that asset holders are indifferent to the composition of their bond portfolios, as long as the expected rate of return on the two countries' bonds is the same, when expressed in any common numeraire and implies uncovered interest parity,

$$i_t - i_t^* = \Delta s_t^e = s_{t+1}^e - s_t \tag{3.4}$$

where, Δs_t^e = expected change in the spot rate and s_{t+1}^e = expected spot rate in the next period.

3.2.1 The Monetary Approach to the Exchange Rate Determination

Given that uncovered interest parity does hold ($i_t - i_t^* = s_{t+1}^e - s_t$), the supply of bonds becomes irrelevant. Now, the responsibility for determining the exchange rate is shifted to money markets. Such models belong to the "monetary approach" to exchange rate determination,[1] which focuses on the demand for and supply of money. Instead of emphasizing trade flows and capital movements, the monetary approach focuses on the stock equilibrium condition in each country's money market.

3.2.1.1 The Monetarist Model (Flexible Prices)

The monetarist model assumes there are no transaction costs, no capital control, and no segmenting international capital markets (domestic and foreign bonds are also perfect substitutes). It is similar to having only one bond in the world. Also, there are no transportation costs, no trade controls, and no segmenting international goods markets (domestic and foreign goods are perfect substitutes). It is also similar to having only one good in the world. This assumption implies purchasing power parity (PPP) that is, $P_t = P_t^* S_t$; where, P_t = the domestic price level, P_t^* = the foreign price level, and S_t = the spot exchange rate.

Because perfect price flexibility is considered and the model assumes PPP, it is called the "monetarist model." Its fundamental equations are:

The PPP equation in logarithm form,

$$s_t = p_t - p_t^* \tag{3.5}$$

where, s_t = the ln of the spot exchange rate (i.e., \$/€), p_t = the ln of the domestic price level (CPI), and p_t^* = the ln of the foreign price level (CPI^*).

The domestic real demand for money equation is,

$$m_t^d - p_t = \alpha + \beta y_t - \gamma i_t + \varepsilon_{1t} \tag{3.6}$$

where, m_t^d = the ln of the domestic money demand, p_t = the ln of the domestic price level, y_t = the ln of domestic real income, i_t = the domestic short-term interest rate, and ε_{1t} = the error term.

The foreign real demand for money equation is,

$$m_t^{*d} - p_t^* = \alpha + \beta y_t^* - \gamma i_t^* + \varepsilon_{2t} \tag{3.7}$$

where, asterisks (*) denote foreign variables and elasticities are assumed to be the same in both countries (constrained model).

Assuming equilibrium in the money markets, we have,

$$m_t^d - p_t = m_t^s - p_t = m_t - p_t \tag{3.8}$$

and

$$m_t^{*d} - p_t^* = m_t^{*s} - p_t^* = m_t^* - p_t^* \tag{3.9}$$

By combining eqs. (3.6), (3.7), (3.8), and (3.9) to eq. (3.5), we have,

$$s_t = (m_t - m_t^*) - \beta(y_t - y_t^*) + \gamma(i_t - i_t^*) + \varepsilon_t \tag{3.10}$$

Equation (3.10) gives a constrained model of exchange rate determination (with three constraints); the unconstrained one is when we allow the elasticities to be different in each country,

$$s_t = \alpha_0 + \alpha_1 m_t + \alpha_2 m_t^* + \alpha_3 y_t + \alpha_4 y_t^* + \alpha_5 i_t + \alpha_6 i_t^* + \varepsilon_t \tag{3.11}$$

where, α_0 = the constant term, $\alpha_1 > 0$ = the domestic money elasticity of the exchange rate, $\alpha_2 < 0$ = the foreign money elasticity of exchange rate, $\alpha_3 < 0$ = the domestic real income elasticity of exchange rate, $\alpha_4 > 0$ = the foreign real income elasticity of exchange rate, $\alpha_5 > 0$ = the domestic interest rate semielasticity of the exchange rate, $\alpha_6 < 0$ = the foreign interest rate semielasticity of the exchange rate, and ε_t = the error term or residual or disturbance.

Under the alternative unconstrained equation (eq. [3.11], we can test the hypothesis that elasticities are the same in both countries (null hypothesis), constrained equation (eq. [3.10])]. By solving both models, we can determine the log likelihood statistic ($\ln L^c$) of the constrained model and the log likelihood statistic ($\ln L^u$) of the unconstrained model. The resulting likelihood ratio statistic,

$$-2(\ln L^c - \ln L^u) \approx \chi^2_{(q)} \tag{3.12}$$

is distributed asymptotically as $\chi^2_{(q)}$, where, q=the number of constraints (three constraints, in this case). Comparison of this statistic with the critical $\chi^2_{(q)}$ then, tests the null hypothesis (i.e., the same elasticities in both countries).[2]

Also, by taking into consideration other economic and financial relationships between the two countries, we can create alternative specifications of the basic monetarist model, eq. (3.10).

(1) The *uncovered interest parity*:

$$i_t - i_t^* = \Delta s_t^e = s_{t+1}^e - s_t \tag{3.13}$$

(2) The *covered interest parity*:

$$i_t - i_t^* = fd_t \text{ or } fp_t = f_t - s_t \tag{3.14}$$

(3) Expected depreciation of the currency is equal to expected inflation differential:

$$\Delta s_t^e = \pi_t^e - \pi_t^{*e} \tag{3.15}$$

(4) The monetarist view: the expected growth of money ($\dot{m}_t^e$) is equal to the expected inflation (π_t^e):

$$\dot{m}_t^e - \dot{m}_t^{*e} = \pi_t^e - \pi_t^{*e} \tag{3.16}$$

Thus, based on eqs. (3.13), (3.14), (3.15), and (3.16), we have alternative specifications of the basic model, eq. (3.10):

$$s_t = (m_t - m_t^*) - \beta(y_t - y_t^*) + \gamma(s_{t+1}^e - s_t) + \varepsilon_t \tag{3.10.1}$$

$$\text{or} \quad s_t = (m_t - m_t^*) - \beta(y_t - y_t^*) + \gamma(f_t - s_t) + \varepsilon_t \tag{3.10.2}$$

$$\text{or} \quad s_t = (m_t - m_t^*) - \beta(y_t - y_t^*) + \gamma(\pi_t^e - \pi_t^{*e}) + \varepsilon_t \tag{3.10.3}$$

$$\text{and} \quad s_t = (m_t - m_t^*) - \beta(y_t - y_t^*) + \gamma(\dot{m}_t^e - \dot{m}_t^{*e}) + \varepsilon_t \tag{3.10.4}$$

The first factor affecting exchange rate is the money differential between the two countries. An increase in the domestic money supply increases the supply of domestic currency (dollars) and the US dollar is depreciated, and the spot rate increases ($s_t\uparrow$). The second factor refers to relative income levels. A boost in domestic real income (ceteris paribus) creates an excess demand for the domestic money stock. In an attempt by domestic residents to increase real money balances, they reduce expenditure, and prices fall until the money market equilibrium is achieved. Through PPP ($p_t\downarrow - \overline{p}_t^* = s_t\downarrow$), the fall in domestic prices (with foreign prices constant) implies an appreciation of the domestic currency ($s_t\downarrow$). The third factor is the relative short-term interest rate in the two countries. An increase in the domestic interest rate denotes the market expectation of the exchange rate. The domestic currency is expected to depreciate and the country increases the interest rate to cover the forward discount with its higher interest rate, so it could attract investment. Thus, the causal effect is from: $s^e_{t+1} \uparrow \Rightarrow (i_t \uparrow - \bar{i}^*_t)$.

3.2.1.2 *The Exchange Rate Dynamics or Overshooting Model (Sticky Prices)*

The monetarist model assumes instantaneous adjustment in all markets. An important modification was set forth by Dornbusch (1976), who assumed that asset markets adjust instantaneously, whereas prices in goods markets adjust slowly (gradually). The resulting exchange rate dynamics model retains all the long-run equilibrium or steady state properties of the monetary approach, but in the short run, the real exchange rate and the interest rate can diverge from their long-run levels. Then, the monetary policy can have effects on real variables in the system. Thus, exchange rate dynamics or "overshooting" can occur in any model, in which some markets do not adjust instantaneously.

This sticky price version is a Keynesian model of the monetary approach. Purchasing power parity ($p_t = s_t p^*_t$) may be a good approximation in the long run, but it does not hold in the short run. There are long-term contracts, imperfect information, high cost of acquiring information, inertia in consumer habits, and other restrictions, which do not allow prices to change instantaneously, but adjust gradually. This gives us a model of exchange rate determination, in which changes in the nominal money supply are also changes in the real money supply $\left(\frac{M^s\uparrow}{\bar{P}} = \frac{M^s}{P}\uparrow\right)$ because prices are sticky, so the effect is real:

$$\frac{M^s \uparrow}{\bar{P}} \Rightarrow \frac{M^s}{P} \uparrow \Rightarrow D_{Bonds} \uparrow \Rightarrow P_{Bonds} \uparrow \Rightarrow i \downarrow \Rightarrow K_{outflow}$$

$$\Rightarrow S_{S-R} \uparrow\uparrow\uparrow \Rightarrow X \uparrow$$

In the short run, because prices are sticky, a monetary expansion has a liquidity effect; thus, the interest rate falls, generating an incipient capital outflow, which causes the currency to depreciate instantaneously more than it will in the long run, as shown in figure 3.2. The currency depreciates just enough, so that the rationally expected rate of future appreciation precisely cancels out the interest differential. This is known as "overshooting" of the spot exchange rate.

The overshooting results are consistent with perfect foresight. The assumptions of the model are that goods' prices are sticky (price inertia in

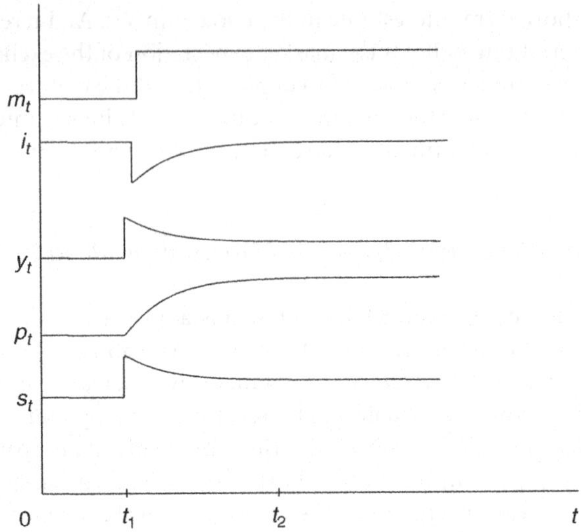

Figure 3.2 The overshooting model. (exchange rate dynamics)

Note: m_t = money supply, i_t = interest rate, y_t = real output (production), p_t = price level, and s_t = spot exchange rate. $M^s \uparrow \Rightarrow (\overline{P}) \Rightarrow \frac{M^s}{P} \uparrow \Rightarrow D_{Bonds} \uparrow \Rightarrow P_{Bonds} \uparrow \Rightarrow i \downarrow \Rightarrow$ capital outflows $\Rightarrow$ currency depreciates instantaneously more than it will in the long term.

the short run), prices of currencies are flexible, arbitrage in asset markets holds (uncovered interest parity [UIP]), and expectations of exchange rate changes are rational. Initial shocks are unanticipated, but when they occur, overshooting clears the way for a time path of the domestic interest rate and the exchange rate that is consistent with perfect foresight on the part of market participants. Given that an unanticipated increase in the domestic money supply in period t_1 would temporarily lower the domestic interest rate (liquidity effect), expectations of currency appreciation are necessary in order to induce individuals to continue to hold domestic securities and money.

When a monetary shock occurs in period t_1 (unanticipated increase in the money supply); the market will adjust to a new equilibrium, which will be between prices and quantities. Due to price stickiness in the goods market, the short-run equilibrium will be achieved through shifts in financial market prices. As prices of goods increase gradually toward the new equilibrium in period t_2, the foreign exchange continuous repricing approaches its long-term equilibrium level. Then, a new long-run equilibrium will be attained in the domestic money, currency exchange, and goods markets. As a result, the exchange rate will initially overreact (overshoot), due to a monetary shock. Over time, goods prices will respond, allowing the foreign exchange rate to restrain its overreaction and the economy will reach its new long-run equilibrium in all markets in period t_2(figure 3.2).

The overshooting model can be presented with the following equations:

The money demand function,

$$m_t = \overline{p}_t + \alpha + \beta y_t - \gamma i_t + \varepsilon_{1t} \tag{3.6'}$$

The uncovered interest parity,

$$i_t - i_t^* = \Delta s_t^e = s_{t+1}^e - s_t \tag{3.4'}$$

The long-run PPP,

$$\overline{s}_t = \overline{p}_t - \overline{p}_t^* \tag{3.5'}$$

The bars (i.e., $\overline{p}$) over the variables mean that the relationship holds in the long run.

The long-run monetarist exchange rate equation,

$$\overline{s}_t = (\overline{m}_t - \overline{m}_t^*) - \beta(\overline{y}_t - \overline{y}_t^*) + \gamma(\Delta\overline{p}_t^e - \Delta\overline{p}_t^{*e}) + \varepsilon_t \tag{3.17}$$

We assume that expectations are rational and the system is stable. Income growth is exogenous, random with $E(g_y) = 0$, and monetary growth follows a random walk. Thus, the relative money supply and, in the long run, the relative price level and exchange rate, are all rationally expected to follow paths that increase at the current rate of relative money growth $(g_{m_t} - g_{m_t^*}\ or\ \dot{m}_t - \dot{m}_t^*)$.

Then, eq. (3.17) becomes,

$$\overline{s}_t = (m_t - m_t^*) - \beta(y_t - y_t^*) + \gamma(g_{m_t} - g_{m_t^*}) + \varepsilon_t \tag{3.18}$$

In the short run, when the exchange rate deviates from its equilibrium path, it is expected to close that gap with a speed of adjustment of Θ(theta). In the long run, when the exchange rate lies on its equilibrium path, it is expected to increase at $(g_{m_t} - g_{m_t^*})$.

$$\Delta s_t^e = -\Theta(s_t - \overline{s}_t) + g_{m_t} - g_{m_t^*} \tag{3.19}$$

By combining (19) with (4′), we obtain,

$$i_t - i_t^* = -\Theta(s_t - \overline{s}_t) + g_{m_t} - g_{m_t^*} \tag{3.20}$$

and putting the growth of money equal to the expected inflation,

$$g_{m_t} - g_{m_t^*} = \pi_t^e - \pi_t^{*e} \tag{3.21}$$

we have,

$$s_t - \bar{s}_t = -\frac{1}{\Theta}[(i_t - \pi_t^e) - (i_t^* - \pi_t^{*e})] \tag{3.22}$$

Equation (3.22) shows that the gap between the exchange rate and its equilibrium value is proportional to the real interest rate differential. When a tight domestic monetary policy causes the interest differential to rise above its equilibrium level, an incipient capital inflow causes the value of the domestic currency to rise (spot rate falls) proportionately above its equilibrium level.

Now, by combining eq. (3.18), which represents the long-run monetary equilibrium path, with eq. (3.22), representing the short-run overshooting effect, we can obtain a general monetary equation of exchange rate determination,

$$s_t = \bar{s}_t - \frac{1}{\Theta}[(i_t - \pi_t^e) - (i_t^* - \pi_t^{*e})] + \varepsilon_t \tag{3.23}$$

and

$$s_t = (m_t - m_t^*) - \beta(y_t - y_t^*) + \gamma(g_{m_t} - g_{m_t^*}) - \frac{1}{\Theta}[(i_t - \pi_t^e) - (i_t^* - \pi_t^{*e})] + \varepsilon_t \tag{3.24}$$

Equation (3.24) is an expansion of the monetarist equation with the addition of the fourth variable, the real interest differential between the two countries. If the monetarist model is correct, the last variable must have a coefficient of zero, which means that the speed of adjustment (Θ) is infinite. By considering that the level of the money supply, rather than the change in the money supply, is a random walk, the expected long-run inflation differential ($\pi_t^e - \pi_t^{*e}$) is zero.

Equation (3.24) becomes,

$$s_t = (m_t - m_t^*) - \beta(y_t - y_t^*) - \frac{1}{\Theta}(i_t - i_t^*) + \varepsilon_t \tag{3.25}$$

Equation (3.25) is the Dornbusch equation, which can be tested econometrically by estimating eq. (3.24). A question remains, here: whether or not the domestic and foreign bonds are perfect substitutes. The violation of this assumption means that the interest differential will differ from the expected rate of currency depreciation. This difference may arise due to transaction costs, expectation errors, or a risk premium, as most financial analysts consider being the case.

3.2.2 *Portfolio-Balance Approach of the Exchange Rate Determination*

The correlation between current account deficits (CA_t) and exchange rates (s_t) has been undeniably strong ($\rho_{CA,s} > 0$). The current account developments have been largely dominated by imports of oil, and for small countries, except oil, by imports of industrial and manufacturing products. As the world oil trade is done in US dollars, a sharp increase in world oil prices raises the demand for the dollar at the expense of the other currencies (euro, yen, pound, etc.).[3] On the other hand, some economists argue that the huge US national debt, the Middle East crises, and the easy money policy of the Fed have depreciated the dollar.

Further, the release by the US government of unexpected figures on the trade balance and the current account appear to have had large immediate "announcement effects" on the exchange rate (dollar depreciates or depreciates depending on "bad" or "good" news). The current account figures reveal information about shifts in the long-run terms of trade. Of course, the important point is that only the unexpected component (CA^u) of the current account ($CA = CA^e + CA^u$) has a large effect; the expected component (CA^e) has already been taken into account by the foreign exchange market:

$$CA_{t+1} = CA^e_{t+1} + CA^u_{t+1} \tag{3.26}$$

where, CA_{t+1} = the actual current account balance, CA^e_{t+1} = the expected current account balance based on information today [$CA^e_{t+1} = E(CA_{t+1} | I_t)$], and CA^u_{t+1} = the unexpected part of the current account balance, the "surprise," the "news," the risky part of the CA_{t+1}.

In addition, a current account surplus is a transfer of wealth from foreign residents to domestic residents (and a transfer of unemployment from the domestic economy to the foreign one). The increase in domestic wealth ($W_t \uparrow$) can appreciate the currency ($S_t \downarrow$).

(1) It can raise domestic expenditure by increasing domestic consumption:

$$C_t = f(\overset{+}{W_t}) \tag{3.27}$$

where, C_t = consumption and W_t = domestic wealth.

Then, aggregate demand will increase, which will affect production and income. This higher income will increase the demand for money (M^d_t).

(2) It can raise the demand for domestic money directly if wealth enters the money demand function:

$$M_t^d = \alpha_0 + \alpha_1 W_t + \alpha_2 P_t - \alpha_3 i_t + \varepsilon_t \tag{3.28}$$

where, M_t^d = demand for money, P_t = price level, i_t = nominal interest rate (opportunity cost of capital), and ε_t = the error term.

(3) If domestic bonds and foreign bonds are imperfect substitutes, domestic residents have a greater tendency to hold wealth in the form of domestic bonds; then, the increase in domestic wealth will raise the demand for domestic bonds:

$$B_t^d = f(\overset{+}{W_t}) \tag{3.29}$$

where, B_t^d = demand for domestic bonds.

We assume that there are no barriers segmenting international capital markets, but we have imperfect capital substitutability, which means that there is a risk premium (RP_t),

$$RP_t = fd_t - E(\Delta s_t) = i_t - i_t^* - E(\Delta s_t) = (f_t - s_t) - (s_{t+1}^e - s_t) \tag{3.30}$$

where, RP_t = risk premium, fd_t = forward discount, $E(\Delta s_t)$ = expected change in the spot exchange rate, $i_t - i_t^*$ = interest rate differential, and f_t = ln of the forward exchange rate.

Thus, investors allocate their bond portfolios between the two countries in proportions that are functions of the expected rates of return (i_t^e and i_t^{*e}). The two assets are imperfect substitutes because there are differences between the two countries in liquidity, in tax rates, in default risk, in political risk, in exchange rate risk, and in other factors. We assume that there are perfect international bond markets and the two bonds differ, due to their currency denomination (one is in dollars and the other is in a foreign currency).

A shock in the economy, in the form of a change in wealth, produces a wealth effect, which is an increase in the demand for each financial asset, and a substitution effect, substituting a high-return financial asset for the low-return alternative. Consequently, the exchange rate and interest rates have to adjust to ensure portfolio equilibrium. The portfolio balance approach states that the exchange rate and interest rates are determined simultaneously by the portfolio equilibrium conditions for asset holders in these two different countries.

A simple version of the portfolio balance model can be presented with the following equations:

Demand for money:

$$M_t^d = m(i_t, i_t^*, W_t) \tag{3.31}$$

Demand for domestic bonds:

$$B_t^d = b(i_t, i_t^*, W_t) \tag{3.32}$$

Demand for foreign bonds evaluated in the domestic currency:

$$S_t B_t^{*d} = f(i_t, i_t^*, W_t) \tag{3.33}$$

The supply of these assets is given as follows: M_t^s, B_t^s, and B_t^{*s}, and we assume equilibria,

$$M_t^d = M_t^s = M_t \tag{3.34}$$

$$B_t^d = B_t^s = B_t \tag{3.35}$$

$$B_t^{*d} = B_t^{*s} = B_t^* \tag{3.36}$$

where, B_t^d = demand for bonds, B_t^s = supply of bonds, B_t = the equilibrium amount of bonds, and an asterisk (*) denotes the foreign variable.

The financial portfolio makes up the total wealth (W_t), which is equal to the sum of the three assets,

$$W_t = M_t + B_t + S_t B_t^* \tag{3.37}$$

At any point in time, the existing stocks of these assets are fixed, and the domestic interest rate (i_t) and exchange rate (S_t) must adjust so that the assets are willingly held by investors (maximization of their return). The stocks of financial assets change over time. When the budget deficit is increasing, the government issues bonds to finance it, which increases the supply of domestic government bonds (B_t). Autonomous growth of money supply (expansionary monetary policy) or monetization of the government debt (open market purchase) increases the stock of money (M_t). Current account surpluses increase the net domestic holdings of foreign (bonds) assets (B_t^*).

Then, the exchange rate (S_t) of the portfolio balance model will be given from eq. (3.33) and eq. (3.37), as follows:

$$S_t = s(M_t, B_t, B_t^*, i_t, i_t^*) \tag{3.38}$$

The foreign interest rate (i_t^*) is determined by the foreign asset market,

$$i_t^* = r(M_t^*, B_t^*) \tag{3.39}$$

Substituting eq. (3.39) into eq. (3.38), we have,

$$S_t = s(\overset{+}{M_t}, \overset{+}{B_t}, \overset{-}{M_t^*}, \overset{+}{B_t^*}, \overset{-}{i_t}, \overset{+}{i_t^*}) \tag{3.40}$$

Equation (3.40) specifies the relationship between exchange rates, assets supplies, and interest rates (returns) in the two countries:

(1) An expansionary monetary policy, as an exogenous increase in money supply (M_t) means an increase in wealth. The wealth effect leads to excess demand for domestic and foreign bonds. With given foreign interest rate ($\bar{i}_t^*$), excess demand for domestic bonds would raise their price, so the domestic interest rate will fall. The excess demand for foreign bonds will increase the demand for foreign currency (foreign currency will appreciate), leading to a depreciation of the domestic currency (spot rate will increase).

(2) An increase in domestic government bonds (B_t) will increase the domestic wealth and through a wealth effect, would increase the demand for foreign bonds and consequently, the demand for foreign currency will go up. This will lead to an appreciation of the foreign currency and a depreciation of the domestic currency. Also, an increase in domestic debt will increase the supply of bonds, which will reduce their price and increase the domestic interest rate. This higher domestic interest rate ($i_t > i_t^*$) would make foreign bonds less attractive. If this substitution effect dominates the previous wealth effect, the domestic currency will appreciate, due to increase in investment on domestic bonds.

(3) An increase, now, in net holdings of foreign bonds (B_t^*), induced by a current account surplus, increases the domestic wealth. This wealth effect will increase the demand for domestic assets, which will increase their prices and the interest rate will fall. This will depreciate the domestic currency (exchange rate will increase).

The monetary approach focuses only on a single asset (money). The portfolio balance approach deals with multiassets, which integrates the analysis of the exchange rate behavior with other financial assets (bonds, stocks, etc.). This second approach allows the current account imbalances ($-CA = KA$) to affect the exchange rate (where, $CA =$ the current account and $KA =$ the capital account). Thus, the portfolio balance model contains features provided by the monetary approach and the balance of payment approach. Residents of both countries hold assets issued by both countries. Domestic residents wish to hold a greater proportion of their wealth in domestic assets and foreign residents wish to hold a greater proportion in foreign assets ("perfect local habitat"). The current account will redistribute world wealth in such a way as to raise net world demand for the surplus country's assets, thus, raising the price of its currency.

3.3 Efficiency in the Foreign Exchange Market and Exchange Rate Movement

The international monetary system had to accommodate extraordinarily large oil-related shocks, trade deficits, and public and private debts that affected capital flows among nations (and risk). Surpluses had to be recycled (invested) by buying financial assets from the deficit countries. The latest global financial crisis has increased uncertainty, and the deregulation of our financial institutions has increased the gap between the market and politicians. The increased interdependence among nations and the realization that economic policies by strong nations exert pressure on other weaker economies have to induce legal responses and cooperation among all nations. But, can any international organization objectively force international justice?

An understanding of efficiency, expectations, and risk in the foreign exchange market is important to government policy makers, international financial managers, and of course, to investors and students of international finance. The government policy makers need to design macropolicies for achieving the goal of maximization of their social welfare through efficient resource allocation. International investors and financial managers need to assess foreign asset returns and risks in order to make optimal portfolio decisions. The foreign exchange market efficiency hypothesis is the proposition that prices (exchange rate movements) fully reflect information available to market participants. There are no opportunities for the hedgers or the speculators to make supernormal profits; thus, both speculative efficiency and arbitraging efficiency exist. Numerous studies have been tested for speculative efficiency and arbitraging efficiency by testing the following two hypotheses respectively: (1) the forward discount is a good predictor of the change in the future spot rate, implying covered interest parity (CIP), uncovered interest parity (UIP), and rational expectations to hold and (2) the forward discount tends to be equal to the interest differential, implying that CIP holds.

Exchange rates are viewed as relative prices of two assets (actually, two central banks' liabilities, their currencies) that are traded in organized markets (the foreign exchange market) and are influenced by many different factors and, of course, by expectations about the future international events ("news"). Therefore, unanticipated events will influence the exchange rates, too, as it happens with other assets. So far, the flexible exchange rate system has been successful in providing national economies with an added degree of insulation from foreign shocks, and it provides policy makers with an added instrument for the conduct of trade policy. Unfortunately, the Euro-zone membernations (due to their acceptance of the euro) have lost this valuable macroeconomic policy tool.

3.3.1 *The Efficiency of the Foreign Exchange Market*

The efficient market hypothesis (EMH) in domestic finance has been developed by Eugene Fama since early 1970. In finance, the EMH asserts that financial markets are "informationally efficient." In consequence of this, one cannot consistently achieve returns in excess of average market returns on a risk-adjusted basis, given the information available at the time the investment is made. In this efficient market, all new information is quickly understood by market participants and becomes immediately incorporated into market prices. Thus, prices of financial assets provide signals for portfolio allocation. Market efficiency is associated with the rationality of market expectations.

To examine market efficiency, we must determine whether market participants could systematically earn an excess profit. If we designate R_{t+1} as a series of asset returns next period and R^e_{t+1} as market expectations of these returns, and that there are no systematic unexploited profits over time, we can write,

$$E[R_{t+1} - R^e_{t+1} \,|\, \Pi_t] = 0 \tag{3.41}$$

where, R_{t+1} = the actual return next period, R^e_{t+1} = the expected return derived from forecasting it one period ahead, E = is the expectations operator conditioned on the information set Π_t ($\Pi = \pi\lambda\eta\rho o\phi o\rho\iota\alpha\iota$, very broad information) available at the end of period t.

In case there are systematic forecast errors in R^e_{t+1}, the information would be incorporated into the forecast process. Investors inspect the forecast errors ($R_{t+1} - R^e_{t+1} = \varepsilon_{t+1}$) to see whether there are unexploited patterns that may be used to improve their investment strategy. Thus, the systematic information will be exploited and the resulting error becomes "white noise."[4] To satisfy the efficiency condition, eq. (3.41), an optimal forecast of asset prices is consistent with rational expectations behavior.

In the foreign exchange markets, the efficient markets hypothesis has been applied to the spot market and to the forward market. Equation (3.41) can be used to express the spot exchange rate as follows,

$$E[s_{t+1} - s^e_{t+1} \,|\, \Pi_t] = 0 \tag{3.42}$$

where, s_{t+1} = the ln of the spot exchange rate and s^e_{t+1} = the ln of the expected spot rate based on information available at time t.

Equation (3.42) states that the expectation errors will be zero on average, so that no excess profits can be exploited in the foreign exchange markets. The difficulty lies in forming the optimal forecast value that results in residuals displaying no informational content.

3.3.1.1 *The Random Walk Hypothesis*

Let the current value of s_t be equal to last period's value plus a white-noise term,

$$s_t = s_{t-1} + \varepsilon_t \quad \text{or} \quad s_t - s_{t-1} = \varepsilon_t \tag{3.43}$$

The random walk model is clearly a special case of the AR(1) process: $s_t = \alpha_0 + \alpha_1 s_{t-1} + \varepsilon_t$, when $\alpha_0 = 0$ and $\alpha_1 = 1$. In practice, the investor does not need all the information in Π_t that are based on experience, empirical knowledge, market conditions, true wisdom, and have very high information costs. Then, a rational investor may use a smaller set of information I_t to form exchange rate expectations. Economists have observed that the exchange rate follows a random walk process, which means that the expected exchange rate next period s^e_{t+1} is equal to the current spot rate s_t. Thus,

$$s^e_{t+1} = s_t \tag{3.44}$$

Now, substituting eq. (3.44) into eq. (3.42) and using information I_t, we get,

$$E[s_{t+1} - s_t | I_t] = 0 \tag{3.45}$$

Equation (3.45) suggests that if the foreign exchange market is efficient, the current exchange rate will reflect all the available information and the unexpected change in the spot rate $(s_{t+1} - s_t)$ is essentially caused by the random shock ε_{t+1}, which hits the market between time t and time $t+1$. Market rationality suggests that the investor finds no particular pattern from the history of ε_{t+1}. This random walk (market efficiency) can be tested as follows:

$$s_t = \alpha_0 + \alpha_1 s_{t-1} + \varepsilon_t \tag{3.46}$$

If $\alpha_0 \cong 0$ and $\alpha_1 \cong 1$, the foreign exchange market is efficient. This random walk hypothesis explains the erratic behavior of exchange rate movements. Exchange rates respond to "news" (surprises), which are unpredictable. Thus, exchange rates move randomly because they respond sensitively to the unexpected events that randomly hit the markets.

3.3.1.2 The Unbiased Forward Rate Hypothesis

Another way to measure the expected exchange rate is to use the forward exchange rate. The forward rate has been viewed as an unbiased predictor of the future spot rate ("The Unbiased Forward Rate Hypothesis"). The validity of this UFRH implies that the investor is risk neutral, transaction costs are insignificant, and the arrival of important informational events is random. This hypothesis is derived from an efficient arbitrage activity by investors and it is expressed as,

$$s_{t+1}^{e} = f_t \tag{3.47}$$

Substituting s_{t+1}^{e} in eq. (3.42) with f_t and a smaller information set I_t (due to lack of complete information because of its enormous cost), we have,

$$E[s_{t+1} - f_t \,|I_t] = 0 \tag{3.48}$$

Equation (3.48) states that the forecast errors resulting from using forward rates to predict the future spot rates will be zero on average. A nonzero value, $E[s_{t+1} - f_t \,|I_t] \neq 0$, suggests the rejection of the unbiased forward rate hypothesis, due to high transaction costs associated with arbitrage; a risk premium if investors are not risk neutral; and a specification error if the model is not well specified. This UFRH (market efficiency) can be tested as follows:

$$s_t = \alpha_0 + \alpha_1 f_{t-1} + \varepsilon_t \tag{3.49}$$

If $\alpha_0 \cong 0$ and $\alpha_1 \cong 1$, the foreign exchange market is efficient; last period's forward rate predicts the current spot rate. Prices reflect all relevant available information; thus, the residuals in eq. (3.49) should contain no information and, therefore, should be serially uncorrelated $[E(\varepsilon_t, \varepsilon_{t-1}) = 0]$. Further, under the assumption of risk neutrality, if the forward exchange rate is an unbiased predictor of the future spot exchange rate $[f_t = s_{t+1}]$; then, the constant term should be closed to zero $[\alpha_0 \cong 0]$ and the slope coefficient (actually, elasticity) should be closed to unity $[\alpha_1 \cong 1]$.

Also, if forward exchange rates prevailing at period $t - 1$ summarize all relevant information available at that period, these exchange rates should also contain the information that is summarized in data corresponding to period $t - 2$ and so on. It follows that including additional lagged values of the forward rates in eq. (3.49) should not greatly affect the coefficients of determination and the sum of these coefficients must not differ significantly from unity (the inclusion of additional lagged variables does not improve the fit):

$$s_t = \alpha_0 + \alpha_1 f_{t-1} + \alpha_2 f_{t-2} + \varepsilon_t \tag{3.50}$$

Hence, if $\alpha_0 \cong 0$ and $\alpha_1 + \alpha_2 \cong 1$ the foreign exchange market is efficient; last periods' forward rates predict the current spot rate.

3.3.1.3 The Composite Efficiency Hypothesis

The composite efficiency hypothesis combines the previous two hypotheses (the random walk and the unbiased forward rate hypotheses). It suggests that the expected future spot exchange rate is a weighted average of the current spot rate and the forward rate, as follows,

$$s_{t+1}^e = ws_t + (1 - w)f_t \tag{3.51}$$

where, w = the weight of the spot rate.

Equation (3.51) is based on the information contained in the spot and forward rates. We assume rational expectations here too. The information contained in the spot rate (s_t) reflects current market conditions and summarizes all historical information that affects exchange rates. The forward rate (f_t) reflects all the information concerning factors that are expected to determine future exchange rates. Therefore, the composite efficiency hypothesis contains two sets of information affecting the future spot exchange rate: first, past historical information and second, rational expectations of the market participants. One problem might still exist: What will be the value of each one of the weights on the spot and forward rates?

3.3.1.4 Exchange Rate Volatility and Predictability

The exchange rates have been very volatile since the 1970s, when the exchange rates became flexible. As an example, the standard deviation of the spot exchange rate between the US dollar and the euro has been, $\sigma_s = \pm 2.8\%$ per month, as graph 3.1 shows. Thus, the predictability of the exchange rate has become very difficult. These two characteristics of exchange rates (volatility and unpredictability) are typical of auction asset markets and have worsened after 2008 with the global financial crisis and the new systemic risk that our economies are facing. In our foreign currency markets, current spot exchange rates reflect expectations concerning the future course of events (market, political, economic, international) and new information (global news are instantaneously known to everyone), which induces changes in expectations and are immediately reflected in corresponding changes in exchange rates (and all asset prices), thus reducing unexploited profit opportunities from arbitrage. However, speculators are thriving and proving at the same time inefficiency in all the assets markets.

The strong dependence of current prices (spot exchange rates) on expectations about the future is unique to the determination of asset prices. This strong dependence causes many problems in our economy and our

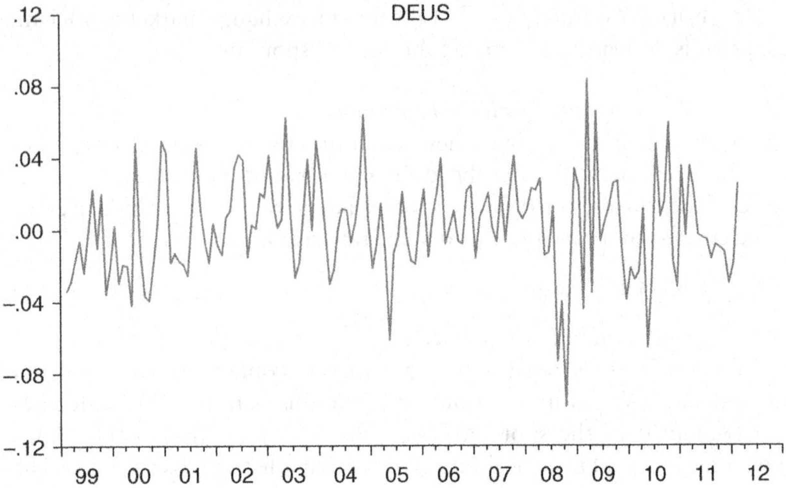

Graph 3.1 Volatility of the spot exchange rate (\$/€).

Note: DEUS $= \Delta s_t = s_t - s_{t-1}$ (the growth of the \$/€ spot exchange rate) measured on the vertical axis and years depicted on the horizontal axis (from 1999 to 2012).

Source: *Economagic.com.*

social welfare; especially in periods that are dominated by uncertainties, new information, rumors (propagandas), announcements, and "news" (the media plays a major role in today's social welfare). All these, mostly, negative "news" change our expectations (make us, mostly, pessimistic) and are the prime cause of fluctuations in asset prices. Consequently, since the information, which alters expectations is new ("news"), the resulting fluctuations in price (exchange rate) cannot be predicted by lagged forward exchange rates, which are based on past information. During these uncertain periods, we should expect exchange rates (and all other asset prices) to exhibit large fluctuations. Thus, past prices, which are based on past information, might be imprecise to forecast future prices. The new information cannot be anticipated, and these "surprises" affect the spot exchange rates.

This view on exchange rate movements can be exploited using the following model:

$$s_t = \Phi_t + \delta E_t(s_{t+1} - s_t) \tag{3.52}$$

where, Φ_t represents only the economic fundamentals, which affect the exchange rate in period t [i.e., eq. (3.10′)] and $E_t(s_{t+1} - s_t)$ captures the expected percentage change in the exchange rate between the current period (t) and the next period $(t+1)$, based on the information available today (t).

The economic fundamentals are the well-known factors presented previously in eq. (3.10):

$$\Phi_t \equiv s_t = (m_t - m_t^*) - \beta(y_t - y_t^*) + \gamma(i_t - i_t^*) + \varepsilon_t \qquad (3.10')$$

Equation (3.52) represents a more general exchange rate determination formula, which may be viewed as a *reduced form* that can be derived not only from eq. (3.10′), but from a variety of other models of exchange rate determination. Assuming that expectations are rational in eq. (3.52), the current exchange rate and current expectations of future exchange rates are linked, and both depend on expectations concerning the future fundamentals $(E_t\Phi_{t+1})$. Thus, the spot exchange rate depends on the current exchange rate and on the expected percentage change in the future. Due to profit opportunities from arbitrage, this link, eq. (3.52), must be strong, at least, for the exchange rates expected in the near future. Based on the above argument, we expect a high correlation between movements of spot and forward rates. The correlation coefficient between the spot and forward rate (\$/€) is so far $(\rho_{s,f} = +0.97)$, because both rates respond at the same time to the same flow of new information (permanent or transitory). Also, the contemporaneous spot and forward exchange rates are approximately equal, showing that the market's best forecast of the future spot rate is the current spot rate. This phenomenon reveals that exchange rates follow a random walk process.

3.3.2 Exchange Rate Expectations and Unanticipated Events ("News")

An important characteristic of the rational expectations hypothesis is that unanticipated events, surprises, and "news" are affecting assets' returns, prices, and real variables in our economies, which are sensitive to information. The recognition, in the last half of the century, that expectations are extremely important to the economic decision-making process has led to a major revolution in macroeconomic and financial analysis, but at the same time has increased instability and uncertainty. The rational expectations hypothesis developed initially by Muth (1961) has played a critical role in our market-oriented system, and it states that expectations reflected in market behavior will be optimal forecasts using all available information. In the context of exchange rate determination, it is emphasized that the predominant cause of exchange rate movements is the unanticipated "news" (surprises).[5] Thus,

$$s_t = \text{"the expected exchange rate"} + \text{"the unexpected part of the exchange rate"}$$

or

$$s_t = s_t^e + s_t^u$$

As was mentioned earlier, the forward exchange rate summarizes the information that is available to the market when this forward rate is being set $[f_t = E(s_{t+1}|I_t)]$. Therefore, the spot rate can be expressed as a function of factors, which are known in advance and are summarized by the lagged forward rate, plus a function of the "news" and a serially uncorrelated error term, as follows:

$$s_t = \alpha_0 + \alpha_1 f_{t-1} + \alpha_2 \text{"News"}_t + \varepsilon_t \tag{3.53}$$

where, "$News$"$_t$ = variables used in measuring the "news."

Equation (3.53) can be applied to an empirical analysis of the role of unanticipated events "news" as a determinant of the spot exchange rate. The difficulty is in identifying the variables that can be used in measuring the "news." Important variables that are affecting the exchange rate can be the interest rates in the two countries because they are market determined, and "news" affects them promptly. Then, by making the assumption that the (financial) asset market clears fast, and that the "news" is immediately reflected in unexpected changes in the interest rates, eq. (3.53) can be rewritten with an extra term, which represents the surprise element between the interest differential and the expected interest differential between the two countries.

$$s_t = \alpha_0 + \alpha_1 f_{t-1} + \alpha_2[(i_t - i_t^*) - E_{t-1}(i_t - i_t^*)] + \varepsilon_t \tag{3.54}$$

where, $\alpha_0 + \alpha_1 f_{t-1}$ = the expected exchange rate, $\alpha_2[(i_t - i_t^*) - E_{t-1}(i_t - i_t^*)]$ = the unexpected (the innovation) part of the exchange rate ("news"), $(i_t - i_t^*)$ = the actual interest differential in the two countries, and $E_{t-1}(i_t - i_t^*)$ = the expected interest differential based on information available in period $t-1$.

By taking into consideration the most important relationship in international finance, the IRP, the expected interest differential can be computed from a regression by using lagged values of the spot and forward rates, and lagged values of the interest differential, as follows,

$$E_{t-1}(i_t - i_t^*) \equiv (i_t - i_t^*) = \beta_0 + \beta_1 s_{t-1} + \beta_2 s_{t-2} + \beta_3 f_{t-2} + \beta_4 f_{t-3} + \beta_5(i_{t-1} - i_{t-1}^*) + \beta_6(i_{t-2} - i_{t-2}^*) + \varepsilon_t \tag{3.55}$$

Now, we take the difference between the actual interest differential minus the computed expected interest differential, which represents the "news." These two values are used in eq. (3.54); and by running this regression, the computer will give its coefficients. If $\alpha_0 \cong \alpha_2 \cong 0$ and $\alpha_1 \cong 1$, the foreign exchange market is efficient. In the case that $\alpha_2 \neq 0$, this means that the current exchange rate is affected by expectations concerning the future course of events and that the unanticipated changes in the exchange rate are primarily due to innovations. Most of the actual changes in exchange rates are unanticipated, which means that most of the actual changes in exchange rates are due to "news."

3.3.3 *Money Market and Exchange Rate*

Many researchers such as Kallianiotis (2010) have used the spot exchange rate as an independent variable in the money market equilibrium equation, as follows,

$$\frac{M_t}{P_t} = L(Q_t, i_t, S_t) \tag{3.56}$$

$$L_Q > 0, L_i < 0, L_S > 0$$

where, M_t = the money supply, P_t = the price level, Q_t = real income, i_t = nominal rate of interest, and S_t = the spot exchange rate.

An increase in the spot exchange rate (dollar is depreciated) reduces the demand for US dollar (investors and speculators do not want to hold a weak currency). This depreciated dollar will put pressure on the US interest rate to increase in order to attract foreign investment (covering the forward discount of the dollar). The US central bank will in all likelihood, increase the money supply to keep the interest rate at a moderate level. Solving eq. (3.56) for the spot exchange rate and taking the natural logarithm of the variables, we have:

$$s_t = \beta_0 - \beta_1 q_t + \beta_3 i_t + \beta_4 (m_t - p_t) + \varepsilon_t \tag{3.57}$$

The bilateral value of money in the two countries (not only the money supply in a single economy) plays a significant role in the determination of the exchange rate in many theories. The efficient markets approach emphasizes the efficiency of markets reacting to information, rather than market structure. The rational expectations approach, in contrast, emphasizes the structure of the model that explains fundamental market reactions. But, there is also substitutability of currencies across countries.

Thus, currency portfolio substitution or diversification does in fact take place. Money demand, money supply, and exchange rates should be analyzed from an international rather than a country-specific perspective. Starting from a simple closed-economy monetary model with rational expectations, a second currency can be introduced. The two monies are assumed to be substitutes in demand, and an exchange rate exists between them. This model permits the description of the behavior of the exchange rate in terms of anticipated and unanticipated changes in money supplies, money demands, and income:

$$m_t^d - p_t = \beta_0 + \beta_1 q_t - \beta_2 i_t + \varepsilon_t \tag{3.58}$$

$$m_t^s - p_t = exogenous \tag{3.59}$$

where, m_t^d = the ln of money demand, p_t = the ln of price level, m_t^s = the ln of money supply, β_1 = the income elasticity of demand for real balances, β_2 = the interest rate semielasticity of demand for real balances, i_t = the opportunity cost of holding money, q_t = the ln of a measure of real economic activity (income).

A similar system of equations exists for the foreign country. Fluctuations in real incomes lead to aggregate disturbances in the money markets. Given current available information, participants in each market use the structure of the economy, which is known to everyone, to form rational operational forecasts of the general price level. From the above equations (3.58) and (3.59), we can get the spot exchange rate as follows,

$$s_t = f[(m_t - m_t^*), (m_t^d - p_t) - (m_t^{*d} - p_t^*), s_{t+1}^e \,|I_t]\tag{3.60}$$

where, $m_t - m_t^*$ = the nominal stock of money differential in the two countries and $(m_t^d - p_t) - (m_t^{*d} - p_t^*)$ = the real demand for money differential in the two countries.

One result for s_t in eq. (3.60) is that, since any real disturbance leads to an equiproportionate change in the demand for the two currencies (given the assumption of strict money neutrality), real disturbances have no effect on the determination of the exchange rate. In this model, the exchange rate is truly a monetary phenomenon. The exchange rate in this model is also affected by concurrent events, which the market has not anticipated.[6]

Another model takes into consideration the equation of exchange ($MV = QP$) in natural logarithm (ln) terms,

$$m_t + v_t = q_t + p_t \tag{3.61}$$

and the PPP ($S = \frac{P}{P*}$) in natural logarithms,

$$s_t = p_t - p_t^* \tag{3.62}$$

From eq. (3.62), by substituting p_t and p_t^* with their values from eq. (3.61) and a similar one for the foreign country, we get,

$$s_t = (v_t - v_t^*) + (m_t - m_t^*) - (q_t - q_t^*) \tag{3.63}$$

This model is tested in first differences:

$$s_t - s_{t-1} = [(v_t - v_t^*) - (v_{t-1} - v_{t-1}^*)] + [(m_t - m_t^*) - (m_{t-1} - m_{t-1}^*)] \\ - [(q_t - q_t^*) - (q_{t-1} - q_{t-1}^*)] \tag{3.64}$$

where, v_t = the ln of velocity of money, m_t = the ln of stock of money, q_t = the ln of the real output (income), and p_t = the ln of the price level.

3.3.4 *Exchange Rate and Risk (Freezing Funds Risk Premium, Wars, Debt Crises)*

This current ex ante analysis includes an international portfolio balance theory and its implications are used for exchange rate determination.[7] A starting point is the hypothesis that real money demand depends not only on real income, the conventional transactions variable, but also on interest rate and on exchange rate, eq. (3.56), the speculative demand. The internationalization of business and investment opportunities induce speculators to diversify their portfolios of assets denominated in a variety of currencies so that they can maximize their expected return (i_t^e) and minimize its risk (σ_i^2). Many times, we have experienced drastic effects on the value of currencies because these speculators decided to change overnight the content of their portfolios.[8]

These shifts in investments induced by current account imbalances or portfolio diversification create monetary imbalances leading to adjustments in long-run price-level expectations and thus, to exchange rate movements. With perfect mobility of capital, these specifications of money demand imply that the real money demand of a country with a surplus or acquiring its assets rises in the home country while it falls abroad. The relative price level of the country with a surplus or with a high demand of its assets declines and, therefore, exchange rates for given terms of trade tend to appreciate. The demand for monies is affected by an international redistribution of wealth, due to different returns and exchange rate fluctuations. Portfolio effects can arise in the context of imperfect asset substitutability. With uncertain returns, portfolio diversification makes assets imperfect substitutes and gives rise to determinate demands for the respective securities and to yield differentials or a higher risk premium that one currency offers relative to the others.

A portfolio model can provide an explanation for the unanticipated euro (€) appreciation that is only poorly accounted for by speculation, high risk of holding US dollar assets, huge deficits and debts, future uncertainty, and global instability. The system of flexible exchange, the macroeconomic policies, the recent disturbances, and the Iraqi and Afghan crises and the new Syrian and Iranian crisis have created an incentive for portfolio diversification, that the euro would occupy a large share in an efficiently diversified portfolio, and that the resulting portfolio shift or capital flows account for some of the unanticipated appreciation of this new currency and not the EMU fundamentals.

The returns and risks of investors (American, European, and foreign) on assets denominated in dollars and euros are measured, here. The nominal interest rate for a foreign investor (investing abroad) must be as follows (with ex ante calculation), depending on whether the currency is at a forward discount or at a forward premium:

$$i^e_{At+1} = i^{*e}_{t+1} + fp^e_{t+1} \tag{3.65}$$

or

$$i^e_{At+1} = i^{*e}_{t+1} - fd^e_{t+1} \tag{3.66}$$

and

$$fd^e_{t+1} \text{ or } fp^e_{t+1} = f_t - s_t \cong s^e_{t+1} - s_t \tag{3.67}$$

For a domestic investor, the risk-free rate of interest has two components:

$$i^e_{Dt+1} = r^e_{t+1} + \pi^e_{t+1} \tag{3.68}$$

where, i_D = the nominal interest rate (return) for investing domestically, i_A = the interest rate (rate of return) for investing abroad, r = the real rate of interest, π = the inflation rate, fd = the forward discount of the currency, fp = the forward premium, s = the ln of spot exchange rate, f = the ln of forward exchange rate, (^{e}) the expected value of the variable, and an asterisk (*) denotes the foreign country.

These ex ante interest rates can be measured by using a combined regression-time series model as a function of lagged values of interest differential, lagged values of exchange rate, lagged values of inflation differential, and an autoregressive moving-average model (lagged values of the dependent variable and lagged values of the error term):

$$i^e_{t+1} = E(i_{t+1}|I_t) \cong i_t = k + \sum_{j=1}^{m} \alpha_j (i_{t-j} - i^*_{t-j}) + \sum_{j=1}^{n} \beta_j (\pi_{t-j} - \pi^*_{t-j})$$
$$+ \sum_{j=1}^{T} \gamma_j s_{t-j} + \sum_{j=1}^{\Phi} \delta_j i_{t-j} + \sum_{j=1}^{\Psi} \theta_j \varepsilon_{t-j} \tag{3.69}$$

where, $i^e_{t+1} = i^e_{Dt+1}$ *or* i^{*e}_{t+1}

In order to measure the interest rate risk (σ_i^2), a Bollerslev's (1986) model is used, which is an extension of Engle's (1982) original work by developing a technique that allows the conditional heteroscedastic variance to be an ARMA process. This process is the Generalized ARCH (p, q), called the GARCH (p, q), in which the variance is given by

$$\sigma^2_{it} = \omega + \sum_{j=1}^{q} \alpha_j \varepsilon^2_{t-j} + \sum_{j=1}^{p} \beta_j \sigma^2_{t-j} \tag{3.70}$$

where, ε_t = the disturbances or estimated residuals and σ_t^2 = the variance of $\{\varepsilon_t\}$.

The GARCH model has been used extensively by many researchers to characterize patterns of volatility in US dollar foreign exchange markets, in the European Monetary System, and the interest rate risk.

Now, the utility function of an investor, who wants to maximize his next-period return (i_{t+1}) by investing on home (i^A_D *or* i^E_D) and foreign (i^A_A *or* i^E_A) securities and minimize its interest rate risk (σ_i^2) is taken into consideration, as follows,

$$\text{Max } U = u\left[E(i_{t+1}), \sigma_i^2\right] \tag{3.71}$$

where, U = the utility function, $E(i_{t+1})$ = the next-period expected return, and σ_i^2 = the variance of return, i^A_D or i^E_D = return of an American or European investor investing domestically, and i^A_A or i^E_A = the return of an American and a European investing abroad.

The solution of eq. (3.69) will be to construct four different portfolios of four different assets ($i^A_D, i^E_D, i^A_A, i^E_A$) for four different types of investors (American investing in the United States, Europeans investing in the EU, Americans investing abroad, and Europeans investing abroad), which will maximize their returns, $E(i_{t+1})$, and minimize their risks, σ_i^2. If investors choose to invest in the United States or in the EU, due to high return and low risk, the high demand for this country's assets would increase the demand for its currency and the currency will appreciate:

$$E(i^A_{Dt+1}) = i^e_{Dt+1} \tag{3.72}$$

$$E(i^E_{Dt+1}) = i^{*e}_{Dt+1} \tag{3.73}$$

$$E(i^A_{At+1}) = i^{*e}_{t+1} + fp^e_{t+1} \tag{3.74}$$

$$E(i^E_{At+1}) = i^e_{t+1} - fd^e_{t+1} \tag{3.75}$$

where $fp^e_{t+1} \equiv hfp_{t+1}$ = historic forward premium and $fd^e_{t+1} \equiv hfd_{t+1}$ = historic forward discount.

Also, the expected return to variability ratios of these four investment opportunities are calculated, and the objective is to maximize them:

$$\text{Max } E(RVR) = \frac{E(i_{t+1})}{\sigma_i} \tag{3.76}$$

where, $E(RVR)$ = expected return to variability ratio, $E(i_{t+1})$ = expected nominal return of asset j (in the United States or the EU) for an American or a European investor, and σ_i = the standard deviation of the nominal return of this asset j.

Currency market participants are heterogeneous and act on their own bits of private information, as well as on public information. Examples of private information include participants' expectations of future economic variables, perceptions of official and private sector demand, and perceptions of developing shifts in global liquidity and risk taking. Speculators act immediately in advance of exchange rate movements in a way that anticipates the direction of exchange rates and the rate of return. From international finance, we know, "The currency with the higher interest rate will sell forward at a discount, and the currency with the lower interest rate will sell forward at a premium." There is a rule of thumb here. If the currency is at a premium ($S \downarrow$ and $\$ \uparrow$), the interest rate will decline ($i \downarrow$). Then, a correlation exists between S_{t+1} and i_{t+1}. The causality between i_t and S_t ($i \Rightarrow S$) is tested too. If the interest rate causes the exchange rate to change, we can determine the trend of the exchange rate by predicting the future interest rate in the countries in question.

The objective is to seek data that will help us understand what is driving the exchange rate in any given time period. Variables that are viewed as fundamental to dictating currency values (relative money supply, output, inflation rates, interest rate differentials, risk premiums, current accounts and budget deficits, unemployment rates, growth in financial markets, etc.) are constantly analyzed and forecast. Various transaction data are also examined to determine demand changes in different currencies. The results suggest that the expected rate of return and risk in different countries merit inclusion in policy analysis and in ongoing research on exchange rate trend, its dynamics, and its determination. Here, the goal is to forecast the rate of return in different financial assets and their risk and to derive the long-term trend of these interest rates by using the Hodrick-Prescott (HP) filter. In a country when the interest rate increases and the risk falls (increase in RVR), its currency will appreciate.

This filter is a two-sided linear filter that computes the smoothed series I (HPTREND) of i ($i_D^A, i_D^E, i_A^A, i_A^E$) by minimizing the variance of i around I, subject to a penalty that constrains the second difference of I. Then, the HP filter chooses I to minimize the following function,

$$\text{Min} \sum_{t=1}^{T} (i_t - I_t)^2 + \lambda \sum_{t=2}^{T-1} [(I_{t+1} - I_t) - (I_t - I_{t-1})]^2 \qquad (3.77)$$

where, $\lambda =$ the penalty parameter that controls the smoothness of the series (the larger theλ, the smoother the series, as $\lambda \to \infty$, I approaches a linear trend). Here, $\lambda = 14{,}400$ (because data are monthly), as Hodrick and Prescott (1997) mention.

Even though the US dollar had depreciated drastically from 2001 to 2008 (−87.58 percent with respect to the euro), the current account deficits had assumed extraordinary proportions. A current account deficit is matched by a capital account surplus. In other words, a country with a current account deficit surrenders claims on future income (physical assets, stocks, and bonds) to foreigners. The ongoing US current account deficit translates into an average of billion dollars in net capital imports per business day. That is, foreign investors have been accumulating US assets at an unusually high rate. Foreign investors have already started to become wary of holding increasingly larger portions of their wealth in US assets. In order to promote continued investment in the United States, US assets would then have to become more attractive. One way of attracting foreign investments is to lower the price of the asset in foreign currency terms. A decline in the foreign exchange value (depreciation) of the dollar would do just that. Therefore, a large current account deficit might be expected to depress the value of the dollar over time.

Also, at the end of 2002, the exchange rate of the US dollar with respect to the euro was about one (1),[9] but the interest rate began to fall in the United States as preparations for the Iraqi war started. It seems that many investors had begun to invest in the Euro-zone by taking their funds out from the United States. Thus, Arabs and the other Muslim investors, shocked by the war and afraid that the US government might freeze their funds, transferred them to Europe. For a Middle East investor to invest in

US assets he requires a return, which will compensate him for the expected depreciation of the dollar plus a risk premium due to the possibility of freezing his funds.[10] Then, the interest rate in the United States must be:

$$i_{US_t} > i^*_{EU_t} + fd_{\$_t} + FFRP_t \tag{3.78}$$

where, i_{US} = US interest rate on financial assets, i^*_{EU} = Euro-zone interest rate, $fd_{\$}$ = forward discount of the dollar, and $FFRP$ = freezing funds risk premium.

Even though the return is lower in the United States (inequality, eq. 3.78, is not satisfied), investors invest here because of the unparalleled safety, efficiency, stability, transparency, certainty, and liquidity of the US financial markets. Then, inequality, eq. (3.78), is actually as follows:

$$i_{US_t} + SR_t > i^*_{EU_t} + fd_{\$_t} + FFRP_t \tag{3.79}$$

where, SR_t = safety reward.

Thus, investors still find that dollar-denominated claims are an attractive element of any international portfolio. This process of investors seeking the most beneficial combination of risk and return, rebalancing portfolios when opportunities arise, gives rise to a source of capital account dynamics that is unrelated in any direct way to the pattern of trade in goods and services. Of course, the price of oil (see, also, Section 3.3.5), the national debt, the trade deficit, the ongoing wars, and high risk are negatively affecting the value of the dollar. The latest European debt crisis is negatively affecting the spot exchange rate ($S \downarrow$: \$ ↑ and €↓), as is discussed in the next section:

$$s_t = \alpha_0 + \alpha_1 p_{oil_t} + \alpha_2 nd_t + \alpha_3 td_t + \alpha_4 p_{Gold_t} + \alpha_5 WD + \varepsilon_t \tag{3.80}$$

where, p_{oil} = price of oil, nd = national debt, td = trade deficit, p_{Gold} = price of gold (measurement of uncertainty), WD = war dummy (taking values of zero [0] before the third month of 2003 and one [1] after that date).

In other words, financial economists try to establish a relationship between exchange risk premiums and the measure of risk. One popular approach is the consumption-based international asset pricing model, which was built on the premise that the economic agent chooses an optimal time path of consumption and assets that yield uncertain returns. Some empirical results have shown that movements in the conditional risk premiums of returns on the US stock market are similar to those of the conditional risk premiums in the forward foreign exchange markets. Attempts have been made to establish an empirical link between the exchange risk premium and these financial variables.

Some researchers have related the realized return in the foreign exchange markets to the nominal interest rates as follows,[11]

$$s_{t+1} - s_t - (i_t - i_t^*) = \gamma_0 + \gamma_1 i_t + \gamma_2 i_t^* + \varepsilon_{t+1} \tag{3.81}$$

where, $\gamma_1 < 0$, $\gamma_2 > 0$, and $s_t - (i_t - i_t^*) = f_t$ is the covered interest parity condition.

Thus, increases in foreign exchange risk premiums, that is, higher values of $(s_{t+1} - f_t = rp_s)$ are reliably associated with decreases in US interest rates and increases in foreign interest rates. Chiang (1991) has developed a model to link the risk premiums in foreign exchange markets to the equity risk premiums in the stock markets. Returns in the foreign exchange market and the stock market move together over time. The equation can be the following:

$$s_{t+1} - s_t - (i_t - i_t^*) = \delta_0 + \delta_1 (RP^e_{m,t+1} - i_t) + \delta_2 (RP^{*e}_{m^*,t+1} - i_t^*) + \varepsilon_{t+1} \tag{3.82}$$

where, i_t = the three-month T-bill rate, $\delta_1 > 0$, $\delta_2 < 0$, $RP^e_{m,t+1} - i_t$ = the expected equity risk premium in the domestic market, and $RP^{*e}_{m^*,t+1} - i_t^*$ = the expected equity premium in the foreign market.

Empirical evidence supports the hypothesis that exchange risk premiums are empirically associated with the relative expected equity risks in stock markets.

3.3.5 *Oil Prices and Exchange Rate*

The two most watched prices since the 1970s have been the price of gold and the price of oil, which are related to the value of the dollar (its exchange rate). Increases in the price of gold and the price of oil have been caused due to the depreciation of the US dollar.[12] An oil price increase offers an interesting example of possible conflict between an asset market and a goods market view of the exchange rate.[13]

Even though the price of oil continues to go up and the US interest rate (return) is closed to zero,[14] investors are still finding that dollar-denominated claims are an attractive element of any international portfolio (Euro-zone was getting some momentum with the passing of time, but lately, it seems that it is lessened due to the Euro-zone debt crisis). This process of investors seeking the most beneficial combination of risk and return by rebalancing portfolio, when opportunities arise gives rise to a source of capital account dynamics that is unrelated in any direct way to the pattern of trade in goods and services. In the 2000s, the price of oil, the national debt, the trade deficit, the ongoing wars, and the high risk were negatively affecting the value of the dollar. But during the latest global financial crisis, a lot of speculations against the euro had benefited the dollar up to a degree. Of course, until the US economy completely recovers (which should take a couple of years, due to the high unemployment), the dollar cannot appreciate. Another equation, beyond eq. (3.80), which takes into consideration the price of oil and the Euro-zone debt crisis, can be the following:

$$s_t = \alpha_0 + \alpha_1 p_{oil_t} + \alpha_2 nd_t + \alpha_3 td_t + \alpha_4 p_{Gold_t} + \alpha_5 WD + \alpha_6 EDCD + \varepsilon_t \tag{3.83}$$

where, p_{oil_t} = price of oil, nd_t = national debt, td_t = trade deficit, p_{Gold_t} = price of gold (measurement of uncertainty), WD = war dummy (taking values of zero [0] before the third month of 2003 and one [1] after that date), and $EDCD$ = European debt crisis dummy (taking zero [0] before the tenth month of 2009 and one [1] after).

In addition, the effect of the above factors on the current account deficit can be tested with the following equation:

$$ca_t = \beta_0 + \beta_1 TED_t + \beta_2 p_{oil_t} + \beta_3 p_{Gold_t} + \beta_4 nd_t + \beta_5 tot_t + \beta_6 gdp_t + \beta_7 g_t + \varepsilon_t \tag{3.84}$$

where, ca_t = the current account, TED_t = TED spread ($= i_{LIBOR} - i_{RF}$), tot_t = terms of trade ($s_t + p_t^* - p_t$), gdp_t = gross domestic product, and g_t = government spending.

3.3.6 *Monetary, Fiscal, and Trade Policies and Exchange Rate*

The objective of public policies is well known (the citizens' well-being) since the beginning of civilization and the foundation of the city-state by the leadership of a government. Public policies can be fiscal (through taxes and government spending), monetary (with the use of interest rate and money supply), and trade (by intervening in the foreign exchange market). All these policies affect the value of the currency (exchange rate) through the factors mentionedearlier when the exchange rate determination was discussed. A country must have an exchange rate under its control (this is the current problem with the Euro-zone; the member nations do not control the euro's exchange rate) and through this exchange rate, the ultimate objective of public policy is satisfied; which is the maximization of the social welfare of the country. During periods of recessions and high unemployment, public policies must be such that the currency is depreciated and exports are improved, so domestic production is encouraged and increased. Citizens must have incentives to buy domestic products. The opposite policies must be pursued during periods of an overheating economy with high inflation. The currency must appreciate and imports must be encouraged from countries with low cost of production and low prices. Also, other trade restrictions must be eased in this case. The role of government and of the other national authorities cannot be ignored, because this is responsible for the well-being of a nation and its citizens.

Furthermore, we can run a vector autoregression (VAR) estimate to see the effect of monetary (and fiscal) policies on the three most interrelated time series (s, i_{FFF}, i^*_{ONDF}) and to analyze the dynamic impact of random disturbances on the system of our variables. We take the three-variable case VAR, spot exchange rate (s_t), the expected (forecasted) federal funds rate (i_{FFF_t}), and the expected (forecasted) overnight deposit rate ($i^*_{ONDF_t}$), which are affected by past realizations of the variables sequence (endogenous variables) and the i_{FF_t} and $i^*_{OND_t}$ as exogenous (policy instruments) variables, as follows:

$$\begin{aligned} s_t &= \alpha_0 + \alpha_{11} s_{t-1} + \alpha_{12} s_{t-2} + \beta_{11} i_{FFF_{t-1}} + \beta_{12} i_{FFF_{t-2}} \\ &\quad + \gamma_{11} i^*_{ONDF_{t-1}} + \gamma_{12} i^*_{ONDF_{t-2}} + \delta_1 i_{FF_t} + \zeta_1 i^*_{OND_t} + \varepsilon_{1t} \\ i_{FFF_t} &= \beta_0 + \alpha_{21} s_{t-1} + \alpha_{22} s_{t-2} + \beta_{21} i_{FFF_{t-1}} + \beta_{22} i_{FFF_{t-2}} \\ &\quad + \gamma_{21} i^*_{ONDF_{t-1}} + \gamma_{22} i^*_{ONDF_{t-2}} + \delta_2 i_{FF_t} + \zeta_2 i^*_{OND_t} + \varepsilon_{2t} \\ i^*_{ONDF_t} &= \gamma_0 + \alpha_{31} s_{t-1} + \alpha_{32} s_{t-2} + \beta_{31} i_{FFF_{t-1}} + \beta_{32} i_{FFF_{t-2}} \\ &\quad + \gamma_{31} i^*_{ONDF_{t-1}} + \gamma_{32} i^*_{ONDF_{t-2}} + \delta_3 i_{FF_t} + \zeta_3 i^*_{OND_t} + \varepsilon_{3t} \end{aligned} \tag{3.85}$$

where, $\alpha, \beta, \gamma, \delta$, and ζ are parameters to be estimated.

The coefficients δ_1 and ζ_1 will determine the effect of the monetary policy on the spot exchange rate (s_t). The above VAR can be expanded by incorporating some fiscal policy variables, like taxes (T_t) and government spending (G_t) for the two countries, as is done below.

Table A3.10 gives the VAR results and we see that the spot rate depends only on its lagged values. The policy rates (i_{FF} and i^*_{OND}) do not affect the exchange rate. The forecasting US federal funds rate depends on its one period lagged value and on the exogenous federal funds rate. The European overnight rate depends on its one period lagged value and on its own policy rate. The impulse responses appear in figure A3.3. A shock to the j-th variable not only directly affects the j-th variable, but is also transmitted to all the other endogenous variables through the dynamic (lag) structure of the VAR. The impulse response function traces the effect of a one-time shock to one of the innovations on current and future values of the endogenous variables. An increase in the i_{FFF} reduces the spot rate ($\$\uparrow$) and after three months flattens out. An increase in the European overnight deposit rate (i^*_{ONDF}) reduces the spot rate ($euro\downarrow$) and after three months the effect stops.

Of course, central banks and governments can stabilize the economies and reduce uncertainty through their independent public policies and controls over this impersonal global financial system. Political stability, foreign policies, government uprightness, and business ethics are necessary factors to improve an economy and increase confidence toward nations and their assets, which will affect positively the value of their currencies. The response of the two-policy rates (i_{FF} *and* i^*_{OND}) on the exchange rate is negative and lasts for three months, then remaining constant. This means $[i \downarrow (M^s\uparrow) \Rightarrow S \uparrow (\$ \downarrow\ and\ euro\uparrow)]$ for three months (overshoots)[15] and then, stabilizes at a lower level. Testing the effectiveness of monetary policy on the exchange rate shows that it is noneffective $[i_{FF} \downarrow \Rightarrow S \uparrow (\$\downarrow)\ and\ i^*_{OND} \uparrow \Rightarrow S \downarrow (euro\downarrow)]$.[16] Taking into consideration the effect of the FFRP (section 3.3.4) on the exchange rate, it is found that $[FFRP \uparrow \Rightarrow S \uparrow (\$ \downarrow\ and\ euro\uparrow)]$,[17] which is reasonable for our state of the economy, due to the Middle East crises. The results show that the dollar could appreciate with respect to the euro, if the US economy were to show signs of growth (reduction in unemployment) and the Euro-zone were to show signs of deterioration of its deficits, except when it is any other domestic (like an increase in the federal funds rate or ECB rate, due to fear of inflation) or external shock (like, increase in the price of oil) on the two economies (especially in Europe).

Lastly, two other VARs are used, first, for the same endogenous variables (s, i_{FFF}, i^*_{ONDF}) and the four exogenous variables ($i_{FF}, i^*_{OND}, g,$ *and* g^*), and second, for the other interest rates in the two economies and the spot rate by taking six variables as endogenous ($s, i_{STT3M}, i_P, i_{GB}, i^*_{3MDL}, i^*_{GB}$), and two exogenous ones (i_{FF} *and* i^*_{OND}). The results appear in tables A3.11 and A3.12. The spot exchange rate (s) depends on governments' spending (g *and* g^*). The T-bill rate (i_{STT3M}) depends on the lagged exchange rate, on its lagged values, and the second lagged value of the European three-month deposit rate (i^*_{3MDL}) and on the exogenous federal funds rate (i_{FF}). The prime rate (i_P) depends on the lagged T-bill rate (i_{STT3M}), on the second lag of the European government bonds' rate (i^*_{GB}), and on the exogenous federal funds rate (as long as the FOMC raises the Fed funds rate, and the prime follows). At the end, the European three-month deposit rate (i^*_{3MDL}) depends on lagged values of the exchange rate (s), on the second lagged prime rate (i_P), its own one period lagged rate, and on the exogenous federal funds (i_{FF}) and overnight rates (i^*_{OND}).

3.4 Summary

In this chapter different theories of exchange rate determination were developed and efficiency in the foreign exchange market was discussed and tested. First, the balance of payments approach was presented. This model, however, focuses largely on tradable goods and services, ignoring the increasing role of global capital flows. Then, some asset market models were covered in more detail by considering currencies as an important asset class for constructing investment portfolios. Asset prices are influenced mostly by people's willingness to hold the existing quantities of assets, which in turn depends on their expectations regarding the future worth of these assets. The asset market model of exchange rate determination states that "the exchange rate between two currencies represents the price that just balances the relative supplies of, and demand for, assets denominated in those currencies."

The models developed so far do not discuss and do not explain exchange rates and volatility in the longer time frames. It is understood from the above models that many macroeconomic factors affect exchange rates, and in the end, currency prices are a result of the dual forces of demand and supply. The world's currency markets can be viewed as a huge assets market in a large and ever-changing mix of current events, supply and demand factors, information and expectations, and of course, risks constantly shifting and becoming systemic; thus, the price of one currency in relation to another shifts accordingly. No other market encompasses as much of what is going on in the world at any given time as the foreign exchange market. Supply and demand for any given currency, and thus its value, are not influenced by any single element, but rather by several. These elements generally fall into three categories: economic factors (fundamentals), political conditions (government and central bank interventions, public policies: fiscal, monetary, and trade policies, political stability, and uncertainty), and market psychology (expectations, information, and risk). For all these reasons, exchange rate determination is a difficult and dynamic process that needs continuous improvement. The forecasting of the exchange rate still remains a problem.

Appendix 3

A3.1 Exchange Rate Determination: Empirical Results

The objective here is to provide some evidence concerning the theories of exchange rate determination and market efficiency. Least squares regression analyses are used, which provide a method for fitting the mathematical functions discussed in theory earlier to observed data. Also, testing of hypothesis, correlations, pairwise Granger causality tests, GARCH methods of measuring volatility of exchange rate, Hodrick-Prescott filter, VAR, and impulse responses are presented to help the readers understand the theories and be able to do empirical research by using the existing data in our economies.

A3.1.1 Empirical Results of Eq. (3.2)

By taking monthly data between the United States and the Euro-zone (1999:01–2006:12) and running the regression for eq. (3.2), we receive the following results:

$$\begin{aligned} s_t = {} & \underset{(0.873)}{6.458^{***}} - \underset{(1.454)}{3.114^{**}}(p_t - p_t^*) - \underset{(0.419)}{2.573^{***}}(y_t - y_t^*) \\ & - \underset{(0.082)}{0.210^{**}}(i_t - i_t^*) \end{aligned}$$

$$R^2 = 0.404, \quad SSR = 1.116, \quad F = 20.820, \quad D - W = 0.110,$$

$$N = 96$$

The above equation has a very low *D-W* statistic, which means that there is serial correlation of the error term; as a result, the coefficients are biased. We rerun the same regression by correcting the serial correlation of the ε_t:

$$
\begin{aligned}
s_t = \underset{(0.240)}{0.723^{***}} & - \underset{(0.309)}{0.595^{**}}(p_t - p_t^*) - \underset{(0.106)}{0.220^{**}}(y_t - y_t^*) \\
& - \underset{(0.018)}{0.021}(i_t - i_t^*) + \underset{(0.102)}{1.196^{***}} s_{t-1} - \underset{(0.099)}{0.249^{***}} s_{t-2}
\end{aligned}
$$

$R^2 = 0.976, \quad SSR = 0.044, \quad F = 720.645, \quad D - W = 1.860,$

$N = 94$

According to the theory, the signs of the coefficients α_1 and α_3 are wrong, but the overall equation is a good one, based on the resulting statistics.

A3.1.2 Empirical Results of Eqs. (10) and (11)

The results of the constrained model, eq. (3.10), are as follows:

$$
s_t = -\underset{(0.333)}{3.304^{***}}(m_t - m_t^*) + \underset{(0.028)}{0.327^{***}}(y_t - y_t^*) + \underset{(0.048)}{0.280^{***}}(i_t - i_t^*)
$$

$R^2 = 0.539, \quad SSR = 0.863, \quad \ln L^c = 89.955, \quad D - W = 0.228,$

$N = 96$

Now, the unconstrained model, eq. (3.11), gives the following results:

$$
\begin{aligned}
s_t = \underset{(9.218)}{14.824} & - \underset{(0.804)}{4.688^{***}} m_t + \underset{(0.489)}{4.489^{***}} m_t^* + \underset{(1.061)}{2.678^{***}} y_t \\
& - \underset{(1.273)}{5.034^{***}} y_t^* - \underset{(0.070)}{0.120^{*}} i_t + \underset{(0.065)}{0.069}\, i_t^*
\end{aligned}
$$

$R^2 = 0.781, \quad SSR = 0.409, \quad \ln L^u = 125.726, \quad F = 53.022,$

$D - W = 0.434, \quad N = 96$

Testing the hypothesis that the elasticities are the same in both countries, we measure the likelihood ratio statistic, which gives: $-2(\ln L^c - \ln L^u) = -2(89.955 - 125.726) = 71.542$ and is distributed as $\chi^2_{(3)}$ because there are three (3) constraints. The critical value of $\chi^2_{(3)}$ at the 99 percent is 11.34; thus, the null hypothesis (same elasticities) is rejected because, $\chi^2_{(3)} = 71.542 > 11.34$. Consequently, the elasticities are different in these two economies (United States and Euro-zone).

The critical values of the $\chi^2_{(q)}$ distribution are:

Q	90%	95%	99%
3	6.25	7.81	11.34
4	7.78	9.49	13.28
5	9.24	11.07	15.09

Source: Chi-square Distribution Table, http://www.medcalc.org/manual/chi-square-table.php.

As the *D-W* statistics show, the error terms of the above two equations are serially correlated. We can correct the serial correlation by using a $MA(q)$ process. First, eq. (3.10) becomes:

$$\underset{}{s_t = -}\underset{(0.383)}{0.748^{**}}(m_t - m_t^*) + \underset{(0.030)}{0.087^{***}}(y_t - y_t^*) - \underset{(0.018)}{0.030}(i_t - i_t^*)$$

$$+\underset{(0.094)}{1.635^{***}}\varepsilon_{t-1} + \underset{(0.177)}{1.786^{***}}\varepsilon_{t-2} + \underset{(0.204)}{1.493^{***}}\varepsilon_{t-3}$$

$$+\underset{(0.885)}{0.885^{***}}\varepsilon_{t-4}$$

$R^2 = 0.957,\quad SSR = 0.081,\quad \ln L^c = 203.730,$

$D - W = 1.719,\quad N = 96$

The same technique is applied for eq. (3.11) to improve the *D-W* statistic:

$$s_t = -\underset{(2.005)}{8.536^{***}} - \underset{(0.489)}{0.017}\, m_t + \underset{(0.377)}{0.468}\, m_t^* + \underset{(0.358)}{0.843^{**}}\, y_t$$

$$-\underset{(0.428)}{0.420}\, y_t^* - \underset{(0.020)}{0.010}\, i_t + \underset{(0.018)}{0.006}\, i_t^*$$

$$+\underset{(0.093)}{1.653^{***}}\varepsilon_{t-1} + \underset{(0.129)}{1.503^{***}}\varepsilon_{t-2} + \underset{(0.085)}{0.672^{***}}\varepsilon_{t-3}$$

$R^2 = 0.962,\quad SSR = 0.071,\quad \ln L^u = 209.836,\quad F = 242.563,$

$D - W = 1.787,\quad N = 96$

Using similar data, we can run the other specifications of eq. (3.10), which are eqs. (3.10.1), (3.10.2), (3.10.3), and (3.10.4).

A3.1.3 Empirical Results of the "Overshooting Equation," Eq. (3.24)

Equation (3.24) is tested to see whether the monetarist or the overshooting model is correct. First, the equation is a running one as it is in the theory:

$$s_t = -\underset{(0.337)}{3.258^{***}}(m_t - m_t^*) + \underset{(0.036)}{0.397^{***}}(y_t - y_t^*) - \underset{(1.401)}{0.396}(g_{m_t} - g_{m_t^*})$$

$$+ \underset{(0.044)}{0.273^{***}}[(i_t - \pi_t^e) - (i_t^* - \pi_t^{*e})]$$

$R^2 = 0.559, \quad SSR = 0.826, \quad D - W = 0.242,$

$N = 96$

The coefficient $\frac{1}{\Theta} \neq 0$, reveals that the speed of adjustment is small ($\Theta = 3.663$). But the statistics show a high serial correlation of the error term ($D - W \neq 2$) and a correction must take place by using some $MA(q)$ processes:

$$s_t = -\underset{(0.407)}{2.319^{***}}(m_t - m_t^*) + \underset{(0.031)}{0.225^{***}}(y_t - y_t^*)$$

$$+ \underset{(0.232)}{1.232^{***}}(g_{m_t} - g_{m_t^*}) + \underset{(0.022)}{0.043^{**}}[(i_t - \pi_t^e) - (i_t^* - \pi_t^{*e})]$$

$$+ \underset{(0.079)}{1.697^{***}}\varepsilon_{t-1} + \underset{(0.154)}{1.684^{***}}\varepsilon_{t-2} + \underset{(0.156)}{1.183^{***}}\varepsilon_{t-3} + \underset{(0.081)}{0.672^{***}}\varepsilon_{t-4}$$

$R^2 = 0.956, \quad SSR = 0.082, \quad D - W = 1.857, \quad N = 96$

The above equation shows that the results are unbiased and the last term (the real interest differential) is statistically significant (at the 5 percent level) different from zero ($\frac{1}{\Theta} = 0.043 \Rightarrow \Theta = 23.253$). Then, the speed of adjustment ($\Theta \neq \infty$) is finite and the monetarist model is not correct. The empirical results show that we have gradual adjustment, and "overshooting" is taking place.

A3.1.4 Empirical Results of the Portfolio-Balance Approach, Eq. (3.40)

The regression of eq. (3.40) is shown here by taking the US national debt as a proxy for domestic bonds (there are no data for Euro-zone bonds). The results are as follows:

$$s_t = -4.252^{***} - 2.283^{***} m_t + 2.474^{***} nd_t + 0.288 m_t^*$$
$$(0.661) \quad (0.352) \quad (0.173) \quad (0.360)$$
$$- 0.086^{***} i_t + 0.034 i_t^*$$
$$(0.026) \quad (0.024)$$
$$R^2 = 0.915, \quad SSR = 0.201, \quad F = 214.802, \quad D - W = 0.501,$$
$$N = 106$$

A correction for the serial correlation of the error term takes place and the results become:

$$s_t = -4.820^{***} - 1.617^{***} m_t + 1.768^{***} nd_t + 0.402 m_t^*$$
$$(0.811) \quad (0.422) \quad (0.235) \quad (0.390)$$
$$- 0.041^{**} i_t + 0.007 i_t^* + 0.952^{***} \varepsilon_{t-1} + 0.488^{***} \varepsilon_{t-2}$$
$$(0.022) \quad (0.020) \quad (0.097) \quad (0.100)$$
$$R^2 = 0.964, \quad SSR = 0.086, \quad F = 371.194, \quad D - W = 1.654,$$
$$N = 106$$

This regression shows relatively good results according to the theory of the portfolio balance approach. There are two wrong signs, in the domestic and in the Euro-zone money supply, with respect to the theory.

A3.2 Foreign Exchange Market Efficiency: Empirical Results

The theories of this section appeared in 3.3 above.

A3.2.1 Testing for Random Walk, Eq. (3.46)

The random walk (market efficiency) between the US dollar and euro (\$/€) is tested as follows:

$$s_t = 0.003 + 0.988^{***} s_{t-1}$$
$$(0.003) \; (0.013)$$
$$R^2 = 0.973, \quad SSR = 0.119, \quad F = 5{,}651.128, \quad D - W = 1.606,$$
$$N = 157$$

Here, $\alpha_0 \cong 0$(statistically insignificant) and $\alpha_1 = 0.988 \cong 1$(statistically significant at the 1 percent level); then, the market for this s_t is efficient.

A3.2.2 Testing for the Unbiased Forward Rate Hypothesis (UFRH), Eqs. (49) and (50)

The UFRH is tested with eq. (3.49) as follows:

$$s_t = \underset{(0.014)}{0.006} + \underset{(0.044)}{0.972^{***}} f_{t-1}$$

$R^2 = 0.876$, $SSR = 0.053$, $F = 479.709$, $D-W = 1.536$, $N = 70$

The $\alpha_0 \cong 0$ (statistically insignificant) and $\alpha_1 = 0.972 \cong 1$ (statistically significant at the 1 percent level); then, the foreign exchange market for (\$/€) exchange rate is efficient.

Also, the UFRH is tested with eq. (3.50) as follows:

$$s_t = \underset{(0.014)}{0.009} + \underset{(0.101)}{1.074^{***}} f_{t-1} - \underset{(0.101)}{0.114} f_{t-2}$$

$R^2 = 0.878$, $SSR = 0.052$, $F = 237.578$, $D-W = 1.690$, $N = 69$

The $\alpha_0 \cong 0$ (statistically insignificant) and $\alpha_1 + \alpha_2 = 1.074 - 0.114 = 0.960 \cong 1$ (with α_1 statistically significant at the 1 percent level; then, this foreign exchange market is efficient.

A3.2.3 Exchange Rate Predictability, Eq. (3.52)

Testing eq. (3.52) by using $(s_t - s_{t-1})$ for the term $E_t(s_{t+1} - s_t)$, we have the following results:

$$s_t = -\underset{(0.334)}{3.285^{***}}(m_t - m_t^*) + \underset{(0.029)}{0.323^{***}}(y_t - y_t^*) + \underset{(0.049)}{0.271^{***}}(i_t - i_t^*) + \underset{(0.412)}{0.460}(s_t - s_{t-1})$$

$R^2 = 0.547$, $SSR = 0.847$, $D-W = 0.196$, $N = 95$

Now, correcting for the serial correlation of the error term, we have:

$$s_t = -\underset{(0.341)}{1.545^{***}} - \underset{(0.138)}{0.427^{***}}(m_t - m_t^*) + \underset{(0.180)}{0.867^{***}}(y_t - y_t^*)$$

$$+ \underset{(0.008)}{0.023^{***}}(i_t - i_t^*) + \underset{(0.022)}{0.533}(s_t - s_{t-1}) + \underset{(0.082)}{2.210^{***}}\varepsilon_{t-1}$$

$$+ \underset{(0.210)}{2.784^{***}}\varepsilon_{t-2} + \underset{(0.302)}{2.568^{***}}\varepsilon_{t-3} + \underset{(0.301)}{1.922^{***}}\varepsilon_{t-4}$$

$$+ \underset{(0.206)}{1.271^{***}}\varepsilon_{t-5} + \underset{(0.077)}{0.607^{***}}\varepsilon_{t-6}$$

$R^2 = 0.988$, $SSR = 0.022$, $D - W = 1.621$, $N = 95$

A3.2.4 Exchange Rate Expectations and "News," Eq. (3.54)

We start by first running eq. (3.55) to forecast the $E_{t-1}(i_t - i_t^*)$. We generate, $ID_t = (i_t - i_t^*)$and the results of this regression are:

$$ID_t = \underset{(0.155)}{0.176} + \underset{(1.355)}{0.432}\, s_{t-1} + \underset{(2.814)}{1.118}\, s_{t-2} - \underset{(2.408)}{0.304}\, f_{t-2}$$

$$- \underset{(1.470)}{2.311}\, f_{t-3} + \underset{(0.126)}{0.871^{***}}\, ID_{t-1} - \underset{(0.125)}{0.078}\, ID_{t-2}$$

$R^2 = 0.771$, $SSR = 5.312$, $D - W = 1.964$, $N = 69$

The computer gives us the $IDF_t \equiv E_{t-1} ID_t = E_{t-1}(i_t - i_t^*)$from the above equation. With this forecasting interest differential IDF_t, we run eq. (3.54) and the results are:

$$s_t = \underset{(0.013)}{0.008} + \underset{(0.044)}{0.966^{***}} f_{t-1} + \underset{(0.012)}{0.015}(ID_t - IDF_t)$$

$R^2 = 0.883$, $SSR = 0.049$, $F = 244.560$, $D - W = 1.538$,

$N = 68$

This equation shows that $\alpha_0 \cong \alpha_2 \cong 0$(both coefficients statistically insignificant) and $\alpha_1 = 0.966 \cong 1$(statistically significant at the 1 percent level). Thus, the exchange rate market is efficient.

A3.2.5 Money Market and Exchange Rate, Eqs. (3.60) and (3.64)

We take instead of s^e_{t+1} the f_t and the results of eq. (3.60) are:

$$s_t = 0.103\,(m_t - m^*_t) + 0.050\,[(m^d_t - p_t) - (m^{*d}_t - p^*_t)] + 1.032^{***} f_t$$
$$(0.066) \qquad (0.039) \qquad (0.058)$$
$$R^2 = 0.964, \quad SSR = 0.003, \quad D-W = 1.876, \quad N = 32$$

Then, we leave out the velocity differential term and we run eq. (3.63) in first differences $[AR(1) : s_t - s_{t-1}]$, which gives the results of eq. (3.64):

$$s_t = -\,0.252 - 0.568\,(m_t - m^*_t) + 0.239\,(q_t - q^*_t) + 0.987^{***} AR(1)$$
$$(1.288)\;(0.363) \qquad (0.623) \qquad (0.021)$$
$$R^2 = 0.970, \quad SSR = 0.056, \quad D-W = 1.363, \quad N = 95$$

A3.2.6 Exchange Rate and Risks

Table A3.1 presents the exchange rate [USEUS ($/€)]. The sample is divided into two sub-periods, 1999:01–2001:12 (before the introduction of the euro-notes), and 2002:01–2009:11 (after the circulation of the euro-notes). Also, the four rates of returns are calculated by taking into consideration the forward discount (*fd*) or premium (*fp*) of the currencies. The return for an American investor investing in EU was –3.76 percent and for a European investing in the United States was 13.67 percent. The highest return was in the United States, followed by the Euro-zone. During this period, the dollar was at a premium and the euro was at a discount. After 2002, the highest return was in the Euro-zone (8.34 percent), followed by the United States (–4.39 percent return for a European investing in the United States). The dollar was at a discount with respect to the euro and the euro was at a premium. Table A3.1 shows ex post that the high returns in the US assets before 2002 had attracted speculators, and this excess demand for financial assets in the United States had appreciated the US dollar ($S \downarrow$). After 2002, the rate of return was higher in the Euro-zone and this demand for European assets had appreciated the euro ($S \uparrow$). A question still remains here: Was the currency at a premium (before 2002) and then, was the interest rate expected to decline and investment went abroad (after 2002)? Or was the interest rate higher than that abroad and had this caused the appreciation of the dollar? This causality is examinednext.

Tables A3.2, A3.3, and A3.4 give the average return ($\bar{x}$), standard deviation (risk) of the return ($\bar{x}$), and the return to variability ratio ($\frac{i_x}{\sigma_x}$). The

Table A3.1 Spot exchange rates, rates of return, natural logarithms, and forward discounts or premiums

	(1999:01–2009:11)					(1999:01–2001:12)							(2002:01–2009:11)					
	$\bar{S}$	σ_S	$\bar{s}$	σ_s	$fd(+)$	σ_{fd}	$\bar{S}$	σ_S	$\bar{s}$	σ_s	fp(−)	σ_{fp}	$\bar{S}$	σ_S	$\bar{s}$	σ_s	fd(+)	σ_{fd}
USEUS	1.175	0.20	0.15	0.17	2.29	33.15	0.962	0.09	−0.04	0.09	−9.01	30.34	1.255	0.17	0.22	0.14	6.45	33.32

	(1999:01–2009:11)				(1999:01–2001:12)				(2002:01–2009:11)			
	$\bar{i}_j^I$	$\sigma_{i_j^I}$	$\bar{fd}$ or $\bar{fp}$	$\sigma_{fd\ or fp}$	$\bar{i}_j^I$	$\sigma_{i_j^I}$	$\bar{fd}$ or $\bar{fp}$	$\sigma_{fd\ or fp}$	$\bar{i}_j^I$	$\sigma_{i_j^I}$	$\bar{fd}$ or $\bar{fp}$	$\sigma_{fd\ or fp}$
i_{US}^A	2.94	1.84			4.67	1.23			2.28	1.59		
i_{US}^E	0.51	33.61	2.29	33.15	13.67	30.50	−9.01	30.34	−4.39	33.54	6.45	33.32
i_{EU}^E	3.76	1.83			5.25	1.40			3.11	1.62		
i_{EU}^A	4.72	31.34	−2.29	33.15	−3.76	30.24	9.01	30.34	8.34	31.28	−6.45	33.32

Note: USEUS = dollar/euro spot exchange rate ($/€), $\bar{S}$ = the mean spot rate, $\bar{s}$ = the mean of the ln S, σ_S = the standard deviation, *fd* = the forward discount, *fp* = the forward premium, i_{US}^A = US interest rate for an American investor, i_{US}^E = US interest rate for a European investor, i_{EU}^E = EU interest for a European investor, and i_{EU}^A = EU interest for an American investor (investments in *T*-bills).

Source: Economic Time Series Page by Eveline Tainer at http://www.economagic.com and hhttp://www.imfstatistics.org.

Table A3.2 Investments in US and Euro-zone assets: Return, risk, and return to variability ratio (1999:01–2009:11)

	i_{US}^{A}	i_{US}^{E}	i_{EU}^{E}	i_{EU}^{A}
$\bar{x}$	3.207	2.235	3.748	4.721
σ_x	1.700	31.868	1.838	31.345
$\frac{i_x}{\sigma_x}$	1.886	0.070	2.039	0.151

Note: See table A3.1; $\dot{S}$=growth of the US \$/€ exchange rate ($\dot{S}\uparrow \Rightarrow \$\downarrow$), and $\frac{i_x}{\sigma_x}$ =the return to variability ratio.
Source: See table A3.1.

Table A3.3 Investments in US and Euro-zone assets: Return, risk, and return to variability ratio (1999:01–2001:12)

	i_{US}^{A}	i_{US}^{E}	i_{EU}^{E}	i_{EU}^{A}
$\bar{x}$	4.672	13.683	5.248	−3.764
σ_x	1.231	30.495	1.398	30.244
$\frac{i_x}{\sigma_x}$	3.795	0.449	3.754	−0.124

Note: See table A3.1; $\dot{S}$=growth of the U.S \$/€ exchange rate ($\dot{S}\uparrow \Rightarrow \$\downarrow$), and $\frac{i_x}{\sigma_x}$ =the return to variability ratio.
Source: See table A3.1.

Table A3.4 Investments in US and Euro-zone assets: Return, risk, and return to variability ratio (2002:01–2009:11)

	i_{US}^{A}	i_{US}^{E}	i_{EU}^{E}	i_{EU}^{A}
$\bar{x}$	2.582	−2.652	3.108	8.342
σ_x	1.477	31.357	1.622	31.284
$\frac{i_x}{\sigma_x}$	1.748	−0.085	1.916	0.267

Note: See table A3.1; $\dot{S}$=growth of the U.S (\$/€) exchange rate ($\dot{S}\uparrow \Rightarrow \$\downarrow$), and $\frac{i_x}{\sigma_x}$ =the return to variability ratio.
Source: See table A3.1.

highest return, before 2002, was for $i_{US}^{E}=13.683\%$ and the lowest was for $i_{EU}^{A}=-3.764\%$. The lowest risk is for an American investor investing in US T-bills ($\sigma_{i_{US}^{A}}=\pm 1.231\%$), the highest risk was for the European investor investing in the United States ($\sigma_{i_{US}^{E}}=\pm 30.495\%$). The return to variability ratio ranks, first $i_{US}^{A}=3.795$, second $i_{EU}^{E}=3.754$, third $i_{US}^{E}=0.449$, and lastly $i_{EU}^{A}=-0.124$. The high RVR in the United States had appreciated the US dollar and depreciated the euro. The highest return after 2002 was in the EU by an American investor ($i_{EU}^{A}=8.342\%$) and the lowest in the United States for a European investor ($i_{US}^{E}=-2.652\%$). The risk was smaller in the United States for an American investor ($\sigma_{i_{US}^{A}}=1.477\%$) and worst in the United States for a European investor ($\sigma_{i_{US}^{E}}=31.357\%$). The return to variability ratio ranks first in the EU for a European investor (1.916 percent), second in the United States for an American investor (1.748 percent), third in the EU for an American investor (0.267 percent), and least in the United States for an European investor (−0.085 percent). The best country for investors was the EU. This might be the reason why the US dollar depreciated during that period and the euro gained value.

Tables A3.5, A3.6, and A3.7 represent the average expected values, eq. (3.69), and standard deviations, eq. (3.70), of interest rates and exchange rates from 1999:01 to 2009:11; also, their correlation coefficients and the causality between interest rates and exchange rates are given. The United States had higher returns relative to the Euro-zone during that period. The highest correlation of the exchange rate was with the European overnight rate ($\rho=-0.876$) and the European government bonds ($\rho=-0.764$). The euro appreciated and the European interest rate fell (but, when the dollar appreciated, the US interest rate increased, which is a paradox for the US economy). The causality is stronger between exchange rate and interest rates ($S \Rightarrow i$); $[S\uparrow (\$\downarrow) \Rightarrow i_{US}\downarrow \textit{ and } S\uparrow (euro\uparrow) \Rightarrow i_{EU}\downarrow]$.

Table A3.8 forecasts the interest rates, their risk, and the expected return to variability ratios. The results show that Americans would invest abroad (in the EU) because the returns were higher (i.e., 4.251%<4.988%). Also, Europeans would invest domestically because the returns were expected to be higher in the Euro-zone (i.e., 2.543%<3.280%). By considering the risk (interest rate and exchange rate), Americans would invest domestically and Europeans in Europe $[E(RVR)_{US} = 3.026\% \textit{ and } E(RVR)_{EU} = 2.262\%]$, but Europeans would never invest in the United States because

Table A3.5 Statistics of the expected interest rates in financial assets (1999:01–2009:11), eqs. (69) and (70)

Variables	S	s	i_{FF}^{e}	i_{RF}^{e}	i_{P}^{e}	i_{GB}^{e}	i_{OND}^{*e}	i_{3MDL}^{*e}	i_{GB}^{*e}
$\bar{X}$	1.175	0.146	3.204	3.016	6.333	5.498	2.989	3.410	4.803
$\sigma_{\bar{X}}$	0.199	0.173	1.906	1.763	2.100	0.425	0.950	1.961	0.507

Source: See table A3.1.

Table A3.6 Correlation matrix of the expected returns and exchange rate

Variables	*S*	*s*	i^e_{FF}	i^e_{RF}	i^e_P	i^e_{GB}	i^{*e}_{OND}	i^{*e}_{3MDL}	i^{*e}_{GB}
S	1.000								
s	0.999	1.000							
i^e_{FF}	−0.499	−0.489	1.000						
i^e_{RF}	−0.479	−0.468	0.996	1.000					
i^e_P	−0.510	−0.501	0.999	0.996	1.000				
i^e_{GB}	−0.464	−0.451	0.724	0.750	0.732	1.000			
i^{*e}_{OND}	−0.876	−0.881	0.621	0.589	0.632	0.344	1.000		
i^{*e}_{3MDL}	−0.468	−0.457	0.996	0.999	0.996	0.749	0.580	1.000	
i^{*e}_{GB}	−0.763	−0.762	0.644	0.651	0.660	0.808	0.664	0.646	1.000

Source: See table A3.1.

Table A3.7 Pairwise Granger causality tests (1999:01–2009:11)

S($/€)	i^e_{FF}	i^e_{RF}	i^e_P	i^e_{GB}	i^{*e}_{OND}	i^{*e}_{3MDL}	i^{*e}_{GB}
$X \Rightarrow S$	4.485**	4.002**	4.551**	2.594*	3.266**	3.937**	2.722*
$S \Rightarrow X$	5.608***	6.150***	1.308	4.363**	2.167	5.532***	5.628***
$X \Rightarrow s$	4.990***	4.415**	4.672**	2.257	3.615**	4.330**	2.492*
$s \Rightarrow X$	5.770***	6.549***	1.382	4.013**	2.395*	5.906***	5.422***

Note: S=Spot exchange rate, s=ln of S, i^e_{FF}=expected federal funds rate, i^e_{RF}=expected risk-free rate of interest, i^e_P=expected prime rate, i^e_{GB}=expected government bonds rate, i^{*e}_{OND}=expected EU overnight rate, i^{*e}_{3MDL}=expected EU three-month deposit rate (LIBOR), i^{*e}_{GB}=expected EU government bonds rate, $\bar{X}$ =the mean value of the variable, $\sigma_{\bar{X}}$ =the standard deviation of the variable, $X \Rightarrow S$=X causes S, ***=significant at the 1percent level, **=significant at the 5 percent level, and *=significant at the 10 percent level.
Source: See table A3.1.

$[E(RVR)_{US} = 0.448\% < E(RVR)_{EU} = 0.878\%]$. As a result, it was difficult for the dollar to appreciate.

Figure A3.1 shows the natural logarithm of the spot exchange rate and the two monetary policy variables (interest rates) in the United States, the federal funds rate (USFFR), and in the EMU, the overnight deposit rate (EUOND). The correlations are here: $\rho_{s,i_{FF}} = -0.238$ *and* $\rho_{s,i^*_{OND}} = -0.321$. The correlations between the actual and the forecasting interest rates are very high, $\rho_{i_{FF},i_{FFF}} = 0.997$ *and* $\rho_{i^*_{OND},i^*_{ONDF}} = 0.990$, which means that the forecasting is very good. Finally, $\rho_{i_{FF},i^*_{OND}} = 0.599$ *and* $\rho_{i_{FFF},i^*_{ONDF}} = 0.587$. The causality between the spot rate and these two policy rates goes both ways, but it is

Table A3.8 Expected (forecasting) interest rates, eq. (3.69), their risk, eq. (3.70), and expected return to variability ratio, eq. (3.76)

	U.S. Financial Assets			*EU Financial Assets*	
Variables	i_D^A	i_A^E	*Variables*	i_D^E	i_A^A
$E(i_{FF})$	4.251%	2.543%	$E(i^*_{OND})$	3.280%	4.988%
$E(\sigma_{i_{FF}})$	1.975%	32.166%	$E(\sigma_{i^*_{OND}})$	2.102%	32.293%
hfd or hfp	−1.708%	−1.708%	*hfd or hfp*	+1.708%	+1.708%
$E(RVR)$	3.026%	0.448%	$E(RVR)$	2.262%	0.878%
$E(i_{TB})$	5.005%	3.297%	$E(i^*_{3MDL})$	4.336%	6.044%
$E(\sigma_{i_{TB}})$	3.209%	33.400%	$E(\sigma_{i^*_{3MDL}})$	2.732%	32.923%
hfd or hfp	−1.708%	−1.708%	*hfd or hfp*	+1.708%	+1.708%
$E(RVR)$	2.794%	0.570%	$E(RVR)$	2.623%	1.053%
$E(i_P)$	7.219%	5.511%			
$E(\sigma_{i_P})$	2.707%	32.898%			
hfd or hfp	−1.708%	−1.708%			
$E(RVR)$	4.388%	0.961%			
$E(i_{GB})$	4.844%	3.136%	$E(i^*_{GB})$	4.307%	6.015%
$E(\sigma_{i_{GB}})$	3.300%	33.491%	$E(\sigma_{i^*_{GB}})$	2.094%	32.285%
hfd or hfp	−1.708%	−1.708%	*hfd or hfp*	+1.708%	+1.708%
$E(RVR)$	2.665%	0.542%	$E(RVR)$	2.977%	1.059%

Note: See tables A3.1 and A3.7; $\sigma_{hfd} = \pm 30.191\%$, $\sigma_{i_A^E}$ or $\sigma_{i_A^A} \equiv \sigma_{i^*} = \sigma_i + \sigma_{hfd}$

Source: See table A3.1.

stronger from the spot rate to the interest rate ($S \Rightarrow i$). Both interest rates were falling lately, and this fall in interest rates causes the spot exchange rate to increase [$i \downarrow \Rightarrow S \uparrow$ (\$ $\downarrow$, *euro* $\uparrow$)]. Any time that there is a decrease of $\Delta i = -1\%$ the dollar will depreciate by $\Delta S = +0.238\%$ (capital outflow depreciates the dollar) and when there is a change of $\Delta i^* = -1\%$, the euro will appreciate by $\Delta S = +0.321\%$ (expectations of appreciation of the euro reduces the European interest rate).

Next, a smooth estimate of the long-term trend of the rate of return in the two different economies (US and EMU) and the spot exchange rate using a Hodrick-Prescott filter, eq. (3.77), takes place. Figure A3.2 shows that the trend for the US interest rate is negative and this decline in interest rate will keep the exchange rate flat (dollar will continue to stay at the current rate). The trend of the interest rate in the Euro-zone is negative too,

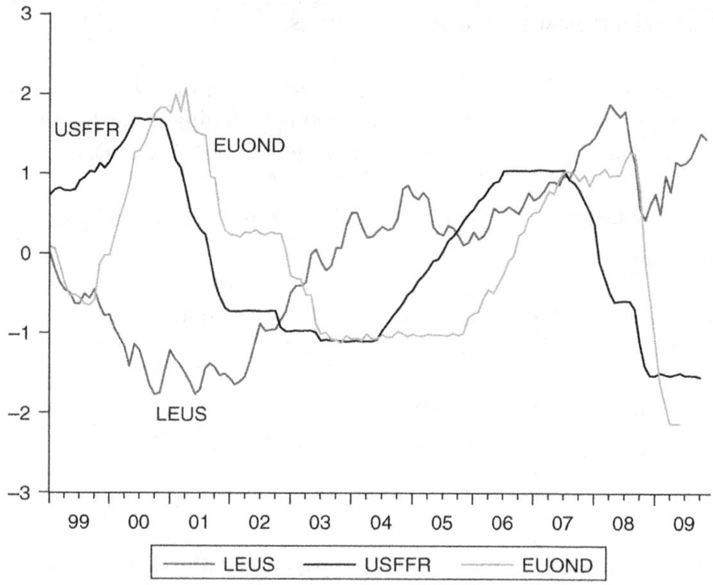

Figure A3.1 Exchange rate and policy rates.

Note: LEUS = ln of S ($/€), USFFRF = forecasting U.S. federal funds rate, and EUONDF = forecasting ECB overnight deposit rate. Also, $\rho_{s,i_{FF}} = -0.238$ and $\rho_{s,i^*_{OND}} = -0.321$, and depreciation of the US dollar causes the US interest rate to fall and an appreciation of the euro causes the Euro-zone rate to fall.

Source: See table A3.1.

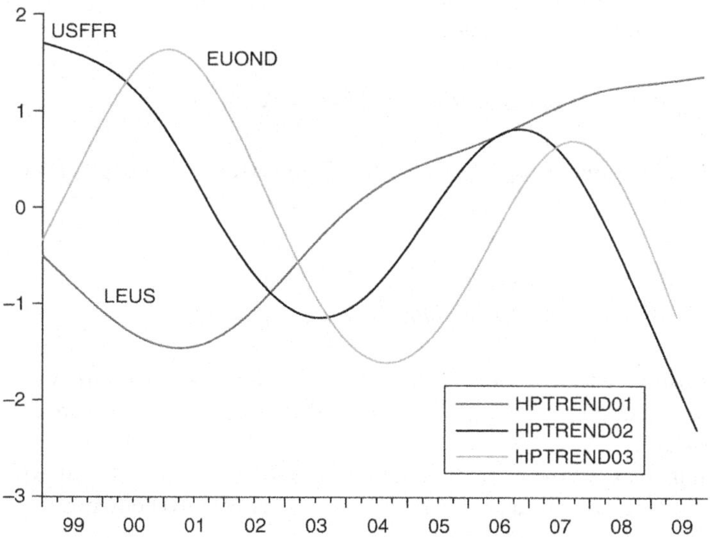

Figure A3.2 Smooth estimate of the *L-T* Trend of the policy rates and exchange rate (Hodrick-Prescott Filter).

Note: HPTREND01 = LEUS (ln of the spot exchange rate), HPTREND02 = USFFR (U.S. federal funds rate), and HPTREND03 = EUOND (ECB overnight deposit rate). As $s \uparrow \Rightarrow i_{FF} \downarrow$ *and* $i_{OND} \downarrow$, the trend was at that time (2009): $i_{FF} \downarrow \Rightarrow \bar{s} \uparrow (\bar{\$} \downarrow)$ *and* $i_{OND} \downarrow \Rightarrow \bar{s} \uparrow (\bar{euro} \uparrow)$, both effects were going in the same direction, then, the euro might continue to appreciate a little with respect to the US dollar.

which means that the euro might appreciate a little or will stay as it was at that time. Lastly, the exchange rate trend is flattening out, which means that the exchange rate will stay as it was (with some appreciation of the dollar).

Then, we test eq. (3.80), to see the effects of war on the exchange rates, which gives:

$$\begin{aligned} s_t = & -\underset{(0.850)}{2.827^{***}} + \underset{(0.025)}{0.061^{**}} p_{oil_t} + \underset{(0.102)}{0.312^{***}} nd_t + \underset{(0.149)}{0.421^{***}} ca_t \\ & + \underset{(0.030)}{0.141^{***}} WD + \underset{(0.062)}{0.792^{***}} \varepsilon_{t-1} \end{aligned}$$

$$R^2 = 0.936, \quad SSR = 0.217, \quad F = 336.171$$

The war dummy (WD), the price of oil (p_{oil}), the national debt (ND), and the current account deficit (ca) depreciate the dollar $(s_t \uparrow)$ and

$$\begin{aligned} s_t = & -\underset{(0.898)}{3.034^{***}} + \underset{(0.021)}{0.106^{***}} p_{oil_t} + \underset{(0.113)}{0.243^{**}} nd_t + \underset{(0.041)}{0.094^{**}} p_{Gold_t} \\ & + \underset{(0.025)}{0.043^{*}} WD + \underset{(0.031)}{0.896^{***}} s_{t-1} \end{aligned}$$

$$R^2 = 0.979, \quad SSR = 0.075, \quad F = 1,120.72$$

The price of gold (p_{Gold}), as a measure of uncertainty has depreciated the dollar, too.

A3.2.7 *Oil Prices and Exchange Rate*

The positive effect of the price of oil on the spot exchange rate was presented in section A3.2.6, eq. (3.80). Now, the results of eq. (3.83) are shown in table A3.9.

An increase in the price of oil depreciates the US dollar. The oil exporting countries try to keep their oil proceeds constant (knowing the US' inelastic demand for oil).

A3.2.8 Public Policies and Exchange Rate

Furthermore, we run a vector autoregression (VAR) estimate, eq. (3.85), to forecast the system of the three most interrelated time series (s, i_{FFF}, i^*_{ONDF}) and to analyze the dynamic impact of random disturbances on the system of our variables. Table A3.10 gives the VAR results and we see that the spot rate depends only on its lagged values. The policy rates (i_{FF} and i^*_{OND}) do not affect the exchange rate. The impulse responses appear in figure A3.3. An increase in the i_{FFF} reduces the spot rate (\$↑) and after three months it flattens out. An increase in the i^*_{ONDF} reduces the spot rate (*euro*↓) and after three months it stops.

The empirical results show that the two monetary policy rates (i_{FF} and i^*_{OND}) have no effect on the spot exchange rate (s_t).

Figure A3.3 shows response of the forecasting policy rates in the United States and the EMU to the spot exchange rate (s).

Also, tables A3.11 and A3.12 give two more VARs estimates, which show the effect of public policies (monetary and fiscal) on the spot exchange rates and on different interest rates.

Table A3.11 reveals that fiscal policy (g and g^*) is effective in both economies; an increase in government spending depreciates their currencies (their deficits increase).

Target rates (i_{FF} *and* i^*_{OND}) affect the other interest rates. Interest rates must stay low in our economies because they increase the cost of production, prices, inflation, deficits, and debts and cause a redistribution of wealth from borrowers to lenders. Lastly, graph A3.1 shows the US dollar volatility with respect to the major currencies of the world, which has increased drastically after 1973.

Table A3.9 Estimation of the US/Euro-zone spot exchange rate, eq. (3.83)

Variables	s_t	s_t	s_t	s_t	s_t
α_0	0.897	−2.544***	1.695**	−1.211	−2.662***
	(0.566)	(0.585)	(0.791)	(0.756)	(0.612)
p_{oil_t}	0.111***	0.132***	0.048**	0.097***	0.130***
	(0.020)	(0.021)	(0.025)	(0.023)	(0.021)
nd_t	−0.129**	0.237***	−0.357***	0.047	0.252***
	(0.066)	(0.068)	(0.121)	(0.109)	(0.072)
ca_t	0.686***	−0.148	0.466***	0.120	−0.116
	(0.132)	(0.146)	(0.137)	(0.145)	(0.149)

continued

Table A3.9 Continued

Variables	s_t	s_t	s_t	s_t	s_t
p_{Gold_t}	–	–	0.234***	0.087*	–
			(0.068)	(0.052)	
WD	0.264***	0.057***	0.237***	0.119***	0.058**
	(0.026)	(0.024)	(0.026)	(0.027)	(0.025)
EDCD	–	–	−0.057**	−0.047*	−0.026
			(0.028)	(0.028)	(0.026)
MA(1)	–	1.276***	–	1.073***	1.257***
		(0.075)		(0.077)	(0.076)
MA(2)	–	–	–	–	1.048***
					(0.100)
R^2	0.849	0.969	0.867	0.958	0.969
SSR	0.614	0.127	0.538	0.170	0.126
D − *W*	0.265	1.719	0.310	1.530	1.729
F	190.552	586.632	145.865	377.290	513.154
N	141	141	141	141	141

Note: s_t = spot exchange rate, p_{oil_t} = price of oil, nd_t = national debt, ca_t = current account, p_{Gold_t} = price of gold, *WD* = war dummy, *EDCD* = European debt crisis dummy, *AR* = autoregessive process, *MA* = moving average process, R^2 = R-squared, *SSR* = sum of squared residuals, *D* − *W* = Durbin-Watson statistic, *F* = *F*-statistic, *N* = number of observations, (*), (**), and (***) = significant at the 10 percent, 5 percent, and 1 percent level, standard errors in parentheses, and the lower case letters are the natural logarithms (ln) of the capital ones.

Source: See table A3.1.

Table A3.10 Vector autoregression estimates (s, i_{FFF}, i^*_{ONDF}), eq. (3.85) (exogenous variables: i_{FF}, i^*_{OND})

Variables	s	i_{FFF}	i^*_{ONDF}
s_{t-1}	1.167***	0.277	−0.338
	(0.114)	(0.518)	(0.454)
s_{t-2}	−0.264***	−0.276	0.175
	(0.114)	(0.520)	(0.455)
$i_{FFF_{t-1}}$	−0.005	0.249***	0.075
	(0.021)	(0.093)	(0.082)
$i_{FFF_{t-2}}$	−0.015	0.094	−0.057
	(0.016)	(0.074)	(0.065)
$i^*_{ONDF_{t-1}}$	0.028	0.078	0.310***
	(0.028)	(0.126)	(0.110)
$i^*_{ONDF_{t-2}}$	−0.019	−0.079	0.150
	(0.021)	(0.096)	(0.085)
C	0.034	0.156	0.061
	(0.025)	(0.114)	(0.100)

continued

Table A3.10 Continued

Variables	s	i_{FFF}	i^*_{ONDF}
i_{FF}	0.014	0.679***	0.009
	(0.014)	(0.062)	(0.054)
i^*_{OND}	−0.013	−0.074	0.492***
	(0.016)	(0.072)	(0.063)
R^2	0.975	0.997	0.992
SSR	0.039	0.803	0.616
F-Statistic	354.938	3364.964	1100.894

Note: s = ln of S, i_{FFF} = expected federal funds rate, i^*_{ONDF} = expected EU overnight deposit rate, i_{FF} = actual federal funds rate, i^*_{OND} = actual EU overnight deposit rate, *** = significant at the 1 percent level, ** = significant at the 5 percent level, and * = significant at the 10 percent level.
Source: See table A3.1.

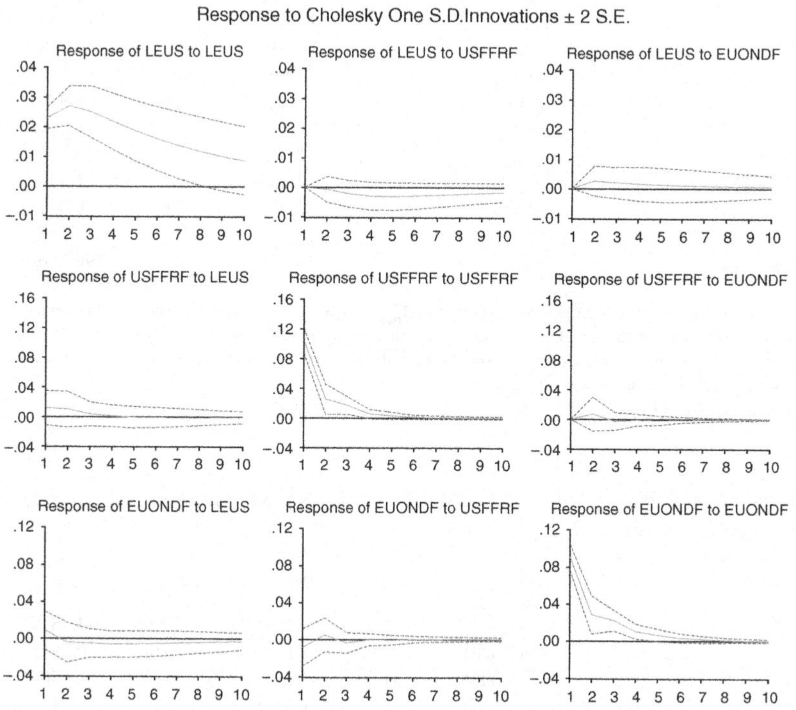

Figure A3.3 The impulse response functions.

Note: See table A3.10; LEUS = ln of S ($/€), USFFRF = US federal funds rate forecasting, and EUONDF = EU overnight deposit rate forecasting.

Source: See table A3.1 and table A3.10.

Table A3.11 Vector autoregression estimates (s, i_{FFF}, i^*_{ONDF}) (exogenous–ariables: $i_{FF}, i^*_{OND}, g, g^*$)

Variables	s	i_{FFF}	i^*_{ONDF}
s_{t-1}	1.099***	0.179	−0.596
	(0.119)	(0.565)	(0.487)
s_{t-2}	−0.319***	−0.202	−0.113
	(0.123)	(0.582)	(0.502)
$i_{FFF_{t-1}}$	0.003	0.259***	0.103
	(0.021)	(0.101)	(0.087)
$i_{FFF_{t-2}}$	−0.010	0.090	−0.029
	(0.017)	(0.081)	(0.070)
$i^*_{ONDF_{t-1}}$	0.028	0.095	0.276***
	(0.028)	(0.133)	(0.115)
$i^*_{ONDF_{t-2}}$	−0.030	−0.111	0.147
	(0.022)	(0.104)	(0.089)
C	−0.016	2.580	−3.793
	(0.025)	(0.114)	(0.100)
i_{FF}	0.001	0.652***	−0.022
	(0.015)	(0.070)	(0.061)
i^*_{OND}	−0.009	−0.039	0.468***
	(0.019)	(0.090)	(0.078)
g	0.696***	1.498	0.976
	(0.323)	(1.529)	(1.318)
g^*	−0.894**	−2.365	−0.593
	(0.476)	(2.256)	(1.945)
R^2	0.976	0.997	0.992
SSR	0.034	0.762	0.566
F-Statistic	259.504	2453.761	790.450

Note: s = ln of S, i_{FFF} = expected federal funds rate, i^*_{ONDF} = expected EU overnight rate, i_{FF} = actual federal funds rate, i^*_{OND} = actual EU overnight deposit rate, g = the ln of US government spending, g^* = the ln of the EU government spending, *** = significant at the 1% level, ** = significant at the 5 percent level, and * = significant at the 10 percent level.
Source: See table A3.1.

Table A3.12 Vector autoregression estimates (s, $i_{STT3M}, i_P, i_{GB}, i^*_{3MDL}, i^*_{GB}$) (exogenous variables: i_{FF}, i^*_{OND})

Variables	s	i_{STT3M}	i_P	i_{GB}	i^*_{3MDL}	i^*_{GB}
s_{t-1}	1.172***	−2.104**	−0.045	−4.758***	−2.706***	−3.481***
	(0.927)	(0.670)	(0.190)	(1.139)	(0.616)	(0.881)
s_{t-2}	−0.254*	1.308*	−0.070	3.134**	1.850**	1.856**
	(0.137)	(0.640)	(0.181)	(1.087)	(0.588)	(0.841)
$i_{STT3M_{t-1}}$	−0.016	0.360*	0.162***	−0.274	−0.144	−0.187
	(0.036)	(0.169)	(0.048)	(0.288)	(0.156	(0.223)
$i_{STT3M_{t-2}}$	0.035	−0.290	−0.097*	−0.144	−0.095	−0.365
	(0.038)	(0.176)	(0.050)	(0.298)	(0.162)	(0.231)

continued

Table A3.12 Continued

Variables	s	i_{STT3M}	i_P	i_{GB}	i^*_{3MDL}	i^*_{GB}
$i_{P_{t-1}}$	0.027	−0.298	0.145**	0.751*	0.068	0.883**
	(0.051)	(0.237)	(0.067)	(0.403)	(0.218)	(0.312)
$i_{P_{t-2}}$	−0.046	−0.243*	−0.032	−0.278	−0.253*	−0.328*
	(0.032)	(0.143)	(0.040)	(0.242)	(0.131)	(0.187)
$i_{GB_{t-1}}$	0.003	−0.029	0.028	0.658**	0.023	−0.042
	(0.031)	(0.146)	(0.041)	(0.247)	(0.134)	(0.191)
$i_{GB_{t-2}}$	0.019	0.077	−0.041	−0.106	−0.181	0.022
	(0.029)	(0.136)	(0.039)	(0.231)	(0.125)	(0.179)
$i^*_{3MDL_{t-1}}$	0.049	−0.010	−0.025	0.116	0.308*	−0.382
	(0.039)	(0.184)	(0.052)	(0.313)	(0.169)	(0.242)
$i^*_{3MDL_{t-2}}$	−0.038	0.612***	0.068	0.199	0.267	0465*
	(0.038)	(0.179)	(0.051)	(0.304)	(0.165)	(0.235)
$i^*_{GB_{t-1}}$	−0.001	0.039	−0.070	0.094	0.063	1.018***
	(0.037)	(0.173)	(0.049)	(0.293)	(0.159)	(0.227)
$i^*_{GB_{t-2}}$	−0.029	−0.048	0.096*	−0.019	0.206	−0.143
	(0.038)	(0.175)	(0.050)	(0.297)	(0.161)	(0.230)
c	0.064	1.806*	2.682***	1.357	1.085	−0.243
	(0.195)	(0.909)	(0.257)	(1.544)	(0.836)	(1.195)
i_{FF}	−0.020	0.786***	0.790***	−0.314	0.894***	−0.067
	(0.028)	(0.131)	(0.037)	(0.223)	(0.121)	(0.172)
i^*_{OND}	0.017	−0.137*	−0.032	−0.312**	−0.335***	−0.277**
	(0.016)	(0.073)	(0.021)	(0.124)	(0.067)	(0.096)
R^2	0.967	0.998	0.999	0.884	0.998	0.973
SSR	0.026	0.565	0.045	1.633	0.478	0.977
F-Statistic	101.316	1446.212	20877.30	26.117	2123.423	56.598

Note: See table A3.10; i_{STT3M} = the US three-month *T*-Bill rate, i_P = the US prime rate, i_{GB} = the US (ten-year maturity) government bonds rate, i^*_{3MDL} = the European three-month deposit LIBOR, and i^*_{GB} = the European (ten-year maturity) government bonds rate.
Source: See table A3.1.

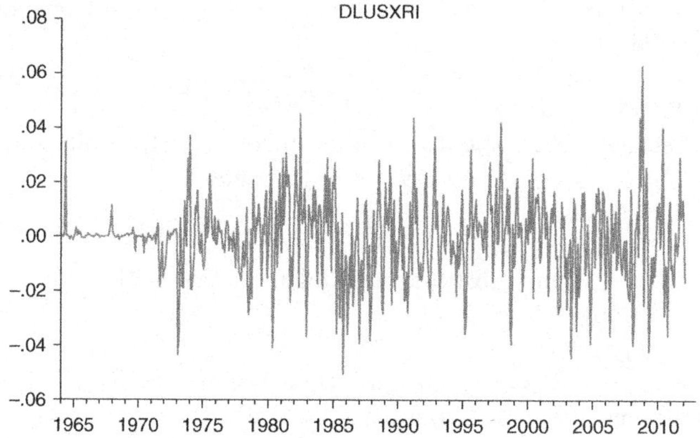

Graph A3.1 US dollar volatility with respect to the major currencies.

Note: *USXRI* = US trade-weighted xxchange rate index (FC/$) and *DLUSXRI* = $\ln USXRI_t - \ln USXRI_{t-1}$ (the rate of growth of the exchange rate index).

Source: *Economagic.com*.

Notes

1. See, Bilson (1978) and Kallianiotis (1988).
2. See, Mishkin (1983, pp. 17–20).
3. The price of oil from 1950 to 2012 has a mean value of ($\bar{P}_{oil}$ = \$21.87) per barrel and a standard deviation of ($\sigma_{P_{oil}} = \pm\$24.84$); its minimum price was \$2.57 and its maximum price was \$144.15 (July 2008). The increase of its price was 5,509 percent or 94.98 percent per annum, which has contributed to the global inflation, risk, and recessions. (*Economagic.com*).
4. White noise process is a sequence $\{\varepsilon_t\}$ if each value in the sequence has a mean value of zero, a constant variance, and is serially uncorrelated. If the notation $E(R)$ denotes the theoretical mean value of R, the sequence $\{\varepsilon_t\}$is a white-noise process for each time period t, $E(\varepsilon_t) = 0$, $E(\varepsilon_t^2) = \sigma^2$, and $E(\varepsilon_t, \varepsilon_{t-1}) = 0$.
5. See, Dornbusch (1978), Bilson (1978), Frenkel and Mussa (1980), Isard (1980), and Frenkel (1984).
6. See, Canto and Miles (1984).
7. See, Kallianiotis and Bianchi (2009).
8. This caused the Southeast Asian crisis in June 1997. See, http://www.westga.edu/~bquest/2003/asian.htm.
9. On December 31, 2002, it was 1.0194 \$/€. (*Economagic.com*).
10. For example, by looking at the average policy rates in the US and Euro-zone from 1999:01 to 2006:12, we have: $\bar{i}_{FF} = 3.43\%, \sigma_{i_{FF}} = \pm 1.88\%$; $\bar{i}^*_{OND} = 2.98\%, \sigma_{i^*_{OND}} = \pm 0.91$; $\bar{fd}_\$ = 0.0014, \sigma_{fd_\$} = 0.025$; and $FFR\bar{P} = 0.434\%, \sigma_{FFRP} = \pm 1.594\%$. During 2003–2004, the interest rate in the United States was 1 percent and the interest rate in the EMU was 1.97 percent plus 0.17 percent the $fd_\$$ and 0.434 percent the average FFRP, which gave a total return of 2.574 percent for investing in the Euro-zone. Consequently, no one could have invested in US assets.
11. See, Giovannini and Jorion (1987).
12. The causality and correlation between spot exchange rate (\$/€) and price of oil and gold are:

    (i) $F = 3.528^{**}$, $S \uparrow (\$ \downarrow) \Rightarrow P_{oil} \uparrow$ and $\rho_{S,P_{oil}} = +0.843$

    (because the payments of oil are made with US dollars and the OPEC countries want a constant revenue)

    (ii) $F = 1.660^{*}$, $S \uparrow (\$ \downarrow) \Rightarrow P_{gold} \uparrow$ and $\rho_{S,P_{gold}} = +0.719$

    (because of the substitution of dollar reserves with gold)

    (iii) $F = 3.045^{***}$, $P_{oil} \uparrow \Rightarrow P_{gold} \uparrow$ and $\rho_{P_{oil},P_{gold}} = +0.802$

    (because risk is going up and people invest in precious metals).
13. See, Krugman (1984) and Ghosh and Kallianiotis (2012).

14. The three-month US T-Bill rate was $i_{T-Bill}=0.100\%$ and the target rate $i_{FF}=0.25\%$, but the effective federal funds rate was $i_{FF}^{eff}=0.14\%$. (*The Wall Street Journal*, August 13, 2012, p. C5).
15. See, Dornbusch (1976), and Kallianiotis and Bianchi (2009).

$$s_t = 0.301^{***} - 0.019^{**}\, i_{FF_t} - 0.031^{**}\, i^*_{ond_t}$$
$$(0.039) \qquad (0.009) \qquad (0.016)$$
$$+\, 1.456^{***}\varepsilon_{t-1} + 0.770^{***}\varepsilon_{t-2}$$
$$(0.053) \qquad (0.054)$$

16. The regression is:

$$R^2 = 0.886, \quad SSR = 0.468, \; F = 271.249$$

17. These results are as follows:

$$s_t = 0.240 + 0.005^{*}\, i^*_{OND_t} + 0.007^{***} FFRP_t + 0.001^{***} fd_{\$_t}$$
$$(0.203)\;(0.002) \qquad (0.002) \qquad (0.001)$$
$$+\, 0.984^{***} s_{t-1} + 1.205^{***}\varepsilon_{t-1} + 0.217^{**}\varepsilon_{t-2}$$
$$(0.016) \qquad (0.088) \qquad (0.087)$$
$$R^2 = 0.994, \quad SSR = 0.026, \quad F = 3{,}543.402$$

Bibliography

Arize, Augustine C., Theologos H. Bonitsis, Ioannis N. Kallianiotis, Krishna M. Kasibhatla, and John Malindretos (2000), *Balance of Payments Adjustment: Macro Facets of International Finance Revisited*, Westport, CT: Greenwood Press.

Bhandari, Jagdeep S. and Bluford H. Putnam (1984), *Economic Interdependence and Flexible Exchange Rates*, Cambridge, MA: The MIT Press.

Bilson, John (1978), "Rational Expectations and the Exchange Rate," in *The Economics of Exchange Rates*, edited by J. Frenkel and H. G. Johnson, Reading MA: Addison-Wesley.

Bollerslev, Tim (1986), "Generalized Autoregressive Conditional Heteroscedasticity," *Journal of Econometrics*, Vol. 31, pp. 307–327.

Canto, Victor A. and Marc A. Miles (1984), "Exchange Rates in a Global Monetary Model with Currency Substitution and Rational Expectations," in *Economic Interdependence and Flexible Exchange rates*, edited by J. S. Bhandari and B. H. Putnam, Cambridge, MA: The MIT Press, pp. 157–175.

Chiang, T. (1991), "International Asset Pricing and Equity Market Risks," *Journal of International Money and Finance*, Vol. 10, September, pp. 365–391.

Dornbusch, Rudiger (1976), "Expectations and Exchange Rate Dynamics," *Journal of Political Economy*, Vol. 84, No. 6, December, pp. 1161–1176.

Dornbusch, Rudiger (1978), "Monetary Policy under Exchange Rate Flexibility," in *Managed Exchange-Rate Flexibility: The Recent Experience*, Federal Reserve Bank of Boston Conference Series, No. 20.

Enders, Walter (1995), *Applied Econometric Time Series*, New York, NY: John Wiley & Sons, Inc.

Engle, Robert F. (1982), "Autoregressive Conditional Heteroscedasticity with Estimates of the Variance of United Kingdom Inflation," *Econometrica*, Vol. 50, July, pp. 987–1007.

Fama, E. (1970), "Efficient Capital Markets: A Review of Theory and Empirical Work," *Journal of Finance*, 25, May, pp. 383–417.

Frenkel, Jacob A. (1984), "Flexible Exchange Rates, Prices, and the Role of 'News': Lessons from the 1970s," in *Economic Interdependence and Flexible Exchange Rates*, edited by J. S. Bhandari and B. H. Putnam, Cambridge, MA: The MIT Press, pp. 3–41.

———. (1983), *Exchange Rates and International Macroeconomics*, National Bureau of Economic Research, Chicago: The University of Chicago Press.

Frenkel, Jacob A. and Michael L. Mussa (1980), "The Efficiency of Foreign Exchange Markets and Measures of Turbulence," *American Economic Review*, Vol. 70, pp. 374–381.

Ghosh, Satyajit and Ioannis N. Kallianiotis (2012), "Uncertainty, Oil Prices, Debts, Deficits, and Exchange Rates Dynamics," unpublished manuscript, *University of Scranton*, June, pages 24.

Giovannini, A. and Philippe Jorion (1987), "Interest Rates and Risk Premia in the Stock Market and in the Foreign Exchange Market," *Journal of International Money and Finance*, Vol. 6, No. 1, March, pp. 107–124.

Hodgson, Douglas J., Oliver Linton, and Keith Vorkink (2004), "Testing Forward Exchange Rate Unbiasedness Efficiently: A Semiparametric Approach," *Journal of Applied Economics*, Vol. 7, No. 1, May, pp. 325–353.

Hodrick, R. J. and E. C. Prescott (1997), "Postwar U.S. Business Cycles: An Empirical Investigation," *Journal of Money, Credit, and Banking*, Vol. 29, pp. 1–16.

Isard, Peter (1980), "Expected and Unexpected Changes in Exchange Rates: The Role of Relative Price Levels, Balance-of-Payments Factors, Interest Rates and Risk," Federal Reserve Board, International Finance Discussion Papers, No. 156.

Kallianiotis, Ioannis N. (2010), "Greece's Interdependence with the European Union and Her Loss to Society Function," *European Research Studies*, Vol. 13, No. 4, pp. 3–30.

———. (1988), "A Theoretical Monetary and Real Approach to the Balance of Payments," *Greek Economic Review*, Vol. 10, No. 2, December, pp. 383–404.

Kallianiotis, Ioannis N. and Karen Bianchi (2009), "Speculation, Uncertainty, Financial Assets Expected Return and Risk, and Exchange Rate Determination," unpublished manuscript, *University of Scranton*, November, pages 31.

Krueger, Anne O. (1983), *Exchange-Rate Determination*, Cambridge Surveys of Economic Literature, New York: Cambridge University Press.

Krugman, Paul (1984), "Oil and the Dollar," in *Economic Interdependence and Flexible Exchange Rates*, edited by J. S. Bhandari and B. H. Putnam, Cambridge, MA: The MIT Press, pp. 179–190.

Mishkin, Frederic S. (1983), *A Rational Expectations Approach to Macroeconomics: Testing Policy Ineffectiveness and Efficient-Markets Models*, National Bureau of Economic Research, Chicago: The University of Chicago Press.

Muth, J. F. (1961), "Rational Expectations and the Theory of Price Movements," *Econometrica*, Vol. 29, pp. 315–335.

Neely, Christopher and Lucio Sarno (2002), "How Well Do Monetary Fundamentals Forecast Exchange Rates?" *Review*, The Federal Reserve Bank of St. Louis, September/October, pp. 51–72.

Tucker, Alan L, Jeff Madura, and Thomas C. Chiang (1991), *International Financial Markets*, St. Paul, MN: West Publishing Company.

4

Exchange Rate Forecasting

In the previous chapter, we discussed theories of exchange rate determination and we looked at some of the macroeconomic variables (fundamentals) that influence and are influenced by the exchange rate. We can envision a "true" model of the two economies (domestic and foreign) that include all of these variables, incorporate full information, and expectations and in the context of economic optimization and random events generate the time path of foreign exchange rate between two currencies. Forecasting can be thought of as the formal process of generating expectations by using economic theory, mathematics, statistics, and econometric analysis. When expectations for future economic variables are derived, we have an implicit forecast of the variable in question, the exchange rate. The rational expectations theory says that people form expectations of future values of the exchange rate and other variables in the same way that the "true" model of the economy generates these variables. Forecasting is very common and necessary in our times. People take forecasting into consideration when they make economic decisions. These decisions then influence the direction in which the economy will move. Cash flows of all international transactions are affected by the expected value of the exchange rates; therefore, forecasting exchange rate movements is very important for businesses, investors, and policy makers.

Multinational corporations (MNCs) need forecasts of exchange rates for their *hedging decision.* Firms face the decision of whether or not to hedge future payables and receivables, which are in foreign currencies. *Short-term financial and investment decisions* require exchange rate forecasting to determine the ideal currency for borrowing money and to allocate the one that maximizes the return on an investment. *Capital budgeting decisions* need forecasting of exchange rate to determine the expected cash flows and make an accurate decision for these foreign investments. Also, *long-term financial decisions* require forecasting of currencies to decide from where to borrow money (which will reduce the cost if the currency is depreciated) and whether it is better to issue a bond denominated in foreign currency. Furthermore, *earnings assessments* need to forecast the foreign currency in which the earnings are coming and decide if earnings are going to be remitted back to the parent company or be invested abroad.

4.1 Technical Forecasting Techniques and Practices

Technical forecasting involves use of historical exchange rate data (S_t) to predict future values. It is sometimes conducted in a "judgmental" manner, without statistical analysis. From a corporate point of view, the use of technical forecasting may be limited in focusing on the near future, which is not very helpful in developing corporate policies. Many researchers represent the general solution to a linear stochastic difference equation as consisting of four distinct parts:[1]

$$s_t = trend + cyclical + seasonal + irregular$$

The exchange rate series has no obvious tendency for mean reversion.[2] A critical task for econometricians is to develop simple stochastic difference equation models that can mimic the behavior of trending variables. The key feature of a trend is that it has a permanent effect on a series. Since the irregular component is stationary, the effects of any irregular components will "die out" while the trending elements will remain in long-term forecasts.

4.1.1 *Time-Series Trends*

One approach to forecasting the variance is to explicitly introduce an independent variable that helps to predict volatility. Consider the simplest case in which,

$$S_{t+1} = \varepsilon_{t+1} X_t \tag{4.1}$$

where, S_{t+1} = the spot exchange rate (the variable of interest), ε_{t+1} = a white-noise disturbance term with variance σ^2, and X_t = an independent variable that can be observed at period t. If $X_t = X_{t-1} = X_{t-2} = \cdots =$ constant, the $\{S_t\}$ sequence is the familiar white-noise process with a constant variance. If the realization of the $\{X_t\}$sequence are not all equal, the variance of S_{t+1} conditional on the observable value of X_t is

$$Var(S_{t+1} | X_t) = X_t^2 \sigma^2 \tag{4.2}$$

4.1.1.1 Deterministic Trends

One of the basic characteristics of S_t that can be described relatively easily is its long-term growth pattern. Despite the short-run up-and-down movement, it is possible that S_t might exhibit a clear-cut long-term trend. There are many models that describe this deterministic trend and can be used to forecast, for example, extrapolate, S_t. They are the following:

(1) Linear time trend:

$$S_t = \alpha_0 + \alpha_1 t + \varepsilon_t \tag{4.3}$$

(2) Log linear time trend:

$$s_t = \beta_0 + \beta_1 t + \varepsilon_t \tag{4.4}$$

(3) Quadratic time trend:

$$s_t = \gamma_0 + \gamma_1 t + \gamma_2 t^2 + \varepsilon_t \tag{4.5}$$

(4) Polynomial time trend:

$$s_t = \delta_0 + \delta_1 t + \delta_2 t^2 + \cdots + \delta_n t^n + \varepsilon_t \tag{4.6}$$

Where, S_t = the spot exchange rate, t = time trend (1, 2, 3, ...), n = a nth-degree polynomial, and $s_t = \ln S_t$ (lowercase letters are the natural logarithms of the uppercase counterparts).

4.1.1.2 Models of Stochastic Trend

The deterministic trend models can be augmented with lagged values of the $\{s_t\}$ sequence and $\{\varepsilon_t\}$ sequence. These equations now become models with stochastic trends. Some of these models are the following:

(1) The random walk model:
The random walk model[3] is a special case of the AR(1) process (discussed in section 4.1.2.1 later), which is:

$$s_t = \alpha_0 + \alpha_1 s_{t-1} + \varepsilon_t \tag{4.7}$$

with $\alpha_0 = 0$ and $\alpha_1 = 1$, the above equation becomes,

$$s_t = s_{t-1} + \varepsilon_t \tag{4.8}$$

where, $s_t - s_{t-1} = \Delta s_t = \varepsilon_t$
The conditional mean of $s_{t+\lambda}$ (for any $\lambda > 0$) is

$$E_t s_{t+\lambda} = s_t + E\sum_{i=1}^{\lambda} \varepsilon_{t+i} = s_t \tag{4.9}$$

The variance is time dependent,

$$Var(s_t) = Var(\varepsilon_t + \varepsilon_{t-1} + \cdots + \varepsilon_1) = t\sigma^2 \tag{4.10}$$

and since the variance is not constant, the random walk process is nonstationary; as $t \to \infty$, $Var(s_t) \to \infty$, too.
The forecast function will be,

$$E_t s_{t+\lambda} = s_t \tag{4.11}$$

Hence, the constant value of s_t is the unbiased estimator of all future values of $s_{t+\lambda}$ for all $\lambda > 0$.

(2) The random walk plus drift model:
The random walk plus drift model augments the random walk model by adding a constant α_0. Then, the s_t becomes partially deterministic and partly stochastic:

$$s_t = s_{t-1} + \alpha_0 + \varepsilon_t \tag{4.12}$$

The general solution for s_t is:

$$s_t = s_0 + \alpha_0 t + \sum_{i=1}^{t} \varepsilon_i \tag{4.13}$$

where, s_0 = the initial condition and

$$E_t s_{t+\lambda} = s_0 + \alpha_0 (t + \lambda) \tag{4.14}$$

The forecast function by λ periods yields:

$$E_t s_{t+\lambda} = s_0 + \alpha_0 \lambda \tag{4.15}$$

(3) The random walk plus noise model:
The s_t, here, is the sum of a stochastic trend and white-noise component, represented by

$$s_t = \mu_t + \eta_t \tag{4.16}$$

and

$$\mu_t = \mu_{t-1} + \varepsilon_t \tag{4.17}$$

where, $\{\eta_t\}$ is a white-noise process with variance σ_n^2; ε_t and η_{t-j} are independently distributed for all t and j [i.e., $E(\varepsilon_t \eta_{t-j}) = 0$]; and $\{\mu_t\}$ sequence represents the stochastic trend.
The solution for this model can be written as:

$$s_t = s_0 - \eta_0 + \sum_{i=1}^{t} \varepsilon_i + \eta_t \tag{4.18}$$

The forecast function, by taking the conditional expectation, is:

$$E_t s_{t+\lambda} = s_t - \eta_t \tag{4.19}$$

(4) The general trend plus irregular model:
We replace eq. (4.17) with the so-called trend plus noise model,

$$\mu_t = \mu_{t-1} + \alpha_0 + \varepsilon_t \tag{4.20}$$

where, α_0 is a constant and $\{\varepsilon_t\}$ is a white-noise process.
The solution is,

$$s_t = s_0 - \eta_0 + \alpha_0 t + \sum_{i=1}^{t} \varepsilon_i + \eta_t \tag{4.21}$$

Let $A(L)$be a polynomial in the lag operator L; it is possible to augment a random walk plus drift process with the stationary noise process $A(L)\eta_t$. Then, we have the "general trend plus irregular model":

$$s_t = \mu_0 + \alpha_0 t + \sum_{i=1}^{t} \varepsilon_i + A(L)\eta_t \tag{4.22}$$

(5) The local linear trend model:
The local linear trend model is built by combining several random walk plus noise processes. Let $\{\eta_t\}$, $\{\varepsilon_t\}$, and $\{u_t\}$ be three mutually uncorrelated white-noise processes. The local linear trend model can be represented by the equations,

$$\begin{aligned} s_t &= \mu_t + \eta_t \\ \mu_t &= \mu_{t-1} + \alpha_t + \varepsilon_t \\ \alpha_t &= \alpha_{t-1} + u_t \end{aligned} \tag{4.23}$$

The local linear trend model consists of the noise term η_t plus the stochastic term μ_t. What is interesting about the model is that the change in the trend is a random walk plus noise. From all the above models, this is the most detailed one. The other processes are special cases of the local linear trend model.

$$\Delta\mu_t = \mu_t - \mu_{t-1} = \alpha_t + \varepsilon_t \tag{4.24}$$

The forecast function of $s_{t+\lambda}$ is the current value of s_t less the transitory component η_t, plus λmultiplied by the slope of the trend term in t:

$$E_t s_{t+\lambda} = (s_t - \eta_t) + \lambda(\alpha_0 + u_1 + u_2 + \cdots + u_t) \tag{4.25}$$

4.1.2 *Time-Series Models*

In this section, stochastic processes are introduced and some of their properties and their use in forecasting are discussed. The objective is to develop models that "explain" the movement of the time series s_t. Unlike the regression model, however, a set of explanatory variables will not be used. Instead we explain s_t by relating it to its own past values and to a weighted sum of current and lagged random disturbances.

4.1.2.1 *The Autoregressive [AR(p)] Model*

In the autoregressive process of order (p), the current observation s_t is generated by a weighted average of its past observations going back p periods, together with a random disturbance in the current period. This process is denoted as $AR(p)$ and its equation is written as:

$$s_t = \phi_1 s_{t-1} + \phi_2 s_{t-2} + \cdots + \phi_p s_{t-p} + \delta + \varepsilon_t \tag{4.26}$$

where, δ is a constant term, which relates to the mean of the stochastic process.

The first-order process $AR(1)$is,

$$s_t = \phi_1 s_{t-1} + \delta + \varepsilon_t \tag{4.27}$$

Its mean is: $\mu = \frac{\delta}{1-\phi_1}$ and is stationary[4] if $|\phi_1| < 1$.

Updating one period, we obtain,

$$s_{t+1} = \phi_1 s_t + \delta + \varepsilon_{t+1} \tag{4.28}$$

By running the regression, eq. (4.27), we make the coefficients δ and ϕ_1 known to us; then, we can forecast s_{t+1} conditioned on the information available at period t as,

$$E_t s_{t+1} = \hat{\phi}_1 s_t + \hat{\delta} \tag{4.29}$$

where, $E_t s_{t+1}$ = the forecasted s_{t+1} one period ahead, s_t = the current spot rate, $\hat{\delta}$ = the estimated constant term, and $\hat{\phi}_1$ = the estimated coefficient.

In the same way $AR(p)$ can be used to forecast the spot rate next period by using as many lags as are statistically significant.

4.1.2.2 *The Moving Average [MA(q)] Model*

In the moving-average process of order (q), each observation s_t is generated by a weighted average of random disturbances going back q periods. We denote this process as $MA(q)$ and its equation is written as,

$$s_t = \mu + \varepsilon_t + \theta_1 \varepsilon_{t-1} + \theta_2 \varepsilon_{t-2} + \cdots + \theta_q \varepsilon_{t-q} \tag{4.30}$$

where the parameters $\theta_1, \ldots, \theta_q$ may be positive or negative.

The moving-average process of order 1, $MA(1)$ is:

$$s_t = \mu + \varepsilon_t + \theta_1 \varepsilon_{t-1} \tag{4.31}$$

The same way, here, as with the $AR(1)$ process above, by updating one period, we obtain,

$$s_{t+1} = \mu + \varepsilon_{t+1} + \theta_1 \varepsilon_t \tag{4.32}$$

By running the regression, eq. (4.31), we know the coefficients μ and θ_1; then, we can forecast s_{t+1} conditioned on the information available at period t as,

$$E_t s_{t+1} = \hat{\mu} + \hat{\theta}_1 \varepsilon_t \tag{4.33}$$

where, $E_t s_{t+1}$ = the forecasted s_{t+1} one period ahead, s_t = the current spot rate, $\hat{\mu}$ = the estimated constant term, and $\hat{\theta}_1$ = the estimated coefficient.

In the same way $MA(q)$ can be used to forecast the spot rate next period by using as many lags as are statistically significant, and usually, there will be many lagged errors.

4.1.2.3 The Mixed Autoregressive Moving-Average [ARMA(p,q)] Model

Many stationary random processes cannot be modeled as purely autoregressive or moving average, since they have the qualities of both types of processes. The logical extension of the models presented in the last two sections can be the mixed autoregressive moving-average process of order (p,q) and is represented by the following equation:

$$s_t = \phi_1 s_{t-1} + \phi_2 s_{t-2} + \cdots + \phi_p s_{t-p} + \delta + \varepsilon_t + \theta_1 \varepsilon_{t-1} + \cdots + \theta_q \varepsilon_{t-q} \tag{4.34}$$

where, its mean is: $\mu = \phi_1 \mu + \cdots + \phi_p \mu + \delta$

or $\mu = \dfrac{\delta}{1 - \phi_1 - \cdots - \phi_p}$.

The $ARMA(1,1)$ process is,

$$s_t = \phi_1 s_{t-1} + \delta + \varepsilon_t + \theta_1 \varepsilon_{t-1} \tag{4.35}$$

Estimating the coefficients in eq. (4.35), we can use them to forecast one period ahead of the expected spot exchange rate, $E_t s_{t+1}$:

$$E_t s_{t+1} = \hat{\phi}_1 s_t + \hat{\delta} + \varepsilon_{t+1} + \hat{\theta}_1 \varepsilon_t \tag{4.36}$$

Formally, the $ARMA(p,q)$ process is forecasting the spot rate next period based on past values of the exchange rate and the error terms:

$$E_t s_{t+1} = E(s_{t+1} \mid s_t, s_{t-1}, \ldots, s_{t-p}, \varepsilon_t, \varepsilon_{t-1}, \ldots, \varepsilon_{t-q}) \tag{4.37}$$

4.1.2.4 The Autoregressive Integrated Moving-Average [$ARIMA(p,d,q)$] Model

In time-series analysis, an autoregressive integrated moving-average $ARIMA(p,d,q)$ model is a generalization of an autoregressive moving-average $ARMA(p,q)$ model. These models are fitted to time-series data either to better understand the data or to predict future points in the series (forecasting). They are applied in some cases, where data show evidence of nonstationarity and where an initial differencing step (corresponding to the "integrated" part of the model) can be applied to remove the nonstationarity. The model is generally referred to as an $ARIMA(p,d,q)$ model, where p, d, and q are non-negative integers that refer to the order of the autoregressive, integrated, and moving-average parts of the model, respectively. $ARIMA(p,d,q)$ models form an important part of the Box-Jenkins approach to time-series modeling, which has the following formula:

$$s_t = \alpha_0 + \sum_{j=1}^{p} \alpha_j s_{t-j} + \sum_{j=0}^{q} \beta_j \varepsilon_{t-j} \tag{4.38}$$

If the characteristic roots of eq. (4.38) are all in the unit circle, $\{s_t\}$ is called an $ARMA$ model for s_t. If one or more characteristic roots are greater than or equal to unity, the $\{s_t\}$ sequence is said to be an $ARIMA$ model, where p are the AR coefficients, q the MA coefficients, and d the number of nonseasonal differences.

For example, an $ARIMA(0,1,2)$ model is:

$$s_t = s_{t-1} + \alpha_0 + \varepsilon_t + \beta_1 \varepsilon_{t-1} + \beta_2 \varepsilon_{t-2} \tag{4.39}$$

The exchange rate time series are nonstationary, so that the characteristics of the underlying stochastic process change over time. We say that s_t is homogeneous nonstationary of order d if

$$w_t = \Delta^d s_t \tag{4.40}$$

is a stationary series. Here, Δ denotes differencing, for example, $\Delta s_t = s_t - s_{t-1}$ and $\Delta^2 s_t = \Delta s_t - \Delta s_{t-1}$ and so forth.

If we have a series w_t, we can get back to s_t, by summing w_t a total of d times. We write this as,

$$s_t = \sum^{d} w_t \tag{4.41}$$

After we have differenced the series s_t to produce the stationary series w_t, we can model w_t as an $ARMA$ process. If $w_t = \Delta^d s_t$, and w_t is an $ARMA(p,q)$ process; then, we say that s_t is an integrated autoregressive moving-average process of order (p,d,q) or simply $ARIMA(p,d,q)$. We can write the equation for the process $ARIMA(p, d, q)$ using the backward shift operator, as

$$\phi(B)\Delta^d s_t = \delta + \theta(B)\varepsilon_t \tag{4.42}$$

with $\phi(B) = 1 - \phi_1 B - \phi_2 B^2 - \cdots - \phi_p B^p$ and $\theta(B) = 1 - \theta_1 B - \theta_2 B^2 - \cdots - \theta_p B^p$ where, $\phi(B)$ is the autoregressive operator and $\theta(B)$ is the moving-average operator.

The mean of $w_t = \Delta^d s_t$ and it is given by

$$\mu_w = \frac{\delta}{1 - \phi_1 - \cdots - \phi_p} \tag{4.43}$$

The first difference of any $ARIMA(p, 1, q)$ series has the stationary infinite-order moving average representation:

$$s_t - s_{t-1} = \alpha_0 + \varepsilon_t + \beta_1 \varepsilon_{t-1} + \beta_2 \varepsilon_{t-2} + \cdots \tag{4.44}$$

So, the solution for the forecast function can be written as,

$$E_t s_{t+n} = s_t + \alpha_0 n + \sum_{j=1}^{n} e_{t+j} \tag{4.45}$$

where, n=number of periods ahead and $e_t = \varepsilon_t + \beta_1 \varepsilon_{t-1} + \beta_2 \varepsilon_{t-2} + \beta_3 \varepsilon_{t-3} + \cdots$

4.2 Fundamental Forecasting

Fundamental forecasting is based on fundamental relationships between economic variables and exchange rates. Then, all the previous theories of exchange rate determination, in Chapter 3, can be used to forecast the value of the exchange rate next period. This type of analysis is called fundamental analysis, due to the economic fundamentals that are used in the forecasting process. Thus, fundamental forecasting is the practice of using fundamental analysis to predict future exchange rates. This involves looking at all quantitative and qualitative aspects that might affect exchange rates, including macroeconomic data and political factors. Critics contend that fundamental forecasting is limited as some of the data it includes are difficult to quantify and it may miss some data that have an immediate effect of exchange rates.

4.2.1 An Augmented Monetary Model of Exchange Rate Forecasting

An augmented monetary model that was used in Chapter 3 can be considered here for fundamental forecasting, which is a descendant of the original models of Bilson (1978), Kallianiotis (1985, 1988), and Neely and Sarno (2002). It starts with the conventional money demand functions for both the domestic and foreign economies and through the PPP determines the current spot exchange rate by using lag values of the independent variables, as follows,

$$\begin{aligned} s_t &= \alpha + \psi(m_{t-1} - m^*_{t-1}) + \beta(y_{t-1} - y^*_{t-1}) + \gamma(i_{t-1} - i^*_{t-1}) \\ &\quad + \delta(w_{t-1} - w^*_{t-1}) + \zeta(ca_{t-1} - ca^*_{t-1}) \\ &\quad + \theta(nd_{t-1} - nd^*_{t-1}) + \lambda(I_{t-1} - I^*_{t-1}) + \phi(p_{t-1} - p^*_{t-1}) + \cdots + \varepsilon_t \end{aligned} \tag{4.46}$$

where, s_t = the ln of the current spot rate, m_{t-1} = the ln of the domestic money supply last period, y_{t-1} = the ln of domestic real income last period, i_{t-1} = the domestic short-term interest rate last period, w_{t-1} = the wage rate last period, ca_{t-1} = the ln of the current account last period, nd_{t-1} = the ln of the national debt last period, I_{t-1} = the ln of investment last period, and p_{t-1} = the ln of the domestic price level last period, ε_t = the error term, and an asterisk (*) denotes the foreign country.

Running the above regression, eq. (4.46), we receive estimates for the coefficients of all the independent variables $(\hat{\alpha}, \hat{\psi}, \hat{\beta}, \hat{\gamma}, \hat{\delta}, \hat{\zeta}, \hat{\theta}, \hat{\lambda}, \hat{\phi}, \cdots)$; then, we forecast the $E_t s_{t+1}$ by using the current values of the independent variables times the estimates of their coefficients:

$$\begin{aligned} E_t s_{t+1} &= \hat{\alpha} + \hat{\psi}(m_t - m^*_t) + \hat{\beta}(y_t - y^*_t) + \hat{\gamma}(i_t - i^*_t) \\ &\quad + \hat{\delta}(w_t - w^*_t) + \hat{\zeta}(ca_t - ca^*_t) \\ &\quad + \hat{\theta}(nd_t - nd^*_t) + \hat{\lambda}(I_t - I^*_t) + \hat{\phi}(p_t - p^*_t) + \cdots + \varepsilon_t \end{aligned} \tag{4.47}$$

The above equation is a constrained one; an unconstrained model (allowing different elasticities in each country) can be used, too, and it is expected to give better results:

$$\begin{aligned} s_t &= \alpha_0 + \alpha_1 m_{t-1} + \alpha_2 m^*_{t-1} + \alpha_3 y_{t-1} + \alpha_4 y^*_{t-1} + \alpha_5 i_{t-1} \\ &\quad + \alpha_6 i^*_{t-1} + \alpha_7 w_{t-1} + \alpha_8 w^*_{t-1} + \alpha_9 ca_{t-1} \\ &\quad + \alpha_{10} ca^*_{t-1} + \alpha_{11} nd_{t-1} + \alpha_{12} nd^*_{t-1} + \alpha_{13} I_{t-1} + \alpha_{14} I^*_{t-1} \\ &\quad + \alpha_{15} p_{t-1} + \alpha_{16} p^*_{t-1} + \cdots + \varepsilon_t \end{aligned} \tag{4.48}$$

By taking the values from the estimated coefficients $(\hat{\alpha}_0, \hat{\alpha}_1, \hat{\alpha}_2, \ldots, \hat{\alpha}_{16})$ and the current values of the independent variables, the $E_t s_{t+1}$ can be forecasted the same way as in eq. (4.47).

4.2.2 *Combining Regression Analysis with a Time-Series Model: Transfer Function Models*

Suppose we want to forecast the variable $E_t s_{t+1}$ using a regression model. Presumably such a model would include all those independent variables, which could provide an explanation for movements in s_t, but which are not themselves collinear. Let us suppose that the best regression model contains the following independent variables:

$$s_t = f[(m_{t-1} - m^*_{t-1}), (y_{t-1} - y^*_{t-1}), (i_{t-1} - i^*_{t-1}), (p_{t-1} - p^*_{t-1}), (tb_{t-1} - tb^*_{t-1}), (bd_{t-1} - bd^*_{t-1})] + \alpha_0 + \varepsilon_t \tag{4.49}$$

This equation has an implicit additive error term (ε_t) that accounts for unexplained variance in s_t. It accounts for that part of the variance of s_t that is not explained by the other independent variables. Eq. (4.49) can be estimated and an R^2 will result, which will be less than 1. The equation can, then, be used to forecast $E_t s_{t+1}$. One source of forecast error would come from the additive noise term, whose values cannot be predicted.

Subtracting the estimated value of $E_t s_t = \hat{s}_t$ from the actual value s_t, we can calculate a residual series u_t, which represents unexplained movements in s_t, a pure noise ($s_t - \hat{s}_t = u_t$). One effective application of time-series analysis is to construct an *ARIMA* model for the residual series u_t of the regression. We would then substitute the *ARIMA* model for the implicit error term in the original regression equation. When using the equation to forecast $\hat{s}_t$, we would also be able to make a forecast of the error term ε_t by using the *ARIMA* model. The *ARIMA* model provides some information as to what future values of ε_t are likely to be; it helps explain the unexplained variance in the regression equation. The combined regression-time series model is:

$$s_t = \alpha_0 + \mathrm{A}X_{t-1} + \Phi^{-1}(\mathrm{B})\theta(\mathrm{B})n_t \tag{4.50}$$

where, X_t represents the independent variables and n_t is a normally distributed error term, which may have a different variance from ε_t.

This model is likely to produce better forecasts than the regression eq. (4.49) alone or a time-series model alone, since it includes a structural (economic) explanation of that part of the variance of s_t that can be explained structurally and a time-series explanation of that part of the variance of s_t that cannot be explained structurally. Equation (4.50) is referred to as a *transfer function* model or a *multivariate autoregressive moving-average* model (*MARMA*).[5] This combined use of regression analysis with a time-series model of the error term is a particularly powerful approach to forecasting that in some cases can provide the best of both worlds.

4.2.3 *Multiequation Time-Series Models*

One of the most fertile areas of contemporary time-series research concerns multiequation models. Many economic systems do exhibit feedback from other variables. It is not always known if the time path of a series designated to be the "independent" variable has been unaffected by the time path of the "dependent" variable. There is a type of analysis that treats all variables symmetrically without making reference to the issue of dependence versus independence, this is a vector autoregression (*VAR*) analysis.

4.2.3.1 *Vector Autoregression (VAR) Analysis*

When we are not confident that a variable is actually exogenous, a natural extension of transfer function analysis is to treat each variable symmetrically. In the two variable case, we can let the time path of $\{s_t\}$ be affected by current and past realizations of the $\{f_t\}$ sequence and let the time path of the $\{f_t\}$ sequence be affected by current and past realizations of the $\{s_t\}$ sequence.

A *VAR* is a system of equations that makes each endogenous variable a function of its own past and of the past of the other endogenous variables in the system. *VAR* has been proven to be a successful technique for forecasting systems of interrelated time series variables. We use, here, a slight generalization of the simple *VAR* by allowing for the possibility that there may be exogenous variables that help determine the endogenous variables (the simplest exogenous variable can be a time trend or any public policy instruments).

Our methodology involves estimating spot (s_t) and forward (f_t) exchange rates in a *VAR* framework with a time trend component as,

$$\begin{aligned} s_t &= \alpha_{10} + \mathrm{A}_{11}(L)\, s_{t-1} + \mathrm{A}_{12}(L) f_{t-1} + \mathrm{A}_{13} t + \varepsilon_{st} \\ f_t &= \alpha_{20} + \mathrm{A}_{21}(L)\, s_{t-1} + \mathrm{A}_{22}(L) f_{t-1} + \mathrm{A}_{23} t + \varepsilon_{ft} \end{aligned} \tag{4.51}$$

where, α_{10} and α_{20} = constants, A_{ij} = the polynomials in the lag operator L, and t = time trend.

We can also use, as exogenous variables, for the above *VAR* system the monetary policy instruments for the two economies (i_{FF} and i^*_{OND}), in our case here.

4.2.3.2 *The Impulse Response Function*

The solution of eq. (4.51) can be used to examine the interaction between the $\{s_t\}$ and $\{f_t\}$ sequences. The coefficients can be used to generate the effects of ε_{st} on ε_{ft} shocks on the entire time paths of the $\{s_t\}$ and $\{f_t\}$

sequences. The six sets of coefficients are called the *impulse response functions.* Plotting the impulse response functions is a practical way to visually represent the behavior of the $\{s_t\}$ and $\{f_t\}$ series in response to the various shocks. The Appendix provides a figure (graph A4.5) that traces out the effects of one-unit shocks on ε_{st} and ε_{ft}.

4.3 Market-Based Forecasting

A very simple way to develop future forecasting for the exchange rate is for someone to follow the market indicators, the spot rate (s_t) and the forward rate (f_t). This type of forecasting is called the market-based forecasting.

4.3.1 The Current Spot Rate as a Forecasting Indicator

The current spot exchange rate (s_t) can be used to forecast the spot rate next period (s^e_{t+1}). Rational market participants observe the trend of a currency (exchange rate) based on market expectations. This market is also an efficient market, where complete information exists. Then,

$$s^e_{t+1} = E_t s_{t+1} = s_t + v_t \mid I_t \tag{4.52}$$

where, I_t = the set of information available at time t and v_t = an observation trend of the value of the currency and a weaker definition of rationality allows for a zero observation trend error.

Thus,

$$E(s_{t+1} - s^e_{t+1} \mid I_t) = 0 \tag{4.53}$$

If the market expects the euro (€↓) to depreciate against the dollar ($ ↑) in the near future, speculators will buy dollars with euros today in anticipation of its appreciation. This excess demand for dollars will immediately increase the dollar value and cause the euro to fall because of its excess supply. Thus, the current value of the euro reflects the expectations of the euro's value in the near future. Spot rates can be used as a very good estimate of the spot rates at a future time in an efficient foreign exchange market.

4.3.2 The Forward Exchange Rate as a Forecasting Indicator

Forward rates are quoted for a specific date in the future (F_1, F_3, F_6, F_{12}, *etc.*). A one-month (F_1) forward rate provides a forecast for the spot rate in one month (S^e_{t+1}); then, it is a forecasting indicator of the spot rate next period. In general,

$$F_j = E(S_{t+j} \mid I_t) \tag{4.54}$$

where, F_j = the j-month forward rate quoted now and S_{t+j} = the spot rate j months from today.

The forward rate, as a reflector the market expectations, is a very good market-based forecast because market participants (speculators and businesses) follow it to the expected level regarding the future spot rate. Let's say that the one-month forward rate is quoted as, $F_1 = 1.2411$ \$/€ and the spot rate is $S_1 = 1.2529$ \$/€. The market expects the US dollar to appreciate and the euro to depreciate. Then, market participants will start buying dollars and selling euros. This excess demand for dollars will appreciate the dollar, which will start going up (the spot rate will fall) until its exchange rate reaches 1.2411 \$/€. Thus, the participants' actions caused the dollar to appreciate and through their reaction proved that the forward rate is a very good predictor of the future spot rate and must be considered for their forecasting. Actually, we forced the spot rate to reach the quoted forward rate. Unfortunately, there is no escape from the market expectations. Everyone trust and follows the market; then, if someone decides to go against the market, he will lose (because he did not follow the market and instead of buying dollars, he was buying euros). Actually, we are "captives" of the forward and futures market for all the assets (financial, real, commodities, etc.).

$$F_1 \downarrow \Rightarrow S^e_{t+1} \downarrow \Rightarrow EX\,D(\$) \Rightarrow \$ \uparrow \Rightarrow S_{t+1} \downarrow$$

Further, long-term exchange rate forecasting can be derived from long-term forward rates. Forward rates are available for periods up to five (5) years, but the bid/ask spreads are wider, due to limited trading volume. These long-term forward exchange rates are determined based on the interest rate parity (IRP) between the two countries.[6]

4.4 Forecasting with the Use of Currency Betas (β_s)

This type of forecasting is based on a similar argument as the market beta of a financial asset. Currency betas (β_s) measure the responsiveness of a particular currency to a market index of foreign currencies. To estimate currency betas (β_s), we use the following equation:

$$\dot{s}_t = \alpha + \beta \dot{e}_{XRI_t} + \varepsilon_t \tag{4.55}$$

where, $\dot{s}_t$ = the percentage change of the spot exchange rate, as a percentage per annum $[\%\Delta S_t = \frac{S_t - S_{t-1}}{S_{t-1}} \frac{12}{n} 100 = (s_t - s_{t-1}) \frac{12}{n} 100]$, $\dot{e}_{XRI_t}$ = the percentage change of a market index for foreign currencies, as a percentage per annum, α = the vertical intercept, β = the sensitivity (responsiveness) between the currency and the currency index (slope of the line), and ε_t = the error term.

By using a least squares regression, we can determine (estimate) the $\hat{\alpha}$ and the $\hat{\beta}$ of the specific currency (exchange rate) with respect to the market index of foreign currencies.

4.5 Mixed Forecasting

Some forecasts are superior to the others, but no one knows with certainty which one is the best forecast. Thus, the best way to forecast exchange rate is to use a combination of forecasting techniques. For this reason, the current method is called as mixed forecasting. We can use a technical, a fundamental, a market-based forecast, and a currency beta (β) method, and from all these different values, we can take the average or we can assign different weights for each one of the forecasting techniques and derive from there a weighted average value for the future spot rate.

4.6 Forecasting Evaluation

Forecasts are made with errors because the economy is dynamic, our information is restrained, our models are only approximations of reality, and our knowledge is limited. Suppose the true model is given by,

$$s_t = \chi_t\beta + \varepsilon_t \tag{4.56}$$

where, β is a vector of unknown parameters, and ε_t is an independent and identically distributed with mean zero random disturbance $[E(\varepsilon_t) = 0]$.

The true model generating s_t is not known, but we obtain estimates $\hat{\beta}$ of the unknown parameters β. Then, setting the error term equal to its mean value (zero), the forecasts of s_t are obtained as follows:

$$\hat{s}_t = \chi_t\hat{\beta} \tag{4.57}$$

The forecast error (e_t) is the difference between the actual and the forecasted value,

$$e_t = s_t - \chi_t\hat{\beta} \tag{4.58}$$

Assuming that the model is correctly specified, there are two sources of forecast errors: (1) residual or innovation uncertainty and (2) coefficient uncertainty.

(1) *Residual or Innovation Uncertainty.* This first source of errors arises because the innovations ε_t in the equation are unknown for the forecast period and are replaced with their expectations. While the residuals are zero in expected value, the individual values are nonzero; the larger the variation in the individual errors, the greater the overall error in the forecasts. The standard measure of this variation is the "Standard Error of the Regression" (SSR) in the equation output. Residual uncertainty is usually the largest source of forecast errors. Our criterion, here, will be minimization of the SSR because the smaller the SSR in our output, the better the forecast of this model.

(2) *Coefficient Uncertainty.* The second source of forecast error is coefficient uncertainty. The estimated coefficients $\hat{\beta}$ of the equation deviate from the true coefficients β in a random fashion. The standard error of the estimated coefficient, given with the output from the regression, is a measure of the precision with which the estimated coefficients measure the true coefficients. The effect of coefficient uncertainty depends on the exogenous variables. Since the estimated coefficients are multiplied by the exogenous variables χ_t in the computation of forecasts, the more exogenous variables deviate from their mean values, the greater is the forecast uncertainty.

When we construct a forecast of the $s^e_{t+1} = LEUSF$ using different estimated equations, the computer output will show different forecast evaluation options (root mean squared error, mean absolute error, mean absolute percentage error, Theil inequality coefficient, etc.). The output will show the actual (s_t) and the forecasted value ($\hat{s}_t$) of the variable, with an *F* at the end (i.e., *LEUS* and *LEUSF*). The reported forecast error statistic that we can look is the Root Mean Squared Error (RMSE) and it is computed as follows:

$$RMSE = \sqrt{\sum_{t=T+1}^{T+n} (\hat{s}_t - s_t)^2 / n} \tag{4.59}$$

This statistic (RMSE) depends on the scale of the dependent variable and it is used as a relative measure to compare forecasts for the same series across different models; the smaller the error, the better the forecasting ability of that model according to the RMSE criterion. Statistical programs offer dynamic and static forecasting. Dynamic forecasting is a multistep forecast of $\hat{s}_{t+n}$. Static forecasting performs a series of one-step ahead forecast of the dependent variable $\hat{s}_{t+1}$. Both methods will always yield identical results in the first period of a multiperiod forecast.

4.7 Unit Root or Stationarity Test

There are important differences between stationary and nonstationary time series. Shocks to a stationary series are necessarily temporary; over time, the effects of the shocks will dissipate and the series will revert to its long-run mean level. As such, long-term forecasts of a stationary series will converge to the unconditional mean of the series.

A covariance stationary series:

(1) exhibits *mean reversion*, it fluctuates around a constant long-run mean;
(2) has a finite variance that is time-invariant; and
(3) has a theoretical correlogram that diminishes as lag length increases.

A nonstationary series necessarily has permanent components. The mean and/or variance are time dependent. In a nonstationary (which contains unit roots) series:

(1) there is no long-run mean to which the series returns;
(2) the variance is time dependent and goes to infinity as time approaches infinity; and
(3) theoretical autocorrelations do not decay but, in finite samples, the sample correlogram dies out slowly.

Suppose we know that a series is generated from the following first-order process:

$$s_t = \alpha_1 s_{t-1} + \varepsilon_t \tag{4.60}$$

where, $\{\varepsilon_t\}$ is generated from a white-noise process.

We wish to test the null hypothesis that $\alpha_1 = 0$. We can estimate eq. (4.60) by using thed OLS method. The fact that ε_t is a white-noise process and $|\alpha_1| < 1$ guarantees that the $\{s_t\}$ sequence is stationary, the estimate of α_1 is efficient. The situation is quite different if we want to test the hypothesis $\alpha_1 = 1$. Now, under the null hypothesis, the $\{s_t\}$ sequence is generated by the nonstationary process:

$$s_t = \sum_{j=1}^{t} \varepsilon_{j''} \tag{4.61}$$

Thus, if $\alpha_1 = 1$, the variance becomes infinitely large as t increases. Under the null hypothesis, it is inappropriate to use classical statistical method to estimate and perform significance tests on the coefficient α_1. If the $\{s_t\}$ sequence is generated as in eq. (4.61), the OLS estimate of eq. (4.60) will yield a biased estimate of α_1. Thus, standard inference procedures do not apply to regressions, which contain an integrated dependent variable or integrated regressors. The order of integration $[I(d)]$ is the number of unit roots contained in the series or the number of differencing operations it takes to make the series stationary. A stationary series is $I(0)$.

For verifying the stationarity of a series, Augmented Dickey-Fuller (ADF) and Phillips-Perron (PP) tests[7] can be used. Let us consider an $AR(1)$ process of the s_t,

$$s_t = \alpha_o + \alpha_1 s_{t-1} + \varepsilon_t \tag{4.62}$$

where, α_o and α_1 are parameters and ε_t is assumed to be white noise.

The variable s_t is a stationary series if $0 < \alpha_1 < 1$. If $\alpha_1 = 1$, s_t is a nonstationary series (a random walk with drift), and its variance increases steadily with time and goes to infinity. If $|\alpha_1| > 1$, the s_t series is explosive.

First, the test regression for the simple Dickey-Fuller (DF) test is a slightly different $AR(1)$ process, after subtracting s_{t-1} from both sides of eq. (4.62), as follows,

$$\Delta s_t = \beta_o + \beta_1 s_{t-1} + \varepsilon_t \tag{4.63}$$

where, $\beta_1 = \alpha_1 - 1$ and the null (unit root, nonstationary) and the alternative (stationary) hypotheses are,

$$H_0 : \beta_1 = 0 \text{ and } H_1 : \beta_1 < 0$$

The simple DF unit root test is valid only if the series is an $AR(1)$ process. If the series is correlated at higher order lags, the assumption of white-noise disturbances ε_t is violated. The ADF approach controls for higher-order correlation by adding lagged difference terms of the dependent variable s_t to the right-hand side of the regression,

$$\Delta s_t = \gamma_o + \beta_1 s_{t-1} + \gamma_1 \Delta s_{t-1} + \gamma_2 \Delta s_{t-2} + \cdots + \gamma_p \Delta s_{t-p} + \varepsilon_t \tag{4.64}$$

The test is now, $H_0 : \beta_1 = 0$ and $H_1 : \beta_1 < 0$.

Second, Phillips-Perron (PP) propose an alternative (nonparametric) method of controlling for serial correlation when testing for a unit root. The PP method estimates the nonaugmented DF test eq. (4.63), and modifies the t-ratio of the β_1 coefficient so that serial correlation does not affect the asymptotic distribution of the test statistic. The Phillips-Perron procedure can be applied to mixed processes in the same way as the Dickey-Fuller tests.

The unit root issue arises naturally in the context of the standard regression model. Consider the following regression equation,

$$s_t = \delta_o + \delta_1 m_t + \varepsilon_t \tag{4.65}$$

The assumptions of the classical regression model necessitate that both the $\{s_t\}$ and $\{m_t\}$ sequences be stationary $[I(0)]$ and the errors have a zero mean and finite variance. In the presence of nonstationary variables, there might be a *spurious regression.* A spurious regression has a high R^2, $t-$statistics that appear to be significant, but the results are without any economic meaning. The econometrician has to be very careful in working with nonstationary variables. In terms of eq. (4.65), there are four cases to consider:

1. Both $\{s_t\}$ and $\{m_t\}$ are stationary. When both variables are stationary, the classical regression model is appropriate.
2. The $\{s_t\}$ and $\{m_t\}$ sequences are integrated of different orders. Regression equations using such variables are meaningless.
3. The nonstationary $\{s_t\}$ and $\{m_t\}$ sequences are integrated of the same order and the residual sequence contains a stochastic trend. This is the case, in which the regression is spurious. The results from such spurious regressions are meaningless in that all errors are permanent. In this case, it is often recommended that the regression equation be estimated in first differences. Since $\{s_t\}$, $\{m_t\}$, and $\{\varepsilon_t\}$each contain unit roots, the first difference of each is stationary. Thus, the usual asymptotic results apply. But, if one of the trends is deterministic and the other is stochastic, first differencing each is not appropriate.
4. The nonstationary $\{s_t\}$ and $\{m_t\}$ sequences are integrated of the same order and the residual sequence is stationary. In this circumstance, $\{s_t\}$ and $\{m_t\}$ are *cointegrated.*

4.8 Cointegration Test

The finding that many macrotime series may contain a unit root has spurred the development of the theory of nonstationary time-series analysis. Engle and Granger (1987) pointed out that a linear combination of two or more nonstationary series may be stationary. If such a stationary linear combination exists, the nonstationary time series is said to be *integrated.* The stationary linear combination is called the *cointegration equation* and may be interpreted as a long-run equilibrium relationship among the variables.

The purpose of the cointegration test is to determine whether groups of nonstationary series are cointegrated or not. Let us consider a simple model of money demand. In logarithms, an econometric specification for such an equation can be as follows,

$$m_t = \beta_0 + \beta_1 p_t + \beta_2 y_t + \beta_3 i_t + \varepsilon_t \tag{4.66}$$

where, m_t = money demand, p_t = price level, y_t = real income, i_t = interest rate (opportunity cost of holding money), ε_t = stationary disturbance term, and β_j = parameters to be estimated.

The hypothesis that the money market will clear allows the researcher to collect time-series data of the money supply ($m_t^s = m_t^d$ assuming that the money market always clears), the price level (CPI), real income (real GNP), and an appropriate short-term interest rate. The behavioral assumptions require that $\beta_1 = 1$, $\beta_2 > 0$, and $\beta_3 < 0$. Of course, the properties of the unexplained portion of the demand for money (the $\{\varepsilon_t\}$ sequence) are an integral part of the theory. If the theory is to make any sense at all, any deviation in the demand for money must necessarily be temporary in nature. If ε_t has a stochastic trend, the errors in the model will be cumulative so that deviations from money market equilibrium will not be eliminated. Hence, a key assumption of this theory is that the $\{\varepsilon_t\}$ sequence is stationary [$I(0)$].

But, there is a problem that the researcher has to confront, and this is that the real GNP, the money supply, the price level, and the interest rate are not stationary; they can all be characterized as nonstationary [$I(1)$] variables. As such, each of these variables can meander without any tendency to return to a long-run level. However, the theory expressed in eq. (4.66) asserts that there exists a linear combination of these nonstationary variables that is stationary. Solving eq. (4.66) for the error term, we have,

$$\varepsilon_t = m_t - \beta_0 - \beta_1 p_t - \beta_2 y_t - \beta_3 i_t \tag{4.67}$$

Since $\{\varepsilon_t\}$ must be stationary, it follows that the linear combination of the integrated variables given by the right-hand side of eq. (4.67) must also be stationary. Thus, the economic theory necessitates that the time paths of the four nonstationary variables $\{m_t\}$, $\{p_t\}$, $\{y_t\}$, and $\{i_t\}$be linked. This crucial insight has dominated the macro-econometric literature in the recent years. "Equilibrium theories involving nonstationary variables require the existence of a combination of the variables that is stationary."[8] In Economics and Finance there are many cases (models) of stationary combinations of nonstationary variables. Within any equilibrium framework, their deviations from equilibrium are considered to be temporary.[9]

A formal analysis of cointegration begins by considering a set of economic variables in their long-run equilibrium when,

$$\beta_1 x_{1t} + \beta_2 x_{2t} + \cdots + \beta_n x_{nt} = 0 \tag{4.68}$$

If β and x_t denote the vectors $(\beta_1, \beta_2, \ldots, \beta_n)$ and $(x_{1t}, x_{2t}, \ldots, x_{nt})'$, the system is in long-run equilibrium when $\beta x_t = 0$. The deviation from long-run equilibrium (called the *equilibrium error)* is ε_t, so we have,

$$\varepsilon_t = \beta x_t \tag{4.69}$$

If the equilibrium is meaningful, it must be the case that the equilibrium error process is stationary. The components of the vector $x_t = (x_{1t}, x_{2t}, \ldots, x_{nt})'$ are said to be *cointegrated of order d, b,* denoted by $x_t \sim CI(d, b)$if (1) all components of x_t are integrated of order d and (2) there exists a vector $\beta = (\beta_1, \beta_2, \ldots, \beta_n)$ such that linear combination $\beta x_t = \beta_1 x_{1t} + \beta_2 x_{2t} + \cdots + \beta_n x_{nt}$ is integrated of order $(d - b)$, where $b > 0$. The vector β is called the *cointegrating vector.*

In terms of eq. (4.66), if the money supply, price level, real income, and interest rate are all $I(1)$and the linear combination $m_t - \beta_0 - \beta_1 p_t - \beta_2 y_t - \beta_3 i_t = \varepsilon_t$ is stationary, then the variables are cointegrated of order (1, 1). The deviation from long-run money market equilibrium is ε_t; and since $\{\varepsilon_t\}$ is stationary, this deviation is temporary in nature. A cointegration test by using an Engle and Granger (1987) testing procedure for a *VAR* model is shown in the Appendix A5.8.[10]

4.9 Summary

In this chapter different techniques of exchange rate forecasting were given and their forecast evaluation was discussed. Multinational corporations and all the other professionals involved in international finance need exchange rate forecasting to make decisions on their investment, their financing, capital budgeting, on hedging payables and receivables, and other short-term and long-term financial decisions. The most common forecasting techniques are: technical forecasting, fundamental forecasting, market-based forecasting, forecasting with the use of currency betas, and mixed forecasting. Finally, forecast evaluation has been considered to test the accuracy of forecasting by using specific criteria like *SSR*, standard errors of the coefficients, *RMSE*, and others. Of course, it is almost impossible to predict future exchange rates with perfect accuracy, but it is better to have an estimate (an objective approximation), instead of having no values for the future movements of a currency.

Appendix 4

A4.1 Exchange Rate Forecasting: Empirical Results

In this appendix some empirical results of the models used in the chapter are presented and a few tests are performed. It is important that students and other professionals are in a position to do empirical, analytical, and forecasting work for exchange rates. The criteria for the best forecasting are: (1) minimization of *SSR*, (2) minimization of the standard error of the coefficients, (3) minimization of the *RMSE*, and the other statistics reported with the regression's output. Data are monthly and can be found at *Economagic.com*. The econometric software used here is the *EViews 7*.

A4.1.1 Deterministic Trends

The first equation presented here is the linear time trend, eq. (4.3), which gives the following results:

$$S_t = \underset{(0.017)}{0.929^{***}} + \underset{(0.001)}{0.003^{***}}\, t$$

$$R^2 = 0.682, \quad SSR = 1.915, \quad F = 340.736, \quad D - W = 0.098,$$

$$N = 161, \quad RMSE = 0.109055$$

Next, the log linear time trend, eq. (4.4), is given (graph A4.1),

$$s_t = \underset{(0.015)}{-0.070^{***}} + \underset{(0.001)}{0.003^{***}}\, t$$

$$R^2 = 0.689, \quad SSR = 1.394, \quad F = 344.901, \quad D - W = 0.087,$$

$$N = 158, \quad RMSE = 0.093945$$

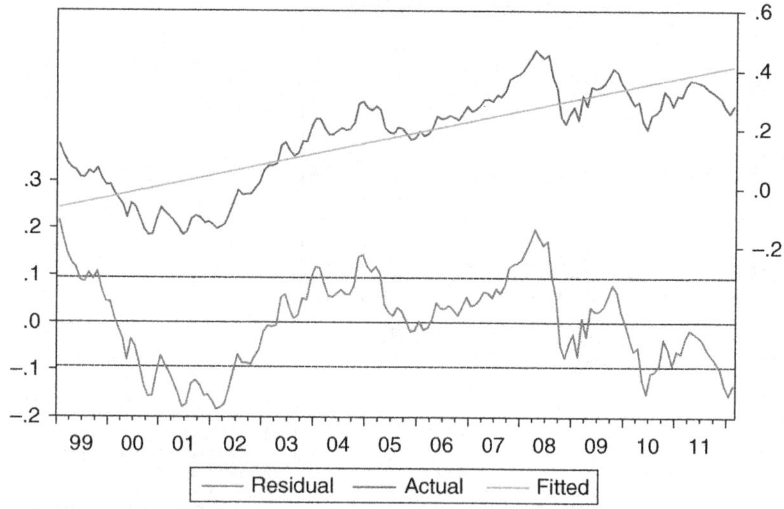

Graph A4.1 Log linear time trend of the spot exchange rate (s_t), eq. (4.4).

Note: Actual = ln of the spot rate (s_t) and Fitted = the estimated log linear trend.

Source: *Economagic.com.*

Now, the quadratic time trend, eq. (4.5), is shown,

$$s_t = \underset{(0.022)}{-0.125^{***}} + \underset{(0.001)}{0.005^{***}}\, t - \underset{(0.001)}{0.001^{***}}\, t^2$$

$R^2 = 0.709$, $SSR = 1.303$, $F = 188.898$, $D-W = 0.093$,

$N = 158$, $RMSE = 0.090797$

A4.1.2 Models of Stochastic Trend

The following regression is the random walk model (graph A4.2), eq. (4.7):

$$s_t = \underset{(0.003)}{0.003} + \underset{(0.013)}{0.988^{***}}\, s_{t-1}$$

$R^2 = 0.973$, $SSR = 0.120$, $F = 5{,}651.128$, $D-W = 1.606$,

$N = 157$, $RMSE = 0.027590$

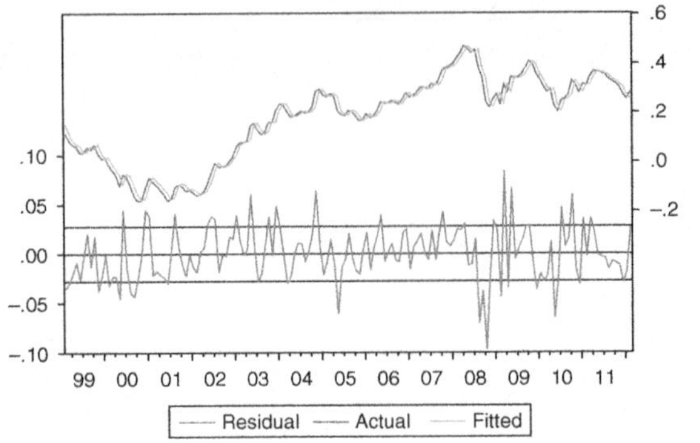

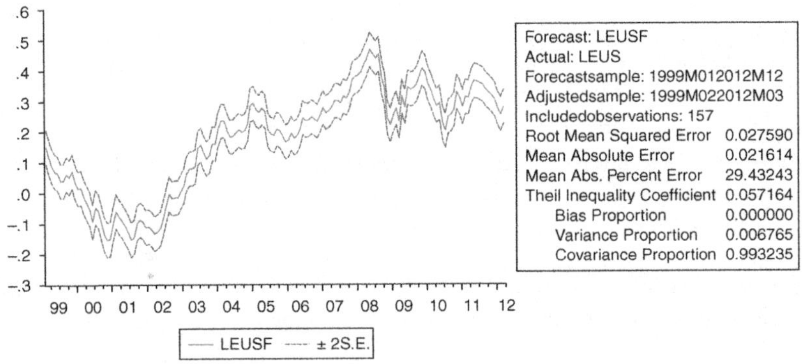

Graph A4.2 The random walk of the s_t and its forecasting, eq. (4.7).

Note: Actual (LEUS) = ln of the spot rate (s_t), Fitted = the estimated s_t (from the random walk model), and LEUSF = the static forecast of the s_t.

Source: *Economagic.com.*

A4.1.3 The Autoregressive [AR(p)] model

We starts with the first-order process, $AR(1)$ model, eq. (4.27), which is actually a random walk model and gives the same results with eq. (4.7),

$$\underset{}{s_t = \underset{(0.003)}{0.003} + \underset{(0.013)}{0.988^{***}} s_{t-1}}$$

$R^2 = 0.973$, $SSR = 0.120$, $F = 5{,}651.128$, $D-W = 1.606$,

$N = 157$, $RMSE = 0.027590$

Then, an autoregressive process of order (p) is presented, eq. (4.26), with only two significant lagged values, $AR(2)$, as follows,

$$\underset{(0.003)}{s_t = 0.004} \; + \underset{(0.013)}{1.178^{***} s_{t-1}} - \underset{(0.079)}{0.193^{**} s_{t-2}}$$

$R^2 = 0.975$, $SSR = 0.114$, $F = 2{,}929.702$, $D - W = 2.017$,

$N = 156$, $RMSE = 0.027013$

The forecasting criteria (statistics) are a little better in the second equation, the $AR(2)$model, compared to the $AR(1)$.

A4.1.4 The Moving Average [$MA(q)$] Model

The moving average $MA(1)$process for the s_t, eq. (4.31), gives the following results (graph A4.3),

$$s_t = \underset{(0.014)}{0.174^{***}} + \underset{(0.035)}{0.898^{***} \varepsilon_{t-1}}$$

$R^2 = 0.692$, $SSR = 1.378$, $F = 350.763$, $D - W = 0.391$,

$N = 158$, $RMSE = 0.093400$

Next, the moving average $MA(q)$ process for the s_t, eq. (4.30), by using $q = 14$(only the statistically significant coefficients), gives the following results,

$$\begin{aligned} s_t = {} & \underset{(0.024)}{0.231^{***}} + \underset{(0.079)}{1.265^{***} \varepsilon_{t-1}} + \underset{(0.121)}{1.393^{***} \varepsilon_{t-2}} + \underset{(0.165)}{1.456^{***} \varepsilon_{t-3}} \\ & + \underset{(0.188)}{1.648^{***} \varepsilon_{t-4}} + \underset{(0.199)}{1.793^{***} \varepsilon_{t-5}} + \underset{(0.207)}{1.927^{***} \varepsilon_{t-6}} + \underset{(0.209)}{1.886^{***} \varepsilon_{t-7}} \\ & + \underset{(0.198)}{1.861^{***} \varepsilon_{t-8}} + \underset{(0.178)}{1.735^{***} \varepsilon_{t-9}} + \underset{(0.165)}{1.696^{***} \varepsilon_{t-10}} + \underset{(0.163)}{1.297^{***} \varepsilon_{t-11}} \\ & + \underset{(0.112)}{0.770^{***} \varepsilon_{t-12}} + \underset{(0.076)}{0.750^{***} \varepsilon_{t-13}} + \underset{(0.150)}{0.379^{***} \varepsilon_{t-14}} \end{aligned}$$

$R^2 = 0.975$, $SSR = 0.110$, $F = 405.332$, $D - W = 1.946$,

$N = 158$, $RMSE = 0.026393$

The output statistics of this $MA(14)$ model are relatively very good ones.

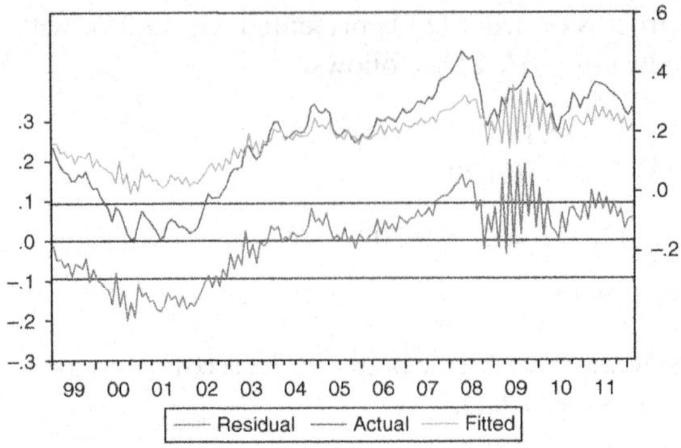

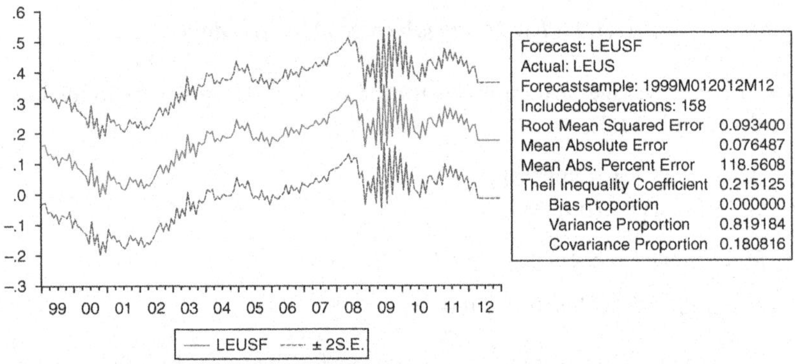

Graph A4.3 The moving average $MA(1)$process of s_t and its forecasting, eq. (4.31).

Note: Actual (LEUS) = ln of the spot rate (s_t), Fitted = the estimated s_t [from the $MA(1)$ model], and LEUSF = the static forecast of the s_t.

Source: *Economagic.com.*

A4.1.5 The Mixed Autoregressive-Moving Average [ARMA(p, q)] Model

We start with the estimation of an $ARMA(1,1)$process, eq. (4.35):

$$s_t = \underset{(0.162)}{0.224} + \underset{(0.015)}{0.983^{***}} s_{t-1} + \underset{(0.081)}{0.178^{**}} \varepsilon_{t-1}$$

$$R^2 = 0.974, \quad SSR = 0.115, \quad F = 2{,}908.241, \quad D-W = 1.963,$$

$$N = 157, \quad RMSE = 0.027120$$

Now, we run eq. (4.34), where there are only two significant lagged values, $ARMA(2,2)$:

$$\underset{(0.143)}{s_t = 0.370^{**}} + \underset{(0.023)}{1.906^{***}} s_{t-1} - \underset{(0.024)}{0.908^{***}} s_{t-2} - \underset{(0.082)}{0.849^{***}} \varepsilon_{t-1} - \underset{(0.089)}{0.226^{**}} \varepsilon_{t-2}$$

$$R^2 = 0.978, SSR = 0.098, F = 1{,}687.831, D - W = 2.094,$$

$$N = 156, RMSE = 0.025046$$

The statistics are improved a little in the $ARMA(2,2)$ compared to the $ARMA(1,1)$ process.

A4.1.6 The Autoregressive Integrated Moving Average [ARIMA(p, d, q)] Model

The empirical results below show eq. (4.39). This is an $ARIMA(0,1,2)$ process:

$$s_t = \underset{(0.017)}{0.981^{***}} s_{t-1} + \underset{(0.004)}{0.004} + \underset{(0.082)}{0.194^{**}} \varepsilon_{t-1} + \underset{(0.082)}{0.079} \varepsilon_{t-2}$$

$$R^2 = 0.974, \quad SSR = 0.115, \quad F = 1{,}937.785, \quad D - W = 1.988,$$

$$N = 157, \quad RMSE = 0.027041$$

A4.2 Fundamental Forecasting

To use this technique, we must take into consideration the economic variables (fundamentals) between the two countries and the theories of the exchange rate determination with which to forecast the future values of exchange rates.

A4.2.1 An Augmented Monetary Model of Exchange Rate Forecasting

We start forecasting the constrained function, eq. (4.46), which gives the following results:

$$\begin{aligned} s_t = &\underset{(1.655)}{1.210} - \underset{(0.481)}{2.795^{***}} (m_{t-1} - m^*_{t-1}) + \underset{(0.553)}{1.048^{*}} (y_{t-1} - y^*_{t-1}) \\ &- \underset{(0.061)}{0.005} (i_{t-1} - i^*_{t-1}) + \underset{(0.303)}{0.152} (ca_{t-1} - ca^*_{t-1}) \\ &- \underset{(1.472)}{5.194^{***}} (p_{t-1} - p^*_{t-1}) \end{aligned}$$

$$R^2 = 0.688, \quad SSR = 0.594, \quad F = 40.221, \quad D-W = 0.232,$$
$$N = 97, \quad RMSE = 0.078277 \quad \ln L^c = 109.471$$

Now, we run the same equation, but in an unconstrained form, [eq. (4.48)], which gives the estimates,

$$\begin{aligned} s_t = {} & \underset{(7.960)}{14.553^*} - \underset{(0.997)}{0.130}\, m_{t-1} + \underset{(0.446)}{4.058^{***}}\, m^*_{t-1} + \underset{(1.045)}{4.323^{***}}\, y_{t-1} \\ & - \underset{(1.188)}{5.736^{***}}\, y^*_{t-1} - \underset{(0.062)}{0.057}\, i_{t-1} + \underset{(0.056)}{0.032}\, i^*_{t-1} \\ & - \underset{(0.339)}{0.040}\, ca_{t-1} + \underset{(0.305)}{0.447}\, ca^*_{t-1} - \underset{(1.417)}{1.732}\, p_{t-1} \\ & - \underset{(1.909)}{7.852^{***}}\, p^*_{t-1} \end{aligned}$$

$$R^2 = 0.846, \quad SSR = 0.293, \quad F = 47.332, \quad D-W = 0.599,$$
$$N = 97, \quad RMSE = 0.054992 \quad \ln L^c = 143.718$$

Testing the null hypothesis that elasticities are the same in both countries, we use the likelihood ratio statistic, $-2(\ln L^c - \ln L^u) = -2(109.471 - 143.718) = 68.494$ and is distributed as $\chi^2_{(5)} = 68.494 > 15.09$ (exceeds the critical value). Thus, the null hypothesis is rejected; the elasticities are different in these two economies (US and Euro-zone). Also, the forecasting criteria (statistics) are not very good using the economic fundamentals.

A4.2.2 The Transfer Function Models

We run, now, a combining regression, which includes the fundamental variables plus time-series. This is eq. (4.50) in the text above, where it is shown as constrained model, first and then as unconstrained one:

$$\begin{aligned} s_t = {} & \underset{(1.468)}{1.789} - \underset{(0.335)}{0.400}\,(m_{t-1} - m^*_{t-1}) - \underset{(0.628)}{0.749}\,(y_{t-1} - y^*_{t-1}) \\ & - \underset{(0.021)}{0.044^{**}}\,(i_{t-1} - i^*_{t-1}) + \underset{(0.054)}{0.004}\,(ca_{t-1} - ca^*_{t-1}) \end{aligned}$$

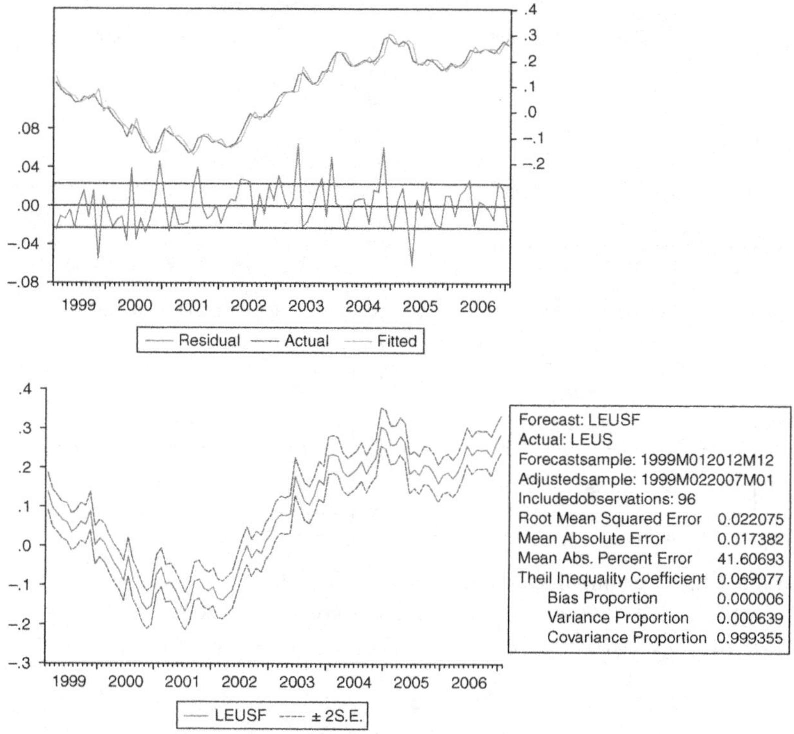

Graph A4.4 The transfer function model, eq. (4.50).

Note: Actual (LEUS) = ln of the spot rate (s_t), Fitted = the estimated s_t (from the transfer function model), and LEUSF = the static forecast of the s_t.

Source: *Economagic.com.*

$$\begin{aligned}
&-\underset{(0.563)}{0.155}(p_{t-1}-p^*_{t-1})+\underset{(0.021)}{0.987^{***}}s_{t-1}+\underset{(0.101)}{0.381^{***}}\varepsilon_{t-1}\\
&R^2=0.975,\quad SSR=0.047,\quad F=498.732,\quad D-W=1.966,\\
&N=96,\quad RMSE=0.022075
\end{aligned}$$

Further, eq. (4.50), as an unconstrained model, gives the following results (graph A4.4):

$$\begin{aligned}
s_t=\ &\underset{(5.084)}{0.167}+\underset{(0.421)}{0.044}\,m_{t-1}+\underset{(0.350)}{0.724^{**}}m^*_{t-1}-\underset{(0.778)}{1.086}y_{t-1}\\
&-\underset{(0.721)}{0.055}y^*_{t-1}-\underset{(0.024)}{0.019}\,i_{t-1}+\underset{(0.022)}{0.036}\,i^*_{t-1}
\end{aligned}$$

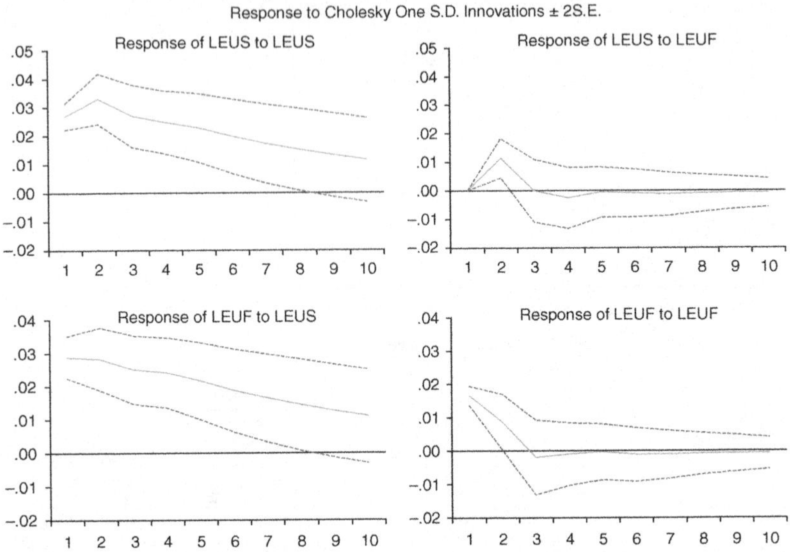

Graph A4.5 The impulse response function of eq. (4.51).

Note: LEUS = ln of the spot rate (s_t) and LEUF = ln of forward exchange rate (f_t).

Source: *Economagic.com* and Table A4.1.

$$\begin{aligned} &- \underset{(0.233)}{0.075}\, ca_{t-1} + \underset{(0.071)}{0.031}\, ca^*_{t-1} - \underset{(0.803)}{0.005}\, p_{t-1} \\ &+ \underset{(0.777)}{0.823} p^*_{t-1} + \underset{(0.036)}{0.929^{***}}\, s_{t-1} + \underset{(0.107)}{0.408^{***}}\, \varepsilon_{t-1} \end{aligned}$$

$$R^2 = 0.977, \quad SSR = 0.044, \quad F = 291.150, \quad D-W = 1.974,$$

$$N = 96, \quad RMSE = 0.021446$$

This equation gives better statistics compared to the constrained model.

A4.2.3 Multiequation Time-Series Models: (VAR) Analysis, Eq. (4.51)

The estimation of the spot (s_t) and forward (f_t) rates by using a *VAR* with time trend model, eq. (4.51), is as follows (table A4.1) and its impulse response function appears in graph A4.5:

A shock on the spot rate overshoots the spot and the forward rate and then they fall to their previous levels. A shock on the forward rate undershoots it a little and reduces the value of the spot rate.

Table A4.1 Vector autoregression estimates, eq. (4.51)

Date: 09/04/12 Time: 11:05
Sample (adjusted): 2005M05 2010M12
Included observations: 68 after adjustments
Standard errors in ( ) & *t*-statistics in [ ]

	LEUS	*LEUF*
LEUS(−1)	0.494469	0.498516
	(0.24134)	(0.29973)
	[2.04887]	[1.66322]
LEUS(−2)	0.426802	0.560948
	(0.20041)	(0.24890)
	[2.12967]	[2.25374]
LEUF(−1)	0.683122	0.517509
	(0.19865)	(0.24671)
	[3.43885]	[2.09763]
LEUF(−2)	−0.697569	−0.731988
	(0.23231)	(0.28852)
	[−3.00270]	[−2.53703]
C	0.007720	0.038910
	(0.02016)	(0.02503)
	[0.38301]	[1.55431]
TIME1	0.000181	0.000100
	(0.00019)	(0.00023)
	[0.97041]	[0.43254]
R-squared	0.895937	0.826295
Adj. *R*-squared	0.887545	0.812287
Sum sq. resids	0.044163	0.068118
S. E. equation	0.026689	0.033146
F-statistic	106.7583	58.98559
Log likelihood	153.0512	138.3169
Akaike AIC	−4.325036	−3.891673
Schwarz SC	−4.129197	−3.695834
Mean dependent	0.292987	0.296431
S. D. dependent	0.079587	0.076505
Determinant resid covariance (dof adj.)		1.94E-07
Determinant resid covariance		1.62E-07
Log likelihood		338.7067
Akaike information criterion		−9.609020
Schwarz criterion		−9.217342

Note: LEUS = ln of the spot rate (s_t), LEUF = ln of forward exchange rate (f_t), and TIME1 = time trend.
Source: *Economagic.com*.

A4.2.4 The Current Spot Rate as a Forecasting Indicator

The empirical results of eq. (4.52) are:

$$\underset{}{s_t = \underset{(0.009)}{0.997^{***}}\, s_{t-1}}$$

$R^2 = 0.973$, $SSR = 0.120$, $D-W = 1.611$, $N = 157$,

$RMSE = 0.027668$

Thus, $s^e_{t+1} = 0.997\, s_t$ (the current spot forecasts the spot rate next period).

A4.2.5 The Forward Exchange Rate as a Forecasting Indicator

The empirical results of eq. (4.54) appear below:

$$s_t = \underset{(0.011)}{0.990^{***}}\, f_{t-1}$$

$R^2 = 0.876$, $SSR = 0.053$, $D-W = 1.565$, $N = 70$,

$RMSE = 0.027513$

Consequently, $s^e_{t+1} = 0.990 f_t$ (the current forward rate forecasts the next period's spot exchange rate).

A4.3 Forecasting with the Use of Currency Betas (β_s)

The estimation of the currency β, eq. (4.55), by taking the ln of the variables, is given below (graph A4.6),

$$s_t = \underset{(0.135)}{5.481^{***}} + \underset{(0.030)}{1.190^{***}}\, e_{XRI_t}$$

$R^2 = 0.908$, $SSR = 0.051$, $D-W = 0.101$, $N = 158$,

$RMSE = 0.051047$

Then, we run the same equation by taking the growth of the two variables $\dot{s}_t$ and $\dot{e}_{XRI_t}$, which gives the results:

$$\dot{s}_t = \underset{(0.001)}{-0.001} + \underset{(0.076)}{1.322^{***}}\, \dot{e}_{XRI_t}$$

$R^2 = 0.661$, $SSR = 0.041$, $D-W = 2.347$, $N = 157$,

$RMSE = 0.016114$

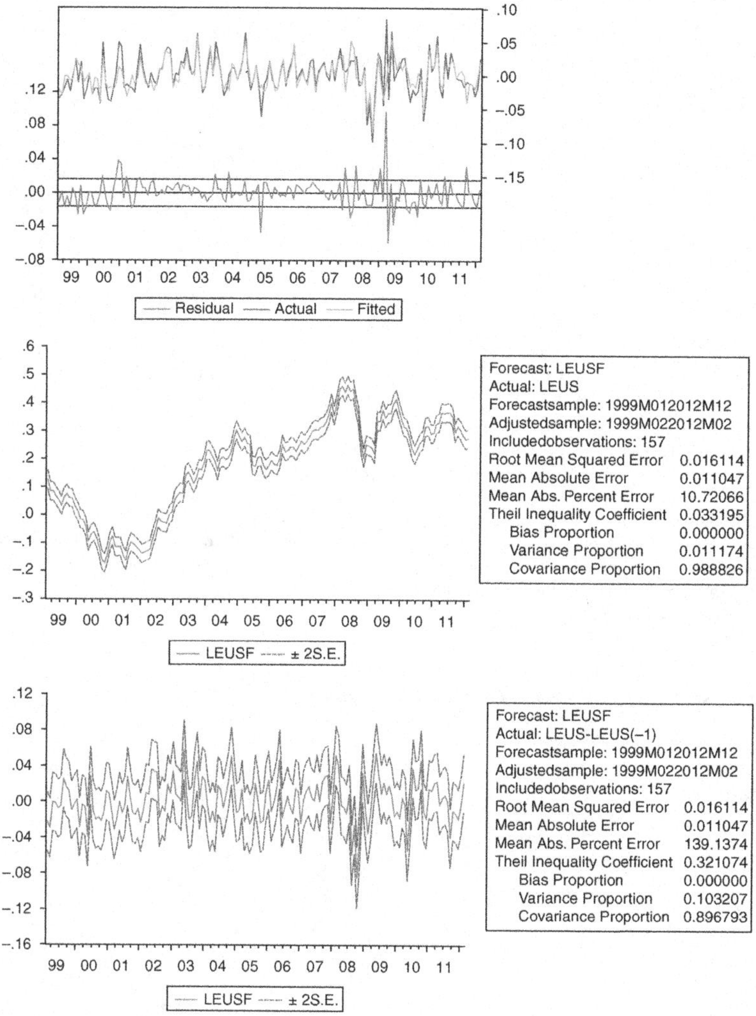

Graph A4.6 The estimate of currency beta, eq. (4.55).

Note: Actual (LEUS) = ln of the spot rate (s_t) and Fitted (LEUF) = ln of forward exchange rate (f_t).

Source: *Economagic.com.*

A4.4 Unit Root (Stationarity) Test

The Augmented Dickey-Fuller (ADF) and Phillips-Perron (PP) unit root (stationarity) tests of the variables used in our regressions are shown in table A4.2 below.

Table A4.2 Augmented Dickey-Fuller and Phillips-Perron unit root tests

Variables	*ADF*	I(d)	*PP*	*I(d)*
S	−1.093	I(1)	−1.306	I(1)
s	−1.170	I(1)	−1.109	I(1)
F	−1.910	I(1)	−2.035	I(1)
f	−1.937	I(1)	−2.033	I(1)
usxri	−0.763	I(1)	−0.682	I(1)
m	−1.003	I(1)	−1.003	I(1)
m^*	2.683*	I(0)	6.525***	I(0)
q	−1.553	I(10	−2.733*	I(0)
q^*	1.138	I(1)	0.733	I(1)
i_{TB}	−1.490	I(1)	−1.147	I(1)
i_{3MDDL}	−1.216	I(1)	−1.204	I(1)
ca	−0.611	I(1)	−0.771	I(1)
ca^*	−10.048***	I(0)	−10.050***	I(0)
p	−1.051	I(1)	−1.030	I(1)
p^*	−2.707*	I(0)	−7.400***	I(0)

Note: * = significant at the 10 percent level, ** = significant at the 5 percent level, and *** = significant at the 1 percent level, S = spot exchange rate ($/€), s = ln of spot rate, F = the forward exchange rate, f = the ln of the forward rate, *usxri* = the ln of the US exchange rate index, m = the ln of the US money supply, m^* = the ln of the Euro-zone money supply, q = the ln of the US real income, q^* = the ln of the European real income, i_{TB} = the US T-bill rate, i^*_{3MDL} = the three-month deposit LIBOR, ca = the ln of the US current account balance, ca^* = the ln of the European current account balance, p = the ln of the price level (CPI) in the United States, and p^* = the ln of the Euro-zone price index.
Source: *Economagic.com* and *Eurostat.*

Table A4.3 Cointegration test of the VAR model

Eq. (4.51); Variables: s_t and f_t

(Maximum lag in VAR=2)

Type of Tests	*Null*	*Alternative*	*Eigenvalue*[1]	*Statistics*	*Critical Values 95%*
Trace Test	$r=0$	$r>0$	0.299	29.844***	15.495
	$r\leq 1$	$r>1$	0.087	6.072**	3.841
Maximum Eigenvalue Test	$r=0$	$r=1$	0.299	23.772***	14.265
	$r=1$	$r=2$	0.087	6.072**	3.841

Note: s_t = the ln of spot rate, f_t = the ln of the forward rate, r = determines the number of cointegrating relations (conditional on the assumptions made about the trend), *trace statistics* = the number of cointegrating relations under the null hypothesis, *maximum eigenvalue statistics* = the ordered eigenvalues of the coefficient matrix of the VAR; trace test indicates 1 cointegrating equation at 1 percent level and 1 cointegrating equation at the 5percent level. Maximum eigenvalue test indicates 1 cointegrating equation at the 1 percent level and 1 cointegrating at the 5 percent level.

[1] An *eigenvector* of a square matrix is a nonzero vector that, when multiplied by the matrix, yields a vector that is parallel to the original. For example, if three-element vectors are seen as arrows in three-dimensional space, an eigenvector of a 3 × 3 matrix A is an arrow whose direction is either preserved or exactly reversed after multiplication by A. The corresponding eigenvalue determines how the length and sense of the arrow is changed by the operation. Specifically, a nonzero column vector v is a *right eigenvector* of a matrix A if (and only if) there exists a number λ such that $Av=\lambda v$. If the vector satisfies $vA=\lambda v$ instead, it is said to be a *left eigenvector*. The number λ is called the *eigenvalue* corresponding to that vector.

Source: See table A4.2.

Then, the first table reported here is table A4.2, which presents an Augmented Dickey-Fuller and Phillips-Perron unit root test for the variables of our models. The only stationary series are: q for the United States and m^*, ca^*, p^* for the Euro-zone. The rest of the variables contain a unit root, they are integrated of order one [I(1)]. Table A4.3 gives the results of the cointegration test of the VAR system, eq. (4.51). Trace tests and maximum eigenvalue ones indicate that our equations are cointegrating (stationary).

A4.5 Cointegration Test

The finding that s_t and f_t series contain a unit root (are nonstationary) led us to test their linear combination (VAR model) if it is stationary. If such a stationary linear combination exists, these two nonstationary time series are *cointegrated*. This stationary linear combination is called the cointegrating equations and is interpreted as a long-run equilibrium relationship between these two variables. The test output for the two-variable (VAR) system is as follows (table A4.3):

Notes

1. See, Enders (1995) and Chatfield (1985).
2. *Mean reversion* is a mathematical concept sometimes used for stock investing, but it can be applied to other assets (not to exchange rates). In general terms, the essence of the concept is the assumption that both a stock's high and low prices are temporary and that a stock's price will tend to move to the average price over time. Mean reversion involves first identifying the trading range for a stock, and then computing the average price using analytical techniques, as it relates to assets, earnings, etc. When the current market price is less than the average price, the stock is considered attractive for purchase, with the expectation that the price will rise. When the current market price is above the average price, the market price is expected to fall. In other words, deviations from the average price are expected to revert to the average.
3. The random walk model seems to approximate the behavior of the exchange rates shown in the appendix A4.1.2. The various exchange rates series have no particular tendency to increase or decrease over time; neither do they exhibit any tendency to revert to a given mean value.
4. The random walk with drift is a first-order autoregressive process that is not stationary.
5. A transfer function model simply relates a dependent variable to lagged values of itself, current, and lagged values of one or more independent variables, and an error term, which is partially explained by a time-series model. The technique of transfer function modeling involves examination of partial and

total autocorrelation functions for the independent variables X_t as well as the dependent variable s_t in an effort to specify the lag polynomials. The structural part of the model is arrived at through the mixture of the monetary approach theory and other econometric methods, while the time-series part of the model is arrived at through an analysis of the residuals of the structural model.
6. Interest Rate parity (IRP): $i_t - i_t^* = \frac{F_{t+n} - S_t}{S_t} \frac{12}{n} 100$, where n=the number of months of the forward rate.
7. See, Dickey and Fuller (1979), Phillips and Perron (1988), and Kallianiotis (2002).
8. See, Enders (1995, pp. 356–362).
9. Some examples of stationary combinations of nonstationary variables are: (1) the money demand function, (2) the consumption function theory, (3) the unbiased forward market hypothesis, (4) the commodity market arbitrage and purchasing power parity, and many others.
10. See also Kallianiotis (2007).

Bibliography

Arize, Augustine C., Elias C. Grivoyannis, Ioannis N. Kallianiotis, and Valerie Englander (2000), "The Traditional Approach to Balance of Payments Adjustment under Flexible Exchange Rates," in *Balance of Payments Adjustment: Macro Facets of International Finance Revisited*, edited by A. C. Arize, T. H. Bonitsis, I. N. Kallianiotis, K. M. Kasibhatla, and J. Malindretos, Westport, CT: Greenwood Press, pp.171–199.

Bilson, John F. (1978), "Rational Expectations and the Exchange Rate," in *The Economics of Exchange Rates*, edited by Jacob A. Frenkel and Harry G. Johnson, Reading, MA: Addison-Wesley, pp. 75–96.

Chatfield, C. (1985), *The Analysis of Time Series: An Introduction*, 3rd Edition, New York: Chapman and Hall.

Dickey, D. A. and W. A. Fuller (1979), "Distribution of the Estimators for Autoregressive Time Series with a Unit Root," *Journal of the American Statistical Association*, Vol. 74, pp. 427–431.

Enders, Walter (1995), *Applied Econometric Time Series*, New York: John Wiley & Sons, Inc.

Engle, Robert F. and C. W. J. Granger (1987), "Co-integration and Error Correction: Representation, Estimation, and Testing," *Econometrica*, Vol. 55, pp. 251–276.

Johansen, Soren (1991), "Estimation and Hypothesis Testing of Cointegration Vectors in Gaussian Vector Autoregressive Models," *Econometrica*, Vol. 59, pp. 1551–1580.

Kallianiotis, Ioannis N. (2007), "Transmission Mechanism through Aggregate Demand and Supply and Public Policy Effectiveness between the U.S.A. and the EMU," unpublished manuscript, *University of Scranton*, July, pages 34.

Kallianiotis, Ioannis N. (2002), "Saving and Investment: The Forecast Function of Interest Rate," *American Business Review*, Vol. 20, No. 1, January, pp. 50–58.

———. (1988), "A Theoretical Monetary and Real Approach to the Balance of Payments," *Greek Economic Review*, Vol. 10, No. 2, December, pp. 383–404.

———. (1985), *Exchange Rates and Rational Expectations*, PhD Dissertation, Graduate Center, CUNY, New York.

Kallianiotis, Ioannis N. and Anton Boutchev (1996), "Foreign Currency Forecasts: A Combining Analysis," unpublished manuscript, *University of Scranton*, January, pages 35.

Neely, Christopher J. and Lucio Sarno (2002), "How Well Do Monetary Fundamentals Forecast Exchange Rates?," *Review*, Federal Reserve Bank of St. Louis, September/October, pp. 51–72.

Phillips, P. C. B. and P. Perron (1988), "Testing a Unit Root in Time Series Regression," *Biometrika*, Vol. 75, pp. 335–346.

5

Foreign Currency Derivatives

A *foreign currency derivative* is a financial derivative whose payoff depends on the foreign exchange rates of two (or more) currencies. These instruments are commonly used for hedging foreign exchange risk or for currency speculation and arbitrage. Specific foreign exchange derivatives include: *foreign currency forward contracts*, *foreign currency futures*, *foreign currency swaps*, *currency options*, and *foreign exchange binary options*. These instruments are called derivatives because their value is derived from an underlying asset, a foreign currency. The financial managers of MNCs purchase these financial derivatives in order to reduce the risk associated with cash flows denominated in foreign currency, hedging this exchange rate risk or to take positions in the expectation of profit, speculation, or arbitrage. Financial derivatives are powerful tools of hedging (redistributing) foreign exchange risk, but at the same time, they are very risky instruments for inexperienced financial managers. Lately, there were many cases in which financial managers generated enormous losses for their companies (mostly banks) and led them to bankruptcy. Of course, the rule is always moderation and prudence. If we want to go one step further, the rule is the maximization of the social welfare of a nation.

5.1 Foreign Currency Forward and Futures Contracts

In finance, a *forward contract* or simply a *forward* is a nonstandardized contract between two parties to buy or sell an asset (foreign currency) at a specified future time at a price agreed upon today. This is in contrast to a spot contract, which is an agreement to buy or sell a foreign currency today. The party agreeing to buy the underlying currency in the future assumes a long position, and the party agreeing to sell the asset in the future assumes a short position. The price agreed upon is called the delivery price (exchange rate), which is equal to the forward exchange rate at the time the contract is entered into. The currency forward market offers private contracts that are tailored to the specific needs of customers. The forward contracts have existed for many centuries and some authors trace their practice to the classical Greek , Egyptian, and Roman period.[1]

A *currency future*, also *FX future* or *foreign exchange future*, is a futures contract to exchange one currency for another at a specified date in the future at a price (exchange rate) that is fixed on the purchase date. Typically, one of the currencies is the US dollar. The *price* of a future is then in terms of US dollars per unit of other currency. This can be different from the standard way of quoting in the spot foreign exchange markets. The *trade unit* of each contract is then a certain amount of other currency; for example, ¥12,500,000, CAD100,000, £62,500, CHF125,000, AUD100,000, MXN500,000, and €125,000. Most contracts have physical delivery, so for those held at the end of the last trading day, actual payments are made in each currency. They represent an institutionalized form of currency forward contracting, like the International Monetary Market (IMM). However, most contracts are closed out before their maturity. Investors can close out the contract any time prior to the contract's delivery date. Foreign currency futures contracts differ from forward contracts in a number of ways; exhibit 5.1 provides a comparison between them.

5.1.1 *Foreign Currency Forward Contracts*

A *forward contract* is an agreement between an MNC and a bank (foreign currency dealer) that specifies the currencies to be exchanged, the exchange rate (forward rate), and the date at which the transaction will occur. The forward rate is the exchange rate specified within the forward contract at which the currencies will be exchanged. The forward market represents the market in which the forward contracts are traded. With these contracts, MNCs hedge their payables and receivables, as will be discussed in detail in Chapter 6. The liquidity of the forward market varies among currencies with the forward market for hard currencies (i.e., euros) being more liquid because of the size of the trade with these currencies, and less liquid with other currencies that have less international trade and capital flow participation. For some weak currencies, there is no forward market.

The forward exchange rate of such a contract is commonly contrasted with the spot exchange rate, which is the price at which the currency changes hands on the spot date. The difference between the spot and the forward rate is the forward premium or forward discount, generally considered in the form of a profit, or loss, by the purchasing party. Forwards,

Exhibit 5.1 Comparison of currency forward and futures markets

Characteristic	*Forward*	*Futures*
Size of contract	Tailored to individual needs	Standardized
Delivery date	Tailored to individual needs	Standardized
Method of transaction	Established by the bank or broker via telephone contact with limited number of buyers and sellers	Determined by open auction among many buyers and sellers on the exchange floor
Participants	Banks, brokers, and MNCs; public speculation not encouraged	Banks, brokers, and MNCs; qualified public speculation encouraged.
Commissions (Transaction costs)	Set by "spread" between bank's buy and sell price; not easily determined by customer	Published small brokerage fee and negotiated rates on block trades
Security deposit	None as such, but compensating bank balances required	Published small security deposit required
Clearing operation (financial integrity)	Handling contingent on individual banks and brokers;no separate clearinghouse function	Handled by exchange clearinghouse; daily settlements to the market
Marketplace	Over the telephone worldwide	Central exchange floor with worldwide communications
Economic justification	Facilitates world trade by providing hedge mechanism	Same as forward market; in addition, provides a broader market and an alternate hedging mechanism via public participation
Accessibility	Limited to very large customers who deal in foreign trade	Open to anyone who needs hedge facilities or has risk capital to speculate with
Regulation	Self-regulating	April 1975: Regulated under the Commodity Futures Trading Commission
Frequency of delivery	More than 90% settled by actual delivery.	Theoretically, no deliveries in a perfect market. In reality, less than 1%

continued

Exhibit 5.1 Continued

Characteristic	*Forward*	*Futures*
Price fluctuations	No daily limit	No daily limit
Market liquidity	Offsetting with other banks	Public offset Arbitrage offset
Liquidation	Most settled by actual delivery Some by offset, at a cost	Most by offset, very few by delivery.
Maturity	Any maturity up to one year, sometimes longer	Fixed maturities, longest typically being one year
Pricing	Prices are determined by bid and ask quotes	Open outcry process on the exchange floor
Margin/Collateral	No explicit commission; banks earn effective commissions through the bid-ask spreads	Initial margin that is marked to market on a daily basis
Trading Hours	Negotiated by phone or Internet, 24 hours a day, through bank global networks	Traditionally traded during exchange hours; some exchanges have moved to 24 hours
Counterparties	Parties are in direct contact in settling forward specifications	Unknown to each other due to the auction market structure
Liquidity	Liquid and relatively large in sales volume compared to futures contracts	Liquid but relatively small in total sales volume and value

like other derivative securities, can be used to hedge risk (typically currency or exchange rate risk), as a means of speculation, or to allow a party to take advantage of the quality of the underlying instrument that is time sensitive. Large banks and private currency brokers' network trade these contracts electronically to meet their customers' needs. MNCs may require a forward contract for two or three or more years, which can be obtained through direct negotiations with their banks. Mostly, the negotiations are done over the telephone and the banks may require compensating balances or lines of credit to insure the MNCs' obligation. These currency forward contracts are valued at over $1 million.

A closely related contract is a futures contract (see, section 5.1.2); they differ in certain respects, as exhibit 5.1 shows. Forward contracts are very similar to futures contracts, except that they are not exchange traded, or defined on standardized assets. Forwards also typically have no interim partial settlements or "true-ups" in margin requirements like futures (the parties do not exchange additional property securing the party at gain and the entire unrealized gain or loss builds up while the contract is open). However, being traded over the counter (OTC), forward contracts specification can be customized and may include mark-to-market and daily margining. Hence, a forward contract arrangement might call for the loss party to pledge collateral or additional collateral to better secure the party at gain.

The forward contracts on foreign currencies are traded in the forward market, which are created by financial institutions (commercial banks). When MNCs anticipate a future need (payables or receivables) of a foreign currency, they can set up forward contracts to lock in the exchange rate, at which they can purchase or sell a foreign currency. Forward contracts are not used by individuals or small firms, but by large corporations because the transactions are amount to millions of dollars. These large denomination forward contracts are negotiated between the firm and a financial institution and are tailored to meet the specific needs of the firm. In case a bank does not know the corporation, an interest-free compensating balance (deposit) is required. The most common forward contracts are 1, 2, 3, 6, and 12 months, although other periods, up to five years, can also be found.

An example of a forward contract can be the following. A MNC needs £10,000,000 in three months (90 days) to purchase some imports from England. It can wait 90 days to buy pounds in the spot market at that time, but the exchange rate is fluctuatingd and the cost will be uncertain. To avoid the exchange rate risk, it can buy the pounds three months forward at the current forward rate, $F_3 = 1.6091$ \$/£, and thus, it locks in the exchange rate. Then, the cost will be £10,000,000 × 1.6091 \$/£ = \$16,091,000, which is known with certainty from then on.

5.1.2 *Foreign Currency Futures Contracts*

A *foreign currency futures contract* is an alternative to a forward contract that calls for future delivery of a standard amount of foreign currency at a fixed time, place, and price. These futures contracts are similar to commodities, interest bearing deposits, precious metals, stock indices, treasury securities, and other futures. Currency futures are traded on an organized market, which is a physical trading floor, where standardized (listed) contracts are traded face to face. They are commonly used by MNCs to hedge their foreign currency positions and by speculators, who capitalize on their expectations of exchange rate movements. Actually, a buyer of a futures contract locks in the exchange rate to be paid for a foreign currency at a future date. The majority of forward contracts are settled by actual delivery of the underlying currency, whereas the majority of futures contracts are settled via reversing trades (speculators), such that delivery never occurs.

Currency futures were first created in 1970 at the International Commercial Exchange in New York. But the contracts did not "take off," due to the fact that the Bretton Woods system was still in effect. They did so a full two years before the Chicago Mercantile Exchange (CME) was established in 1972, less than a year after the gold exchange standard was abandoned. Some commodity traders at the CME did not have access to the interbank exchange markets in the early 1970s, when they believed that significant changes were about to take place in the currency market. The CME established the International Monetary Market (IMM) and launched trading in seven currency futures on May 16, 1972. Before 1972, only agricultural and metallurgical futures were traded on organized exchanges. Today, the IMM is a division of CME. In the fourth quarter of 2009, CME Group FX volume averaged 754,000 contracts per day, reflecting average daily notional value of approximately $100 billion. Currently most of these are traded electronically.

Currency futures are traded on exchanges that provide regulation in terms of centralized pricing and clearing. The market price for a currency futures contract will be relatively the same regardless of which broker is used. The CME Group offers 49 currency futures contracts, making it the largest regulated currency futures marketplace in the world. Besides the IMM, there are many other futures exchanges that trade currency futures, like the Philadelphia Board of Trade, the London International Financial Futures Exchange, the Singapore International Monetary Exchange, the Sydney Futures Exchange, the Euronext.liffe,[2] the Tokyo Financial Exchange (TFX), the Intercontinental Exchange, the Brazilian Mercantile and Futures Exchange (BM&F), and several other organized exchanges worldwide. At each of these exchanges, trading occurs in areas called *pits.* Traders in the pits offer to buy or sell through a system of open outcry or often by using sophisticated hand signals, but lately, the incorporation of electronic trading platforms is changing this standard way.

5.1.2.1 Contract Specifications

The international foreign exchange market is the largest market in the world with over $4 trillion traded daily, according to the Bank for International Settlements (BIS) data. The foreign exchange market is not the only way for investors and traders to participate in foreign exchange. The currency futures market also has a respectable daily average closer to $100 billion. Currency futures, also called forex futures or foreign exchange futures, are similar to other futures products; they are traded in terms of contract months with standard maturity dates typically falling on the third Wednesday of March, June, September, and December.

A wide variety of currency futures contracts are available. Aside from the popular contracts such as the EUR/USD (euro/US dollar currency futures contract), there are also E-Micro Forex Futures contracts that trade at 1/10th the size of regular currency futures contracts, as well as emerging market currency pairs such as the PLN/USD (Polish zloty/US dollar futures contract) and the RUB/USD (Russian ruble/US dollar futures contract). Different contracts trade with varying degrees of liquidity; for example, the daily volume for the EUR/USD contract might be 400,000 contracts versus 33 contracts for an emerging market like the BRL/USD (Brazilian real/US dollar). Traders and investors are drawn to markets with high liquidity since these markets provide better opportunity for profit. The emerging markets typically have very low volume and liquidity, and they will need to gain traction before becoming competitive with the other established contracts. The G10 contracts, the E-mini, and the E-Micro contracts are the most heavily traded and have the greatest liquidity.

Futures contracts, including currency futures, must list specifications including the size of the contract, the minimum price increment, and the corresponding tick value.[3] These specifications help traders determine position sizing and account requirements, as well as the potential profit or loss for different price movements in the contract. The euro/US dollar contract, for example, shows a minimum price increment of .0001, and a corresponding tick value of $12.50. This indicates that each time there is a .0001 movement in price, the value of the contract will change by $12.50 with the value dependent on the direction of the price change. For instance, if a long trade is entered at 1.3958 and moves to 1.3959, that .0001 price move would be worth $12.50 to the trader (assuming one contract). If that same long trade moves to 1.3968, the price move would be worth $125.00 (=$12.50 × 10 ticks or pips).[4]

There are two primary methods of settling a currency futures contract. In the vast majority of instances, buyers and sellers will offset their original positions before the last day of trading (a day that varies depending on the contract) by taking an opposite position. When an opposite position closes the trade prior to the last day of trading, a profit or loss is credited to or debited from the trader's account. Less frequently, contracts are held until the maturity date, at which time the contract is cash settled or physically delivered, depending on the specific contract and exchange. Most currency futures are subject to a physical delivery process four times a year on the third Wednesday during the months of March, June, September, and December. Only a small percentage of currency futures contracts are settled in the physical delivery of foreign exchange between a buyer and seller. When a currency futures contract is held to expiration and is physically settled, the appropriate exchange and the participant each have duties to complete the delivery.

The CME is responsible for establishing banking facilities in the United States and in each country represented by its currency futures contracts. These agent banks, as they are called, act on behalf of the CME and maintain a US dollar account and a foreign currency account to accommodate any physical deliveries. In addition, futures contracts do not exist directly between clients (e.g., a buyer and a seller). Instead, each participant has a contract with a clearing house, greatly reducing the risk for buyers and sellers in case a counterparty fails to meet the terms of the contract. Buyers (participants holding long positions) make arrangements with a bank to pay dollars into the IMM delivery account, a division of the CME. The IMM is also the account from which sellers (participants holding short positions) are paid. The transfer of foreign currency occurs similarly in other countries. Essentially, a participant's delivering bank transfers the currency to the IMM delivery account, which then transfers the currency to the appropriate account.

Futures brokers, including those that offer currency futures, most follow regulations enforced by governing agencies including the Commodity Futures Trading Commission (CFTC) and the National Futures Association (NFA), as well as rules set forth by the exchanges. For example, the CME Group, the largest futures exchange in the world, ensures that self-regulatory duties are fulfilled through its Market Regulation Department, including market integrity protection by maintaining fair, efficient, competitive, and transparent markets. Currency futures markets have a great deal more oversight than the spot foreign exchange markets, which are at times criticized for things like noncentralized pricing and foreign exchange brokers trading against their clients.

Currency futures are exchange-traded futures. Traders typically have accounts with brokers that direct orders to the various exchanges to buy and sell currency futures contracts. A margin account is generally used in the trading of currency futures; otherwise, a great deal of cash would be required to place a trade. With a margin account, traders borrow money from the broker in order to place trades, usually a multiplier of the actual cash value of the account. The buying power is the amount of money in the margin account that is available for trading. Different brokers have varying requirements for margin accounts. In general, currency futures accounts allow a rather conservative degree of margin (leverage) when compared to foreign exchange accounts that can offer as much as 400:1 leverage. The liberal margin rates of many foreign exchange accounts provide traders the opportunity to make impressive gains, but more often they suffer catastrophic losses. They are very risky, too.

There are many differences between the currency futures and the foreign exchange: (1) The foreign exchange spot market is the largest market in the world. Currency futures trade at a fraction of the volume, with many currency futures contracts trading under high volume and good liquidity. (2) Currency futures are exchange-traded and are regulated like other futures markets. Foreign exchange has less regulation and trading is conducted over the counter through foreign exchange dealers (there is no central marketplace for foreign exchange). (3) Currency futures can be traded using modest leverage; foreign exchange offers the ability to trade with a great deal of leverage, leading to large wins and, of course, large losses. (4) The tax treatment for profits and losses incurred from currency futures trading and foreign exchange trading may differ, depending on the particular situation. (5) Commissions and fees differ: currency futures typically involve a commission (paid to the broker) and other various exchange fees. Though foreign exchange traders do not pay these commissions and fees, they are subject to exchange rate spreads through which the foreign exchange dealer profits. (6) Investors and traders interested in participating in the foreign exchange market have a variety of options. Foreign exchange and currency futures offer traders unique vehicles with which to hedge or speculate. The currency futures market is similar to other futures markets and provides participants a means of entering the foreign exchange market with greater regulation and transparency.

5.1.2.2 Speculating Using Foreign Currency Futures

Currency futures are used for speculating on currency movements and an example can be the euro futures traded on the CME, as is quoted from the "Currency Futures" from the *Wall Street Journal*, and it is presented in exhibit 5.2. Each contract is €125,000 and the quotations are direct for the United States or in "American terms" ($/€).

An investor or speculator can speculate on the movement of the euro (€) versus the US dollar ($) by purchasing one of the following strategies:

1. Short Positions:
   If the speculator believes that the euro (€) will fall (depreciate) versus the US dollar ($) by December 2012, he could sell a December futures contract, taking a *short position*. By selling a December contract, he locks in the right to sell €125,000 at a set price. If the price of euro (€) does fall by the maturity date as he expects, he has a

Exhibit 5.2 Euro futures, US \$/€(CME), €125,000

Maturity	*Open*	*High*	*Low*	*Settle*	*Change*	*Open Interest*
Dec '12	1.2929	1.2947	1.2888	1.2909	−0.0016	216,251
March '13	...	1.2958	1.2909	1.2922	−0.0016	699

Note: Maturity = the third Wednesday of March, June, September, and December, Open = the opening price on the day, High = the high price on the day, Low = the lowest price on the day, Settle = the closing price on the day, Change = the change in the settle price from the previous day's close, and Open Interest = the number of contracts outstanding.
Source: Currency futures, *The Wall Street Journal*, October 4, 2012, p. C11.

contract to sell euros at a price above their current price on the spot market. Then, he makes a profit.

Utilizing the quotations from exhibit 5.2, we have the following. Our speculator sells one December futures contract of €125,000 at the closing price (settle price) of 1.2909 \$/€. The value of his position at maturity (at the expiration of the futures contract) is:

$$V_{S-P}^{M} = -A(S_{t+n} - F_n), \tag{5.1}$$

where, V_{S-P}^{M} = value at maturity (short position), A = amount (size of the contract) or notional principal, S_{t+n} = the spot exchange rate at maturity, F_n = the futures exchange rate (settle price), and the negative sign (−) denotes short position.

Let say that today is the third Wednesday of December 2012 (the maturity date of the contract) and the spot rate is $S_{t+n} = 1.2300\$/€$; then, the value of his position on settlement will be,

$$V_{S-P}^{M} = -125{,}000(1.2300 - 1.2909) = \$7{,}612.50$$

If the expectations of this speculator are correct, he is making a profit of \$7,612.50 per futures contract because "he ends up buying at 1.2300 \$/€ and selling at 1.2909 \$/€."

2. Long Positions:
If our speculator expected the euro (€) to rise in value (appreciate) versus the dollar (\$), he could take a *long position*, by buying a December futures on the euro. By buying December futures he is locking in the price, at which he must buy euros at the future (maturity) date. This futures contract at maturity would have the value:

$$V_{L-P}^{M} = A(S_{t+n} - F_n) \tag{5.2}$$

where, V_{L-P}^{M} = value at maturity (long position) and the sign has become positive now denoting long position.

Let say that the spot exchange rate at maturity (December 2012) is $S_{t+n} = 1.3300\$/€$. Then, the value of his position on settlement is:

$$V_{L-P}^{M} = 125{,}000(1.3300 - 1.2909) = \$4{,}887.50$$

The speculator was right in his expectations and he made a profit of $4,887.50 per futures contract by "buying at 1.2902 $/€ and selling at 1.3300 $/€." In case he had been wrong in his expectations about the future spot exchange rate, he would have major speculative loss. Speculation in foreign currencies is a very risky game.

5.1.3 *Foreign Currency Swaps*

A *foreign currency swap* is a foreign exchange agreement between two parties to exchange aspects (namely the principal and/or interest payments) of a loan in one currency for equivalent aspects of an equal in net present value loan in another currency. Currency swaps are motivated by comparative advantage. A standard currency swap entails the exchange of debt denominated in one currency for debt denominated in another currency. Currency swaps are over the counter (OTC) derivatives, and are closely related to interest rate swaps.[5] However, unlike interest rate swaps, currency swaps can involve the exchange of the principal.

For example, suppose a US MNC (MNC^{US}) wants to issue a British pound-denominated bond since it can make payments with British pound (£) inflows generated by its British subsidiary. Also, suppose that there is a British MNC (MNC^{UK}), which seeks to issue a dollar denominated debt. Thus, the MNC^{US} could provide British pound payments, both principal and interest, to the MNC^{UK} in exchange for dollar payments. This swap of currencies allows the two MNCs to make payments to their respective debt holders without having to repatriate foreign currency and be exposed to foreign exchange risk. Then, the MNC^{US} does not need to convert British pounds into dollars. This currency swap is shown in exhibit 5.3.

Another case of currency swap involves a *back-to-back loan* or a *parallel loan* or a *credit swap*, which became popular in Britain in the 1970s.[6] These parallel loans occur when each MNC makes a loan to the other's subsidiary, in its respective currency (the currency of the country where the subsidiary is located). For example, as is illustrated in exhibit 5.4, a US parent firm (MNC^{US}) loans dollars to a British subsidiary located in the United States (MNC^{UK}), and a British parent company (MNC^{UK}) loans pounds to the US subsidiary in the United Kingdom (MNC^{US}). The principal and periodic interest payments on these loans are structured to coincide. Since the loans are repaid with foreign revenues from ongoing operations, the firms

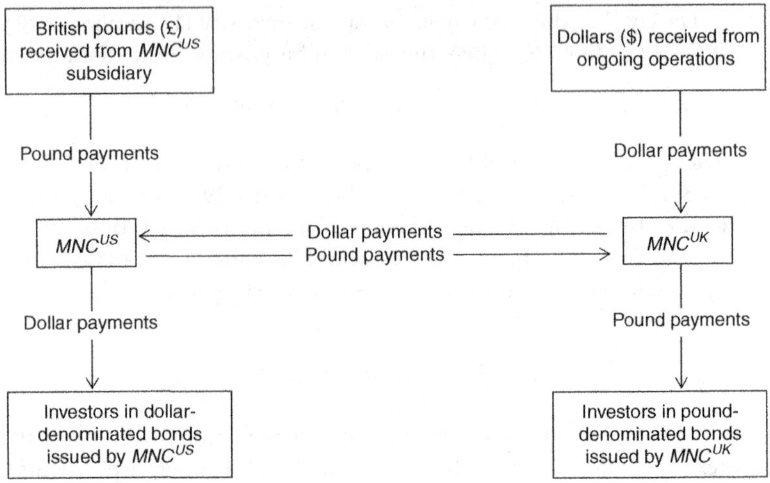

Exhibit 5.3 Currency swap.

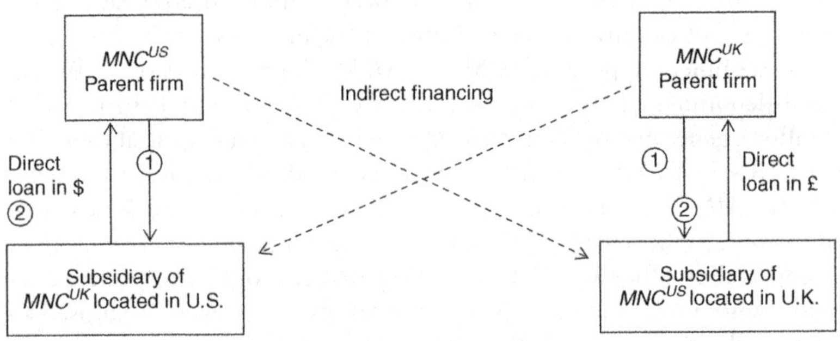

Exhibit 5.4 A parallel loan or credit swap. (back-to-back loan)

Notes: 1. Loans are simultaneously provided by parents of MNCs to the subsidiary of the other MNC. 2. In contemporaneous times the principal and periodic interest payments are repaid in the same currency that was borrowed.

are avoiding the tax on currency translations. The two subsidiaries do not need to convert one currency for the other to pay back their loans; thus, the exchange rate risk is eliminated. This basic structure of a currency swap minimizes the MNCs exposure to exchange rate risk. These parallel loan agreements contain an embedded futures contract, too. If one currency has depreciated greatly during the loan period, the lender of the devalued currency is required to increase its loan to offset its gain.

Actually, there are three different ways in which currency swaps can exchange loans:

(1) The simplest currency swap structure is to exchange only the principal with the counterparty at a specified point in the future at a rate agreed now. Such an agreement performs a function equivalent to a forward or futures contract. The cost of finding a counterparty (either directly or through an intermediary), and drawing up an agreement with them, makes swaps more expensive than alternative derivatives (and thus rarely used) as a method to fix shorter-term forward exchange rates. However for the longer-term future, commonly up to ten years, where spreads are wider for alternative derivatives, principal-only currency swaps are often used as a cost-effective way to fix forward rates. This type of currency swap is also known as an *FX-swap.*

(2) Another currency swap structure is to combine the exchange of loan principal, as above, with an interest rate swap. In such a swap, interest cash flows are not netted before they are paid to the counterparty (as they would be in a vanilla interest rate swap) because they are denominated in different currencies. As each party effectively borrows on the other's behalf, this type of swap is also known as a *back-to-back loan* (exhibit 5.4).

(3) Lastly, it is meant to swap only interest payment cash flows on loans of the same size and term. Again, as this is a currency swap, the exchanged cash flows are in different denominations and so are not netted. An example of such a swap is the exchange of fixed-rate US dollar ($) interest payments for floating-rate interest payments in euro (€). This type of swap is also known as a *cross-currency interest rate swap*, or *cross currency swap.*

The popularity of currency swaps is very high today. One reason for this is the reallocation of the exchange rate risk. Another reason is the regulatory barriers that exist to capital flows. Thus, currency swaps eliminate the exchange rate risk and overcome barriers to international capital movements. In other words, swaps have played an essential role in integrating the international financial markets, butthey also have some negative effects, as the latest global financial crisis revealed to us. This enormous integration and interdependence has made all economies vulnerable to a crisis that appears in one economy (like the current European debt crisis).

Countries and economies must be independent and self-sufficient, if it is possible.

5.2 Foreign Currency Options

A *foreign currency option* (commonly shortened to just *FX option* or *currency option* or *foreign exchange option*) is a derivative financial instrument that gives the owner (the buyer) the right, but not the obligation to purchase or sell a specified currency at a pre-agreed exchange rate (exercise price) on or before a specified expiration (maturity) date.

There are two types of option contracts (*calls*) and (*puts*) and two participants (*buyer* or *holder*) and (*seller* or *writer*), as exhibit 5.5 shows:

Each currency option has different elements, which are defined as follows: *Call option*, the right to buy a foreign currency at a fixed date and price. *Put option*, the right to sell a foreign currency at a fixed date and price. *Strike* or *exercise price*, the exchange rate, at which the investor (holder) can exercise (buy or sell) an option. *Spot price (exchange rate)*, the actual spot exchange rate of the currency in the market at the time of the exercise of the option. *Premium*, the price (cost) of the option, paid in advance by the buyer to the seller. *Maturity date*, the specified expiration date of the option (the third Friday of the month).[7] *American option*, an option that gives to the buyer the right to exercise the option at any time between the date of writing and the expiration or maturity date. *European option*, an option that can be exercised only on its expiration date.[8]

The foreign currency options market is the deepest, largest, and most liquid market for options of any kind. Most trading is over the counter (OTC) through banks (transactions of $1 million or more in custom-tailored option contracts) and is lightly regulated, but a fraction is traded on exchanges like the International Securities Exchange, Philadelphia Stock Exchange,[9] or the Chicago Mercantile Exchange for options on futures contracts. The Philadelphia Stock Exchange introduced trading

Exhibit 5.5 Currency options

		Types	
		Call	*Put*
Parties	Buyer	Contingent right to *buy* at X|E(S)↑	Contingent right to *sell* at X|E(S)↓
	Seller or Writer	Obligation to *sell* at X|E(S)↓	Obligation to *buy* at X|E(S)↑

in standardized foreign currency option contracts in 1982. The global market for exchange-traded currency options was notionally valued by the Bank for International Settlements at $158.3 trillion in 2005. The currency options are used as a hedging tool (redistribution of risk between the two parties) and for speculative purposes.[10]

5.2.1 *Currency Calls*

A *currency call option* grants to the buyer the (contingent) right to buy a specific currency at a designated price (exercise price or strike price) within a specific period of time. The buyer of this call option expects the foreign currency to appreciate ($S \uparrow$ \$/€) and he locks in a maximum price, the exercise price (X) to be paid for the currency in the future. If the spot rate (S) rises above the strike price (X), the holder of the call option can exercise his option by purchasing the currency at the strike price, which will be cheaper than the prevailing spot rate in the market. The owner of the call option can choose to let the option expire on the expiration date without ever exercising it, if the spot rate has declined and his loss will be the premium. The seller of a currency option receives the premium paid by the buyer and he has the obligation to accommodate the buyer in accordance with the rights of this currency call option.

5.2.1.1 Currency Calls: Quotations and Pricing

Currency option quotations are given by many different sources. Here, a list of euro currency options are given by *NASDAQ* and are referred to transactions completed on the Philadelphia Stock Exchange on the previous day (October 9, 2012), as they are shown in exhibit 5.6.

The quotations are direct for the United States (cents/euro) and a column of calls and another of puts are given with their maturity date (October 20, 2012). The different strike prices are shown together with the premium (last) for calls and the premium for puts. On October 12, 2012, a call option with premium of 8.10 cents/€ expires having a strike price of 114.00 cents/€ (1.1400 $/€). Since one option contract on the Philadelphia Stock Exchange consists of €125,000, the total cost of one call option is $10,125.00. The position of the buyer and seller of a call is illustrated in graph 5.1.

A MNC wants to hedge the exchange rate risk by buying the above currency call option, which gives it the right to buy euros (€) at a strike or exercise price of 114.00 cents/€ by paying a premium of 8.10 cents /€ or (€125,000 × 0.0810 S/€= $10,125.00) $10,125.00/contract. The owner has the choice of exercising the option or allowing it to expire unused. The

Exhibit 5.6 Euro currency options detail

Option Chain |Most Active |Greeks
Top of Form
^XDE Options: Type: Symbol Lookup Help
Oct 12 |Nov 12 |Dec 12 |Mar 13 |Jun 13 |Sep 13 |Near Term |All
Bottom of Form

Option Chain for PHLX U.S. Dollar-Settled Euro Currency (^XDE)

Calls	*Last*	*Chg*	*Bid*	*Ask*	*Vol*	*Open Int*	*Root*	*Strike*	*Puts*	*Last*	*Chg*	*Bid*	*Ask*	*Vol*	*Open Int*
Oct 20, 2012			18.85	19.00	0	0	XDE	110.00	Oct 20, 2012				0.04	0	0
Oct 20, 2012			17.85	18.00	0	0	XDE	111.00	Oct 20, 2012				0.04	0	0
Oct 20, 2012			16.85	17.00	0	0	XDE	112.00	Oct 20, 2012				0.04	0	0
Oct 20, 2012			15.85	16.00	0	0	XDE	113.00	Oct 20, 2012				0.04	0	0
Oct 20, 2012	8.10		14.85	15.00	0	1	XDE	114.00	Oct 20, 2012				0.04	0	0
Oct 20, 2012			13.85	14.00	0	0	XDE	115.00	Oct 20, 2012	0.71			0.04	0	21
Oct 20, 2012			12.85	13.00	0	0	XDE	116.00	Oct 20, 2012	0.88			0.04	0	239
Oct 20, 2012	5.60		11.85	12.00	0	11	XDE	117.00	Oct 20, 2012	1.23			0.04	0	403
Oct 20, 2012	4.70		10.85	11.00	0	2	XDE	118.00	Oct 20, 2012	0.95			0.04	0	193
Oct 20, 2012	4.00		9.85	10.00	0	18	XDE	119.00	Oct 20, 2012	1.20			0.04	0	130
Oct 20, 2012			8.85	9.00	0	0	XDE	120.00	Oct 20, 2012	0.25			0.04	0	43
Oct 20, 2012	6.80		7.85	8.00	0	9	XDE	121.00	Oct 20, 2012	1.79			0.04	0	120

Oct 20, 2012			6.85	7.00	0	0	XDE	122.00	Oct 20, 2012	0.58			0.04	0	50
Oct 20, 2012			5.85	6.00	0	0	XDE	123.00	Oct 20, 2012	0.79			0.04	0	140
Oct 20, 2012	6.01		4.85	5.00	0	8	XDE	124.00	Oct 20, 2012	0.14			0.04	0	632
Oct 20, 2012	2.20		3.85	4.00	0	25	XDE	125.00	Oct 20, 2012	0.21			0.04	0	167
Oct 20, 2012	2.00		2.93	3.05	0	67	XDE	126.00	Oct 20, 2012	0.24		0.02	0.06	0	73
Oct 20, 2012			2.01	2.09	0	0	XDE	127.00	Oct 20, 2012			0.11	0.15	0	0
Oct 20, 2012	2.28		1.23	1.28	0	93	XDE	128.00	Oct 20, 2012	0.24		0.31	0.35	0	319
Oct 20, 2012	0.63		0.62	0.67	0	89	XDE	129.00	Oct 20, 2012	1.19		0.70	0.75	0	252
Oct 20, 2012	0.85		0.26	0.30	0	80	XDE	130.00	Oct 20, 2012	1.64		1.32	1.39	0	932
Oct 20, 2012			0.08	0.12	0	0	XDE	131.00	Oct 20, 2012	1.43		2.13	2.22	0	6
Oct 20, 2012	0.51		0.01	0.05	0	6	XDE	132.00	Oct 20, 2012			3.05	3.15	0	0
Oct 20, 2012				0.04	0	0	XDE	133.00	Oct 20, 2012			4.00	4.15	0	0
Oct 20, 2012				0.04	0	0	XDE	134.00	Oct 20, 2012			5.00	5.15	0	0
Oct 20, 2012				0.04	0	0	XDE	135.00	Oct 20, 2012	9.20		6.00	6.15	0	143

Note: ^XDE = Euro currency option, Strike = strike price, Oct. 20, 2012 = maturity date, and Open Int = the number of contracts outstanding.

Source: *NASDAQ*, http://www.nasdaq.com/aspxcontent/optionsWC.aspx?symbol=^XDE&qm_page=25122&qm_symbol=^XDE

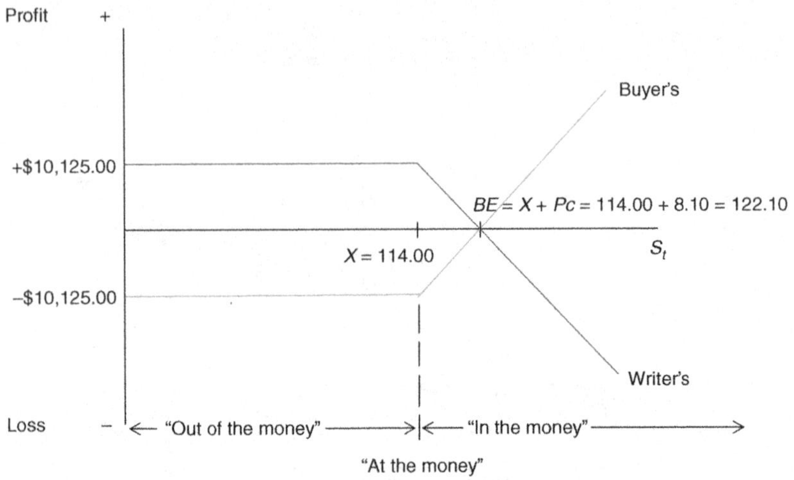

Graph 5.1 Buying and selling a call option on euros (€).

Notes: S_t = spot exchange rate, X = exercise price (X = 114.00 cents/€), BE = Break-even price, Pc = price (premium) of the call (Pc = 8.10 cents/€). The buyer is expected the spot rate to increase [$E(S_t)\uparrow$] and the seller is expected the spot rate to fall [$E(S_t)\downarrow$]. Premium/option contract: €125,000 × 0.0810 \$/€ = \$10,125.00.

Source: NASDAQ, Euro Currency Options, October 10, 2012

owner will exercise the call option only when exercising is profitable (spot rate on maturity above the exercise price, $S_t > X$, "option in the money"). In case the spot rate of the underlying currency moves up, the buyer has the possibility of unlimited profit. The reverse can happen if the spot rate on maturity is equal or less than the strike price, and the buyer can abandon the option and walk away with a loss, never greater than the premium paid (–\$10,125.00). The seller (writer) of the call will have exactly the opposite payoffs. He will have a limited gain (+\$10,125.00) if the spot rate falls below the exercise price and unlimited losses if the spot rate goes to infinity. For example: the spot rate on maturity date is 135.00 cents/€, what is the profit or loss for the two parties?

Buyer's profit:

$$\pi_t = S_t - (X + P_C) \tag{5.3}$$

or profit per euro:

$$\pi_t = 1.3500\$/euro - (1.1400\$/euro + 0.0810\$/euro)$$
$$= 0.1290\$/euro$$

And the profit per contract is:

$$\pi_t = \text{€}\ 125{,}000 \times \$0.1290 = \$16{,}125.00/contract.$$

The buyer can realize a profit through executing an offsetting contract on the options exchange rather than taking delivery of the currency. If he is right on his expectations, his maximum profit is unlimited minus the premium paid. The break-even price is 122.10 cents/€, which is,

$$BE = X + P_C \tag{5.4}$$

Here, the $BE = 114.00 + 8.10 = = 122.10$ cents/€ or 1.2210 $/€

Now, the position of the writer (seller) of the same call option is illustrated in graph 5.1, too. If the spot rate at the expiration of the call option is below the exercise price ($X = 114.00$), the buyer does not exercise his option. What he loses is exactly what the writer gains. When the spot rate is above the exercise price, the buyer will exercise the option and the seller of the call must deliver the underlying currency for 114.00 cents/€. If the writer is "naked" (without owning the currency), he has to buy the currency at spot and sell it at the contractual price; thus, he will take the loss. The amount of loss can be unlimited if the spot rate goes to infinity.

Based on the above example, the loss or profit for the writer will be:

$$\pi_t = P_C - (S_t - X) \tag{5.5}$$

or loss/profit per euro:

$$\pi_t = 0.0810\$/euro - (1.3500\$/euro - 1.1400\$/euro)$$
$$= -0.1290\$/euro$$

At spot rate less than the exercise price ($S_t < X$), the buyer will not exercise the option and the seller will keep the premium (maximum profit). Thus, the payoff for this call option is a *zero-sum game*. In economic theory, a *zero-sum game* is a mathematical representation of a situation, in which a participant's gain (or loss) of utility (or wealth) is exactly balanced by the losses (or gains) of the utility of the other participant. If the total gains of the participant are added up, and the total losses are subtracted, they will sum to zero, actually, transferring the risk to the other party ($\pi_t^B - \pi_t^S = +\$16{,}125.00 - \$16{,}125.00 = 0$).

5.2.1.2 Currency Calls: Pricing of Premium

The *premium* on a call option (P_C) represents the cost to the buyer, who purchases this contract that gives to him the right to buy an underlying currency at a specified price up to specified expiration date. For an MNC that buys call options to hedge the exchange rate risk, the premium reflects a cost of protection against this risk (exposure).

The call option premium (P_C) is affected by six factors:

$$P_C = f(\overset{+}{S}, \overset{-}{X}, \overset{+}{i_{RF}}, \overset{+}{\sigma^2}, \overset{+}{T}, \overset{-}{i^*_{RF}}) \tag{5.6}$$

where, P_C = the call premium (price of the call), S = the spot exchange rate, X = the exercise or strike price, i_{RF} = the domestic interest rate (riskless), σ^2 = the instantaneous variance of the underlying currency, T = the time to maturity (fraction of a year), and i^*_{RF} = the foreign interest rate (riskless).

The relationship between the call option premium and these factors is as follows. The spot rate has a positive effect on the premium because the higher the spot rate the higher the profit to the buyer (call option in the money) and he is willing to pay a higher price (premium). The exercise price has a negative effect on the premium; the higher the exercise price, the higher the loss to the buyer (call option out of the money). The domestic risk-free rate of interest has a small positive effect on premium. The variance of the spot exchange rate has a positive effect on premium because the greater the variability of the spot exchange rate the higher the probability that the spot rate can rise above the strike price and make the option profitable for the buyer. The time to maturity has a positive effect, too. The longer the time to maturity, the greater the probability that the spot rate will exceed the strike price and make the call to be in the money. The last term, the foreign risk-free rate of interest, has a small negative effect on premium.

5.2.2 *Currency Puts*

A *currency put option* is an option contract that gives the holder the right to sell a particular currency at a specified price (exercise rate) within a specified period of time. The holder of a put option is not obligated to exercise the option; therefore, the maximum loss to the owner of the put is the price (premium) paid for this put option contract (P_P). The buyer of this put option expects the foreign currency to depreciate ($S \downarrow \$/€$) and he locks in a maximum price, the exercise price (X) to be paid for the currency in the future. If the spot rate (S) falls below the strike price (X), the holder of the put option can exercise his option by selling the currency at the strike price, which will be higher than the prevailing spot rate in the market. The owner of the put option can choose to let the option expire on the expiration date without ever exercising it, if the spot rate has increased and his loss will be the premium. The seller of the put option receives the premium paid by the buyer and he has the obligation to accommodate the buyer in accordance with the rights of this currency put option, when the spot rate will fall and the buyer will exercise it.

5.2.2.1 Currency Puts: Quotations and Pricing

Exhibit 5.6 takes into consideration the list of euro currency options given by *NASDAQ* and refers to transactions completed on the Philadelphia Stock Exchange on the previous day (October 9, 2012). The quotations are direct for the United States (cents/euro) and a column of puts is given with their maturity date (October 20, 2012). The different strike prices are shown together with the premium (last) for puts. On October 12, 2012, a put option with premium of 0.71 cents/€ expires having a strike price of 115.00 cents/€ (1.1500 $/€). Since one option contract on the Philadelphia Stock Exchange consists of €125,000, the total cost of one put option is $887.50. The position of the buyer and the seller of a put is illustrated in graph 5.2.

The basic terms of this put are similar to those mentioned above with the call option. The buyer of the put wants to be able to sell the underlying currency at the exercise price, when the market price of the currency

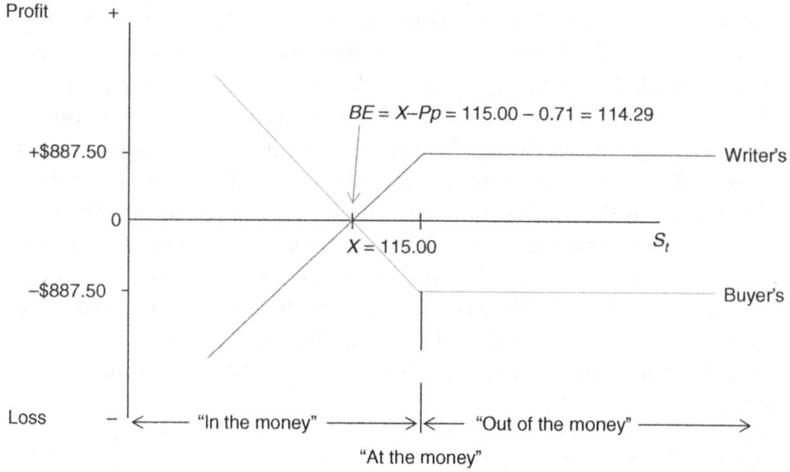

Graph 5.2 Buying and selling a put option on euros (€).

Notes: S_t = spot exchange rate, X = exercise price (X = 115.00 cents/€), BE = Break-even price, P_p = price (premium) of the put (=0.71 cents/€). The buyer is expected the spot rate to fall [E(S_t)↓] and seller is expected the spot rate to increase [E(S_t)↑]. Premium/option contract: €125,000 × 0.0071 $/€ = $887.50.

Source: NASDAQ, Euro Currency Options, October 10, 2012

drops. If the spot rate of euro drops to 113.00 cents/€, the holder of the put will deliver euros to the seller and receive 115.00 cents/€ (the contractual price). The euro can be purchased on the spot market for 1.1300 $/€ and the cost of put was 0.0071 $/€; thus, he will have a net gain of 0.0129 $/€, as follows:

Profit to the buyer of put:

$$\pi_t = X - (S_t + P_P) \tag{5.7}$$

or profit per euro:

$$\begin{aligned}\pi_t &= 1.1500\,\$/euro - (1.1300\,\$/euro + 0.0071\,\$/euro)\\ &= 0.0129\$/euro\end{aligned}$$

And the profit per contract is:

$$\pi_t = € \ 125{,}000 x \$0.0129 = \$1{,}612.50/contract.$$

If the buyer is right in his expectations, his maximum profit is very high as the spot rate falls toward zero minus the premium paid. The break-even price is 114.29 cents/€, which is,

$$BE = X - P_P \tag{5.8}$$

Here, the $BE = 115.00 - 0.71 = 114.29$ cents/€ or 1.1429 $/€

The position of the writer (seller) of the same put option is also illustrated in graph 5.2. If the spot rate at the expiration of this put option is above the exercise price ($X = 115.00$), the buyer does not exercise his option. What he loses is exactly what the writer gains, the premium. When the spot rate is below the exercise price, the buyer will exercise the option and the seller of the put has the obligation to deliver the underlying currency for 115.00 cents/€. If the writer is "naked" (without owning the currency), he has to buy the currency at the exercise price from the holder of the put and sell it at the spot price; thus, he will take the loss. The amount of loss can be unlimited if the spot rate goes to zero.

Based on the above example, the loss or profit for the writer of this put will be:

$$\pi_t = P_P - (X - S_t) \tag{5.9}$$

or loss/profit per euro:

$$\begin{aligned}\pi_t &= 0.0071\$/euro - (1.1500\$/euro - 1.1300\$/euro)\\ &= -0.0129\$/euro\end{aligned}$$

At spot rate higher than the exercise price ($S_t > X$), the buyer will not exercise the option and the seller will keep the premium (maximum profit). Thus, the payoff for this put option is the same as the payoff of a call, a *zero-sum game.*

5.2.2.2 Currency Puts: Factors Affecting the Premium

The *premium* on a put option (P_P) represents the cost to the buyer, who purchases this put contract that gives to him the right to sell an underlying currency at a specified price up to specified expiration date. For a MNC that buys put options to hedge the exchange rate risk, the premium reflects a cost of protection against this risk.

The put option premium (P_P) is affected by the same six factors, as the premium of a call, discussed earlier:

$$P_P = f(\overset{-}{S}, \overset{+}{X}, \overset{-}{i_{RF}}, \overset{+}{\sigma^2}, \overset{+}{T}, \overset{+}{i^*_{RF}}) \tag{5.10}$$

where, P_P = the put premium (price of the put), S = the spot exchange rate, X = the exercise or strike price, i_{RF} = the domestic interest rate (riskless), σ^2 = the instantaneous variance of the underlying currency, T = the time to maturity (fraction of a year), and i^*_{RF} = the foreign interest rate (riskless).

As eq. (5.10) shows, the factors affecting the price of a put have the following effects on P_P. The spot rate has a negative effect on the premium because the higher the spot rate the lower the profit to the buyer (put option out of the money) and he is not willing to pay a higher price (premium). The exercise price has a positive effect on the premium; the higher the exercise price (exceeding the spot price), the higher the profit to the buyer (put option in the money). The domestic risk-free rate of interest has a small negative effect on premium. The variance of the spot exchange rate has a positive effect on premium because the greater the variability of the spot exchange rate the higher the probability that the spot rate can fall below the strike price and make the option profitable for the buyer. The time to maturity has a positive effect, too. The longer the time to maturity, the greater the probability that the spot rate will fall below the strike price and make the put profitable (in the money). The last term, the foreign risk-free rate of interest has a small positive effect on the put premium.

5.2.3 *European Currency Option Pricing Theory*

The foreign currency option model presented here is a closed-form analytic model developed by Black and Scholes (1973) to value European currency call options. The assumptions of the model are the following: (1) there are no taxes, (2) transaction cost is zero, (3) there are no restriction on short selling, (4) the underlying asset exhibits no dividends or other leakages and its returns are log-normally distributed with constant variances, (5) markets operate continuously, and (6) interest rates are constant and risk free. By using these assumptions, they derive a valuation of short position in European call option. Merton (1973) extended the Black and Scholes model to underlying assets that exhibit a continuous dividend leakage, which fits very well to foreign exchange that exhibits continuous leakage. By forming a riskless hedged portfolio, the portfolio manager takes a long position in the underlying currency. Then, this currency can be invested in the foreign risk-free asset, which will yield a continuous foreign riskless rate of interest. The basic theoretical model for the pricing of a European call option is given by the following model:[11]

$$P_C^E = e^{-i_{RF}^* T} S\,N(d) - e^{-i_{RF} T} X\,N(d - \sigma\sqrt{T}) \tag{5.11}$$

$$d = \frac{\ln(S/X) + [i_{RF} - i_{RF}^* + (\sigma^2/2)]\,T}{\sigma\sqrt{T}} \tag{5.12}$$

where, P_C^E=price (premium) of a European call option, e=continuous time discounting (=2.7183), i_{RF}^*=foreign interest rate (riskless), T=time to expiration (maturity in years), S=the spot exchange rate (\$/€),$N(.)$=the standard normal cumulative probability distribution function,[12] i_{RF}=domestic interest rate (riskless), X=exercise or strike price (exchange rate), σ=standard deviation of the spot exchange rate (volatility), and ln =the natural logarithm.

A numerical example and its actual calculation of a European call option premium is in the Appendix A5.2.3. As long as we have the calculation of the price of a call option, we can derive the price (premium) of a European put option (P_P^E) by using the *put-call parity* relationship, which is,

$$P_P^E = P_C^E + X e^{-i_{RF} T} - S e^{-i_{RF}^* T} \tag{5.13}$$

where, P_P^E = price (premium) of a European put option.

5.2.4 *Currency Futures Options*

Currency futures option is an option contract, where the underlying asset is a currency futures contract. That is, a currency futures option gives to the holder the right, but not the obligation, to buy (for a call) or sell (for a put) a currency futures contract; which is a contract to exchange two currencies at an agreed-upon exchange rate at a certain point in the future, regardless of what the exchange rate is at that future time. This helps the holder manage his foreign exchange risk. Exhibit 5.7 gives quotations for currency futures option on euros at the CME.[13]

The division of the Chicago Mercantile Exchange, the IMM, trades listed American options on currency futures contracts. Volume and open interest of currency futures options are similar to those of PHLX-traded spot options. They were introduced in 1984 and gave to the currency

Exhibit 5.7 Currency futures options

EURO (CME) 125,000 Euros, cents per Euro

		Calls			*Puts*	
Strike Price	*Nov*	*Dec*	*Mar*	*Nov*	*Dec*	*Mar*
9000	38.920	38.920	–	–	0.005	–
10000	28.920	28.920	29.050	0.005	0.005	0.015
10500	–	–	24.050	–	–	0.040
10600	22.920	22.920	–	0.005	0.005	–
10800	–	–	–	–	–	–
10900	19.920	19.920	20.090	0.005	0.010	0.090
10950	19.420	19.420	19.600	0.005	0.010	0.100
11000	18.920	18.920	19.110	0.005	0.010	0.110
11050	18.420	18.420	18.620	0.005	0.010	0.120
11100	17.920	17.920	18.130	0.005	0.010	0.130
11150	17.420	17.420	17.650	0.005	0.015	0.150
11200	16.920	16.920	17.160	0.005	0.015	0.160
11250	16.420	16.420	16.670	0.005	0.015	0.170
11300	15.920	15.920	16.200	0.005	0.015	0.190
11350	15.420	15.430	15.710	0.005	0.020	0.200
11400	14.920	14.930	15.230	0.005	0.020	0.220
11450	14.420	14.430	14.740	0.005	0.025	0.230
11500	13.920	13.930	14.260	0.005	0.025	0.250
11550	13.420	13.440	13.780	0.005	0.030	0.270
11600	12.920	12.940	13.310	0.005	0.035	0.300
11650	12.420	12.450	12.840	0.010	0.040	0.330
11700	11.920	11.950	12.370	0.010	0.045	0.360
11750	11.420	11.460	11.910	0.010	0.050	0.400
11800	10.920	10.970	11.450	0.010	0.060	0.440
11850	10.430	10.480	11.000	0.010	0.070	0.480
11900	9.930	10.000	10.550	0.015	0.090	0.530
11950	9.430	9.510	10.100	0.015	0.100	0.580
12000	8.930	9.030	9.660	0.020	0.120	0.640
12050	8.440	8.550	9.220	0.025	0.140	0.700
12100	7.950	8.070	8.780	0.030	0.160	0.760

Source: The Wall Street Journal, http://online.wsj.com/mdc/public/page/2_3024-futopt_currency.html

futures traders the opportunity to trade both futures and options. Capital constraints for currency futures options are lower than those for spot options. To exercise an option on foreign exchange, the trader must have the entire cash value of the exercise price; but, to exercise an option on a currency futures contract, the trader needs only the futures margin. When a call or a put futures option is exercised, settlement is in a currency futures contract priced at the option's exercise price.

5.2.5 Foreign Exchange Binary Options

Binary options are high-risk financial instruments, where a prediction is made regarding the price of an asset (currency) at a certain period of the day. The predictions made relate to very small price modifications, which are extremely hard to predict, hence the high risk factor. The payoff of a binary option is either some fixed amount of some asset or nothing at all. The two main types of binary options are the *cash-or-nothing binary option* and the *asset-or-nothing binary option.* The cash-or-nothing binary option[14] pays some fixed amount of cash if the option expires in-the-money, while the asset-or-nothing pays the value of the underlying security. Thus, the options are binary in nature because there are only two possible outcomes. They are also called *all-or-nothing options, digital options* (more common in forex/interest rate markets), and *fixed return options (FROs)* (on the American Stock Exchange). Binary options are usually European style options.

For example, a trader who thinks that the EUR/USD ($/€) strike price will close at or above 1.2500 at 3:00 p.m. can buy a call option on that outcome. A trader who thinks that the EUR/USD strike price will close at or below 1.2500 at 3:00 p.m. can buy a put option or sell the contract. At 2:00 p.m. the EUR/USD spot price is 1.2490, but the trader believes this will increase, so he buys 10 call options for EUR/USD at or above 1.2500 at 3:00 p.m. at the cost of $40 each. The risk involved in this trade is known. The trader's gross profit/loss follows the "all or nothing" principle. He can lose all the money he invested, which in this case is $\$40 \times 10 = \$400$, or make a gross profit of $\$100 \times 10 = \$1000$. If the EUR/USD strike price will close at or above 1.2500 at 3:00 p.m., the trader's net profit will be the payoff at expiry minus the cost of the option: $\$1000 - \$400 = \$600$. The trader can also choose to liquidate (buy or sell to close) his position prior to expiration, at which point the option value is not guaranteed to be $100. The larger the gap between the spot price and the strike price, the value of the option decreases, as the option is less likely to expire in the money. In this example, if at 3:00 p.m. the spot has risen to 1.2505; the option has expired in the money and the gross payoff is \$1000. The trader's net profit is \$600.[15]

5.2.6 *Currency Option Combinations*

Beyond the basic call and put options in foreign currency, there are also *currency option combinations*, which include both long and short positions and they will be either long or short. They can be used both to hedge cash inflows and outflows denominated in a foreign currency and to speculate on the future movement of foreign currencies. They can be constructed to accommodate expectations of either appreciation or depreciation of foreign currencies. The most popular currency option combinations are *straddles* and *strangles.*[16]

5.2.6.1 *Currency Straddles*

A *currency straddle* is a combination of a call and put option of an underlying foreign currency in that they have the same expiration date and exercise price. First, a *long currency straddle* is constructed when an MNC or an individual buys (take a long position in) both a call and a put option for the same currency, which have the same expiration date and the same striking price. Then, the buyer purchases both the right to buy the foreign currency and the right to sell this currency. A long straddle becomes profitable when the foreign currency either appreciates or depreciates. The individual will benefit from his position as long as the foreign exchange rate does not remain constant. Of course, the disadvantage of a long straddle position is that it is expensive because it involves the purchase of two separate options, payment of two option premiums. Thus, it becomes profitable only if the foreign currency appreciates or depreciates drastically.

Now, a *short currency straddle* is constructed when an individual sells foreign currency (taking a short position in) both a call and a put option for that specific currency and both options have the same expiration date and strike price. The advantage of a short straddle is that it provides to the option writer income from two separate options, but there is a big disadvantage (substantial losses) if the underlying currency moves substantially away from the common strike price. Graph 5.3 shows a long and short currency straddle.

For example, we have a call and a put option for euros (€) with the following information: $P_C = 0.03\$/euro$; $P_P = 0.02\,\$/euro$; strike price, $X = 1.2500\,\$/euro$; one option contract is €125,000. To construct a long straddle, the buyer must purchase a euro call and a euro put option, paying \$0.03/€+\$0.02/€=\$0.05/€. If the exchange rate of the euro at the

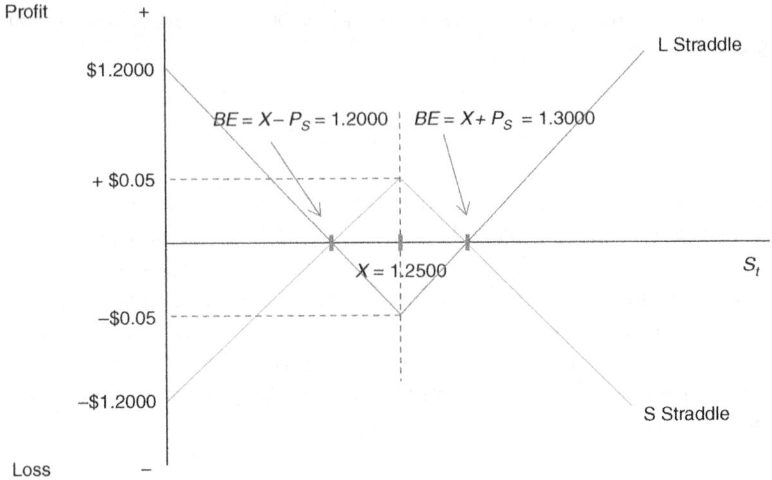

Graph 5.3 Long and short currency straddle.

Notes: P_C = 0.03 $/€, P_P = 0.02 $/€, X = strike price (X = 1.2500 $/€), the long straddle (a euro call and a euro put) costs: P_S = 0.03 + 0.02 = 0.05 $/€.

expiration is above the strike price 1.2500 $/€, the call option is in the money, but the put option is out of the money. On the contrary, if the exchange rate is below 1.2500 $/€, the put option is in the money, but the call is out of the money, as graph 5.3 shows.

There are two break-even (BE) points for a long straddle position (one below the strike price and the other above). The lower BE point is equal to the strike price minus both premiums ($BE_l = X - P_S = 1.2500 - 0.05 = 1.2000\$/euro$). The higher BE point is equal to the strike price plus both premiums ($BE_h = X + P_S = 1.2500 + 0.05 = 1.3000\,\$/euro$). The maximum loss for the buyer of a long straddle can occur if the exchange rate on expiration will be equal to the exercise price ($X = 1.2500\,\$/euro$) and the loss will be 0.05 $/€ or −6,250 $/contract [=€125,000 × (−0.05) $/€]. The short straddle is exactly opposite of the long straddle, as the graph shows too. The short straddle involves writing both a call and a put option on euros (€). There will be two break-even points, which are the same as the long straddle ones. The maximum gain of 0.05 $/€ (=0.03+0.02) occurs at a euro spot value equal to the strike price ($X = 1.2500\,\$/euro$) or 6,250 $/contract (=€125,000 × 0.05 $/€).

Based on their expectations about the future movements of foreign currency, speculators can speculate by using currency straddles, as they do with the other derivatives. A speculator who expects that the euro will appreciate or depreciate substantially can buy a straddle. If the euro appreciates considerably, the speculator will let the put option expire and exercise the call option. On the contrary, if the euro deprecates substantially, he will let the call option expire and will exercise the put option. Also, speculators can profit from short straddles. The writer of a short straddle believes that the exchange rate of the underlying currency will remain close to the exercise price until the expiration of the option. If his expectations are correct, he will collect the premiums from both options (call and put). Of course, this is a very risky position because the currency can appreciate or depreciate drastically, and he will experience losses. If the currency appreciates substantially, the straddle writer will have to sell the currency to the buyer for the low contractual (strike) price, since the buyer will exercise the call option. Now, if the currency depreciates substantially, the straddle writer has to buy the currency from the buyer for the high strike price, since the buyer will exercise his put option.

5.2.6.2 Currency Strangles

A *currency strangle* is a combination of a call and put option of an underlying foreign currency that have the same expiration date, but different exercise prices. To construct a *long currency strangle* an MNC will take a long position in a call option and a long position in a put option for a specific currency and the call option will have the higher exercise price ($X_C > X_P$). The advantage of a long strangle is that it is relatively cheaper to construct compared to a long straddle. But, it has a disadvantage relative to a straddle; the underlying currency has to fluctuate more prior to expiration. The reason for constructing a long strangle is that the speculator expects a substantial currency fluctuation in either direction prior to the expiration date. Graph 5.4 shows a long and a short currency strangle.

Now, a *short currency strangle* is an analogous instrument, where the speculator takes a short position on both the call and the put options for the same currency. The put and the call have the same expiration date, but the call has the higher strike price. The disadvantage of a short strangle is that it provides less income, compared to the straddle, because the call premium is lower. The advantage to the writer is that the short strangle has less risk of him losing his money because the underlying currency has to fluctuate more than in the case of a straddle.

Let us take a call and a put option for euros with a strike price for the call of ($X_C = 1.3000\$/euro$) and premium of ($P_C = 0.025\$/euro$), and an exercise price for the put of ($X_P = 1.2000\$/euro$) and a put option premium of ($P_P = 0.020\$/euro$). One option contract is €125,000. To construct a long strangle, the buyer must purchase a euro call and a euro put option,

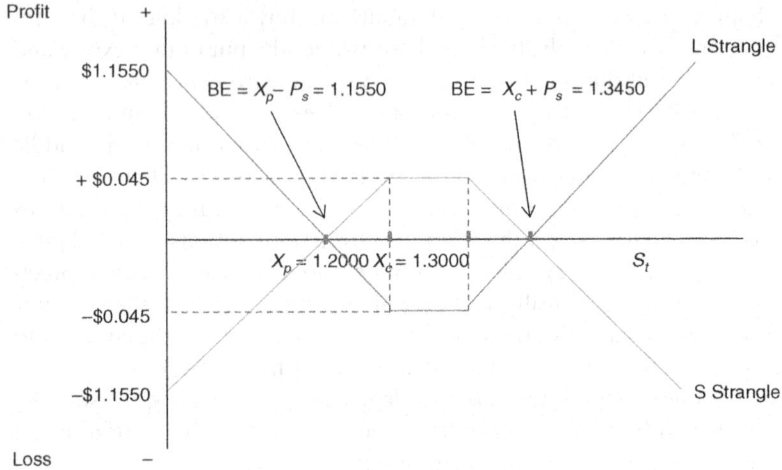

Graph 5.4 Long and short currency strangle.

Notes: P_c=0.025 $/€, P_p=0.020 $/€, X_c=1.3000 $/€, X_p=1.2000 $/€, P_s=0.025+0.020=0.045 $/€.

paying $0.025/€+$0.020/€=$0.045/€. If the exchange rate of the euro at the expiration is above the strike price 1.3000 $/€, the call option is in the money, but the put option is out of the money. On the contrary, if the exchange rate is below 1.2000 $/€, the put option is in the money, but the call is out of the money, as graph 5.4 shows.

In this case, the lower break-even (BE) point is equal to the put strike price minus both premiums ($BE_l = X_P - P_S = 1.2000 - 0.045 = 1.1550\$/euro$). The higher BE point is equal to the strike price of the call plus both premiums ($BE_h = X_C + P_S = 1.3000 + 0.045 = 1.3450\$/euro$). The maximum loss for the buyer of a long strangle can occur if the exchange rate on expiration is between the two strike prices ($1.2000\$/euro \leq S_t \leq 1.3000\$/euro$) and the loss will be 0.045 $/€ or −5,625 $/contract [=€125,000 × (−0.045) $/€]. The short strangle is exactly opposite of the long strangle, as the graph shows. The short strangle involves writing both a call and a put option on euros (€). There will be two break-even points, which are the same as the long strangle ones. The maximum gain of 0.045 $/€ (=0.025+0.020) occurs at a euro spot value between the two exercise prices or 5,625 $/contract (=€125,000 × 0.045 $/€).

Speculation can take place using currency strangles based on individuals' expectations about the future movement of a particular foreign currency. Speculators who expect that the euro will appreciate or depreciate substantially (above the X_C and below the X_P) can construct a long strangle. Speculators can benefit from short strangles if the future spot rate of the underlying currency is between the two exercise prices. Of course, the risk of these hybrid instruments is enormous and because there are no regulations in this market, businesses are having serious financial disasters related to derivatives. These risks are transferred to individuals (taxpayers) because governments have to bail them out in case of a major financial crisis, as it happened with the latest one in 2007, to avoid the negative effect of employment. Prudence, moderation, and regulations are necessary for all our markets.

5.3 Summary

In this chapter the different foreign currency derivatives were presented, which are instruments of hedging foreign currency risk and at the same time used as speculative instruments. They are called derivatives because their values are derived from the underlying asset (a foreign currency, here). MNCs use these currency derivatives in order to take positions in expectations of profit from their international transactions that are in foreign currencies (hedging). But, speculators use them to take a speculative position on a specific foreign currency based on their expectations about the future value of this currency.

There are various currency derivatives and new innovations that have appeared in our financial markets. Here, we present foreign currency forward and futures contracts. Also, foreign currency swaps and option contracts are discussed. First, we started with call options and then, we continued with put currency options. Their valuation and pricing was presented and the mathematics of a European option contract was illustrated and analyzed with the use of a numerical example. Also, foreign currency binary options and currency option combinations (straddles and strangles) were presented and their speculation was covered. All these are valuable instruments for MNCs, but at the same time very risky ones too, due to lack of regulations in the derivative markets.[17] Finally, derivatives play an important role in the economy, but are associated with high risks. The latest American financial and European debt crises have highlighted that these risks are not sufficiently mitigated in the over-the-counter (OTC) part of the market, especially as regards credit default swaps (CDS).[18] Since the beginning of the financial crisis, the European Commission has been working to address these risks, but markets are reacting against any regulations.

Appendix 5

A5.1 European Call Option: A Numerical Example

Assuming the following European call option is given from the PHLX World Currency Options for Euro (XDE) and now, the spot exchange rate, exercise price, interest rates, maturity, and volatility of the exchange rate are:

$S = 1.2929\$/€$, $X = 1.2200\$/€$, $i = 0.20\%$(per annum), $i^* = 0.80\%$ (per annum), $\sigma^2 = 0.10$, $T = 3 - months(0.25\,years)$, and $e = 2.71828$ (infinite discounting).

The basic theoretical model is:

$$P_C^E = e^{-i_{RF}^* T} S N(d) - e^{-i_{RF} T} X N(d - \sigma\sqrt{T})$$

$$d = \frac{\ln(S/X) + [i_{RF} - i_{RF}^* + (\sigma^2/2)]\,T}{\sigma\sqrt{T}}$$

We start with the calculation of the value of the density function $d \equiv d_1$:

$$d = \frac{\ln(1.2929/1.2200) + [0.002 - 0.008 + (0.10/2)](0.25)}{0.3162\sqrt{0.25}}$$

$$= \frac{0.058 + 0.011}{0.1581} = 0.4364 \cong 0.44 = d_1$$

Now, we derive the value of the second density function d_2:

$$d_2 = (d - \sigma\sqrt{T}) = 0.4364 - 0.1581 = 0.2783 \cong 0.28$$

We use table A5.1 to find the probability of the two density functions:

$$N(d_1) = N(0.44) = 0.50 + 0.17003 = 0.67003 \text{ or } (p_1 = 67.003\%)$$

$$N(d_2) = N(0.28) = 0.50 + 0.11026 = 0.61026 \text{ or } (p_2 = 61.026\%)$$

Table A5.1 Attachment Areas under the Standard Normal Distribution Function and implied probabilities.
Cumulative Probabilities of the Standard Normal Distribution Function

d	*0. 00*	*0. 01*	*0. 02*	*0. 03*	*0. 04*	*0. 05*	*0. 06*	*0. 07*	*0. 08*	*0. 09*
	0. 00000	0. 00399	0. 00798	0. 01197	0. 01595	0. 01994	0. 02392	0. 02790	0. 03188	0. 03586
0.1	0. 03983	0. 04380	0. 04776	0. 05172	0. 05567	0. 05962	0. 06356	0. 06749	0. 07142	0. 07535
0.2	0. 07926	0. 08317	0. 08706	0. 09095	0. 09483	0. 09871	0. 10257	0. 10642	0. 11026	0. 11409
0.3	0. 11791	0. 12172	0. 12552	0. 12930	0. 13307	0. 13683	0. 14058	0. 14431	0. 14803	0. 15173
0.4	0. 15542	0. 15910	0. 16276	0. 16640	0. 17003	0. 17364	0. 17724	0. 18082	0. 18439	0. 18793
0.5	0. 19146	0. 19497	0. 19847	0. 20194	0. 20540	0. 20884	0. 21226	0. 21566	0. 21904	0. 22240
0.6	0. 22575	0. 22907	0. 23237	0. 23565	0. 23891	0. 24215	0. 24537	0. 24857	0. 25175	0. 25490
0.7	0. 25804	0. 26115	0. 26424	0. 26730	0. 27035	0. 27337	0. 27637	0. 27935	0. 28230	0. 28524
0.8	0. 28814	0. 29103	0. 29389	0. 29673	0. 29955	0. 30234	0. 30511	0. 30785	0. 31057	0. 31327
0.9	0. 31594	0. 31859	0. 32121	0. 32381	0. 32639	0. 32894	0. 33147	0. 33398	0. 33646	0. 33891
1.0	0. 34134	0. 34375	0. 34614	0. 34849	0. 35083	0. 35314	0. 35543	0. 35769	0. 35993	0. 36214
1.1	0. 36433	0. 36650	0. 36864	0. 37076	0. 37286	0. 37493	0. 37698	0. 37900	0. 38100	0. 38298
1.2	0. 38493	0. 38686	0. 38877	0. 39065	0. 39251	0. 39435	0. 39617	0. 39796	0. 39973	0. 40147
1.3	0. 40320	0. 40490	0. 40658	0. 40824	0. 40988	0. 41149	0. 41308	0. 41466	0. 41621	0. 41774
1.4	0. 41924	0. 42073	0. 42220	0. 42364	0. 42507	0. 42647	0. 42785	0. 42922	0. 43056	0. 43189
1.5	0. 43319	0. 43448	0. 43574	0. 43699	0. 43822	0. 43943	0. 44062	0. 44179	0. 44295	0. 44408
1.6	0. 44520	0. 44630	0. 44738	0. 44845	0. 44950	0. 45053	0. 45154	0. 45254	0. 45352	0. 45449
1.7	0. 45543	0. 45637	0. 45728	0. 45818	0. 45907	0. 45994	0. 46080	0. 46164	0. 46246	0. 46327
1.8	0. 46407	0. 46485	0. 46562	0. 46638	0. 46712	0. 46784	0. 46856	0. 46926	0. 46995	0. 47062
1.9	0. 47128	0. 47193	0. 47257	0. 47320	0. 47381	0. 47441	0. 47500	0. 47558	0. 47615	0. 47670
2.0	0. 47725	0. 47778	0. 47831	0. 47882	0. 47932	0. 47982	0. 48030	0. 48077	0. 48124	0. 48169
2.1	0. 48214	0. 48257	0. 48300	0. 48341	0. 48382	0. 48422	0. 48461	0. 48500	0. 48537	0. 48574
2.2	0. 48610	0. 48645	0. 48679	0. 48713	0. 48745	0. 48778	0. 48809	0. 48840	0. 48870	0. 48899

continued

Table A5.1 Continued

d	*0. 00*	*0. 01*	*0. 02*	*0. 03*	*0. 04*	*0. 05*	*0. 06*	*0. 07*	*0. 08*	*0. 09*
2.3	0. 48928	0. 48956	0. 48983	0. 49010	0. 49036	0. 49061	0. 49086	0. 49111	0. 49134	0. 49158
2.4	0. 49180	0. 49202	0. 49224	0. 49245	0. 49266	0. 49286	0. 49305	0. 49324	0. 49343	0. 49361
2.5	0. 49379	0. 49396	0. 49413	0. 49430	0. 49446	0. 49461	0. 49477	0. 49492	0. 49506	0. 49520
2.6	0. 49534	0. 49547	0. 49560	0. 49573	0. 49585	0. 49598	0. 49609	0. 49621	0. 49632	0. 49643
2.7	0. 49653	0. 49664	0. 49674	0. 49683	0. 49693	0. 49702	0. 49711	0. 49720	0. 49728	0. 49736
2.8	0. 49744	0. 49752	0. 49760	0. 49767	0. 49774	0. 49781	0. 49788	0. 49795	0. 49801	0. 49807
2.9	0. 49813	0. 49819	0. 49825	0. 49831	0. 49836	0. 49841	0. 49846	0. 49851	0. 49856	0. 49861
3.0	0. 49865	0. 49869	0. 49874	0. 49878	0. 49882	0. 49886	0. 49889	0. 49893	0. 49896	0. 49900
3.1	0. 49903	0. 49906	0. 49910	0. 49913	0. 49916	0. 49918	0. 49921	0. 49924	0. 49926	0. 49929
3.2	0. 49931	0. 49934	0. 49936	0. 49938	0. 49940	0. 49942	0. 49944	0. 49946	0. 49948	0. 49950
3.3	0. 49952	0. 49953	0. 49955	0. 49957	0. 49958	0. 49960	0. 49961	0. 49962	0. 49964	0. 49965
3.4	0. 49966	0. 49968	0. 49969	0. 49970	0. 49971	0. 49972	0. 49973	0. 49974	0. 49975	0. 49976
3.5	0. 49977	0. 49978	0. 49978	0. 49979	0. 49980	0. 49981	0. 49981	0. 49982	0. 49983	0. 49983
3.6	0. 49984	0. 49985	0. 49985	0. 49986	0. 49986	0. 49987	0. 49987	0. 49988	0. 49988	0. 49989
3.7	0. 49989	0. 49990	0. 49990	0. 49990	0. 49991	0. 49991	0. 49992	0. 49992	0. 49992	0. 49992
3.8	0. 49993	0. 49993	0. 49993	0. 49994	0. 49994	0. 49994	0. 49994	0. 49995	0. 49995	0. 49995
3.9	0. 49995	0. 49995	0. 49996	0. 49996	0. 49996	0. 49996	0. 49996	0. 49996	0. 49997	0. 49997
4.0	0. 49997	0. 49997	0. 49997	0. 49997	0. 49997	0. 49997	0. 49998	0. 49998	0. 49998	0. 49998

Note: $N(d)$ = areas under normal distribution function. Suppose that $d_1 = 0.44$ and $d_2 = 0.28$. Table A5.1 implies a probability of $p_1 = 0.50000 + 0.17003 = 0.67003$ and $p_2 = 0.50000 + 0.11026 = 0.61026$.

Source: Engineering Statistics Handbook, http://www.itl.nist.gov/div898/handbook/eda/section3/eda3671.htm

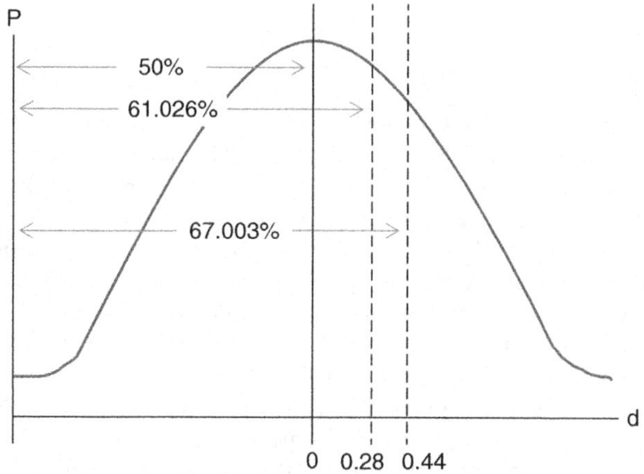

$N(d_1) = N(0.44) = 0.50 + 0.17003 = 0.67003$ probability

$N(d_2) = N(0.28) = 0.50 + 0.11026 = 0.61026$ probability

The premium of this European call for euros (which is in the money) is:

$$\begin{aligned} P_C^E &= e^{-0.008(0.25)}1.2929(0.67003) - e^{-0.002(0.25)}1.2200(0.61026) \\ &= e^{-0.002}(0.86628) - e^{-0.0005}(0.74452) \\ &= 0.998(0.86628) - 0.9995(0.74452) \\ &= 0.86455 - 0.74415 = 0.1204\$/euro \end{aligned}$$

Thus, the call option premium is: $P_C^E = 12.04$cents/€.

Now, by using the *put-call parity* relationship, we can derive the price (premium) of a European put option (P_P^E) for the above example:

$$P_P^E = P_C^E + X e^{-i_{RF}T} - S e^{-i_{RF}^{*}T}$$

The premium of the European put option is:

$$\begin{aligned} P_P^E &= 0.1204 + 1.2200\, e^{-0.002(0.25)} - 1.2929 e^{-0.008(0.25)} \\ &= 0.1204 + 1.2200\, e^{-0.0005} - 1.2929 e^{-0.002} \\ &= 0.1204 + 1.2200(0.99950) - 1.2929(0.99800) \\ &= 0.1204 + 1.21939 - 1.29031 = 0.04948\$/euro \end{aligned}$$

or $P_P^E = 4.948$cents/€.

Notes

1. See Kolb (1988).
2. Euronext.liffe was formed in January 2002 after the takeover of the London International Financial Futures and Options Exchange by Euronext. The derivatives activities of the other constituent exchanges of Euronext (Amsterdam, Brussels, Lisbon, and Paris), were merged into Euronext.liffe. Trading is done electronically through the LIFFE CONNECT platform. Euronext.liffe offers a wide range of futures and option products on short-term interest rates, bonds, swaps, equities, and commodities. In addition to this, it sells its technology to third parties. Since April 2003, the Tokyo International Financial Futures Exchange has run on LIFFE CONNECT. Furthermore, from January 2004 until its merger with the Chicago Mercantile Exchange in 2008, the Chicago Board of Trade provided electronic trading via e-cbot, which was powered by LIFFE CONNECT. As a result, the Kansas City Board of Trade and the Minneapolis Grain Exchange used LIFFE CONNECT for their overnight trading. The e-cbot is an electronic trading platform that gives traders the ability to trade future contracts listed on the Chicago Board of Trade. The CBOT has primarily been regarded as an open outcry market, but the incorporation of electronic trading platforms is changing the standard way in which futures trading is done.
3. The tick-size is the minimum price movement of a trading instrument. The price movements of different trading instruments vary. For example, if the minimum price movement of a stock is 0.01; the stock has a tick value of one cent (each tick is worth one cent for one stock). Futures markets typically have a tick size that is specific to the instrument. For example, the Russell 2000 e-mini futures contract (TF) has a tick size of .10; the value of each tick is $10.00 (each contract is worth $100 multiplied by the index).
4. Pip is the smallest price change that a given exchange rate can make. Since most major currency pairs are priced to four decimal places, the smallest change is that of the last decimal point; for most pairs this is the equivalent of 1/100 of 1 percent, or one basis point.
5. An *interest rate swap* (IRS) is a popular and highly liquid financial derivative instrument in which two parties agree to exchange interest rate cash flows based on a specified notional amount from a fixed rate to a floating rate (or vice versa), or from one floating rate to another. Interest rate swaps are commonly used for both hedging and speculating.
6. These parallel loans introduced in the United Kingdom in 1970s provided a means of circumventing foreign exchange controls implemented to prevent the outflow of UK capital. These controls were in the form of taxes imposed on foreign transactions to discourage the outflow of pounds (£) and encourage domestic investment. These parallel (back-to-back) loans were created to avoid this tax.
7. See *CBOE*, 2012 Options Expiration Calendar, http://www.cboe.com/About CBOE/xcal2012.pdf

8. See *NASDAQ*, http://www.nasdaqtrader.com/Micro.aspx?id=phlxwcoproduct specs#eu
9. See *NASDAQ*, Euro Currency option Quotations (Calls), http://www.nasdaq.com/aspxcontent/optionsWC.aspx?symbol=^XDE&qm_page=81588&qm_symbol=^XDE; Euro Currency option quotations (Puts), http://www.nasdaq.com/aspxcontent/optionsWC.aspx?symbol=^XDE&qm_page=80424&qm_symbol=^XDE; and Euro Currency Options (Calls & Puts), http://www.nasdaq.com/markets/currency-options.aspx?currency=%5EXDE.
10. See *NASDAQ*, http://www.nasdaq.com/includes/currency-help-faqs.stm.
11. See, Tucker, Madura, and Chiang (1991, Appendix 15.A, 15.B, 15.C, and 15.D, pp. 309–313) for the derivations of different currency option pricing models (European options, American options, etc.).
12. See, table A5.1 and http://www.itl.nist.gov/div898/handbook/eda/section3/eda 3671.htm
13. See Ogden and Tucker (1987).
14. For example, a purchase is made of a binary cash-or-nothing call option on XYZ Corporation's stock struck at \$100 with a binary payoff of \$1000. Then, if at the future maturity date, the stock is trading at or above \$100, \$1000 is received. If its stock is trading below \$100, nothing is received.
15. There is a view, according to Bonpasse (2008), that the world would be simpler if we did not have a different currency for each country. It would not be necessary to buy foreign currency, when going on vacation, with all the time and expense that incurs. Countries could trade without the uncertainty of varying exchange rates, which can lead to losses on exchange and an unexpected expense. Everything would be just so much simpler and there would not be the need for forex markets and complex trading mechanisms. But, countries without their own currency lose their monetary policy and their trade policy, and it will lead to a serious socioeconomic crisis. This single currency theory has been expounded for many years, but the Euro-zone has proved, if proof were needed, that it just does not work. The experiment has been an expensive failure although its supporters will not admit it. Having a large number of countries with the same currency causes enormous difficulties. Each of those countries has different economies, some have budget deficits, trade deficits, while others have surpluses, and they are all growing or contracting at different speeds. Consequently, they all really need different exchange rates (their own domestic currency) and different interest rates (monetary policy) to balance it all out. But, because they have the same exchange rate, they cannot and so the situation improves for some (i.e., Germany) and is made worse for the rest (GIPSI nations). From the narrow point of view (his self-interest) of a binary options trader, the removal of different currencies is definitely not an advantage. It removes an opportunity to make money. But, from the social point of view, countries must have their own monetary policy, money, and independent central bank. The very fact that there are lots of different currencies in the world means that there are a huge number of exchange rates between the

various ones. Currency is being bought and sold all the time (for thousands of years) and these are changing constantly, so the possibilities for a binary options trader are almost limitless.

16. See, Madura (2012, Appendix 5B, pp. 160–172), where he discusses currency straddles, currency strangles, and currency spreads.
17. The European Commission tried to regulate them, but it was very difficult owing to their complexity and their innovations. See http://ec.europa.eu/internal_market/financial-markets/docs/derivatives/20100915_summary_impact_assessment_en.pdf. Also, the US regulators tried to regulate this market after the systemic risk of 2007. "Federal regulators outlined plans to regulate the giant market for derivatives, a move aimed at avoiding a repeat of the turmoil created last year by certain financial institutions whose risk-taking in exotic financial instruments went largely unchecked. Under a proposed raft of reforms, regulators could be given authority to force many standard over-the-counter derivatives to be traded on regulated exchanges and electronic-trading platforms. That would make it easier to see prices and make markets more transparent." See Sarah N. Lynch and Serena Ng, "U.S. Moves to Regulate Derivatives Trade," *The Wall Street Journal*, May 14, 2009. See, http://online.wsj.com/article/SB124224226775916215.html.
18. A *credit default swap (CDS)* is a derivative (a financial swap) agreement that the seller of the CDS will compensate the buyer in the event of a loan default or other credit event. The buyer of the CDS makes a series of payments (the CDS "fee" or "spread") to the seller and, in exchange, receives a payoff if the loan defaults. In the event of default the buyer of the CDS receives compensation (usually the face value of the loan), and the seller of the CDS takes possession of the defaulted loan. However, anyone can purchase a CDS, even buyers who do not hold the loan instrument and who have no direct insurable interest in the loan (these are called "naked" CDSs). If there are more CDS contracts outstanding than bonds in existence, a protocol exists to hold a credit event auction; the payment received is usually substantially less than the face value of the loan. Since December 1, 2011, the European Parliament has banned naked CDSs on the debt for sovereign nations. CDSs have existed since the early 1990s, and increased in use after 2003. By the end of 2007, the outstanding CDS amount was $62.2 trillion, falling to $26.3 trillion by mid-2010, but reportedly $25.5 trillion in early 2012. CDSs are not traded on an exchange and there is no required reporting of transactions to a government agency. During the 2007–2010 financial crisis, the lack of transparency in this large market became a concern to regulators as it could pose a systemic risk. In March 2010, the Depository Trust & Clearing Corporation (DTCC) through the Trade Information Warehouse announced it would give regulators greater access to its credit default swaps database. CDS data can be used by financial professionals, regulators, and the media to monitor how the market views credit risk of any entity, on which a CDS is available, which can be compared to that provided by the credit rating agencies. In addition to the basic, single-name swaps, there are basket default swaps (BDSs), index CDSs, funded CDSs (also

called credit-linked notes), as well as loan-only credit default swaps (LCDS). Many economists claim that derivatives such as CDS are potentially dangerous in that they combine priority in bankruptcy with a lack of transparency.

Bibliography

Black, F. and M. Scholes (1973), "The Pricing of Options and Corporate Liabilities," *Journal of Political Economy*, Vol. 81, May/June, pp. 637–659.

Bonpasse, Morrison (2008), *The Single Global Currency: Common Cents for the World*, Newcastle, Maine: Single Global Currency Association.

Gastineau, Gary (1979), *The Stock Options Manual*, 2nd Edition, New York, NY: McGraw-Hill Book Company.

Kolb, Robert W. (1988), *Understanding Futures Markets*, 2nd Edition, Glenview, IL: Scott, Foresman and Company.

Madura, Jeff (2012), *International Financial Management*, 11th Edition, Mason, OH: South-Western, Cengage Learning.

Merton, Robert C. (1973), "Theory of Rational Option Pricing," *Bell Journal of Economics and Management Science*, Vol. 4, No.1, Spring, pp. 141–183.

Ogden, Joseph P. and Alan L. Tucker (1987), "Empirical Tests of the Efficiency of the Currency Futures Options Market," *The Journal of Futures Markets*, Vol. 7, No. 6, pp. 695–703.

Tucker, Alan L. (1991), *Financial Futures, Options, & Swaps*, New York, NY: West Publishing Company.

Tucker, Alan L., Jeff Madura, and Thomas C. Chiang (1991), *International Financial Markets*, New York, NY: West Publishing Company.

6

Foreign Exchange Risk and Its Management

Foreign exchange risk is also known as *exchange rate risk* or *currency risk* or *foreign exchange exposure,* and it is the financial risk posed by an exposure to unanticipated changes in the exchange rates. Investors and MNCs exporting or importing goods and services or making foreign investments throughout the global economy are faced with an exchange rate risk, which can have severe financial consequences on firms' profitability, cash flows, and their market value, if not managed appropriately. Currency-related gains or losses can have enormous impacts on reported earnings, which affect the firm's profitability and consequently, the market's opinion about this firm and its market value, through the demand of its financial assets. MNCs use a number of external techniques of risk (exposure) management and resort to contractual relationships outside their companies in order to reduce (or redistribute) the risk of foreign exchange losses. These hedging techniques are: forward exchange contracts, short-term borrowing, financial futures contracts, currency options, discounting bills receivable, factoring receivables, currency overdrafts, currency swaps, government exchange risk guarantees, and others, which are covered in detail in this chapter.

6.1 Types of Foreign Exchange Exposures and Their Management

Foreign exchange exposures are generally categorized into the following three distinct types: (1) translation exposure, changes in reported owners' equity in consolidated financial statements caused by a change in exchange rates; (2) transaction exposure, impact of settling outstanding obligations entered into before change in exchange rates, but to be settled after change in exchange rates; and (3) economic or operating exposure, change in expected future cash flows arising from an unexpected change in exchange rates. These exposures pose risks to MNCs' cash flows, competitiveness, market value, and financial reporting.

Hedging against exchange rate movements can reduce the uncertainty surrounding future cash flows. The hedging process can stabilize an MNC's revenue, expenses, earnings, and cash flows. Creditors who provide loans to MNCs prefer these MNCs to maintain low exposure to exchange rate risk. Thus, MNCs that hedge their exposure to exchange rate risk might be able to borrow funds at a lower cost of capital. On recognizing that exchange rate risk is relevant for their cash flows, they hedge their positions.

6.2 Translation Exposure

A firm's *translation exposure*, also called *accounting exposure*, is the extent to which its financial reporting is affected by exchange rate movements. MNCs need to "translate" foreign currency financial statements of their foreign subsidiaries into a single reporting currency to prepare worldwide consolidated financial statements. As all firms must prepare consolidated financial statements for reporting purposes, the consolidation process for MNCs entails translating foreign assets and liabilities or the financial statements of foreign subsidiaries from foreign to domestic (parent's company) currency. While translation exposure may not affect a firm's cash flows, it could have a significant impact on a firm's reported earnings and therefore its stock price. Translation exposure is distinguished from transaction risk as a result of income and losses from various types of risk having different accounting treatments. Translation gives special consideration to assets and liabilities with regard to foreign exchange risk, whereas exposures to revenues and expenses can often be managed ex ante by managing transactional exposures when cash flows take place. To translate earnings, MNCs use a process established by the Financial Accounting Standards Board (FASB). The prevailing guidelines are set by FASB #52.[1]

6.2.1 *Translation Methods*

There are two basic methods employed for the translation of foreign subsidiaries financial statements, the *current rate method* and the *temporal method.*

The *current rate method* is the most prevalent one worldwide. Under this method, all financial statement line items are translated at the "current" exchange rate with few exceptions. These line items are:

(1) *Assets and Liabilities*: All assets and liabilities are translated at the current exchange rate, at the exchange rate, which is, in effect, on the balance sheet date.
(2) *Income Statement Items:* All items, including depreciation and cost of goods sold, are translated at either the actual exchange rate on the dates the various revenues, expenses, gains, and losses were incurred or at an appropriately weighted average exchange rate for the period.
(3) *Distributions:* Dividends paid are translated at the exchange rate in effect on the date of payment.
(4) *Equity Items:* Common stock and paid-in capital accounts are translated at historical rates. Year-end retained earnings consist of the original year-beginning retained earnings plus or minus any income or loss for the year.

The *temporal method* translates specific assets and liabilities at exchange rates consistent with the timing of the item's creation and it is still used by a few countries today. Line items are the following:

(1) *Monetary assets (primarily cash, marketable securities, accounts receivable,* and *long-term receivables).* They are translated at current exchange rates.
(2) *Monetary liabilities (primarily current liabilities and long-term debt).* They are translated at current exchange rates.
(3) *Nonmonetary assets and liabilities (primarily inventory and fixed assets).* They are translated at historical rates.
(4) *Income statement items.* They are translated at the average exchange rate for the period, except for items such as depreciation and cost of goods sold that are directly associated with nonmonetary assets or liabilities. These accounts are translated at their historical rate.
(5) *Distributions.* Dividends paid are translated at the exchange rate in effect on the date of payment.
(6) *Equity items.* Common stock and paid-in capital accounts are translated at historical rates. Year-end retained earnings consist of the original year-beginning retained earnings plus or minus any income or loss for the year, plus or minus imbalance from translation.

The functional currency (the currency of the primary economic environment) translation approach adopted in the FASB Statement No. 52 involves:[2]

(1) identifying the functional currency of the entity's economic environment;

(2) measuring all elements of the financial statements in the functional currency;
(3) using the current exchange rate for translation from the functional currency to the reporting currency, if they are different; and
(4) distinguishing the economic impact of changes in exchange rates on a net investment from the impact of such changes on individual assets and liabilities that are receivable or payable in currencies other than the functional currency.

Financial Accounting Standards (FAS) No. 52 has a special provision for translating statements of foreign subsidiaries of US MNCs operating in countries where cumulative inflation has been approximately 100 percent or higher over a three-year period. Financial statements of these subsidiaries must be translated into the reporting currency using the temporal method, mentioned earlier. Many of the world's largest industrial nations follow the same basic translation procedure.[3]

6.2.2 *Managing Translation Exposure*

The main technique to minimize translation exposure is called a *balance sheet hedge*.[4] Some MNCs have attempted to hedge translation exposure in the forward market. Such action amounts to speculating in the forward market in the hope that a cash profit will be realized to offset the noncash loss from translation. Absolute success depends only on a precise prediction of future exchange rates, which is very difficult. A balance sheet hedge requires an equal amount of exposed foreign currency assets and liabilities on a firm's consolidated balance sheet. If this can be achieved for each foreign currency, net translation exposure will be zero. The cost of a balance sheet hedge depends on relative borrowing costs. Even if management chooses to follow an active policy of hedging translation exposure, it is almost impossible to offset both translation and transaction exposure simultaneously. If forced to choose, most managers will choose protection against transaction losses and not translation ones. Transaction losses are realized cash losses and must be managed.

MNCs can use forward contracts or futures contracts to hedge translation exposure. They can sell the currency that their subsidiaries receive as earnings, forward. Thus, they create a cash outflow in the currency to offset the earnings received in that currency. Of course, there are limitations in hedging translation exposure, too:

1. *Inaccurate earnings forecasts*: The future earnings of a subsidiary are uncertain; we cannot accurately forecast them.

2. *Inadequate forward contracts for some currencies*: In some cases, forward contracts are not available for some currencies issued by small countries. Thus, subsidiaries operating in these small countries are not able to obtain forward contracts, so they cannot hedge.
3. *Accounting distortions*: The forward rate gain or loss reflects the difference between the forward rate and the future spot rate, whereas the translation gain or loss is caused by the change in the average exchange rate over the period, in which the earnings are generated. Also, the translation losses are not tax deductible, whereas gains on forward contracts used to hedge translation exposure are taxed.[5]
4. *Increased transaction exposure*: By using forward contracts on translation exposure, an MNC may be increasing its transaction exposure. The translation gain is simply a paper gain if the foreign currency of the country where the subsidiary is operated is appreciated.

6.3 Transaction Exposure

Transaction exposure measures changes in the value of outstanding financial obligations incurred prior to a change in exchange rates, but not due to be settled until after the exchange rate changes. Then, transaction exposure deals with changes in cash flows that result from existing contractual obligations. Consequently, an MNC has transaction exposure whenever it has contractual cash flows (receivables and payables) whose values are subject to unanticipated changes in exchange rates, due to a contract being denominated in a foreign currency. To realize the domestic value of its foreign-denominated cash flows, the MNC must exchange foreign currency for domestic currency. As firms negotiate contracts with set prices and delivery dates in the face of a volatile foreign exchange market with exchange rates constantly fluctuating, the firms face the risk of changes in the exchange rate between the foreign and domestic currency. Firms generally become exposed as a direct result of activities such as importing and exporting or borrowing and investing. Foreign currencies may depreciate or appreciate by a large percentage within any single year, which can significantly affect an MNC's cash flows, meaning an enormous decline in the value of a receivable or a huge rise in the value of a payable. Such outcomes could be troublesome as export profits could be negated entirely, or import costs could rise substantially.

6.3.1 *Measurement of Transaction Exposure*

Transaction exposure refers to gains or losses that arise from the settlement of transactions, whose terms are stated in a foreign currency. These transactions include: (1) purchasing or selling on credit goods or services, whose prices are stated in foreign currencies; (2) borrowing or lending funds denominated in foreign currencies; (3) being a party to an unperformed forward foreign exchange contract; and (4) acquiring assets or incurring liabilities denominated in foreign currencies.

Common examples of transaction exposure are those when an MNC has receivables or payables denominated in foreign currencies. Suppose an American MNC sells merchandise on an open account (an arrangement whereby sales are made with no formal debt contract; the buyer signs a receipt, and the seller records the sale in the sales ledger) to a British firm for £10,000,000, payment to be made in 90 days. The current spot exchange rate is 1.6148 \$/£ and the US firm expects to exchange the pounds received for \$16,148,000 (=£10,000,000 × 1.6184 \$/£), when payment is received.

But, due to transaction exposure the MNC will receive a different amount from the expected one of \$16,148,000. The reason is that the value of the British pound has changed in the 90 days. If the British pound has weakened to 1.5500 \$/£, when paymentis due, the received amount will be \$15,500,000 (=£10,000,000 × 1.5500 \$/£), a loss of \$648,000. If the pound has strengthened to 1.6500 \$/£, the American firm would have received \$16,500,000 (=£10,000,000 × 1.6500 \$/£), an increase by \$352,000 over the amount expected if the exchange rate has remained constant. Thus, this loss or gain to the MNC is due to exchange rate risk (transaction exposure). This risk (transaction exposure) could have been avoided for the American firm only if the US MNC had invoiced the British firm in US dollars, but in that case, the exchange rate risk would have been transferred to the British buyer.

6.3.2 *Management of Transaction Exposure*

Transaction exposure exists when there are contractual transactions that affect the receivables and the payables of MNCs, which are in foreign currency at a specified point in the future. The dollar value can increase or decrease during this period, due to appreciation or depreciation of the foreign currency, which will negatively affect the profit of the firm. For this reason, MNCs consider hedging the contractual transactions denominated in foreign currencies. By managing transaction exposure, financial managers can reduce the uncertainty surrounding their cash flows. There are different techniques to hedge exchange rate exposure: (1) forward market hedge, (2) futures market hedge, (3) money market hedge, and (4) option market hedge.

6.3.2.1 Management of Receivables

An US MNC is selling some equipment to a French firm. The transaction takes place in December for the amount of €10,000,000. The payment is due three months later in March. The following financial information holds in the two economies (United States and France):

The spot exchange rate is: $S_t = 1.3120$ \$/€.

The three-month forward rate is: $F_3 = 1.3000$ \$/€.

The US interest rate is: $i_t = 3.25\%$ per annum or ($i_t/4 = 0.8125\%$per quarter).

The French interest rate is: $i_t^* = 6\%$ per annum or ($i_t^*/4 = 1.5\%$ per quarter).

A March Philadelphia put option: strike price 131 cents/€, 1.50 cents/€ premium.

OTC (bank) put option for €10,000,000, strike price 131 cents/€, 2% premium.

Brokerage cost per option contract: \$120.00.

The US MNC forecasts the spot rate in three months to be: $S_{t+3}^e = 1.3200$\$/€.

The cost of capital for the MNC is: $k_t = 5.25\%$.

The MNC may decide to hedge its receivables by using four different techniques or remain unhedged. The following options to manage the exposure are available:

1. Remain Unhedged:
   The US MNC may decide to accept the foreign exchange risk by trusting its forecasting that the exchange rate in three months will be $S_{t+3}^e = 1.3200$. Then, it expects to receive €10,000,000 × 1.3200 \$/€ = \$13,200,000. But, this is risky because exchange rate can fall to 1.2000 \$/€ or can go up to 1.4000 \$/€. In this case, the MNC can receive an amount ranging from \$12,000,000 to \$14,000,000. Of course, theoretically the spot rate can go down to zero and up to infinity ($0 \leq S_{t+3}^e \leq \infty$), which means an enormous risk if the transaction is left uncovered.
2. Forward Market Hedge:
   The US MNC can sell the three-month forward €10,000,000 at the three-month forward rate $F_3 = 1.3000$ \$/€. In March, when the MNC receives the funds from France, it will deliver them to cover the forward transaction. It will sell the receivables and will obtain

from the bank a certain amount in dollars: €10,000,000 × 1.3000 $/€ = $13,000,000. This amount is $200,000 less than their forecasting amount of $13,200,000; but it is certain, compared with the uncertain amount if the firm has stayed unhedged.

3. Futures Market Hedge:
   The US MNC has to buy futures contracts in euros maturing in March. One futures contract has the size of €125,000. Then, it needs €10,000,000: €125,000 = 80 futures contracts in euros. The futures rate is the same as the forward rate, due to arbitrage in the foreign currency market. Thus, the revenue from the receivables will be the same as before: €10,000,000 × 1.3000 $/€ = $13,000,000. This is a certain amount, and the exchange rate risk is eliminated.
4. Money Market Hedge:
   A money market hedge includes a contract and a source of funds to fulfill the contract. This contract is a loan agreement. The MNC, seeking the money market hedge, borrows in one currency and exchanges the proceeds for another currency. The process is as follows:

   Step 1: The US.MNC borrows from a French bank the present value of its receivables:

   $$PV = \frac{10,000,000}{(1+0.015)} = 9,852,216.749 \text{ euros.}$$

   Step 2: It exchanges this amount of euros for dollars in the spot market and receives in

   $$\text{dollars: } €9,852,216.749 \times 1.3120\$/€ = \$12,926,108.37.$$

   Step 3: This amount is invested in the United States for three months (by buying a *T*-bill) at the interest rate of $i_t/4 = 0.8125\%$ and will give the proceeds of: $12,926,108.37 (1+0.008125) = $13,031,133.00.

   Step 4: Repayment of loan in France (after three months): €9,852,216.749 (1+0,015) = €10,000,000.

   Step 5: The certain proceeds, after three months, from the US *T*-bill are:

   $$\$13,031,133.00 \text{ (this is the value of the receivables for the US MNC).}$$

The money market hedge results in higher amount from the cash receivables from France compared to forward and futures markets hedge.

5. Option Market Hedge:
   The MNC can cover its €10,000,000 receivables by purchasing a put option in euros (it wants to sell this foreign currency, euros, at this contractual price). This put option hedge allows the firm to speculate on the upside potential for appreciation of the euro (€), while limiting downside risk to a known amount, the put strike price ($X = 131.00$ cents/€) minus the option cost/€. The firm has the choice of using the OTC market or the Philadelphia stock exchange for the purchase of its options.

First, the MNC could purchase from a bank (OTC) a three-month put option on €10,000,000 at the strike price of 1.3100 \$/€ and a premium of 2 percent. The cost will be:

$$C_P^{OTC} = S_P^O \, x \, X_P \, x \, P_P^{OTC} \tag{6.1}$$

where, C_P^{OTC} = cost of the OTC put option, S_P^O = size of the put option, X_p = exercise price, and P_P^{OTC} = premium of the OTC put option.

Then, its cost will be: C_P^{OTC} = €10,000,000 × 1.3100 \$/€ × 0.02 = \$262,000.

And consequently, the net proceeds from the receivables would be: \$13,100,000 minus \$262,000 = \$12,838,000.

Also, the MNC can purchase a March Philadelphia put option, which would have the following cost:

One option contract is €125,000 and the amount of receivables is €10,000,000, which means that we need 80 put option contracts (= €10,000,000 : €125,000).

Total cost per put option:

Premium: €125,000 × 0.015 \$/€ =	\$1,875.00
Brokerage cost:	\$120.00

Total cost:	\$1,995.00

Total cost for 80 put option contracts: 80 × \$1,995.00 = \$159,600.

Then, option cost/€: \$1,995.00/€125,000 = 0.01596 \$/€.

Thus, the Philadelphia stock exchange has a lower cost compared to the OTC market by \$102,400 (\$262,000 − 159,600 = \$102,400). The firm will go with a March Philadelphia put option.

If in March the spot rate becomes equal to the strike price ($S_t = X_p = 1.3100$ \$/€), the MNC will leave the option to expire, and it will sell the receivables in the spot market receiving: €10,000,000 × 1.3100

$/€=$13,100,000 minus the total cost of $159,600, an amount of 12,940,400.

If in March the spot rate becomes (=1.29404$/€ (=$X_P - C_P^{Ph}$€= 1.3100 − 0.01596) the MNC will exercise its option selling at the contractual price of 1.3100 $/€, which makes a gross profit of 0.01596 $/€. This is the total cost per euro, which means that this exchange rate of 1.29404 $/€ is the break-even (*BE*) point. This is the minimum amount from its receivables that the MNC will receive:

$$\begin{aligned} \text{Minimum Amount Received} &= S_P^O \, x \, BE \\ &= €10{,}000{,}000 \times 1.29404\$/€ \\ &= \$12{,}940{,}400 \end{aligned} \tag{6.2}$$

$$\begin{aligned} \text{or Minimum Amount Received} &= S_P^O \, x \, X_P - C_P^{Ph} \\ &= €10{,}000{,}000 \times 1.3100\$/€ \\ &\quad - \$159{,}600 \\ &= \$12{,}940{,}400. \end{aligned} \tag{6.3}$$

Where, S_P^O = size of the put option (receivables), $BE = X_P - C_P^{Ph}/€$ = break-even point (strike price minus option cost per euro), X_p = strike or exercise price, and C_P^{Ph} = the Philadelphia put option cost.

The different alternatives available to the MNC give different amount of receivables in dollars, as graph 6.1 presents. They are: (1) If it stays unhedged, an uncertain amount of receivables in dollars will be made depending on the spot rate in March. If their forecasting would have been correct, the receivables would have been $13,200,000.00. (2) If money market hedge has been used, the receivables would have been $13,031,133.00. (3) If the forward or futures contract had been used, the receivables will be $13,000,000.00. (4) If the option market hedge had been used, the receivables would have been at a minimum of $12,940,400.00 (Philadelphia put option) or $12,838,000.00 (OTC put option), but an unlimited maximum depending on the spot exchange rate in March (always minus the total option cost).

If the MNC is correct in its forecasting and will sell the receivables at the actual $S_t + 3$ = 1.3200 $/€, without hedging them, the value of the receivables will be the highest in dollars, $13,200,000. Then, hedging the euro receivables by using a money market hedge, the highest certain amount will be $13,031,133. Next, following a forward or a futures contract, the receivables will be $13,000,000 (certain). Lastly, by using option market hedge, the receivables can be a minimum of $12,940,400 (Philadelphia

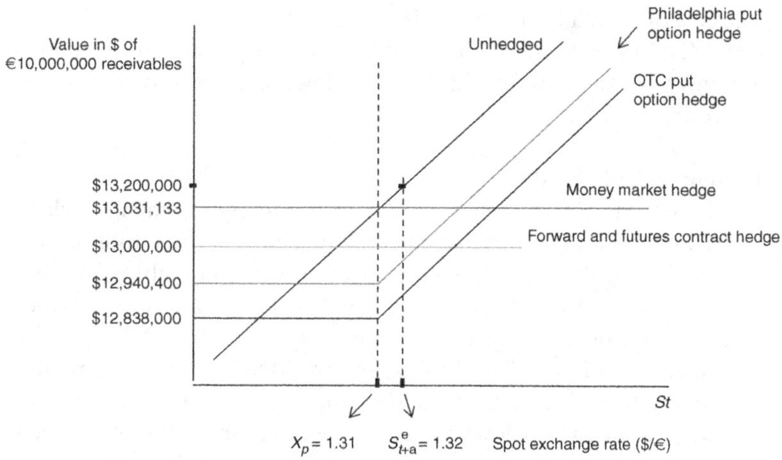

Graph 6.1 Hedging receivables (comparison of alternatives).

Note: X_P = strike or exercise price of the put option, S^e_{t+3} = the forecasting spot rate in March.

put) or $12,838,000 (OTC put), which gives lower value in dollars of these receivables, but the firm has higher flexibility if the spot rate has gone up.

6.3.2.2 *Management of Payables*

We can take, now, the same case as we took above with the US MNC, which has to pay an obligation in foreign currency to a French firm from where it bought some equipment (account payables). The transaction takes place in December for the amount of €10,000,000. The payment is due three months later in March. The following financial information holds in the two economies (United States and France):

The spot exchange rate is: $S_t = 1.3120$ $/€.

The three-month forward rate is: $F_3 = 1.3000$ $/€.

The US interest rate is: $i_t = 3.25\%$ per annum or ($i_t/4 = 0.8125\%$ per quarter).

The French interest rate is: $i_t^* = 6\%$ per annum or ($i_t^*/4 = 1.5\%$ per quarter).

A March Philadelphia call option: strike price 131 cents/€, 1.20 cents/€ premium.

OTC (bank) call option for €10,000,000, strike price 131 cents/€, 2 percent premium.

Brokerage cost per option contract: $120.00.

The US MNC forecasts the spot rate in three months to be: $S^e_{t+3} = 1.3200$$/€.

The cost of capital for the MNC is: $k_t = 5.25\%$.

The MNC may decide to hedge its payables by using four different techniques or to remain unhedged. The following options to manage the exposure are available:

1. Remain Unhedged:
   The US MNC may decide to accept the foreign exchange risk by trusting its forecasting that the exchange rate in three months will be $S^e_{t+3} = 1.3200$ \$/€. Then, it expects its obligation abroad to cost: €10,000,000 × 1.3200 \$/€ = \$13,200,000. This amount is, however, uncertain, because the spot exchange rate can fall to 1.2000 \$/€or can go up to 1.4000 \$/€. In this case, the MNC can receive anything ranging from \$12,000,000 to \$14,000,000. Of course, theoretically the spot rate can go down to zero and up to infinity ($0 \le S^e_{t+3} \le \infty$), which means an enormous risk if the transaction is left uncovered.
2. Forward Market Hedge:
   The US MNC can buy three-month forward €10,000,000 at the three-month forward rate $F_3 = 1.3000$ \$/€. In March, it will deliver the dollars to pay for the forward contract. Its cost will be: €10,000,000 × 1.3000 \$/€ = \$13,000,000. This amount is \$200,000 less than their forecasting amount of \$13,200,000 and it is at the same time, certain, compared with the uncertain amount if the firm had stayed unhedged, as above.
3. Futures Market Hedge:
   The US MNC has to buy futures contracts in euros maturing in March. One futures contract is €125,000. Then, it needs €10,000,000: €125,000 = 80 futures contracts in euros. The futures rate is the same as the forward rate, due to arbitrage in the foreign currency market. Thus, the cost for the payables will be the same as before: €10,000,000 × 1.3000 \$/€ = \$13,000,000. This is a certain amount and the exchange rate risk has been eliminated.
4. Money Market Hedge:
   A money market hedge for payables is different from a money market hedge of receivables. It includes a contract and a source of funds (loan) to fulfill the contract. The MNC, seeking the money market hedge, borrows dollars from a US bank, exchanges this amount for euros, and invests in France. The proceeds from this French investment will be used to pay for the obligation (account payable) in France. The process is as follows:
   Step 1: Amount needed for payables: €10,000,000
   Step 2: Amount to be invested in French *T*-bills (three-month maturity) that will grow to €10,000,000. Then, this will be

the present value of payables:

$PV = \dfrac{10,000,000}{(1+0.015)} = 9,852,216.749$ euros. The proceeds from this T-bill three months later will be used to pay for the payables in France.

Step 3: Amount in dollars needed to be converted to euros:

$$€9,852,216.749 \times 1.3120\$/€ = \$12,926,108.37.$$

Step 4: This amount of $12,926,108.37 will be borrowed from a US bank at

$$i_t/4 = 0.8125\% \text{ for three months.}$$

Step 5: Repayment of loan in US: $12,926,108.37 (1+0.008125)= $13,031,133.00.

Thus, the certain cost of our MNC for the payables in France is: $13,031,133.00.

The money market hedge results in higher cost of payables to France compared to forward and futures markets hedge.

5. Option Market Hedge:
   The MNC can cover its €10,000,000 payables by purchasing a call option in euros (it wants to buy the foreign currency at this contractual price). This call option hedge allows the firm to speculate on the downside potential for depreciation of the euro (€), while limiting upside risk to a known amount the call strike price ($X=$ 131.00 cents/€) plus the call option cost/€. Again, there are two options, here, an OTC call and a Philadelphia call option.

The MNC could purchase from a bank (OTC) a three-month call option on €10,000,000 at the strike price of 1.3100 $/€ and a premium of 2 percent. The cost will be:

$$C_C^{OTC} = S_C^O \, x \, X_C \, x \, P_C^{OTC} \tag{6.4}$$

where, C_C^{OTC} = cost of the OTC call option, S_C^O = size of the call option, X_C = exercise price of the call, and P_C^{OTC} = premium of the OTC call option.

Then, its cost will be: $C_C^{OTC} = €10,000,000 \times 1.3100\$/€ \times 0.02 = \$262,000$.

And consequently, the total cost for the payables would be: $13,100,000 plus $262,000 = $13,362,000.

Also, the MNC can purchase a March Philadelphia call option, which would have the following cost:

One option contract is €125,000 and the amount of payables is €10,000,000, which means that the US MNC needs 80 call option contracts (=€10,000,000 : €125,000).

Total cost per call option:

Premium: €125,000 × 0.012 $/€ =	$1,500.00
Brokerage cost:	$120.00

Total cost:	$1,620.00

Total cost for 80 call option contracts: 80 × $1,620.00 = $129,600.

Then, option cost/€: $1,620.00/€125,000 = 0.01296 $/€.

Thus, the Philadelphia stock exchange has a lower cost compared to the OTC market by $132,400 ($262,000 − 129,600 = $132,400). The firm will go with a March Philadelphia call option.

If in March the spot rate becomes equal to the strike price ($S_t = X_C = 1.3100$ $/€), the MNC will leave the option to expire and it will buy the amount needed for payables in the spot market paying: €10,000,000 × 1.3100 $/€ = $13,100,000 plus the total cost of $129,600, which makes up the total cost of $13,229,600. Also, for any spot rate below the strike price, the MNC will leave the option to expire without exercising it.

If in March the spot rate would be 1.32296$/€ ($=X_C + C_C^{Ph}$€$= 1.3100 + 0.01296$), the MNC will exercise its option buying at the contractual price of 1.3100 $/€, which makes a gross profit of 0.01296 $/€. This is the total cost per euro, which means that this exchange rate of 1.32296 $/€ is the *BE* point. This is the maximum amount for the payables that the MNC will have to pay to France:

$$\begin{aligned}\text{Maximum Amount of Payables} &= S_C^O \, x \, BE \\ &= €10{,}000{,}000 \times 1.32296\$/€ \\ &= \$13{,}229{,}600 \qquad (6.5)\end{aligned}$$

$$\begin{aligned}\text{or Maximum Cost of Payables} &= S_C^O \, x \, X_C + C_C^{Ph} \\ &= €10{,}000{,}000 \times 1.3100\$/€ \\ &\quad + \$129{,}600 = \$13{,}229{,}600. \qquad (6.6)\end{aligned}$$

Where, S_C^O = size of the call option (payables), $BE = X_C + C_C^{Ph}$/€ = break-even point (strike price plus option cost per euro), X_C = strike or exercise price of the call, and C_C^{Ph} = the call option cost.

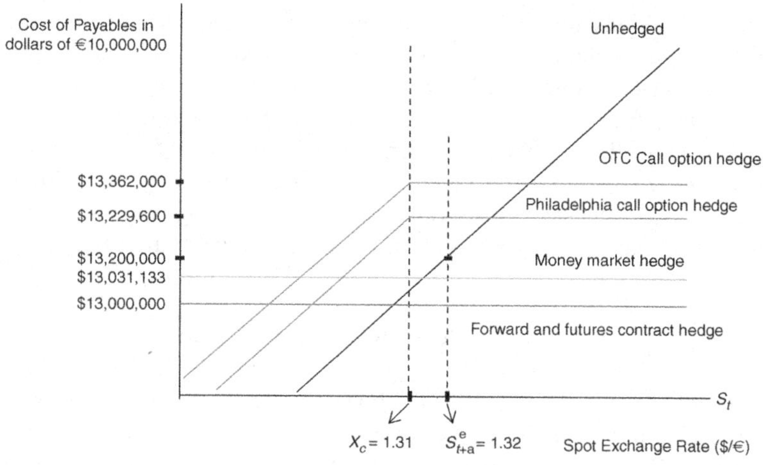

Graph 6.2 Hedging payables (comparison of alternatives).

Note: X_C = strike price of the call option, S^e_{t+3} = the forecasting spot rate three months later in March.

The different alternatives available to the MNC give different amounts of receivables in dollars, as graph 6.2 presents. They are: (1) If it stays unhedged, an uncertain amount of payables in dollars will be made depending on the spot rate in March. If their forecasting turns out to be correct, the payables would be $13,200,000.00. (2) If money market hedge has been used, the payables would be $13,031,133.00. (3) If the forward or futures contract had been used, the payables will be $13,000,000.00. (4) If the option market hedge had been used, the payables would have been at a maximum of $13,229,600.00 (Philadelphia call option) or $13,362,000.00 (OTC call option), but an unlimited minimum depending on the spot exchange rate in March (always plus the total option cost).

As we can see from graph 6.2, the lowest cost for the payables is the one that succeedswith the forward and futures contracts ($13,000,000). Then, comes the cost of the money market hedge with $13,031,133. Staying unhedged (having a perfect forecasting of the future spot rate), the payables will be $13,200,000. Finally, the option markets hedge have higher maximum cost ($13,229,600 for the Philadelphia call option and $13,362,000 for the OTC call option), but more flexibility by leaving the option to expire without exercising it, if the spot rate falls drastically.

All MNCs act conservatively trying to minimize loss by adopting currency risk management. They have to manage their foreign-currency denominated receivables and payables. Conservative hedging policies dictate that contractual hedges be placed only on existing exposures. Some firms use options for their hedging and some others use forward and money market hedging. Also, some firms do not hedge at all. A large number of firms use proportional hedging. They use forward contracts hedging a percentage (i.e., 50 percent or 70 percent) of their existing transaction exposures and do not hedge the remaining proportion of their transactions. Of course, it is very difficult for the financial manager of a MNC to predict accurately the future value of the spot exchange rate. Thus, the foreign exchange risk continues to exist in international transactions.

6.4 Economic or Operating Exposure

A firm has *economic exposure* (also known as *operating exposure* or *competitive exposure* or *strategic exposure*) to the degree that its market value is influenced by unexpected exchange rate fluctuations. Economic exposure measures any change in the firm's present value resulting from changes in future operating cash flows caused by any unexpected change in exchange rates. Such exchange rate adjustments can severely affect the firm's position with regard to its competitors, the firm's future cash flows, and ultimately the firm's value. Thus, economic exposure can affect the present value of future cash flows. Any transaction that exposes the firm to foreign exchange risk also exposes the firm economically; but, economic exposure can be caused by other business activities and investments, which may not be mere international transactions, such as future cash flows from fixed assets. A shift in exchange rate that influences the demand for a good in some country would also be an economic exposure for a firm that sells that good. The objective will be, here, to identify strategic movements or operating techniques that the MNC might wish to adopt to enhance its value, in the presence of unexpected exchange rate changes.

6.4.1 Measurement of Operating Exposure

Measuring operating or economic exposure of a firm requires forecasting and analyzing the firm's future transaction exposures and the future exposures of the firm's competitors. A MNC must determine how it is subject to economic exposure before it can manage its economic exposure. It must measure its exposure to each currency in terms of its cash inflows and cash outflows. The cash flows of the MNC can be divided into *operating cash flows* and *financing cash flows.*

First, operating cash flows arise from intercompany (between unrelated companies) and intracompany (between units of the same company) receivables and payables, rent and lease payments for the use of facilities and equipment, royalty and license fees for the use of technology and intellectual property, and miscellaneous management fees for services provided. Then, financing cash flows are payments for the use of intercompany and intracompany loans (principal and interest) and stockholder equity (new equity and dividends). Each of these cash flows can occur at different time intervals, in different amounts, and in different currencies of denomination, and each has a different predictability of occurrence.

Operating exposure is more important for the long-run growth and performance of a business than changes caused by transaction and translation exposures. But, operating exposure is subjective because it depends on the estimates of future cash flow changes over a long time horizon. Its planning is a management responsibility because it depends on the interaction of strategies in finance, marketing, economics, purchasing, and production. Operating exposure is not only the sensitivity of an MNC's future cash flows to unexpected changes in foreign exchange rates, but also its sensitivity to other key macroeconomic variables. For this reason, this factor has been labeled as *macroeconomic uncertainty.*

Assessing of a firm's economic exposure to currency movements can be done through regression analysis to historical cash flow and exchange rate data, as follows:

$$\Delta RCF_t = \alpha_0 + \alpha_1 \Delta e_t + \varepsilon_t \tag{6.7}$$

where, ΔRCF_t = percentage change in the real cash flow $(\frac{CF_t}{P_t})$, Δe_t = percentage change in the exchange rate (\$/€), α_0 = the constant, α_1 = the sensitivity of ΔRCF_t to movements in Δe_t, and ε_t = the error term.

Other regressions can be run by using different exchange rates because the MNC has businesses and expects cash flows denominated in different currencies. Also, exchange rate indexes can be used as independent variables to assess their effect on the real cash flows:

$$\Delta RCF_t = \alpha_0 + \alpha_1 \Delta e_{1t} + \alpha_2 \Delta e_{2t} + \cdots + \varepsilon_t \tag{6.8}$$

and

$$\Delta RCF_t = \beta_0 + \beta_1 \Delta XRI_t + \varepsilon_t \tag{6.9}$$

or

$$\Delta RCF_t = \beta_0 + \beta_1 \Delta XRI_t + \beta_2 \Delta XRI_{t-1} + \varepsilon_t \tag{6.10}$$

where, ΔXRI_t = percentage change of the exchange rate index.

Furthermore, we can see the effects of exchange rate and stock price indexes on the percentage change of the stock prices.

$$\Delta P_{St} = \gamma_0 + \gamma_1 \Delta S\&P_t + \gamma_2 \Delta e_t + \varepsilon_t \tag{6.11}$$

where, ΔP_{St} = percentage change of stock price of this specific MNC ($\%\Delta P_{St} = \frac{P_t - P_{t-1}}{P_{t-1}} \frac{360}{d} 100$), $\Delta S\&P_t$ = percentage change in the S&P index, and d = number of days.

Other regressions can be used by taking into consideration domestic and foreign stock indexes and exchange rates, depending on where this MNC is operating.

$$\Delta P_{St} = \delta_0 + \delta_1 \Delta HSI_t + \delta_2 \Delta FSI_t + \delta_3 \Delta e_t + \varepsilon_t \tag{6.12}$$

where, ΔHSI_t = percentage change of home stock index and ΔFSI_t = percentage change of foreign stock index.

In addition to the regression analysis, the variability (exchange rate exposure) of a portfolio of currencies can be estimated by using the variance of this portfolio, which includes many different currencies. Then, the dollar cash flows of an MNC are generated from a portfolio of currencies and its risk must be measured by using the portfolio measurement of risk (σ_P^2).

$$\sigma_P^2 = w_{C_1}^2 \sigma_{C_1}^2 + w_{C_2}^2 \sigma_{C_2}^2 + 2 w_{C_1} w_{C_2} \rho_{C_1,C_2} \sigma_{C_1} \sigma_{C_2} \tag{6.13}$$

where, σ_P^2 = the variance of the portfolio of currencies (two different exchange rates, i.e., \$/€ and \$/¥), w_{C_1} = proportion of funds in currency C_1 (€), w_{C_2} = proportion of funds in currency C_2 (¥), σ_{C_1} = standard deviation of exchange rate movement for currency C_1, σ_{C_2} = standard deviation of exchange rate movement for currency C_2, and ρ_{C_1,C_2} = correlation coefficient of the exchange rate movements between currencies C_1 and C_2.

6.4.2 *Management of Operating Exposure*

Operating (economic) and transaction exposure can be managed by adopting operating or financing policies that offset partially anticipated foreign exchange rate exposures. Some of these most commonly employed policies are: (1) long-term forward contracts, (2) matching currency cash flows, (3) risk-sharing agreements, (4) currency swaps, (5) parallel loans (back-to-back loans), (6) leading and lagging, (7) cross-hedging, (8) reinvoicing centers, (9) discounting bills receivables, (10) factoring receivables, (11) currency overdrafts, (12) currency diversification, and (13) government exchange risk guarantees.[6]

6.4.2.1 *Long-Term Forward Contracts*

Long-term forward contracts are contracts that state exchange rate, at which a specified amount of a particular currency can be exchanged at a future date (more than a year from that day). Most large international banks will routinely quote forward rates for terms up to five years for some hard currencies. The long-term forward exchange rate can be quoted and tailored to accommodate the specific needs of an MNC. This is a nonstandardized, over-the-counter agreement, in which one party agrees to buy a certain currency from the other at a certain price (exchange rate), at a certain time more than a year in the future. Because there is a limited secondary market for any forward contract, long-term forward contracts are zero-sum games; one party will win and the other will lose.

6.4.2.2 *Matching Currency Cash Flows*

MNCs exporting products to another country (i.e., England) can offset an anticipated continuous long exposure to that country's currency (British pound) by acquiring debt denominated in that currency (£). The American firm is exporting goods to England and invoices all export sales in pounds (£), which has a long pound position. The American MNC can acquire part of its debt-capital in the British pound markets; it can use the relatively predictable British pounds (£) cash inflows from its exports to service the principal and interest payments on British pound debt (loan) and make a *cash flow matched*, as exhibit 6.1 shows. With this technique, the MNC has hedged an operational cash inflow by creating a financial cash outflow; thus, it does not have to actively manage the exposure with contractual financial instruments, like forward, futures, and other contracts. This form of hedging is referred to as *matching*. It eliminates currency exposure if the cash flow is relatively constant and predictable over time.

The potential matching strategies can be innumerable. If the cash flows were the same in magnitude and timing, the hedging strategy would be a *natural hedge*. Another strategy can be a *currency switching* by paying foreign suppliers with British pounds (£). The American MNC might import components from France and the French firm might welcome payments in pounds because it is short of pounds in its multinational cash flow by doing business in England.

6.4.2.3 *Risk-Sharing Agreements*

Risk-sharing is a contractual agreement, in which the buyer and seller agree to "share" or split currency risk on payments between themselves. The two firms can make a cooperative arrangement to share the burden of currency risk, as follows. A US firm imports automotive parts from a German car manufacture firm every month, and major swings in the dollar/euro

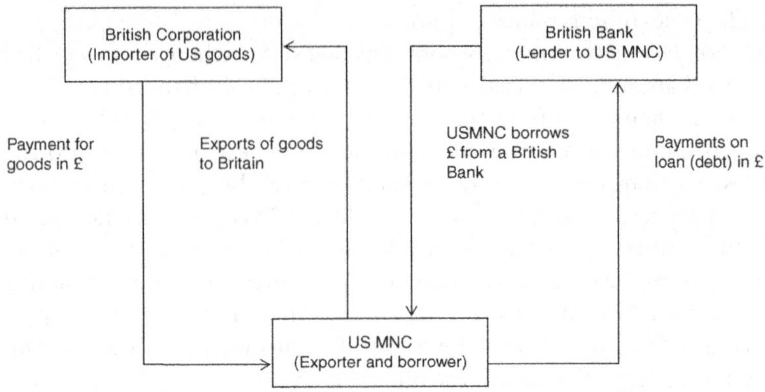

Exhibit 6.1 Matching currency cash flows (financial hedging).

Note: Exposure: The exports to Britain create a foreign currency exposure from the inflow of British pounds (£).
Hedge: The British pound debt payments act as a financial hedge by requiring debt (loan) service in pounds (£), an outflow of £ received from the exports of goods by the US firm to Britain.

exchange rate ($/€) can benefit one party at the expense of the other. The risk-sharing agreement can be signed between the two firms. One potential solution could be that all purchases by the American firm will be made in euros (€) at the spot exchange rate, as long as the spot rate on the date of invoice is between 1.2000 $/€ and 1.3000 $/€. If the exchange rate falls outside of this range on the payment date, the two firms will share the difference equally.

For example, the US importer has an account payable of €5,000,000 at the end of the month. If the spot rate is between the above contractual ranges, the American firm will pay the amount in dollars by multiplying the payables with the spot rate. But, let us say that the euro has appreciated to 1.3600 $/€ at the date of the payment of the above payables, which increases the cost of purchasing for the American firm. Since this exchange rate falls outside the contractual range, they will share the difference (1.3600 $/€–1.3000 $/€= 0.06$/€); so the payment of the US firm will be as follows:

$$\begin{aligned} €5{,}000{,}000[1.3600\$/€ - (0.06\$/€/2)] &= €5{,}000{,}000(1.3300\$/€) \\ &= \$6{,}650{,}000 \end{aligned}$$

The total payment of the American firm will be =$6,650,000, which saves the American firm $150,000 (= €5,000,000 × 0.03 $/€). At a spot rate of 1.3000 \$/€, the cost would have been \$6,500,000 (= €5,000,000 × 1.3000 \$/€). Thus, this risk-sharing agreement has saved the American firm \$150,000. Of course, if the spot rate had fallen below 1.2000 \$/€, the agreement could have benefited the German firm. The risk-sharing arrangement is intended to smooth the impact of the exchange rate volatility on both parties.

6.4.2.4 Currency swaps

Currency swaps are over-the-counter derivatives, and are closely related to interest rate swaps. However, unlike interest rate swaps, currency swaps can involve the exchange of the principal. There are three different ways in which currency swaps can exchange loans:

First, the simplest currency swap structure is to exchange only the principal with the counterparty at a specified point in the future at a rate agreed now. Such an agreement performs a function equivalent to a forward contract or futures. The cost of finding a counterparty (either directly or through an intermediary) and drawing up an agreement with them makes swaps more expensive than alternative derivatives (and thus rarely used) as a method to fix shorter-term forward exchange rates. However for the longer-term future, commonly up to 10 years, where spreads are wider for alternative derivatives, principal-only currency swaps are often used as a cost-effective way to fix forward rates. This type of currency swap is also known as an FX-swap.

Second, another currency swap structure is to combine the exchange of loan principal, as above, with an interest rate swap. In such a swap, interest cash flows are not netted before they are paid to the counterparty (as they would be in a vanilla interest rate swap) because they are denominated in different currencies. As each party effectively borrows on the other's behalf, this type of swap is also known as a *back-to-back loan*. This is a loan agreement between entities in two countries in which the currencies remain separate, but the maturity dates remain fixed. The gross interest rates of the loan are separate as well and are set on the basis of the commercial rates in place when the agreement is signed.

A third currency swap is to swap only interest payment cash flows on loans of the same size and term. The exchanged cash flows are in different denominations and so are not netted. An example of such a swap is the exchange of fixed-rate US dollar interest payments for floating-rate interest payments in euro. This type of swap is also known as a *cross-currency interest rate swap* or *cross currency swap*.

Thus, a type of currency swap is one that accommodates two firms that have different long-term needs. Consider a US MNC, hired to build an oil pipeline in Greece, that expects to receive payment in euros (€) in five years when the job is completed. At the same time, a European firm is hired by a US bank for a long-term consulting project. Assume that payment to this European firm will be in US dollars ($) and that much of the payment will occur in five years. These two firms could arrange a currency swap that allows for an exchange of euros for dollars in five years at some negotiated exchange rate. In this way, the US firm could lock in the number of US dollars the euro payment will convert to in five years.

To create a currency swap, MNCs need to find other firms that can accommodate their needs. Of course, there are brokers employed by large banks and investment firms that act as middlemen for swaps. The brokers receive a fee for their services. The swap agreement may require periodic payments from one party to the other to account for exchange rate movements, so as to reduce the possibility of one party not fulfilling its obligation by the time the swap is supposed to occur.

6.4.2.5 Parallel Loans or Back-to-Back Loans

A *parallel loan* or *back-to-back loan* or *credit swap* involves an exchange of currencies between two parties (MNCs), with a promise to reexchange currencies at a specified exchange rate at a future date. It represents two swaps of currencies, one swap at the inception of the loan contract and another swap at a specified future date. A parallel loan is interpreted by accountants as a loan and is therefore recorded on financial statements. Such a swap creates a covered hedge against exchange loss, since each firm, on its own books, borrows the same currency it repays.

For example, a German parent firm wants to invest funds in its US subsidiary; but, there is an exchange rate risk between the dollar ($) and euro (€) denominated cash flows. Then, the German firm locates an American firm that wants to invest funds in its subsidiary in Germany. The two MNCs come in contact and the German parent company lends money to the US subsidiary in Germany and the US parent company lends money to the German subsidiary in the US. The two loans would be for equal values at the current spot rate and for a specified maturity. Then, at maturity the two loans would each be repaid to the original lender, without any need to use the foreign exchange market. Through this parallel loan, as exhibit 6.2 shows, they have eliminated the exchange rate risk.

Of course, it is difficult for MNCs to find a partner (*counterparty*) for the amount of the currency that they want to invest (or borrow) and the desired time. The exchange rate risk is eliminated, but the default risk of the partners exists. The risk is also minimized because each party of the loan has 100 percent collateral, although in a different currency.

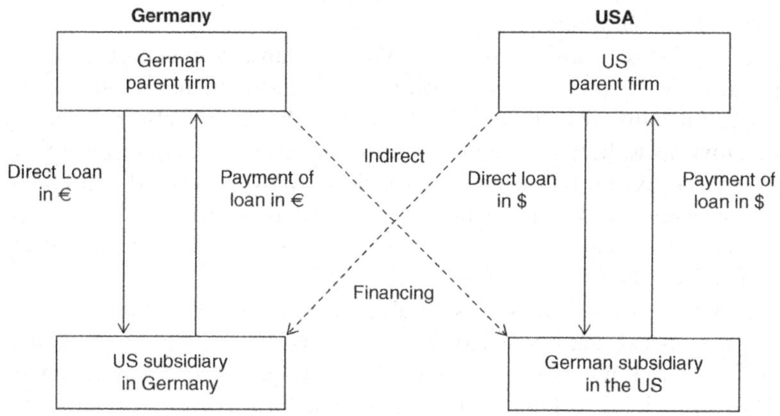

Exhibit 6.2 Parallel loan or back-to-back loan.

Note: German parent firm wishes to invest funds in its US subsidiary and an American parent company wants to invest funds in its German subsidiary.

German parent firm loans euros (€) directly to the US subsidiary in Germany and the German subsidiary in the US borrows dollars ($) from the US parent company. Thus, they avoid the direct currency exposure.

6.4.2.6 Leading and Lagging

MNCs can use *leading* and *lagging* strategies to reduce operating and transaction exposure by accelerating or decelerating the timing of payments or disbursement in foreign currencies, based on their expectations or forecasting of the movement of a currency. Leading and lagging can be done between related firms (intracompany) or with independent firms (intercompany).

Leading is to pay early an obligation that the firm has in foreign currency. For example, suppose the payables are due in two months from now, but the foreign currency is appreciated; then, the best will be to pay this invoice as soon as possible because we will need less dollars to pay this amount of foreign currency. Lagging is to pay late the obligation in foreign currency that we have. The expectations are that the foreign currency is depreciated continuously; thus, by postponing the payment, we will need less units of our hard currency. The use of leads and lags is an obvious technique for minimizing foreign exchange exposure and for shifting the burden of financing to the other party; for this reason there are limits in some countries, or companies have to negotiate the time of payments.

6.4.2.7 *Cross-Hedging*

Cross-hedging is a common method to reduce transaction exposure, when the currency of your receivables cannot be hedged (there are no instruments of hedging this currency). This type of hedging is also referred to as a *proxy hedge* because the hedged position is in another currency that serves as a proxy for the currency in which the MNC is exposed. The effectiveness of cross-hedging depends on the correlation coefficients ($\rho_{X,Y}$) of these two currencies (X and Y). If the $\rho_{X,Y}=+1$, we will have the most effective cross-hedging strategy.

Assume that a US MNC has payables in Saudi Arabian riyals 60 days from now. Because it is worried that this currency may appreciate against the US dollar, it would like to hedge this position. But, forward contracts and other hedging techniques are not possible for this currency; thus, the firm considers cross-hedging, in which case, it needs to first identify a currency that can be hedged and is highly correlated with the riyal. And let us say that this currency with an almost perfect positive correlation with the riyal is the euro. Consequently, the MNC can set up a 60 days forward contract on euros, as a proxy to hedge the riyal exposure.

6.4.2.8 *Reinvoicing Centers*

A *reinvoicing center* is a subsidiary or department of an MNC where all intracompany transactions are centralized and foreign currency related receivables and liabilities are netted. The means of hedging the entire multinational firm's foreign currency exposures are also determined by the reinvoicing center, which serves as a type of middleman between the parent and the foreign subsidiaries in a geographic region.

Employing a reinvoicing center will likely limit the firm's risk to transaction exposure. For example, suppose a US-based MNC has subsidiaries in France and England. The French subsidiary owes the British subsidiary debt in pounds (£) for an intrafirm purchase of processed goods. The US arm of the MNC recently received a payment in British pounds and owes a debt in euros (€). Instead of having each portion of the company engage in its own foreign exchange transaction, a reinvoicing center allows different inflows and outflows of money and makes the process more efficient and stable. The invoice center can also determine a preset foreign exchange rate for hedging purposes. In this case, the most optimal solution would be to have the French subsidiary exchange its euros to the US office for its British pounds.

In another case, a US manufacturing firm (or one of its subsidiaries) sells goods to a distribution subsidiary of the same MNC only by selling to a reinvoicing center, which in turn resells to the distribution subsidiary. The title passes to the reinvoicing center, but the physical movement of

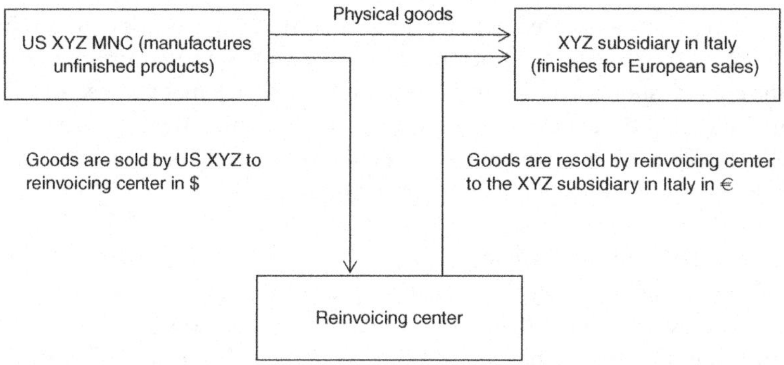

Exhibit 6.3 Reinvoicing center.

Note: US XYZ MNC ships goods directly to its Italian subsidiary. The invoice, which is denominated in US dollars, is passed to the reinvoicing center. The reinvoicing center takes legal title to the products. The reinvoicing center invoices XYZ subsidiary in Italy in euros (€).

goods is direct from the manufacturing plant in the United States to its foreign subsidiary in Italy. The reinvoicing center handles paperwork only, but it has no inventory, as exhibit 6.3 shows.

Thus, all operating units of this MNC deal in their own currency and all transaction exposure lies with the reinvoicing center. These reinvoicing centers are reselling these goods at cost plus a small commission for their services. The resale price of this product is the manufacturer's price times the forward exchange rate for the date on which payment from the buyer is expected. The formation of the reinvoicing center allows managing all foreign exchange transaction exposure.

6.4.2.9 Discounting Bills Receivables

Discounting bills receivables can be converted into cash by selling them to a financial institution at a discount. Bills (and notes) are usually sold (discounted) with recourse, which means the company discounting the bill agrees to pay the financial institution if the maker dishonors the bill. When bill receivable are sold with recourse, the company has a contingent liability that must be disclosed in the bills accompanying the financial statements. A contingent liability is an obligation to pay an amount in the future, if and when an uncertain event occurs.

Thus, discounting can be used to cover export receivables. When an export receivable is to be settled by a bill of exchange,[7] the exporter may discount the bill and thereby receive payment before the settlement date.

The bill may be discounted either with a bank in the importer's country, in which case the foreign currency proceeds can be repatriated immediately at the current spot rate or it can be discounted with a bank in the exporter's country so that the exporter may receive settlement direct in his home currency. Either way, the exporter is covered against exchange rate risk, the cost being the discount rate charged by the bank.

6.4.2.10 Factoring Receivables

Factoring foreign currency denominated receivables can be used for covering export receivables. When the export receivable is to be settled on an open account,[8] rather than by a bill of exchange, the receivable can be assigned as a collateral for bank financing. Commercial banks and specialized factoring institutions offer factoring services. For the exporter, the technique is very straightforward. He simply sells his export receivables to the factor and receives home currency in return. The costs involved include: (1) credit risks, (2) the cost of financing, and (3) the cost of covering exchange rate risk.

Of course, account receivables factoring is a financing method used by many businesses. In effect it is a means of short-term borrowing using outstanding invoices or receivables as collateral. This allows companies of all sizes to obtain working capital they otherwise might not have been able to receive. The credit line for the receivables is decided based on the financial strength of the end customer, who owes money on the products or services purchased, not by the seller of the receivables. Account receivables factoring is not a loan, so there are no payments and no debt is incurred. Any business that generates sales through open credit terms to credit-worthy accounts is eligible for this type of financing.

Each company applying for this type of business funding is assessed on an individual basis to determine which accounts and invoices are eligible for financing. The process is as follows: (1) A company delivers its goods or provides its services to clients and issues an invoice. (2) Said company then sells its invoice to a factoring company and in exchange the company is given up to 90 percent of the invoice's amount in cash within 24 hours. (3) Once the predetermined net terms of 30 to 60 days has passed, the invoice is paid by the end-customer to the factoring company and the remainder of the money from the sale of the invoice is remitted back to the company who sold it, minus a small fee for the financial service that was provided.

6.4.2.11 Currency Overdrafts

Foreign currency overdrafts are available in the London money markets in all major currencies, although banks tend to specialize in currency. An overdraft offers to a firm a short-term finance facility for any fluctuating borrowing requirements that it may have. It can be an ideal source of temporary funding when the firm's business expenses are less predictable. In terms of avoidance of exposure, all that a MNC needs to do is to maintain the amount of its foreign currency receivables in a particular currency equal to the balance on the overdraft in that currency. However, if the company uses the proceeds of the receivables to run down the overdraft, it also needs to draw down as sales denominated in foreign currency are made. Some MNCs find it more convenient to sell the proceeds of the foreign denominated receivables spot rather than perpetually adjust the level of the overdraft.

Currency overdrafts are used for short-term cash flow management. Whether a MNC is importing or exporting, maintaining an onshore overdraft in most major currencies can be very useful, particularly if there is uncertainty in the timing of its overseas trade transactions. It can take advantage of the existing 180-day credit period. There are several key features of currency overdrafts for importers. They are (1) useful in financing transactions over shorter terms; (2) handy if payment to the seller occurs when exchange rates are unfavorable; and (3) a protection against unfavorable exchange rates. For exporters they are (1) useful in financing transactions over shorter terms; (2) useful if one requires an account for receipt of funds from the buyer; and (3) a protection against unfavorable exchange rates. There is an overdraft limit, which is of a minimum of \$20,000.

6.4.2.12 Currency Diversification

Another method for reducing transaction exposure is *currency diversification.* MNCs can minimize their exchange rate exposure by diversifying their business among many different countries, which must have negative correlation in their currencies movements ($\rho_{X,Y} = -1$). Any investment strategy that involves investing in securities denominated in several currencies (or cash flows in different foreign currencies) is considered as currency diversification. For example, one may buy stocks that trade in US dollars, British pounds, euros, Japanese yen, and Swiss francs. One firm conducts a currency diversification strategy to reduce the foreign exchange risk involved in trading with only one or two currencies.

Ancient Greeks had a saying "moderation in all things," but diversification in life is broadly understood to be a wise principle. This is especially true when it comes to investing. Asset allocation is often cited as principle number one, accounting for 90 percent of portfolio returns. To trade successfully in the currency markets, you need to follow the same rules of investing that guide stock market investors—diversify your holdings.

While this plan could lower annual returns somewhat, it is a prudent idea that will safeguard your portfolio against sudden changes in the currency markets. While one part of your portfolio is appreciated, the other depreciates, helping MNCs make a good return (and preserve capital) in all environments.

6.4.2.13 Government Exchange Risk Guarantees

As part of a series of encouragement to exporters, government agencies in many countries offer their businesses insurance against export credit risks and certain export financing schemes. Many of these agencies offer exchange risk insurance to their exporters as well as the usual export credit guarantees. The exporter pays a small premium and in return the government agency absorbs all exchange rate risk (thereby taking profits and absorbing losses). In the United States, the Export-Import Bank (Ex-Im Bank)[9] offers these exchange risk guarantees.

Government agencies, in many countries, provide insurance against export credit risk and introduce special export financing schemes for exporters in order to promote exports. In recent years, a few of these agencies have begun to provide exchange risk insurance to their exporters and the usual export credit guarantees. The exporter pays a small premium on his export sales, and for this premium the government agency absorbs all exchange losses and gains beyond a certain level. Initially, such exchange risk guarantee schemes were introduced to aid capital goods exports where receivable exposures were of long-term nature. Government exchange risk guarantees are also given to cover foreign currency borrowing by public bodies. All these various exposure management techniques are not available in all circumstances. This is mainly because of limitations imposed by the marketplace and by regulatory authorities. Similarly, the availability of internal techniques is largely a function of the international involvement of each company.

6.5 Alternative Exchange Rate Exposures and Hedging Techniques

There are many exchange rate exposures for the MNCs and many external techniques of exposure management, which resort to contractual relationships outside a group of companies in order to reduce the risk of foreign exchange losses.

6.5.1 Contingent Exposure

A MNC has *contingent exposure* when bidding for foreign projects or negotiating other contracts or foreign direct investments. Such an exposure arises from the potential for a firm to suddenly face a transactional or economic foreign exchange risk, contingent on the outcome of some contract or negotiation. For example, a firm could be waiting for a project bid to be accepted by a foreign business or government, which if accepted would result in an immediate receivable. While waiting, the firm faces a contingent exposure from the uncertainty as to whether or not that receivable will happen. If the bid is accepted and a receivable is paid, the firm then faces a transaction exposure, so a firm may prefer to manage contingent exposures.

6.5.2 *Tax Exposure*

Tax exposure is the extent to which an MNC's tax liability is affected by fluctuations in foreign exchange rate. As a general rule, only realized gains or losses affect the income tax liability of a company. Translation losses or gains are normally not realized and are not taken into account in tax liability. Some steps taken to reduce exposure, such as entering into forward exchange contracts, can create losses or gains that enter into tax liability. Other measures that can be taken have no income tax implications.

6.5.3 *Exposure Netting*

Exposure netting is offsetting exposures in one currency with exposures in the same or another currency, where exchange rates are expected to move in such a way that losses or gains on the first exposed position should be offset by gains or losses on the second currency exposure.

In general, *netting* means to allow a positive value and a negative value to set-off and partially or entirely cancel each other out. Netting can be implemented with the joint effort of subsidiaries or by the centralized cash management group. It optimizes cash flows by reducing the administrative and transaction costs that result from currency conversion and eliminates exchange rate exposure at the same time.

Netting offers several key benefits to MNCs. It reduces the number of cross-border transactions between subsidiaries, which means less administrative cost of cash transfers. It reduces the need for foreign exchange conversion and consequently, the conversion cost. It improves reporting and coordination among subsidiaries. Cash flow forecasting becomes easier because only net cash flows are available now, due to less cash flow after the netting.

There is a *bilateral netting system* that involves transactions between two units (parent and a subsidiary or between two subsidiaries) and a *multilateral netting system*, which is a more complex interchange among the parent and several subsidiaries. For large MNCs, a multilateral (centralized) netting system reduces administrative and currency conversion costs and exchange rate risk.

6.6 Summary

Foreign exchange risk (or *exchange rate risk* or *currency risk)* is a financial risk posed by an exposure to unanticipated changes in the exchange rate between two currencies. Investors and MNCs exporting or importing goods and services or making foreign investments throughout the global economy are faced with an exchange rate risk, which can have severe financial consequences if not managed appropriately. Foreign currency exposures are generally categorized into the following three distinct types: (1) transaction exposure, (2) economic exposure, and (3) translation exposure. These exposures pose risks to firms' cash flows, competitiveness, market value, and financial reporting.

Managers of MNCs employ a number of foreign exchange hedging strategies in order to protect against exchange rate risk. Transaction exposure is often managed either with the use of the money markets, foreign exchange derivatives (such as forward contracts, futures contracts, options, and swaps), or with operational techniques such as currency invoicing, leading and lagging of receipts and payments, and exposure netting. MNCs may exercise alternative strategies to financial hedging for managing their economic or operating exposure, by carefully selecting production sites with a mind for lowering costs, using a policy of flexible sourcing in its supply chain management, diversifying its export market across a greater number of countries, or by implementing strong research and development activities and differentiating its products in the pursuit of greater inelasticity and less foreign exchange risk exposure.

Translation exposure is largely dependent on the accounting standards of the home country and the translation methods required by those standards. For example, the United States Federal Accounting Standard Board (FASB) specifies when and where to use certain methods such as the temporal method and current rate method. MNCs can manage translation exposure by performing a balance sheet hedge. Since translation exposure arises from discrepancies between net assets and net liabilities on a balance sheet solely from exchange rate differences. Following this logic, a firm could acquire an appropriate amount of exposed assets or liabilities to balance any outstanding discrepancy. Foreign exchange derivatives may also be used to hedge against translation exposure.

Appendix 6

Investopedia gives a very good Forex Tutorial for anyone who is interested in foreign exchange markets. See the following website:

http://www.investopedia.com/university/forexmarket/default.asp#axzz2H2Rbd26c.

Also, *Gocurrency* provides information about the foreign exchange markets for beginners. See http://www.gocurrency.com/articles/forex-for-beginners.

Further, *IBFX* presents useful information on the foreign exchange market. See http://www.ibfx.com/Trade/The-Foreign-Exchange-Market.

Furthermore, the US Fed supplies data on the foreign exchange. See http://www.ny.frb.org/markets/foreignex.html.

Notes

1. See Selling and Sorter (1983).
2. An entity's functional currency is the currency of the primary economic environment, in which that entity operates. The functional currency can be the dollar or a foreign currency depending on the facts. Normally, it will be the currency of the economic environment in which cash is generated and expended by the entity. An entity can be any form of operation, including a subsidiary, division, branch, or joint venture. See http://www.fasb.org/summary/stsum52.shtml.
3. See Eiteman, Stonehill, and Moffett (2010, p. 351).
4. See, Eun and Resnick (2007, chapter 10, "Management of Translation Exposure"). http://www.ba.metu.edu.tr/~engin/BA4817/ba4817C10.pdf
5. With all these tax deductions that businesses have, poor citizens pay for them and the national debt of the country goes up and very soon the country will find itself in serious debt crisis. These tax systems are socially unfair and unethical, but exist in almost every nation. See http://taxes.about.com/od/businessexpenses/qt/DeductBizExpens.htm
6. See, "Forex Risk Management-Internal and External Techniques," http://drakanshajain.blogspot.com/2011/11/forex-risk-management-internal-and.html.
7. A Bill of Exchange is a non-interest-bearing written order used primarily in international trade that binds one party (the importer) to pay a fixed sum of money to another party (the exporter) at a predetermined future date. Bills of

exchange are similar to checks and promissory notes. They can be drawn by individuals or banks and are generally transferable by endorsements. The difference between a promissory note and a bill of exchange is that this product is transferable and can bind one party to pay a third party that was not involved in its creation. If these bills are issued by a bank, they can be referred to as bank drafts. If they are issued by individuals, they can be referred to as trade drafts.
8. An open account transaction is a sale where the goods are shipped and delivered before payment is due, which is usually in 30 to 90 days. Obviously, this option is the most advantageous to the importer in terms of cash flow and cost, but it is consequently the highest-risk option for an exporter. Because of intense competition in export markets, foreign buyers often press exporters for open account terms. In addition, the extension of credit by the seller to the buyer is more common abroad. Therefore, exporters who are reluctant to extend credit may lose a sale to their competitors. However, though open account terms will definitely enhance export competitiveness, exporters should thoroughly examine the political, economic, and commercial risks as well as cultural influences to ensure that payment will be received in full and on time. It is possible to substantially mitigate the risk of nonpayment associated with open account trade by using such trade finance techniques as export credit insurance and factoring. Exporters may also seek export working capital financing to ensure that they have access to financing for production and for credit while waiting for payment.
9. See, http://www.exim.gov/.

Bibliography

Eiteman, David K., Arthur I. Stonehill, and Michael H. Moffett (2010), *Multinational Business Finance*, 12th Edition, Boston, MA: Prentice Hall, Pearson Education, Inc.

Eun, Cheol S. and Bruce G. Resnick (2007), *International Financial Management*, 4th Edition, New York, NY: McGraw-Hill Companies, Inc.

Madura, Jeff (2012), *International Financial Management*, 11th Edition, Mason, OH: South-Western, Cengage Learning.

Selling, Thomas I. and George H. Sorter (1983), "FASB Statement No. 52 and Its Implications for Financial Statement Analysis," *Financial Analysts Journal*, Vol. 39, No. 3, May/June, pp. 64–69.

Glossary

Absolute advantage: The ability of an individual party or country to produce more of a product or service with the same inputs as another party. It is therefore possible for a country to have no absolute advantage in any international trade activity. See also *Comparative advantage.*

Absolute form of purchasing power parity: The theory that explains how inflation differentials affect exchange rates. It suggests that prices of two products of different countries should be equal when measured by a common currency. And the spot exchange rate is equal to the ratio of price levels between the domestic and the foreign economy.

Accounts receivable currency: Indirect financing provided by exporter for an importer by exporting goods and allowing for payment to be made at a later date.

Accounting exposure: Another name for translation exposure. See *Translation exposure.*

Affiliate: A foreign enterprise, in which the parent company owns a minority interest.

American option: An option that can be exercised at any time up to and including expiration date.

American terms: Foreign exchange quotations for the US dollar, expressed as the number of US dollars per unit of non-US currency. *Direct quotation* for the United States.

Anticipated exposure: A foreign exchange exposure that is believed by management to have a very high likelihood of occurring, but is not yet contractual, and is therefore not yet certain.

Appreciation: In the context of exchange rate changes, a rise in the foreign exchange value of a currency that is pegged to other currencies or to gold. Also called *revaluation.*

Arbitrage: A trading strategy based on the purchase of a commodity or financial assets, including foreign exchange, in one market at one price while simultaneously selling it in another market at a more advantageous price, in order to obtain a risk-free profit on the price differential.

Arbitrageur: An individual or company that practices arbitrage.

Asian dollar market: Market in Asia, in which banks collect deposits and make loans denominated in US dollars.

Ask: The price at which a dealer is willing to sell foreign exchange (the currency that is denominator), securities, or commodities. Also called *offer* price.

Asset market approach: A strategy that determines whether foreigners are willing to hold claims in monetary form, depending on an extensive set of investment considerations or drivers.

At-the-money (ATM): An option whose exercise price is the same as the spot price of the underlying currency.

Back-to-back loan: A loan in which two companies in separate countries borrow each other's currency for a specific period of time and repay the other's currency at an agreed maturity. Sometimes the loans are channeled through an intermediate bank. Back-to-back financing is also called *link financing* or *parallel loan.*

Balance of payments (BofP): A financial statement summarizing the flow of goods, services, and investment funds between residents of a given country and residents of the rest of the world.

Balance of trade (BOT): An entry in the balance of payments measuring the difference between the monetary value of merchandise exports and merchandise imports. Exports of goods minus imports of goods.

Balance on goods and services: Balance of trade, plus the net amount of payments of interest and dividends to foreign investors and from investment, as well as receipts and payments resulting from international tourism and other service transactions.

Balance sheet hedge: An accounting strategy that requires an equal amount of exposed foreign currency assets and liabilities on a firm's consolidated balance sheet.

Bank for International Settlements (BIS): An international organization of central banks that "fosters international monetary and financial cooperation and serves as a bank for central banks." As an international institution, it is not accountable to any single national government. It is in Basel, Switzerland, with representative offices in Hong Kong and Mexico City.

Banker's acceptance: An unconditional promise by a bank to make payment on a draft when it matures. This comes in the form of the bank's endorsement (acceptance) of a draft drawn against that bank in accordance with the terms of a letter of credit issued by the bank.

Barter: International trade conducted by the direct exchange of physical goods, rather than by separate purchases and sales at prices and exchange rates set by a free market.

Basic balance: In a country's balance of payments, the net of exports and imports of goods and services, unilateral transfers, and long-term capital flows.

Beggar-thy-neighbor policy: It is an economic policy through which one country attempts to remedy its economic problems by means that tend to worsen the economic problems of other countries. The term was originally devised to characterize policies of trying to cure domestic depression and unemployment by shifting effective demand away from imports onto domestically produced goods, either through tariffs and quotas on imports or by competitive devaluation. The policy can be associated with mercantilism and neo-mercantilism. These policies were widely adopted by major economies during the Great Depression of the 1930s or is adopted whenever a country is in depression, as seen recently with the global financial crisis of 2007–2013.

Beta: Second letter of the Greek alphabet (β), used as a statistical measure of market risk of a security in the capital asset pricing model. Beta is the covariance between returns on a given asset and returns on the market portfolio, divided by the variance of returns on the market portfolio.

Bid: The price that a dealer or a bank is willing to pay to purchase foreign exchange (the currency that is denominator) or a security.

Bid-ask spread: The difference between a bid and an ask quotation.

Bilateral netting system: Netting method used for transactions between two units.

Bill of exchange (B/E): A written order requesting one party (such as an importer) to pay at a specified time to the writer of the bill. Also called a *draft*. See *Sight draft*.

Black market: An illegal foreign exchange market.

Blocked funds: Funds in one country's currency that may not be exchanged freely for foreign currencies because of exchange controls.

Bretton Woods Conference: An international conference in 1944 that established the international monetary system—the *Bretton Woods Agreement*—that was in effect from 1945 to 1971. The conference was held in Bretton Woods, New Hampshire, United States.

BRIC: A frequently used acronym for the four largest emerging market countries—Brazil, Russia, India, and China.

Bulldogs: British pound-denominated bonds issued within the United Kingdom by a foreign borrower.

Cable: The US dollar per British pound cross rate.

CAD: Cash against documents. International trade term.

Call: An option with the right, but not an obligation, to buy foreign exchange (a currency) or another financial contract at a specified price within a specified time. See *Option.*

Capital account: A section of the balance of payments accounts. Under the revised format of the International Monetary Fund, the capital account measures capital transfers and the acquisition and disposal of nonproduced, nonfinancial assets. Under traditional definitions, still used by many countries, the capital account measures public and private international lending and investment. Most of the traditional definition of the capital account is now incorporated into IMP statements as the financial account.

Capital control: Restrictions, requirements, taxes, or prohibitions on the movements of capital across borders as imposed and enforced by governments.

Capital flight: Movement of funds out of a country because of political risk or to avoid taxes.

Capital markets: The financial markets of various countries in which various types of long-term debt and/or ownership securities or claims on those securities are purchased and sold.

Capital mobility: The degree to which private capital moves freely from country to country in search of the most promising investment opportunities.

Certificate of Deposit (CD): A negotiable receipt issued by a bank for funds deposited for a certain period of time. CDs can be purchased or sold prior to their maturity in a secondary market, making them an interest-earning marketable security.

Clearinghouse: An institution through which financial obligations are cleared by the process of settling the obligations of various members.

Clearinghouse Interbank Payments System (CHIPS): A New York–based computerized clearing system used by banks to settle interbank foreign exchange obligations (mostly US dollars) between members.

Collar option: The simultaneous purchase of a put option and sale of a call option, or vice versa, resulting in a form of hybrid option.

Commercial risk: In banking, the likelihood that a foreign debtor will be unable to repay its debts because of business events, as distinct from political ones.

Common market: An association through treaty of two or more countries that agree to remove all trade barriers among themselves. The best known is the European Common Market, now called the European Union (EU).

Comparative advantage: Theory suggesting that specialization and trade by countries can increase worldwide production.

Competitive advantage: It is defined as the strategic advantage one business entity has over its rival entities within its competitive industry. Achieving competitive advantage strengthens and positions a business better within the business environment. Competitive advantage theory suggests that states and businesses should pursue policies that create high-quality goods to sell at high prices in the market. It emphasizes productivity growth as the focus of national strategies. Competitive advantage rests on the notion that cheap labor is ubiquitous and natural resources are not necessary for a good economy.

Competitive agreement: See *Operating exposure.*

Contingent foreign currency exposure: The final determination of the exposure is contingent upon another firm's decision, such as a decision to invest or the winning of a business or construction bid.

Consignment: Arrangement, in which the exporter ships goods to the importer while still retaining title to the merchandise.

Convertible currency: A currency that can be exchanged freely for any other currency without government restrictions.

Correspondent bank: A bank that holds deposits for and provides services to another bank, located in another geographic area, on a reciprocal basis.

Cost of cover: The cost of hedging.

Counterparty: The opposite party in a double transaction, which involves an exchange of financial instruments or obligations now and a reversal of that same transaction at an agreed-upon later date.

Counterparty risk: The potential exposure any individual firm bears that the second party to any financial contract may be unable to fulfill its obligations under the contract's specifications.

Countertrade: A type of international trade, in which parties exchange goods directly rather than for money, a type of barter.

Country risk: In banking, the likelihood that unexpected events within a host country will influence a client's or a government's ability to repay a loan. Country risk is often divided into sovereign (political) risk and foreign exchange (currency) risk.

Covered interest arbitrage (CIA): The process whereby an investor earns a risk-free profit by (1) borrowing funds in one currency, (2) exchanging those funds in the spot market for a foreign currency, (3) investing the foreign currency at interest rates in a foreign country, (4) selling forward, at the time of original investment, the investment proceeds to be received at maturity, (5) using the proceeds of the forward sale to repay the original loan, and (6) sustaining a remaining profit balance.

Covering: A transaction in the forward foreign exchange market or money market that protects the value of future cash flows. Covering is another term for hedging. See *hedge*.

Crawling peg: A foreign exchange rate system, in which the exchange rate is adjusted very frequently to reflect the prevailing rate of inflation.

Credit risk: The possibility that a borrower's credit worth, at the time of renewing a credit, is classified by the lender.

Cross-border factoring: Factoring by a network of factors across borders. The exporter's factor can contact correspondent factors in other countries to handle the collections of accounts receivable.

Cross-currency interest rate swap: See *Currency swap.*

Cross-currency swap: See *Currency swap.*

Cross-hedging: Hedging an open position in one currency with a hedge on another currency that is highly correlated with the first currency. This occurs when for some reason the common hedging techniques cannot be applied to the first currency. A cross-hedge is not a perfect hedge, but can substantially reduce the exposure.

Cross rate: An exchange rate between two currencies derived by dividing or multiplying each currency's exchange rate with a third currency. Colloquially, it is often used to refer to a specific currency pair such as the euro/yen cross rate, as the yen/dollar and dollar/euro are the more common currency quotations.

Cumulative translation adjustment (CTA) account: An entry in a translated balance sheet, in which gains and/or losses from translation have been accumulated over a period of years.

Currency basket: The value of a portfolio of specific amounts of individual currencies, used as the basis for setting the market value of another currency. Also called *currency cocktail.*

Currency board: System for maintaining the value of the local currency with respect to some other specified currency.

Currency call option: Contract that grants the right to purchase a specific currency at a specific price (exchange rate) within a specific period of time.

Currency diversification: Process of using more than one currency as an investing or financing strategy. Exposure to a diversified currency portfolio typically results in less exchange rate risk than if all of the exposure was in a single foreign currency.

Currency futures contract: Contract specifying a standard volume of a particular currency to be exchanged on a specific settlement date.

Currency option combination: The use of simultaneous call and put option positions to construct a unique position to suit the hedger's or speculator's needs. Two of the most popular currency option combinations are *straddles* and *strangles.*

Currency put option: Contract granting the right to sell a particular currency at a specified price (exchange rate) within a specified period of time.

Currency swap: A transaction in which two counterparties exchange specific amounts of two different currencies at the outset, and then repay over time according to an agreed-upon contract that reflects interest payments and possibly amortization of principal. In a currency swap, the cash flows are similar to those in a spot and forward foreign exchange transaction. See also *Swap.*

Current account: Broad measure of a country's international trade in goods and services.

Current account transactions: In the balance of payments, the net flow of goods, services, and unilateral transfers (such as gifts) between a country and all foreign countries.

Current rate method: A method of translating the financial statements of foreign subsidiaries into the parent country's reporting currency. All assets and liabilities are translated at the current exchange rate.

Depreciation: A market-driven change in the value of a currency that results in reduced value or purchasing power.

Derivative: An asset that derives all changes in value on a separate underlying asset.

Devaluation: The action of a government or central bank authority to drop the spot exchange value of a currency that is pledged to another currency or to gold.

Devalue: To reduce the value of a currency against the value of other currencies.

Direct quote: The price of a unit of foreign exchange expressed in the home country's currency (i.e., $/€). The term has meaning only when the home country is specified.

Direct foreign investment (FDI): Investment in real assets (such as land, buildings, or even existing plants) in foreign countries.

Direct float: A system of floating (i.e., market-determined) exchange rates, in which the government intervenes from time to time to influence the foreign exchange value of its currency.

Direct quotations: Exchange rate quotations representing the value measured by number of dollars per unit of foreign currency.

Discount: In the foreign exchange market, the amount by which a currency is cheaper for future delivery than for spot (immediate) delivery. The currency is expected to depreciate. The opposite of discount is premium.

Dollarization: The use of the US dollar as the official currency of a country.

Draft: An unconditional written order requesting one party (such as an importer) to pay a specified amount of money at a specified time to the order of the writer of the draft. Also called a bill of exchange. Personal checks are one type of draft.

Dumping: Selling products overseas at unfairly low prices (a practice perceived to result from subsidies provided to the firm by its government) to increase competition.

Dynamic hedging: Strategy of hedging in those periods when existing currency positions are expected to be adversely affected, and remaining unhedged in other periods when currency positions are expected to be favorably affected.

Economic exposure: Another name for operating exposure. See *Operating exposure.*

Effective exchange rate: An index measuring the change in value of a foreign currency determined by calculating a weighted average of bilateral exchange rates. The weighting reflects the importance of each foreign country's trade with the home country.

Efficient market: A market, in which all relevant information is already reflected in market prices. The term is most frequently applied to foreign exchange markets and securities markets.

Equilibrium exchange rate: Exchange rate at which demand for a currency is equal to the supply of the currency for sale.

Euro: A new currency unit that has replaced so far the individual currencies of 17 European countries (the Euro-zone) that belong to the European Union; launched electronically on January 1, 1999, and in notes and coins on January 1, 2002.

Eurobank: A bank or bank department that bids for time deposits and makes loans in currencies other than that of the country where the bank is located.

Eurobond: A bond originally offered outside the country in whose currency it is denominated. For example, a dollar-denominated bond is originally offered for sale to investors outside the United States.

Euro-commercial paper (ECP): Short-term notes (30, 60, 90, 120, 180, 270, and 360 days) sold in international money markets.

Eurocredit: Bank loans to MNCs, sovereign governments, international institutions, and banks denominated in Euro-currencies and extended by banks in countries other than the country in whose currency the loan is denominated.

Eurocredit loans: Loans of one year or longer extended by Euro-banks.

Eurocredit market: Collection of banks that accepts deposits and provides loans in large denominations and in a variety of currencies. The banks that comprise this market are the same banks that comprise the Euro-currency market; the difference is that the Eurocredit loans are longer term than so-called Euro-currency loans.

Eurocurrency: A currency deposited (time deposits) in a bank located in a country other than the country issuing the currency.

Eurocurrency market: See *Eurocredit market.*

Eurodollar: A US dollar time deposit deposited in bank outside the United States. A Eurodollar is a type of Euro-currency.

Euronote: Short- to medium-term debt instruments sold in the Eurocurrency market.

European Central Bank (ECB): Conducts monetary policy of the European Economic and Monetary Union (EMU). Its goal is to safeguard the stability of the euro and minimize inflation.

European Currency Unit (ECU): Unit of account that represents a weighted average of exchange rates of member countries within the European Monetary System.

European Monetary System (EMS): A monetary alliance of 15 European countries (same members as the European Union) created in 1979.

European option: An option that can be exercised only on the day on which it expires.

European terms: Foreign exchange quotations for the US dollar, expressed as the number of non-US currency units per US dollar (i.e., €/$).

European Union (EU): The official name of the former European Economic Community (EEC) as of January 1, 1994. The Maastricht Treaty established the European Union under its current name in 1993. The latest amendment to the constitutional basis of the EU, the Treaty of Lisbon, came into force in 2009.

Euro-zone: The countries that officially use the euro as their currency.

Exchange rate: The price of a unit of one country's currency expressed in terms of the currency of some other country.

Exchange Rate Mechanism (ERM): The means by which members of the EMS formerly maintained their currency exchange rates within an agreed-upon range of ±2.25% with respect to the other member currencies.

Exchange rate pass-through: The degree to which the prices of imported and exported goods change as a result of exchange rate changes.

Exercise price: Same as the *strike price*; the agreed-upon rate of exchange within an option contract to buy or sell the underlying asset (currency).

Export credit insurance: Provides assurance to the exporter or the exporter's bank. In case the foreign customer defaults on payment, the insurance company will pay for a major portion of the loss. For example, the Foreign Credit Insurance Association (FCIA).

Export-Import Bank (Ex-Im bank): A US government agency created to finance and otherwise facilitate imports and exports.

Expropriation: Official government seizure of private property, recognized by international law as the right of any sovereign nation provided expropriated owners are given prompt compensation and fair market value in convertible currencies.

Factor income: Income (interest and dividend payments) received by investors on foreign investments in financial assets (securities).

Factoring: Specialized firms, known as factors, purchase receivables at a discount on either a nonrecourse or recourse basis.

FASB 8: A regulation of the Financial Accounting Standards Board requiring US companies to translate foreign affiliate financial statements by the temporal method. FASB 8 was in effect from 1976 to 1981. It is still used under specific circumstances.

FASB 52: A regulation of the Financial Accounting Standards Board requiring US companies to translate foreign subsidiary financial statements by the current rate (closing rate) method. FASB 52 became effective in 1981.

Fiat money: Any currency (bank notes) or check or note of debt is without intrinsic use value as a physical commodity. It derives its value by being declared by a government to be legal tender; that is, it must be accepted as a form of payment within the boundaries of the country, for "all debts, public and private." Such laws in practice cause fiat money to acquire the value of any of the goods and services that it may be traded for within the nation that issues it.

Financial account: A section of the balance of payments accounts. Under the revised format of the International Monetary Fund, the financial account measures long-term financial flows including direct foreign investment, portfolio investments, and other long-term movements. Under the traditional definition, which is still used by many countries, items in the financial account were included in the capital account.

Financial derivative: A financial instrument, such as a futures contract or option, whose value is derived from an underlying asset like a stock or currency.

Financing cash flow: Cash flows originating from financing activities of the firm, including interest payments and dividend distributions.

Fisher Effect: A theory that nominal interest rates in two or more countries should be equal to the required real rate of return to investors plus compensation for the expected amount of inflation in each country. The nominal interest differential in two countries is equal to the expected inflation differential in these two economies.

Fixed exchange rate system: Monetary system, in which exchange rates are either held constant (like the *gold standard* and the *gold exchange standard*) or allowed to fluctuate only within narrow boundaries.

Fixed exchange rates: Foreign exchange rates tied to the currency of a major country (such as the United States), to gold or to a basket of currencies such as Special Drawing Rights.

Flexible exchange rates: The opposite of fixed exchange rates. The foreign exchange rate is adjusted periodically by the country's monetary authorities in accordance with their judgment and/or an external set of economic indicators.

Floating exchange rates: Foreign exchange rates determined by demand and supply in an open market that is presumably free of government interference.

Floating-rate note (FRN): Medium-term securities with interest rates pegged to LIBOR and adjusted quarterly or semiannually.

Foreign affiliate: A foreign business unit that is less than 50 percent owned by the parent company.

Foreign bond: A bond issued by a foreign corporation or government for sale in the domestic capital market of another country, and denominated in the currency of the country where the bond is issued.

Foreign currency intervention: Any activity or policy initiative by a government or central bank with the intent of changing a currency value on the open market. They may include both direct intervention, in which the central bank may buy or sell its own currency, or indirect intervention, in which it may change interest rates in order to change the attractiveness of domestic currency obligations in the eyes of foreign investors.

Foreign currency translation: The process of restating foreign currency accounts of subsidiaries into the reporting currency of the parent company in order to prepare a consolidated financial statement.

Foreign Direct Investment (FDI): Purchase of physical assets, such as plant and equipment, in a foreign country, to be managed by the parent corporation. FDI is distinguished from foreign portfolio investment.

Foreign exchange broker: An individual or firm that arranges foreign exchange transactions between two parties, but is not itself a principal in the trade. Foreign exchange brokers earn a commission for their efforts.

Foreign exchange dealer (or trader): An individual or firm that buys foreign exchange from one party (at a bid price), and then sells it (at an ask price) to another party. The dealer is a principal in two transactions and profits via the spread between the bid and ask prices.

Foreign exchange market: Market composed primarily of banks, serving firms, and consumers who wish to buy or sell various currencies.

Foreign exchange rate: The price of one country's currency in terms of another currency or in terms of commodities such as gold or silver. See also *Exchange rate.*

Foreign exchange risk: The likelihood that an unexpected change in exchange rates will alter the home currency value of foreign cash payments expected from a foreign source. Also, the likelihood that an unexpected change in exchange rates will alter the amount of home currency needed to repay a debt denominated in a foreign currency.

Forfaiting (forfeiting): A technique for arranging nonrecourse medium-term export financing, used most frequently to finance imports into Eastern Europe. A third party, usually a specialized financial institution, guarantees the financing.

Forward contract: An agreement to exchange currencies of different countries at a specified future date and at a specified forward rate.

Forward differential: The difference between spot and forward rates, expressed as an annual percentage. See, *Forward discount or premium.*

Forward discount or premium: The same as forward differential. The expected depreciation or appreciation of a currency as a percentage per annum.

Forward exchange rate: An exchange rate quoted for settlement at some future date. The rate used in a forward transaction.

Forward market: A market that facilitates the trading of forward contracts; commercial banks serve as intermediaries in the market by matching up participants who wish to buy a currency forward with other participants who wish to sell the currency forward.

Forward premium: See *Forward differential.*

Forward transaction: An agreed-upon foreign exchange transaction to be settled at a specified future date, often one, two, or three months after the transaction date.

Freely floating exchange rates: Exchange rates determined in a free market without government interference, in contrast to dirty float.

Fundamental forecasting: Forecasting based on fundamental relationships between economic variables and exchange rate.

Futures or futures contracts: Exchange-traded agreements calling for future delivery of a standard amount of any good, that is, foreign exchange, at a fixed time, place, and price.

Gold Exchange Standard: A fixed exchange rate system adopted in the Bretton Woods agreement. It required the United States to peg the dollar to gold ($35/ 1 oz of gold) and other countries to peg their currencies to the US dollar.

Gold Standard: A monetary system, in which currencies are defined in terms of their gold content (mint parity), and payment imbalances between countries are settled in gold.

Hard currency: A freely convertible currency that is not expected to depreciate in value in the foreseeable future.

Hedge accounting: An accounting procedure that specifies that gains and losses on hedging instruments be recognized in earnings at the same time that the effects of changes in the value of the items being hedged are recognized.

Hedging: Purchasing a contract (including forward foreign exchange) or tangible good that will rise in value and offset a drop in value of another contract or tangible good. Hedges are undertaken to reduce risk by protecting an owner from loss.

Historical exchange rate: In accounting, the exchange rate in effect when an asset or liability was acquired.

Hybrid foreign currency options: Purchase of a put option and the simultaneous sale of a call (or vice versa) so that overall cost is less than the cost of a straight option.

Hyperinflation countries: Countries with a very high rate of inflation. Under United States FASB 52, these are defined as countries where the cumulative three-year inflation amounts to 100 percent or more.

IMM: International Monetary Market. A division of the Chicago Mercantile Exchange.

Import/export letters of credit: Trade-related letters of credit.

In-the-money (ITM): Circumstance in which an option is profitable, excluding the cost of the premium, if exercised immediately.

Indirect quote: The price of a unit of a home country's currency expressed in terms of a foreign country's currency (i.e., €/$).

Interbank market: Market that facilitates the exchange of currencies between banks.

Interest rate parity (IRP): A theory that the differences in national interest rates for securities of similar and maturity should be equal to but opposite in sign (positive or negative) to the forward exchange rate discount or premium for the foreign currency.

Interest rate parity (IRP) line: Diagonal line depicting all points on a four-quadrant graph that represents a state of interest rate parity.

Interest rate parity theory: Theory suggesting that the forward rate differs from the spot rate by an amount that reflects the interest differential between two currencies.

Interest rate risk: The risk to the organization arising from interest-bearing debt obligations, either fixed or floating rate obligations. It is typically used to refer to the changing interest rates, which a company may incur by borrowing at floating rates of interest.

Interest rate swap: A transaction, in which two counterparties exchange interest payment streams of different character (such as floating vs. fixed), based on an underlying notional principal amount.

Internalization: A theory that the key ingredient for maintaining a firm-specific competitive advantage in international competition is the possession of proprietary information and control of human capital that can generate new information through expertise in research, management, marketing or technology.

International Bank for Reconstruction and Development (IBRD or World Bank): International development bank owned by member nations that makes development loans to member countries, established in 1944.

International banking Facility (IBF): A department within a US bank that may accept foreign deposits and make loans to foreign borrowers as if it were a foreign subsidiary. IBFs are free of US reserve requirements, deposit insurance, and interest rate regulations.

International Financial Corporation (IFC): Firm established to promote private enterprise within countries; it can provide loans to and purchase stock of corporations.

International Fisher Effect: A theory that the spot exchange rate should change by an amount equal to the difference in interest rates between two countries.

International Fisher Effect (IFE) line: Diagonal line on a graph that reflects points at which the interest rate differential between two countries is equal to the expected percentage change in the exchange rate between their two respective currencies.

International Monetary Fund (IMF): An international organization created in 1944 to promote exchange rate stability and provide temporary financing for countries experiencing balance of payments difficulties.

International Monetary Market (IMM): A branch of the Chicago Mercantile Exchange that is specialized in trading currency and financial futures contracts.

International Monetary System: The structure within which foreign exchange rates are determined, international trade and capital flows are accommodated, and balance of payments adjustments are made.

Intracompany trade: International trade between subsidiaries that are under the same ownership.

Intrinsic value: The financial gain if an option is exercised immediately.

Investment agreement: An agreement that spells out specific rights and responsibilities of both the investing foreign firm and the host government.

***J*-curve affect:** The adjustment path of a country's trade balance following a devaluation or significant depreciation of the country's currency. The path first worsens as a result of existing contracts before improving as a result of more competitive pricing conditions.

Joint venture (JV): A business venture that is owned by two or more entities, often from different countries.

Lag: In the context of leads and lags, payment of a financial obligation later than is expected or required.

Law of one price: The concept that if an identical product or service can be sold in two different markets, and no restrictions exist on the sale or transportation costs of moving the product between markets, the product's price should be the same in both markets.

Lead: In the context of leads and lags, the payment of a financial obligation earlier than is expected or required.

Lender-of-last-resort: The body or institution within an economy that is ultimately capable of preserving the financial survival or variability of individual institutions. Typically, the country's central bank.

Letter of credit (L/C): An instrument issued by a bank, in which the bank promises to pay a beneficiary upon presentation of documents specified in the letter.

Licensing: Arrangement in which a local firm in the host country produces goods in accordance with another firm's (the licensing firm's) specifications; as the goods are sold, the local firm can retain part of earnings.

Liquid: The ability to exchange an asset for cash at or near its fair market value.

London Interbank Offered Rate (LIBOR): The deposit rate applicable to interbank loans in London. LIBOR is used as the reference rate for many international interest rate transactions.

Long position: A position in which foreign currency assets exceed foreign currency liabilities. The opposite of a long position is a short position.

Long-term forward contracts: Contracts that state any exchange rate, at which a specified amount of a specified currency can be exchanged at a future date (more than one year from today). Also, called *long forwards.*

Maastricht Treaty: A treaty among the 12 European Union countries that specified a plan and timetable for the introduction of a single European currency, called the euro. The Maastricht Treaty (formally, the Treaty on European Union or TEU) was signed on February 7, 1992, by the members of the European Community in Maastricht, Netherlands. On December 9–10, 1991, the same city hosted the European Council, which drafted the treaty. Upon its entry into force on November 1, 1993 during the Delors Commission, it created the European Union and led to the creation of the single European currency, the euro. The Maastricht Treaty has been amended by the treaties of Amsterdam, Nice, and Lisbon.

Macroassessment: Overall risk assessment of a country without considering the MNC's business.

Macrorisk: Country-specific risk.

Macroeconomic uncertainty: Operating exposure's sensitivity to key macroeconomic variables, such as exchange rates and inflation rates.

Managed float: A country that allows its currency to trade within a given band of exchange rates.

Margin: A deposit made as security for a financial transaction otherwise financed on credit.

Margin requirement: Deposit placed on a contract (such as a currency futures contract) to cover the fluctuations in the value of that contract; this minimizes the risk of the contract to the counterparty.

Market-based forecasting: Use of a market-determined exchange rate (such as the spot rate or mostly, the forward rate) to forecast the spot rate in the future.

Marked to market: The condition in which the value of a futures contract is assigned to market value daily, and all changes in value are paid in cash daily. The value of the contract is revalued using the closing price for the day. The amount to be paid is called the "variation margin."

Market liquidity: The degree to which a firm can issue a new security without depressing the existing market price, as well as the degree to which a change in price of its securities elicits a substantial order flow.

Market segmentation: The divergence within a national market of required rates of return. If all capital markets are fully integrated, securities of comparable expected return and risk should have the same required rate of return in each national market after adjusting for foreign exchange risk and political risk.

Matching currency cash flows: The strategy of offsetting anticipated continuous long exposure to a particular currency by acquiring debt denominated in that currency.

Microassessment: The risk assessment of a country as related to the MNC's type of business.

Microrisk: Firm-specific risk.

Mixed forecasting: Development of forecasts based on a mixture of forecasting techniques.

Monetary assets or liabilities: Assets in the form of cash or claims to cash (such as accounts receivable), or liabilities payable in cash. Monetary assets minus monetary liabilities are called net monetary assets.

Money: Any object or record that is generally accepted as payment for goods and services and repayment of debts in a given socioeconomic context or country. The main functions of money are distinguished as: a medium of exchange; a unit of account; a store of value; and, occasionally in the past, a standard of deferred payment. Any kind of object or secure verifiable record that fulfills these functions can be considered money.

Money market hedge: The use of foreign currency borrowing and money market instruments to reduce transaction or accounting foreign exchange exposure.

Money markets: The financial markets in various countries in which various types of short-term debt instruments, including money and bank loans, are purchased and sold.

Moral suasion: A phrase from the Latin words "moral" and "suasio," which denote respectively "conduct or character that is right and virtuous" and "to present in a pleasing manner"; sometimes known as jawboning. It is defined in the economic sphere (mostly, in monetary policy) as "the attempt to coerce private economic activity via governmental exhortation in directions not already defined or dictated by existing statute law." The "moral" aspect comes from the pressure of "moral responsibility" to operate in a way that is consistent with furthering the good of the economy.

Multilateral netting: The process of netting intracompany payments in order to reduce the size and frequency of cash and currency exchanges.

Multinational corporations (MNCs): Firms that engage in some form of international business.

Multinational enterprise (MNE): A firm that has operating subsidiaries, branches, or affiliates located in foreign countries.

Multinational restructuring: Restructuring of the composition of an MNC's assets or liabilities.

Natural hedge: The use or existence of an offsetting or matching cash flow from firm operating activities to hedge a currency exposure.

Negotiable instrument: A written draft or promissory note, signed by the maker or drawer, that contains an unconditional promise or order to pay a definite sum of money on demand or at a determinable future date, and is payable to order or to bearer. A holder of a negotiable instrument is entitled to payment despite any personal disagreements between the drawee and maker.

Nepotism: The practice of showing favor to relatives over other qualified persons in conferring such benefits as the awarding of contracts, granting of special prices, hiring, promotions to various ranks, etc.

Net-transaction exposure: Consideration of inflows and outflows in a given currency to determine the exposure after offsetting inflows against outflows.

Netting: The mutual offsetting of sums due between two or more business entities.

Nominal exchange rate: The actual foreign exchange quotation, in contrast to real exchange rate, which is adjusted for changes in purchasing power (the two-price indexes).

Nondeliverable forward contract (NDF): Like a forward contract, represents an agreement regarding a position in a specified currency, a specified exchange rate, and a specified future settlement date, but does not result in delivery of currencies. Instead, a payment is made by one party in the agreement to the other party based on the exchange rate at that future date.

Nonsterilized intervention: Intervention in the foreign exchange market without adjusting for the change in money supply.

Notional principal: The size of a derivative contract, in total currency value, as used in futures contracts, forward contracts, option contracts, or swap agreements.

Numismatics: The scientific study of moneys and their history in all their varied forms and functions.

Offer: The price at which a trader is willing to sell foreign exchange, securities, or commodities. Also called *ask*.

Official reserve account: Total reserves held by official monetary authorities within the country, such as gold, SDRs, and major currencies.

Offshore finance subsidiary: A foreign financial subsidiary owned by a corporation in another country. Offshore finance subsidiaries are usually located in tax-free or low-tax jurisdictions to enable the parent multinational firm to finance international operations without being subject to home country taxes or regulations.

Operating cash flows: The primary cash flows generated by a business from the conduct of trade, typically composed of earnings, depreciation, and amortization, and changes in net working capital.

Operating exposure: The potential for a change in expected cash flows, and thus in value, of a foreign subsidiary as a result of an unexpected change in exchange rates. Also called *economic exposure*.

Open account transaction: A sale in which the exporter ships the merchandise and expects the buyer to remit payment according to agreed-upon terms.

Option: In foreign exchange, a contract giving the purchaser the right, but not the obligation, to buy or sell a given amount of foreign exchange at a fixed price per unit for a specified time period. Options to buy are calls and options to sell are puts.

Out-of-the-money (OTM): An option that would not be profitable, excluding the cost of the premium, if exercised immediately.

Outright quotation: The full price, in one currency, of a unit of another currency. See its difference as *Points quotation*.

Outsourcing: Represents the process of subcontracting to a third party.

Overdraft: It occurs when money is withdrawn from a bank account and the available balance goes below zero. In this situation the account is said to be "*overdrawn*." If there is a prior agreement with the account provider for an overdraft, and the amount overdrawn is within the authorized overdraft limit, then interest is normally charged at the agreed rate. If the negative balance exceeds the agreed terms, then additional fees may be charged and higher interest rates may apply.

Overhedging: Hedging an amount in a currency larger than the actual transaction amount.

Over-the-counter market: A market for share of stock, options (including foreign currency options), or other financial contracts conducted via electronic connections between dealers. The over-the-counter market has no physical location or address, and is thus differentiated from organized exchanges that have a physical location where trading takes place.

Overvalued currency: A currency with a current foreign exchange (i.e., current price in the foreign exchange market) greater than the worth of that currency. Because "worth" is a subjective concept, overvaluation is a matter of opinion. If the euro has a current market value of $1.20 (i.e., the current exchange rate is $1.20/€) at a time when its "true" value as derived from purchasing power parity or some other method is deemed to be $1.10, the euro is overvalued. The opposite of overvalued is undervalued.

Parallel loan: Another name for a back-to-back loan, in which two companies in separate countries borrow each other's currency for a specific period of time, and repay the other's currency at an agreed maturity to avoid exchange rate risk.

Parallel market: An unofficial foreign exchange market tolerated by a government, but not officially sanctioned. The exact boundary between a parallel market and a black market is not very clear, but official tolerance of what would otherwise be a black market leads to use of the term "parallel market."

Parity conditions: In the context of international finance, a set of basic economic relationships that provide for equilibrium between spot and forward foreign exchange rates, interest rates, and inflation rates.

Pass-through: The time it takes for an exchange rate change to be reflected in market prices of products or services.

Pegged exchange rate: Exchange rate whose value is pegged to another currency's value or to a unit of account.

Petrodollars: Deposits of dollars by countries that receive dollar revenues due to the sale of petroleum to other countries; the term commonly refers to OPEC deposits of dollars in the Eurocurrency market.

Points: The smallest units of price change quoted, given a conventional number of digits in which a quotation is stated.

Points quotation: A forward quotation expressed only as the number of decimal points (usually four decimal points) by which it differs from the spot quotation.

Political risk: The possibility that political events in a particular country will influence the economic well-being of firms in that country. See also *Sovereign risk.*

Portfolio investment: Purchase of foreign stocks and bonds, in contrast to foreign direct investment.

Premium: In a foreign exchange market, the amount by which a currency is more expensive for future delivery than for spot (immediate) delivery. The opposite of premium is discount.

Price-specie-flow mechanism: It is a logical argument by David Hume against the mercantilist (1700–1776) idea that a nation should strive for a positive balance of trade or net exports. The argument considers the effects of international transactions in a gold standard, a system in which gold is the official means of international payments and each nation's currency is in the form of gold itself or of paper currency fully convertible into gold. When a country with a gold standard had a positive balance of trade, gold would flow into the country in the amount that the value of exports exceeds the value of imports. Conversely, when such a country has a negative balance of trade, gold would flow out of the country in the amount that the value of imports exceeds the value of exports. Consequently, in the absence of any offsetting actions by the central bank on the quantity of money in circulation (sterilization), the money supply would rise in a country with a positive balance of trade and fall in a country with a negative balance of trade. Using the quantity theory of money, he argued that in countries where the quantity of money increases, inflation would set in and the prices of goods and services would tend to rise while in countries where the money supply decreases, deflation would occur as the prices of goods and services fell.

Protectionism: A political attitude or policy intended to inhibit the imports of foreign goods and services and to promote the exports of domestic products to increase domestic income and employment. The opposite of free trade policies.

Purchasing power parity (PPP): A theory that the price of internationally traded commodities should be the same in every country, and hence the exchange rate between the two currencies should be the ratio of prices in the two countries.

Purchase power parity (PPP) line: Diagonal line on a graph that reflects points at which the expected inflation differential between two countries is equal to the percentage change in the exchange rate between the two respective currencies.

Put: An option to sell foreign exchange or financial contracts. See *Option.*

Put option on real assets: A project that contains an option of divesting part or all of the project.

Quota: A limit, mandatory or voluntary, set on the import of a product.

Quotation: In foreign exchange trading, the pair of prices (bid and ask), at which a dealer is willing to buy or sell foreign exchange.

Range forward: A complex option position that combines the purchase of a put option and the sale of a call option with strike prices equidistant from the forward rate. Also called flexible forward, cylinder option, option fence, mini-max, and zero-cost tunnel.

Real cost of hedging: The additional cost of hedging when compared to not hedging (a negative real cost would imply that hedging was more favorable than not hedging).

Real cost of hedging payables: Is equal to the cost of hedging payables less the cost of payables if not hedged.

Real interest rate: Nominal (or quoted) interest rate minus the inflation rate.

Real exchange rate: An index of foreign exchange adjusted for relative price-level changes from a base point in time, typically a month or a year. Sometimes referred to as real effective exchange rate, it is used to measure purchasing-power-adjusted changes in exchange rates.

Real options: Implicit options on real assets.

Reference rate: The rate of interest used in a standardized quotation, loan agreement, or financial derivative valuation.

Regression analysis: Statistical technique used to measure the relationship between variables and the sensitivity of a variable to one or more variables.

Regression coefficient: Term measured by regression analysis to estimate the sensitivity (the elasticity) of the dependent variable to a particular independent variable.

Reinvoicing center: A central financial subsidiary used by a multinational firm to reduce transaction exposure by having all home country exports billed in the home currency and then reinvoiced to each operating subsidiary in that subsidiary's local currency.

Relative purchasing power parity: A theory that if the spot exchange rate between two countries starts in equilibrium, any change in the differential rate of inflation between them tends to be offset in the spot exchange rate.

Renminbi (RNMB): The alternative official name (the yuan, CNY) of the currency of the People's Republic of China.

Reporting currency: In the context of translating financial statements, the currency in which a parent firm prepares its own financial statements. Usually this is the parent's home currency.

Repositioning of funds: The movement of funds from one currency or country to another. A MNC faces a variety of political, tax, foreign exchange, and liquidity constraints that limits its ability to move funds easily and without cost.

Representative office: A representative office established by a bank in a foreign country to help clients doing business in that country. It also functions as a geographically convenient location from which to visit correspondent banks in its region rather than send bankers from the parent bank at greater financial and physical cost.

Reserve currency: A currency used by a government or central banking authority as a resource asset or currency to be used in market interventions to alter the market value of the domestic currency.

Revaluation: A rise in the foreign exchange value of a currency that is pegged to other currencies or to gold. Also called *appreciation.*

Revalue: To increase the value of a currency against the value of other currencies.

Risk: The likelihood than an actual outcome will differ from an expected outcome. The actual outcome could be better or worse than expected (two-sided risk), although in common practice risk is more often used only in the context of an adverse outcome (one-sided risk). Risk can exist for any number of uncertain future situations, including future spot rates or the results of political events.

Risk-sharing: A contractual arrangement in which the buyer and seller agree to share or split currency movement impacts on payments between them.

Rules of the game: The basis of exchange rate determination under the international gold standard during most of the nineteenth and early twentieth centuries. All countries agreed informally to follow the rule of buying and selling their currency at a fixed and predetermined price against gold, the mint parity.

Seignorage: The net revenues or proceeds garnered by a government from the printing of its money.

Selling short (shorting): The sale of an asset which the seller does not (yet) own. The premise is that the seller believes he will be able to purchase the asset for contract fulfillment at a lower price before sale contract expiration.

Semistrong-form efficient: Description of foreign exchange markets, implying that relevant public information is already reflected in prevailing spot exchange rates.

Short position: See *Long position.*

SIBOR: Singapore Interbank Offered Rate.

Sight draft: A bill of exchange (B/E) that is due on demand, that is, when presented to the bank. See also *Bill of exchange.*

SIMEX: Singapore International Monetary Exchange.

Smithsonian Agreement: Conference between nations in 1971 that resulted in a devaluation of the dollar against major currencies and a widening of boundaries (2.25 percent in either direction, or a total of 4.5 percent) around the newly established exchange rates.

Snake: Arrangement established in 1972, whereby European currencies were tied to each other within specified limits ($\pm 2.25\%$).

Society of Worldwide Interbank Financial Telecommunications (SWIFT): A dedicated computer network that provides funds transfer messages between member banks around the world.

Soft currency: A currency expected to drop in value relative to other currencies. Free trading in a currency deemed soft is often restricted by the monetary authorities of the issuing country.

Sovereign debt: The debt obligation of a sovereign or governmental authority or body.

Sovereign risk: The risk that a host government may unilaterally repudiate its foreign obligations or may prevent local firms from honoring their foreign obligations. Sovereign risk is often regarded as a subset of political risk.

Sovereign spread: The credit spread paid by a sovereign borrower on a major foreign currency denominated debt obligation. For example, the credit spread paid by the Venezuelan government to borrow US dollars over and above a similar maturity issuance by the US Treasury.

Special Drawing Right (SDR): An international reserve asset, defined by the International Monetary Fund as the value of a weighted basket of four currencies ($, €, £, and ¥).

Speculation: An attempt to make a profit by trading on expectations about future prices.

Spot market: A market in which exchange transactions occur for immediate exchange.

Spot rate: The price at which foreign exchange can be purchased (its bid) or sold (its ask) in a spot transaction. See *Spot transaction.*

Spot transaction: A foreign exchange transaction to be settled (paid for) on the second following business day.

Spread: The difference between the bid (buying) quote and the ask (selling) quote.

Sterilized intervention: Intervention by the Federal Reserve in the foreign exchange market, with simultaneous intervention in the Treasury securities markets to offset any effects on the dollar money supply; thus, the intervention in the foreign exchange market is achieved without affecting the existing dollar money supply.

Straddle: Combination of a put option and a call option with a common strike price and expiration date.

Strangle: A currency option combination; similar to *straddle*, with different strike prices and a common expiration date.

Strategic alliance: A formal relationship, short of a merger or acquisition, between two companies, formed for the purpose of gaining synergies because in some aspect the two companies complement each other.

Strike price: The agreed-upon rate of exchange within an option contract. See *Exercise price.*

Strong-form efficient: Description of foreign exchange markets, implying that all relevant public and private information is already reflected in prevailing spot exchange rates.

Subsidiary: A foreign operation incorporated in the host country and owned 50 percent or more by a parent corporation. Foreign operations that are not incorporated are called branches.

Swap: This term is used in many contexts. In general it is the simultaneous purchase and sale of foreign exchange or securities, with the purchase executed at once and the sale back to the same party carried out at an agreed-upon price to be completed at a specified future date. Swaps include interest rate swaps, currency swaps, and credit swaps.

Swap rate: A forward foreign exchange quotation expressed in terms of the number of points by which the forward rate differs from the spot rate.

SWIFT: See *Society for Worldwide Interbank Financial Telecommunications.*

Syndicated loan: A large loan made by a group of banks to a large multinational firm or government. Syndicated loans allow the participating banks to maintain diversification by not lending too much to a single borrower.

Synthetic forward: A complex option position that combines the purchase of a put option and the sale of a call option or vice versa, both at the forward rate. Theoretically, the combined position should have a net-zero premium.

Synthetic risk: In portfolio theory, it is the risk of the market itself, that is, risk that cannot be diversified away.

Systematic risk: Also called *aggregate risk, market risk,* or *undiversifiable risk* and it is the vulnerability to events that affect aggregate outcomes such as broad market returns, total economy-wide resource holdings, or aggregate income.

Systemic risk: It is the risk of collapse of an entire financial system or entire market, as opposed to risk associated with any one individual entity, group, or component of a system. It can be defined as "financial *system* instability, potentially catastrophic, caused or exacerbated by idiosyncratic events or conditions in financial intermediaries." It refers to the risks imposed by *interlinkages* and *interdependencies* in a system or market where the failure of a single entity or cluster of entities can cause a cascading failure, which could potentially bankrupt or bring down the entire system or market.

Tariff: A duty or tax on imports that can be levied as a percentage of cost or as a specific amount per unit of import.

Tax exposure: The potential for tax liability on a given income stream or on the value of an asset. Usually used in the context of a multinational firm being able to minimize its tax liabilities by locating some portion of operations in a country where the tax liability is minimized.

Technical analysis: The focus on price and volume data to determine past trends that are expected to continue into the future. Analysts believe that future exchange rates are based on the current exchange rate.

Technical forecasting: Development of forecasts using historical prices or trends.

Time-series analysis: Analysis of relationships between two or more variables over periods of time.

Time-series models: Models that examine series of historical data; sometimes used as a means of technical forecasting by examining moving averages, autoregressive processes, and other combinations.

TED Spread: Treasury Eurodollar Spread. The difference in basis points between the 3-month interest rate swap index or the 3-month LIBOR interest rate, and the 90-day US Treasury bill rate. It is sometimes used as an indicator of credit crisis or fear over bank credit quality.

Terms of trade: The weighted average exchange ratio between a nation's export prices and its import prices used to measure gains from trade. Gains from trade refers to increases in total consumption resulting from production specialization and international trade. ($TOT = P_M/P_X = SP^*/P$).

Time draft: A draft that allows a delay in payment. It is presented to the drawee, who accepts it by writing a notice of acceptance on its face. Once accepted, the time draft becomes a promise to by the accepting part. See also *Banker's acceptance.*

Transaction exposure: The potential for change in the value of outstanding financial obligations entered into prior to a change in exchange rates, but not due to be settled until after the exchange rates change.

Translation exposure: The potential for an accounting derived in owners' equity resulting from exchange rate changes and the need to restate financial statements of foreign subsidiaries in the single currency of the parent corporation. See also *Accounting exposure.*

Transparency: The degree to which an investor can discern the true activities and value drivers of a company from the disclosures and financial results reported.

Triangular arbitrage: An arbitrage activity of exchanging currency A for currency B for currency C back to currency A to exploit slight disequilibrium in exchange rates.

Triffin paradox (also Triffin Dilemma): The potential conflict in objectives that may arise between domestic monetary policy and current policy when a country's currency is used as a reserve currency.

Unbiased predictor: A theory that spot prices at some future date will be equal to today's forward rates.

Uncovered interest arbitrage (UIA): The process by which investors borrow in countries and currencies exhibiting relatively low interest rates and convert the proceeds into currencies that offer much higher interest rates. The transaction is "uncovered" because the investor does not sell the higher yielding currency proceeds forward.

Undervalued currency: The status of currency with a current foreign exchange value (i.e., current price in the foreign exchange market) below the worth of that currency. Because "worth" is a subjective concept, undervaluation is a matter of opinion. If the euro has a current market value of $1.20 (i.e., the current exchange rate is $1.20/€) at a time when its "true" value as derived from purchasing power parity or some other method is deemed to be $1.30, the euro is undervalued. The opposite of undervalued is overvalued.

Unilateral transfers: Balance of payments accounting for government and private gifts and grants.

Unsystematic risk: In a portfolio, the amount of risk that can be eliminated by diversification.

Volatility: In connection with options, the standard deviation of daily spot price movement.

Weak-form efficient: Description of foreign exchange markets, implying that all historical and current exchange rate information is already reflected in prevailing spot exchange rates.

Wire transfer: Electronic transfer of funds.

World Bank: Bank established in 1944 to enhance economic development by providing loans to countries.

World Trade Organization (WTO): Organization established to provide a forum for multilateral trade negotiations and to settle trade disputes related to the GATT accord.

Writer: Seller.

Yield to maturity: The rate of interest (discount) that equates future cash flows of a bond (PV), both interest and principal, with the present market price. Yield to maturity is thus the time-adjusted rate of return earned by a bond investor.

Yuan (CNY): The official currency of the People's Republic of China, also termed the *renminbi.*

Index

Made in the USA
Monee, IL
13 September 2026

62976825R00174